American Sports History Series

edited by
David B. Biesel

A related title by the series editor:

Can You Name That Team? A Guide to Professional Baseball, Football, Soccer, Hockey, and Basketball Teams and Leagues by David B. Biesel, 1991

Jimmie Foxx

The Pride of Sudlersville

Mark R. Millikin

Mark R. Millikin

American Sports History Series, No. 11

The Scarecrow Press, Inc.
Lanham, Maryland • Toronto • Oxford

SCARECROW PRESS, INC.

Published in the United States of America
by Scarecrow Press, Inc.
A wholly owned subsidiary of
The Rowman & Littlefield Publishing Group, Inc.
4501 Forbes Boulevard, Suite 200, Lanham, Maryland 20706
www.scarecrowpress.com

PO Box 317
Oxford
OX2 9RU, UK

British Library Cataloguing in Publication Information Available

**The Library of Congress catalogued the hardcover edition of this book
as follows:**

Millikin, Mark R.
    Jimmie Foxx : the pride of Sudlersville / Mark R.
Millikin.
        p.   cm. — (American sports history series : no. 11)
    Includes bibliographical references (p. 267) and index.
    1. Foxx, Jimmie. 2. Baseball players—United States—Bibliography.
I. Title. II. Series.
GV865.F64M55   1998
796.357;092—dc21   98-14707

    ISBN 0-8108-5685-9 (pbk. : alk. paper)

DEDICATION

This book is dedicated to William Mix (Mr. Will), my step-grandfather; my parents, Walter and Rose Marie Millikin; my children, Melissa and Luke Millikin; and my fiancée, Debbie Schaeffer. "Mr. Will" took me as a child to many Oriole games at Memorial Stadium and passed along weekly issues of *The Sporting News* to me for seven years. My parents always supported my addiction to baseball, and my father was my first Little League coach and took me to Fenway Park for my first major league game. My children tolerated many trips to local libraries and the National Baseball Hall of Fame and accompanied me on some of my interviews. Debbie strongly urged me many times to continue the project, especially when I needed encouragement the most.

CONTENTS

ACKNOWLEDGMENTS

I especially wish to acknowledge Barbara Everett, librarian of the Sudlersville Memorial Library in Jimmie Foxx's hometown of Sudlersville, Maryland. Barbara set up many key interviews for me with relatives and friends of Jimmie Foxx and allowed me to conduct the interviews at her library. She also referred me to various articles and other publications containing information on Mr. Foxx and made many initial contacts on my behalf.

I thank Bill Deane, former Senior Research Associate, and Ms. Pat Kelly of the Photography Department of the National Baseball Library of the National Baseball Hall of Fame and Museum, Inc. Bill and Scott Mundore were very helpful at various stages in clarifying what research materials were available at the library. Ms. Joanie Roach of the Calvert County (Maryland) Library System obtained various interlibrary loans for me. Librarians Valerie Taylor and Billie Houghton from Caroline County (Maryland) System supplied some historical information on early baseball played on Maryland's Eastern Shore. Dan Bunch wrote an article on my research on Jimmie Foxx's life in the *Queen Anne's Record Observer* in August 1991 and kindly featured an open invitation in the article for interested readers to contact me if they had additional information on Jimmie Foxx. Dan Rodricks of the *Evening Sun* and WBAL radio (Baltimore) aired his own essay documentary on Jimmie Foxx's life during the 1992 All-Star break; the documentary featured many excerpts from an interview Dan conducted with me.

I am very grateful to the following individuals from Sudlersville and other nearby areas on Maryland's Eastern Shore who agreed to have interviews with me and gave me very useful information about Jimmie Foxx and life on the Eastern Shore during Mr. Foxx's lifetime: Jimmie's cousins, Gladys Smith Truitt, Mattie Jarman Anthony, and William (Winnie) Coleman; his nephew, (Samuel) Dell Foxx III; his schoolmates Tom Gillespie and Bernard Merrick, and his friends, (Lemuel) Bo Benton, Margaret Stack, and Doris Roland Biddle. Marjorie Clements provided me with several old newspaper articles found in the former farm home of Dell and Mattie Foxx, and Ms. Loretta Walls very kindly gave me family charts for the Smith and Foxx families and photographs of Mr. Foxx as a youngster. John George recalled life in Sudlersville in the 1920s and 1930s.

Mr. Foxx's cousin, Lewis Staats, Jr., whose mother, Bessie, was Dell's sister, provided recollections of watching Jimmie at Shibe Park and visiting Dell, Mattie, Jimmie, and Sammy Dell at their home in Sudlersville. Jimmy Dragoo provided recollections about his classmate Helen Heite Foxx, and Ralph Johnson recalled Mr. Foxx's participation in the 1923 Maryland State Olympiad for track and field.

I thank Jimmie's cousin, Ms. Mildred Smith Barracliff, who wrote several very informative letters on her early childhood experiences with Mr. Foxx; and I thank Jimmie's son, William Kenneth Foxx, who gave me information both by telephone and letter on his father. Also, special thanks to Jimmie's stepdaughter, Nanci Canaday, for her helpful information by telephone and mail on Jimmie's life, mostly after playing baseball.

I thank Mr. Gerald Gary, Principal of Sudlersville Elementary School (formerly Sudlersville High School) for allowing me to tour the school, and Ms. Gladys Truitt for conducting the tour.

I especially thank Mr. Al Ruggieri from Flourtown, Pennsylvania, for granting me an interview several hours long on his experiences as the clubhouse errand boy for the Philadelphia Athletics from 1929 through 1936, and Mr. Gil Dunn for his recollections on the formation of his "museum" dedicated to Jimmie Foxx in the Kent Island (Maryland) Pharmacy. Mr. George Jenkins from Claymont, Delaware, showed me his "Foxx's Den" dedicated to Mr. Foxx and recalled the first time he met Jimmie through Foxx's Uncle Benton.

Thanks to Jimmie's former schoolmates, Anna Holden and Robert Farr, his former housekeeper, Ms. Louise Hollett, and relative Margaret Duling, who sent me written replies about Mr. Foxx, and Ms. Anna Roberts Ware for her recollections about Jimmie Foxx's mother.

Relatives of Jimmie Foxx who granted me interviews over the phone were William Heilbron and Dolly Florence Heilbron James.

John Bruehl's son, Colonel Paul Bruehl, wrote a very informative letter on his and his dad's recollections of Jimmie Foxx.

Ms. Helen Tarring Harrison sent me several very informative letters about her relationship with Mr. Foxx, and she and her sister, Dorothy Tarring Willis, wife of Lefty Willis, granted me an interview to give their recollections of Jimmie.

Mr. Ed "Dutch" Doyle of Philadelphia (SABR member) recalled some of his observations of Foxx, the Athletics, and Shibe Park from his days attending A's games beginning in 1929.

Mr. Len Levin, formerly of the *Providence Journal-Bulletin* (SABR member), provided me with extensive information he gathered on Foxx's 1925 season at Providence.

Ms. Jean Toll, archivist for General Mills, Inc., provided information about Mr. Foxx's appearances on Wheaties boxes and in Wheaties advertisements.

Mr. Howard Talbot, Jr., Director, gave a few of his recollections of Jimmie Foxx on the day he was inducted into the Hall of Fame in 1951.

The following former major-league players were very helpful during telephone interviews and gave me their recollections of Mr. Foxx: Joe Hauser, Mel Harder, Willis Hudlin, Ray Hayworth, Ben Chapman, Jack Wilson, Alex Hooks, Eddie Collins, Jr., Bernie Snyder, Jimmy DeShong, Elden Auker, and (Edwin) Dib Williams.

I received written replies to my letters asking about Jimmie Foxx from the following former major-league players: Vern Kennedy, Harlond Clift, Ted Williams, Ken Keltner, Charlie Wagner, Bobbie Doerr, Dom DiMaggio, Charlie Gehringer, Herb Hash, Art Herring, Thornton Lee, Harry Eisenstat, Sid Hudson, Lou Lucier, Rusty Peters, Johnny Berardino, Johnny Babich, Ray Benge, Elden Auker, (Elon) Chief Hogsett, Joe Dobson, Gene Desautels, Rick Ferrell, Lou Clinton, Tony Freitas, Roy Hughes, Bozey Berger, Tony Giuliani, Denny Galehouse, Tony Lupien, Bill Nicholson, Al Milnar, Buster Mills, Marv Owen, Ray Pepper, Hal Spindel, (Luther) Bud Thomas, Gene Woodling, Bill Werber, Bruce Campbell, Ken Silvestri, Al Niemiec, Leo Nonnenkamp, Monte Weaver, and Milt Gaston.

Robert Dean of the Talbot County Historical Society furnished me with the team photograph of the 1924 Easton Farmers from the H. Robins Hollyday Collection.

John E. George, Sr., of Sudlersville, Maryland, provided the Sudlersville Memorial Library with a photograph of the 1902 Sudlersville "town baseball champions."

Peter Curtis of the Hornbake Library of the University of Maryland, College Park campus, provided me access to news clippings from the *Baltimore News Post* and *Baltimore News American*.

Several staff members of the Easton Branch of the Talbot County Library provided me access to copies of the *Easton Star Democrat*.

Staff of the *Queen Anne's Record Observer*, especially Dorothy Monroe, provided me access to weekly issues of the *Centreville Observer* and *Queen Anne's Record*.

Ms. Maureen Gill sent me news clippings about Jimmie Foxx from the morgue of the *Boston Globe*.

Wilma Briggs gave me a wealth of information about the Fort Wayne Daisies' 1952 baseball club. She played for that club, and Jimmie Foxx was its manager.

Steve Adamson provided me with scrapbooks from the sports pages of several Boston newspapers from the early 1940s.

Mike Sparrow and Mark Alvarez loaned me microfilm of *The Sporting News* from the microfilm lending library of the Society of American Baseball Research.

John Holway suggested many former ballplayers I might benefit from contacting who knew Foxx.

Oscar Eddleton (SABR member) sent me two very informative letters on his boyhood recollections of Jimmie Foxx.

Authors Ray Robinson and Ed Linn sent me remarks on some of their recollections of Jimmie Foxx.

Finally, my thanks to my editor, David Biesel, for his interest in my project and his support and guidance, and to Toni Sortor for guiding my manuscript through all of the production process.

PROLOGUE

Town baseball surged in popularity across much of the United States during the 1890s and early 1900s. Older boys and young adult men competed for spots on town teams and the right to represent their town folk in intense rivalries with other nearby teams. Betting on the contests was prevalent and town folk were known to pass around the hat to collect money to reward an especially good performance by a local favorite. Games played in the fall often featured professional players who were added to local teams, usually for a price, to increase the chances for victory for a given team. All of this characterized town baseball on the Eastern Shore of Maryland.

At the same time, professional baseball at the major-league level was gaining in national interest in large cities, where fans could see their favorite teams in person; but was limited to newspaper accounts for fans in most smaller cities and towns. Without radio or television, baseball fans in small towns witnessed major-league teams or players firsthand on rare occasions. Fans living in such areas only saw major-league players in action if an exhibition game was played there by a big-league club while the team traveled north for a series of games after spring training or if an individual player or players barnstorming across the country stopped there in the fall after the regular season.

Dell Foxx, a tenant farmer living in Sudlersville, Maryland, played town ball often and was well-known for his baseball skills, especially his power hitting. He could hit a baseball for long distance, despite having only a wiry, lean build, rather than massive size. Dell never had the chance to play in the major leagues, though many local folk thought he could, but another local boy from nearby Trappe, Maryland, who was ten years younger, received the opportunity that Dell never had. His name was John Franklin Baker, known to locals as Frank and later to baseball fans around the country as "Home Run Baker."

Frank played semipro ball for the Eastern Shore town of Ridgely (Caroline County, Maryland) in 1906 when he was twenty. Dell was thirty at the time, living in Sudlersville, and the two men probably met or played against each other.

Dell determined when he had his firstborn son that his boy would have every opportunity to develop into a first-rate ballplayer and catcher.

It seems almost a certainty that in late October 1915 Dell took his son, James, to a baseball game at nearby Hillsboro twenty-three miles away in Caroline County. Charlie "Buck" Herzog, manager of the Cincinnati Reds, who was living in Caroline County in the off-season, was challenging the Philadelphia Athletics' Frank Baker to a game in which both men chose players from Talbot, Queen Anne's, and Caroline County. Both men played third base and batted cleanup. Herzog stepped onto the field in his light gray Reds' uniform with red cap and stockings and a white band just above the shoe tops. Baker donned his White Elephants' uniform with black and white stripes about the cap and darker gray uniform. Several hundred automobiles lined the field, and more than 2,000 local fans came to see the contest, many of them betting on the outcome. Several times, both Baker and Herzog disagreed with the umpire, Herzog usually having his way.

Herzog's team won the game, 5-4, thanks to a long fly ball hit by Baker being turned into the game's final out by Herzog's center fielder. If young James Foxx was there, he had to be impressed by the two big-name ballplayers, the excitement they generated in the fans, and the closeness of the contest. Dell didn't play in the game; he was past his playing prime at thirty-nine.

The combined skills and baseball knowledge of Dell Foxx and Frank Baker would later serve a very useful purpose—the grooming of one of the most powerful baseball talents ever—James "Jimmie" Foxx—into a topflight major-league player.

1

IN THE BEGINNING: LIFE IN SUDLERSVILLE

Tucked away in fertile farmland on the Eastern Shore of Maryland, the town of Sudlersville, in Queen Anne's County, played host to a community of self-sufficient farmers with a deep-rooted love for baseball from the 1890s through the early 1930s. Grain, vegetables, and dairy products were the mainstay of the farmers who toiled in Queen Anne's County, which lay south of the Chester River and had much flatter farmland than Kent County on the north of the river.

Sudlersville came to be during the middle of the eighteenth century after Walter Smith, from Calvert County, Maryland, sold 800 acres of land to Mr. Joseph Sudler in 1740. The area was first known as Sledmore when a small community began to develop at Sudler's Cross Roads. Before the American Revolutionary War, settlers farmed tobacco and corn; after the war, low tobacco prices forced farmers to emphasize grains and corn as their main crops. The town's name was changed to Sudlersville in 1839, and the arrival of the railroad in 1869 spurred new growth. Before the railroad, Sudlersville had only fifteen houses, one general store, a post office, a Methodist Church, and a blacksmith shop, all connected by dirt roads. Sixteen years later, Sudlersville had thirty-nine homes. Peach orchards became abundant in the area beginning about 1875, with some of the fruit being dried or canned for shipment to distant markets.

Sudlersville is located at the intersection of Route 300, which travels east-west, and Route 313, which travels north-south. The town had a population of 221 in 1900 and 247 in 1910, growing at a rate of 20 to 30 people every decade, up to 443 residents in 1980.

In the early 1900s, there were three corner stores and a bank at the town's center. A milk station, two grain elevators, and two canneries, mostly for tomatoes and peaches grown nearby, made up most of the rest. The corner stores included Jim Knott's store, Charlie Chance's Corner Grocery, and Nat Johnson's store. By the early 1920s, Arthur Truitt had opened his barbershop in the Roe Building near the corner of Church and Main Streets, and the town had its own library. Cox Memorial Hall was a chief meeting place for community events and was located on Church

Street just south of the town's main intersection. The area's farmers often met at Cox Hall on various agricultural issues, and the town's churches, schools, and civic betterment league used the building for various activities, especially for the town's youth, including drama, comedy, lectures, and musicals, almost weekly. Dr. Arthur Sudler was the town physician in the early 1900s, and by about 1920 he had started passing off some of his patients to Dr. C. Metcalffe.

Sudlersville's future claim to fame occurred when James Emory Foxx was born to Martha (Mattie) Smith Foxx and Samuel Dell Foxx on October 22, 1907. As he grew up, he was James to his parents and Jim to his schoolmates.

Most likely, as was customary for the day on the Eastern Shore in the early 1900s, the newborn infant was delivered right in their home by a midwife. In this case, the midwife was probably Mattie Smith Foxx's sister, Lyda Smith, who regularly aided mothers in the Sudlersville area.

Mattie had been born in 1877. Her father, Joseph Emory Smith (born in 1839) and mother, Susanna Rebecca Rutter (born in 1844), were grain farmers near Crumpton (in Queen Anne's County), where they lived and raised wheat, corn, and tomatoes. Mattie had eight brothers: Frank, Thomas, John, Charles, William, Olin, Lee, and Elwood, and three sisters: Lyda, Mary, and Lula.

Dell was born in 1876. The Foxx family hailed from Kennedyville, in Kent County (Maryland). Dell's father, James Benton Foxx, and his mother, Annie D. Pennell, were also grain farmers in Kent County. Dell had one brother, James Benton, Jr., who married but never had children, and five sisters: Sarah, Nellie, Mary Ann, Bessie, and Annie. It was left to Dell to continue the family name.

Dell was a member of the 1902 Sudlersville town ball team, owned and managed by Sudlersville resident John (Johnny) E. George. The Sudlersville team was one of the strongest clubs in a local area that probably spanned parts of Queen Anne's, Kent, and Caroline Counties in Maryland and most of Delaware. The rivalry between Sudlersville and Smyrna (Delaware) was especially intense, with heavy coverage in the *Smyrna Times* of all Smyrna's games. Admission was charged for many, if not all, the games, presumably to pay for meals and the cost of railway transportation to and from the team's games. It's believed that the players typically didn't receive any salary, but on occasion received cash tips or payments from fans.

Dell played mostly in right field for the 1902 Sudlersville team. His position was listed as such on a card associated with the club photograph taken in Smyrna. The *Smyrna Times* listed the names of pitchers and catchers for each team under "batteries" in each game played between Sudlersville and Smyrna, but Ginley was always listed as Sudlersville's catcher. However, Dell may have played catcher for Sudlersville on other occasions that season. Most newspaper accounts in the *Centreville Observer* in the 1920s recalled that he was a catcher during his playing days. He was a handsome man, one of the best-looking men on the team. He had sharp facial features, blue eyes, no mustache, and was not at all heavy or stocky. He had wide shoulders and muscular arms.

There were only nine players in the team photograph, but at least two players (Chance and Leitner) not in the team photograph were mentioned as pitchers for the Sudlersville club in individual game accounts in the *Smyrna Times*. Although the players were generally signed to some sort of "contract," the roster changed often, depending on the availability of players. There was little or no room for injury when only nine or ten players traveled with the club. The catcher, W. Ginley (also spelled McGinley) used a catcher's mask and chest protector. Dell used a dark-colored bat with a thinner handle than those used by some of his teammates. Johnny George wore a heavy handlebar mustache, as did several players on the club. The team had a "mascot," Colonel Bull, an elderly gentleman with a gray mustache, dressed in a suit. The club's umpire, Seward Barwick, dressed in a white dress shirt and bow tie. It's uncertain how many players on the club other than Dell actually lived in Sudlersville. The town teams emphasized home talent but were not averse to filling the roster with high-quality players from other areas. Winning was especially important.

In the early 1900s, horse racing and baseball were the favorite spectator sports for men on the Eastern Shore not lucky enough to be playing on the teams. The *Smyrna Times* reported in 1902, "Baseball enthusiasm has been so much revived that it seems to be the topic of conversation on every street corner. The diversion is popular with our people and the quiet hours of the afternoon find many of our business men enjoying the greatest of American sports."

Prior to marrying Mattie, Dell had been a tenant farmer for some time and lived with Lee Smith, Mattie's brother, in Sudlersville just before Lee married Mary "Mamie" Legar. Mattie and Dell were married on December 27, 1904, at the Calvary Methodist Episcopal Church in Sudlersville. Mattie's parents attended the wedding, but the *Kent News* mentioned that Dell's father was deceased before the marriage and made no mention of his mother. Mattie wore a cream silk tulle and carried carnations, while Dell and his ushers wore black with boutonnieres of carnations. Harry Fallowfield, Dell's cousin, played the wedding march as the bridal party entered the church. The ushers were Walter Stant, Luther Chance, and Mattie's brothers, John and William Smith. Reverend W. O. Bennett, pastor of the church, performed the wedding ceremony, and a wedding reception was held at Mattie's parents' home near Crumpton. Dell and Mattie took up residence immediately on a farm near Sudlersville.

During their early married life, Mattie and Dell were tenant farmers, renting the property they lived on and making enough money from farming to pay the landowner and provide themselves with food and clothing but not much else. Many other families there shared the same lifestyle, tilling the land and growing crops for shares, with the general rule being that the tenant farmer and landowner shared the crop fifty-fifty. The Foxxes took pride in providing for their own family. Mattie Foxx always had a black servant, at least until her son, James, was about twelve. The Foxxes grew grain crops, produced milk, grew and canned vegetables, and cured their own pork products such as ham and sausage. Jim's cousins, Gladys Smith Truitt, daughter of Lee Smith and Mamie Legar, and Mattie Jarman Anthony, daughter of Lyda Smith and William Jarman, recalled that some of the few food products bought by their families and the Foxxes were flour, sugar, coffee, and some fruit. For the most part, they were self-sufficient in terms of food.

In January 1908, a few months after Jim's birth, the Foxxes moved to a farm across the road from the farm of Jim's cousin, Mattie Jarman. The farms were located on either side of the dirt road often referred to at that time as "Church Hill Road" (now Sudlersville Road and Route 300) because it led westward to Church Hill, several miles away.

Mattie Jarman Anthony remembers that "Jim was still in long clothes, typical of a young infant, at the time the Foxx family first moved in the farm across the dirt road. I always stood on my tiptoes to look through the front door when the Foxxes would come down our lane to visit."

Mattie recalls:

Threshing season for the grain crops came every summer, and we had a threshing run. Mr. Louis Anderson had his rig with a steam engine and thresher. I think there were about eight or nine farms on what he called his run. The steam engine required a lot of water. And we had a ditch there, near a stream. We used a water wagon that Jim and I enjoyed riding and we carried three barrels in it. When you got to the ditch, the men dipped a bucket to fill the barrels. It took one or two men all day, just hauling water back and forth.

The Foxxes and Jarmans helped each other during the threshing run. "Lyda and Mattie [Jimmie's mother] always worked together. The hog work was done the same way. See, in the fall, we always did our butchering. When we butchered, Aunt Mattie would be at our home to help," Mattie Jarman added.

Jim's mother's parents celebrated their golden wedding anniversary on January 29, 1917, with a huge poultry dinner at their home near Crumpton. Every family that attended brought a freezer of ice cream that was a different flavor from the others, making it a memorable event for all the grandchildren. "Master James Foxx of Sudlersville" was listed by the *Observer* as one of the ninety-six family members who attended. Jim's grandparents received $75 in gold and numerous other gifts. Jim was just a little more than nine at the time and was impressed by grandfather Smith's tales of his role as a young captain in his mid-twenties in the Union Army during the Civil War (according to Mattie Jarman Anthony and Mildred Smith Barracliff, sister of Gladys Smith Truitt and therefore another cousin of Jimmie Foxx), rather than serving with the Confederate Army under the name Joseph Emory Foxx, as reported frequently in the literature. A story passed down in many newspaper and magazine articles recalls that Jim fantasized about joining the Army for World War I as a drummer boy after hearing grandfather Smith's stories. Only a few months after his fiftieth wedding anniversary, grandfather Smith died, never seeing Jim's younger brother.

Mattie Foxx gave birth to her second child, Sammy Dell Foxx, Jr., in June 1918, when Jim was ten. It's unknown whether she had unsuccessful pregnancies in between the births of her two boys. Sammy Dell, being so much younger than Jim, grew up idolizing his brother for his accomplishments in athletics, especially baseball. Sammy Dell had some athletic ability of his own and the gift of gab, like his father, to the point that some of his classmates felt he talked too much. He was likable, but attached a lot of his own identity to being Jimmie Foxx's brother.

There were two Methodist churches in Sudlersville, the Calvary Methodist Episcopal Church, which the Foxx family attended, and the Asbury Methodist Church. The Foxxes participated in church picnics at Tolchester Beach every summer, where family portraits were sometimes taken.

Jim's cousins Mildred Smith Barracliff and Gladys Smith Truitt lived on the opposite side of town from Jim and Mattie Jarman, about 1.5 miles east of Sudlersville. Mildred remembers:

> We always took our own picnic baskets at Tolchester Beach. They were usually packed with fried chicken, bread and butter, pickles, ham, bananas, and cake and cookies. We had gallons of lemonade. I can recall that some of us were usually stung by yellow jackets that wanted the lemonade. There were a few small concessions and a hotel where food and "ades" were made available, but most of us really could not afford it. Perhaps we were allowed a nickel for an ice cream cone. There were small, open-air pavilions—dancing to nickelodeon music, roller skating, bowling duck pins and a sort of arcade for games. We seldom participated in very much due to lack of money, but we walked around and watched others. Of course, for about two hours in the afternoon, we all went bathing in the Chester

River. We were carefully watched by our mothers who sat and rocked on the long veranda of the hotel. Our fathers swam with us.

Virtually the entire town of gathered for its annual Fourth of July Firemen's Carnival. At first, one whole block of town was roped off for games such as bingo, wheels of chance, ring toss, ball throwing at milk bottles, darts thrown at balloons, and sometimes a baseball game. Eventually, the community moved the carnival to the more spacious grounds in back of the high school. Then a merry-go-round was rented. The money taken in was usually divided between the firemen and the owners of the amusements.

In August of 1919, the town of Sudlersville held an extra carnival as a fundraiser to help pay for some of the costs for Cox Memorial Hall. Some of the carnival's features that young James Foxx and other townfolk enjoyed along the midway were the "African dip," wheels of fortune, "hit the coon," "swat the Kaiser," "ring the cane," and the "hurdy gurdy." In the big tent, Professor Peak of Philadelphia performed magic tricks, and the well-known "Human Water Tank," Sam Johnson, gave two shows nightly. Richard Pastell captivated the crowd each evening with his skill and daring on the trapeze.

Heavy snows in winter fostered horse-drawn sleigh races between some of the men in town, and the children ice skated at McFadden's mill pond, located near Dudley's Corner. Dell Foxx was especially fond of horse racing and competed in trotter races and sleigh-ride races whenever he could. He competed in harness racing at Sudlersville Driving Park, a local racetrack located near Racetrack Road just a few miles south and east of the town. Horse-drawn sleigh races occurred right in the town of Sudlersville. Usually three men would compete in a given sleigh race and they were one of the highlight events in town following any heavy snowfall. The races would start about three-quarters of a mile south of town on Elevators Road, an extension of South Church Street. The horses and sleighs created quite a racket and commotion, with snow being kicked up by the horses during the run and loud clanging from jingle bells. The finish line was the center of town, sometimes referred to as "four corners."

Mattie Foxx was a steadying influence on both Dell and Jimmie. According to Lemuel "Bo" Benton, longtime Sudlersville resident, Mattie often had a hand on one of Dell's shoulders, as if to say, "Calm down. Take it easy." Mattie was a member of the Sudlersville Community Betterment Club, which organized many of the town's activities. She also sang in the church choir and performed janitorial work at the church while her mother played the organ. More importantly, Mattie was the homemaker of the Foxx family, with some athletic ability of her own. She enjoyed playing baseball at Dudley Elementary School, especially batting. In modern terms, she played a role similar to a designated hitter for at least one of the other girls at the school who was fast afoot, but lacked hitting ability. Mattie would bat and the other girl would run the bases.

Dell Foxx was a competitor who liked to win, whether it was baseball, horse races, or whatever. Dell frequently played baseball in the town ball games during the early 1900s, and when he became too old to participate as a player, he umpired many of the games that Jim played in for both the town and the high school teams. He occasionally organized the games. Some people regarded Dell, a highly animated man, a great umpire-baiter. Dell loved baseball. He determined early in Jim's childhood to give his son every opportunity to learn the game and practice it. Every night after farm work was completed, Dell and Jim would go out to a side field and throw a baseball. Gladys Truitt remembers:

> He [Dell] lived baseball for Jim, and Jim lived baseball for him [Dell] or for both of them. Jim was athletic in every way and he developed through athletics. And from the time he could sit up, his father would throw a ball to him, while he was propped up by pillows. And his father was an athlete himself. He wasn't as big as Jim, but he was an athlete. He played baseball and was considered to be very good. And that was Jim's first and last love, anything that had to do with sports, especially baseball.

Mildred Barracliff recalls vividly that:

> As to baseball, Jim grew up with it. His father was a good sandlot player and he wanted his son to play ball, too. When Jim could sit up in a high chair, his father would pitch a soft rubber ball up on the tray of the chair. He insisted, from the first, that Jim pick up the ball in his hands. He taught him to throw it. By the time Jim was two, he could often catch the ball. By about three, they often played outdoors with a hard ball. For Jim, the object that was thrown didn't have to be a ball. Anything he could pick up when he was small, he threw. His family came to see us one Sunday and Jim used my beloved teddy bear for a ball until I cried so hard he gave it back to me. I think I was only about three and he was about five. Afterward, whenever I saw the Foxx carriage turn in our lane, I quickly hid my dolls, teddy bear and all. As soon as Jim's hands got a little size to them, his father put one of his gloves on him and lessons progressed until Jim could catch a hard thrown ball. I recall one Sunday afternoon when Jim proudly showed us his new baseball glove. I think he must have been about eight years old then. His father at that time threw hard balls to him and Jim never missed. My father said, "By gum, Dell,

you're throwing that ball too hard. If he misses one it will kill him."
Dell answered, "He won't miss it. He'll catch it. He's going to be a
big league catcher."

The first mention of Jim Foxx in an athletic event appears to have been
in the *Observer* on May 24, 1919. "J. Fox" (sic) (from Sudlersville High) won
the baseball throw in the County Athletic meet on May 21 with a peg of
183 feet, 5 inches for the 95-pound class (less than 115 pounds). He was
eleven and one-half years old.

It didn't matter how many miles Dell had to travel to make sure his son
James played ball. Dell would take him by horse and buggy and later by
auto to play for local teams when Jimmie was only a young teenager. The
youngster was in high demand as a baseball player at a very young age.

Jim and Mattie Jarman walked eastward together for several years
about one mile to the Dudley School (it's uncertain whether Jim switched
to Sudlersville Grammar School in town for a year or two before attending
Sudlersville High). Dudley School was referred to as a "country school"
by local residents and was much like other one-room schoolhouses:
warmed by a wood stove, roughly twenty-five seats, slate tablets for
writing with pencils, a map of the United States, a picture of George
Washington on the wall, and a U.S. flag placed near the teacher's desk at
the front of the room. Miss Mary Sparks was their first teacher, followed
by Miss Lillian Leager. Foxx and the other boys had to keep the floor
cleaned, the water bucket filled, and plenty of wood handy for heating
during the winter months.

It was probably as a very young teenager that James Foxx realized he
was stronger and quicker than boys his age and many boys even a few
years older. He recalled years later:

> Although it never occurred to me to wonder why, I found that in
> our races across the pastures, I was usually several steps ahead of
> the others, and in short fierce wrestling matches of the school yard
> I had the strength of back and arms to do somewhat better than hold
> my own. I was rather proud of my strength and took a boyish delight
> in turning down the hand of the older boys with a quick snap of the
> wrist and the brawny paws and big forearms that had been made
> hard from years of milking [cows] stood me in good stead.

Beginning in the fall of 1921, Jim attended Sudlersville High School,
which was in the center of town on South Church Street, several miles from
his home. At about the same time, the family moved away from its farm

across the road from the Jarmans to another farm on Roe Road, just west of Benton Corners Road. Jim now had almost a three-mile walk to school. The dark red brick building that was Sudlersville High from 1921 through 1924 still stands. Its facade is now the front portion of Sudlersville Elementary School, on South Church Street. The school had double doors at the front and rear, two main floors, a basement with a coal-fired furnace, and a storage attic. When Jim attended Sudlersville High, it included students from the towns of Sudlersville, Barclay, Ingleside, Templeville, and Crumpton.

The storage attic on the third floor had a small walk-in doorway. Official school records, textbooks, extra books, and costumes for plays were stored here. The first two floors had four classrooms each. The second floor had a long, narrow cloak room with a high ceiling and was connected to a large balcony inside the building that faced through a large window toward Church Street and inward to the foyer on the first floor. The balcony held about eight to ten students easily. This is where the bigger boys, such as Foxx, ate lunch.

During warm weather, some of the boys occasionally left school early through the opened back windows, climbing onto brick ledges and jumping to the ground. Even Jim, who was well-behaved normally, used this escape route to sneak out early. Like other farm boys, Jim typically started school later than town children. His first obligation was to help with the crop harvest. Often he had to leave school early in April to prepare the farm for planting.

All of the students collected in the assembly room for at least several minutes on Fridays, special days such as Lincoln's Birthday, any time the principal wanted to talk to the entire student body about behavior, maybe to get together to sing a patriotic song, or simply for poetry reading. The students usually marched in singing patriotic songs to the music of a piano.

The school was staffed by three full-time teachers. Miss Anna Harrison, the principal at the end of Jimmie's stay in 1924, taught English grammar, literature, and French. Mr. Haupt (in 1921) and Mr. Harry Rasin (in 1922-24) taught geometry, science, and chemistry. Mrs. Fannie Merrick taught history, Latin, and algebra. Once each week, Professor John T. Bruehl came to Sudlersville High to teach manual training (industrial arts) to the boys while Miss Branner taught home economics to the girls. Professor Bruehl was also the Athletic Director for Queen Anne's County and the high school baseball coach for Centreville. He had originally considered the ministry, but later chose to influence boys through educating them about athletics and industrial arts.

Jim had average grades in Latin, math, chemistry, and history, but did better in English, agriculture, manual training, and conduct. He missed many days of school each year, helping out with never-ending farm work.

For reasons known only to him, Jim was especially sensitive about the spelling of his first name. Mildred Barracliff recalls that "He always insisted that it be spelled with an 'ie' at the end, not a 'y.' "

John Bruehl admired Jim Foxx's athletic abilities. He was thrilled to have Foxx on the 1923 County All-Star baseball team after the regular high school baseball season, and the fact that Bruehl organized the club and its schedule gave Foxx and other teammates a chance to showcase their talents throughout the state.

On one occasion when Sudlersville High entered its softball team for a tournament at the County Field Day, Bruehl, representing Centreville's team, tried to convince Miss Harrison to withdraw Jim from the Sudlersville team. Miss Harrison replied, "I certainly am not! He is only sixteen and is eligible. Don't you wish Centreville had him?"

Jim's high school athletic career began in the spring of 1921, apparently while he was still finishing elementary school. At the age of thirteen, Foxx was batting second in the lineup and was the regular catcher on the baseball team. Sudlersville played Centreville, Tri-County, and Stevensville from Queen Anne's County, Chestertown High from Kent County, and Ridgely High and Greensboro High from Caroline County. Sudlersville High was the dominant team during the 1921 season, though the actual game accounts in the *Observer* were spotty.

Jim's last name was often spelled with one "x" rather than two in newspaper accounts. After he joined professional baseball at the major-league level, some stories about Foxx claimed he had added the second "x" after he was born. He did not. Jim's last name was spelled "Foxx" from birth, just as his father's and his father's before him.

In the 1921 spring County track-and-field meet, Jim won the junior unlimited division 80-yard dash with a time of ten seconds. He also placed first in the division's running high jump (4 feet, 9 and 3/4 inches), and soon advanced to the State of Maryland's Olympiad, held in Baltimore on June 11. The state track-and-field competition included contestants from Baltimore City and the twenty-three counties of Maryland. Jim had idolized Olympic sprinter Charley Paddock and aspired to be a champion runner of the same caliber. His early accomplishments in track and field encouraged him to hold onto those dreams.

Prior to the state track and field meet, the boys from Queen Anne's County were taken care of by members of the Parents-Teachers Association of Govans and Cedarcroft in Baltimore, staying in homes there for two nights and one day, "sleeping in good beds and enjoying home cooking," as a strategy to better prepare for the competitions. In the 1921 State Olympiad, Jim finished fourth in the junior unlimited division's 80-yard dash and running high jump.

The first event of the Fourth of July weekend celebration in Sudlersville that year was a baseball game on Saturday, July 2, between the married men and single men of the town. The single men were the winners, and although the players' names weren't listed in the *Observer*, it seems almost certain that Jim played against Dell in this game.

From June through September of 1921, Jim, just shy of fourteen, kept busy playing catcher for Sudlersville in the summer baseball league. He batted fourth and fifth in a lineup with some boys three and four years older. Sudlersville played against Eastern Shore towns in Maryland, including teams from Millington, Barclay, Ridgely, Denton, Massey, and Kennedyville, and from Bridgetown, Delaware.

One of the teams' coaches was Jim's uncle, Olin Smith, who sported a heavy mustache and wore a straw hat with a wide band during practices and games. With only ten players and a mascot, the team had little room for injury; the players had to be dependable and dedicated to their cause. The most prominent players on the club were Foxx, Stanley Atkinson, Wallace Ross, and Kenneth Knotts. Although money was usually scarce for team equipment for town teams, the Sudlersville club managed to raise enough funds to furnish uniforms for the players. A picture exists of the team, and Foxx appears to be one of the youngest players on the squad. Their uniforms were pinstriped with dark trim around the edge of the sleeves and collar. A dark bill provided a clear contrast to their fully pinstriped caps.

Jim played baseball for Sudlersville High again during the spring of 1922. It was a rebuilding year for Sudlersville, so despite his young age, the fourteen-and-one-half-year-old Foxx was already one of the team's leaders. Sudlersville played against high school teams from Centreville, Tri-County (also called Queen Anne's then), and Stevensville.

Foxx continued to excel in organized track-and-field events. During the 1922 county meet at Centreville on May 17, Jim won the 80-yard dash in just 9 seconds and took first place in the running high jump (5 feet, 1 inch) for the junior unlimited class. Then on June 9, in the eighth annual State Olympiad held at Baltimore, he established new state records in the 80-yard dash for the junior unlimited division (8.8 seconds in the first heat and 8.6 seconds in the second).

A week later, when school closed for the summer, Jim began playing town ball for the Eastern Shore town of Goldsboro. Information about this activity is scanty, but some reports indicate that this was the first time Foxx was paid to play baseball. He was at his usual position as catcher and batted fourth. In one game he opposed Alton Scott, a local fastball pitcher from Price, Maryland. The two boys crossed paths many times as team mates and opponents.

In October 1922, Foxx was busy playing soccer for Sudlersville High along with ten other boys, including one of his best friends, Leon Stack, and his cousin Claude Smith. The team was an excellent defensive squad, but typically it scored very few goals. It won its first contest by one goal and then tied its next three games, two of which were scoreless.

Also during the 1922-23 school year, young Jim played on the high school volleyball and basketball teams during the winter months. He led Sudlersville to the county volleyball championship over Centreville in that town's armory on February 8, 1923.

Throughout Jim's high school baseball career, league schedules consisted of six or eight games for each school, because there were four or five county teams, depending on the particular year. Games between league rivals were hotly contested, then as now. Centreville always drew the biggest crowds at Sudlersville.

Harry Rasin performed in a loose fashion as the baseball coach for Sudlersville and was well-liked by the players. Dell Foxx often came onto the playing field during practice to offer advice and even umpired many of the high school games.

Because baseball games were often scheduled for Friday afternoons, school was dismissed at one o'clock, instead of the usual three o'clock dismissal. If the game was at home, most of the Sudlersville High students remained to watch and support their team, as did many people from town. Often as many as 100 or more people would attend a Friday afternoon game, a good size crowd, considering the size of the town. Some of the students brought chairs from the school, but most spectators simply sat on the grass or stood. Mildred Barracliff remembers that she never missed a game while Jim was playing.

On very warm days, some students watched from open windows of the school's assembly room, because it faced the catcher's back and was closest to home plate. The border of the outfield was marked by a wire fence with overgrown weeds and shrubbery. The right field corner was located on a line close to the back right corner of the school building, while home plate was closest to the back left corner. A wire backstop was in place to block foul balls, wild pitches, and passed balls directly beyond home plate. A mix of dirt and gravel made up the infield, which was the lowest part of the field. It didn't take much rain to make the field unplayable.

At home games, Sudlersville High fans eagerly waited for Jim Foxx to belt an opposing pitcher's offering into a farmer's corn field well beyond the outfield. "Jim hit many homers into that corn field. The field wasn't big enough for him," recalled Mildred Barracliff, laughing.

Jim was a menacing presence at the plate for opposing high school pitchers. He stood in the batter's box with those big arms and shoulders, blue eyes coldly staring out at the mound, waiting for the next pitch. He was feisty on the base paths, too, often taunting the pitcher while leading off the base with short, quick steps, daring the pitcher to try to pick him off. He was aggressive and the team leader, and his performance set the tone and level of confidence for the rest of his team.

As usual, Jim excelled in the twentieth annual Queen Anne's County track-and-field meet in late May 1923. He set new records for the junior unlimited class for the county when he ran the 220-yard dash in 24.4 seconds and placed first in the running high jump at 5 feet, 6 inches. Foxx also played speedball for Sudlersville High in a tournament at the county track-and-field meet, leading his team of ten players to the championship.

During the 1923 high school baseball season, Foxx played mostly at catcher and usually batted cleanup when Sudlersville played Centreville, Stevensville, Church Hill, and Tri-County. The season opener between Sudlersville and Church Hill was especially frustrating for pitcher Alton Scott, who lost 2-1 to Sudlersville despite holding Foxx hitless and allowing only one hit the whole game.

The day after Sudlersville captured the 1923 county high school baseball pennant, Jim began playing catcher and occasionally pitcher for the Queen Anne's County All-Stars with manager Bruehl and coach E. Clyde Walls. Bruehl typically wore his billed cap and Norfolk jacket to the games so he was easily recognized by onlookers.

The season opener for the All-Stars on April 28 was at Centreville. Foxx smashed a triple and homer to lead his club to a 5-0 win over City College, a high school from Baltimore. The game was typical of the kind of hitting Foxx produced during the All-Stars' schedule of roughly 30 games, as he batted over .400 for the season.

Foxx was only fifteen and one-half, yet he was his team's captain and top hitter, leading his club to a winning season over teams with mostly seventeen- and eighteen-year-olds. The All-Stars played against other high schools, as well as small colleges, freshman college teams, and even semipro teams. Jack Wesley, sports editor for the *Observer* in 1923, made sure that the All-Stars' game accounts were covered in the paper, usually with a box score and often with a short narrative summary, to the delight of local baseball fans.

Bruehl taught Jim an important piece of sportsmanship very much in line with Foxx's personality: if there's an argument or rhubarb with the umpire, never argue with the umpire. Just go sit on a base until the argument is over. Foxx did just that.

Other standouts on the All-Stars were the hard-hitting Carlton Mandrell from Centreville, who batted fourth while Foxx batted third, and "speed marvel" Alton Scott from nearby Price. Several of Jim's teammates from the Sudlersville High School team joined the All-Stars, including Claude Smith, Roy Godwin, James Roe, Thomas Jones, and Ed Walraven.

This was an exciting time for Jim and his teammates, seeing parts of Maryland on the Eastern and Western shores for the first time, and the tour by the Queen Anne's County All-Stars spread awareness of Jim Foxx's baseball talents among high school and college baseball coaches throughout the state of Maryland.

When the All-Stars played against City College, Jim broke his favorite bat, a heavy model made of hickory. Professor Bruehl was obliged to drive Jim to several stores before they found a replacement. Bruehl recalled, "Jim could swing it like any other player would swing a lighter one made of ashwood."

Jim pitched several times with Bruehl's All-Star club, but seldom with much effectiveness, losing 11-5 to Cambridge High and 10-0 to Mount St. Mary's of Emmitsburg, Maryland.

One of the highlights of young Jim's athletic career occurred on June 8, when he won both events that he entered in the 1923 State of Maryland Olympiad in Baltimore. He placed first in the junior running high jump (5 feet, 8 inches) and the 220-yard run (23 seconds—a new state record). Several different athletes were pictured in the *Baltimore Morning Sun* on June 9, but only "James E. Fox [sic]" was depicted in a closeup photograph.

Assuredly, boys from around the state admired Foxx after the track-and-field meet. On the ferry ride back from Baltimore to Love Point, Ralph Johnson, from Federalsburg High School (Caroline County), said to Jim, "Boy, they were really chasing a 'fox' today they couldn't catch."

Jim's performance prompted observers to select him as the most promising athletic prospect in the State of Maryland. Writer Hy Dykeman of the *Baltimore American* was particularly impressed with Foxx. Dykeman wrote, "A muscular 165-pounder, this boy is a star on the baseball club representing the county, playing the hardest position on the club, catcher." Because of rules governing the Olympiad, Foxx could only compete in two events at the state meet; otherwise, he may have been even more dominant.

Two days after the County All-Stars played their last scheduled game, the Queen Anne's County "Has Beens" challenged the All-Star contingent of high school boys to a game on June 18 at Centreville. As with many of the other games played by the All-Stars at Centreville, the *Observer* advertised the upcoming contest with a half-page ad announcing an admission charge of a quarter, probably to help defray operating costs of the club. The boys easily beat the "Has Beens," 24-7, but the *Observer* praised Jimmie's father for his part in the game. "Del [sic] Foxx of Sudlersville, who has caught many a hard-fought contest performed at short, and frequently showed flashes of his old-time form." The article was not nearly so complimentary of the other "Has Beens." By then, Dell was forty-six or forty-seven.

During the same period, Dell was one of five catchers listed on a preseason roster of twenty-five players for Centreville's club that played in the newly formed Tri-County League during the summer of 1923. But Dell didn't appear in the partial listing of lineups that were published thereafter in the *Observer*.

Jim's prominence in state athletic contests enabled Professor Bruehl to arrange scholarship funding with H. C. "Curley" Byrd, track-and-field coach at the University of Maryland, in case Jim decided to attend college. Byrd probably saw Jim play for Bruehl's baseball All-Stars against the University of Maryland freshmen team in mid-May of 1923 at College Park, Maryland. The Queen Anne's County All-Stars lost 3-2, but Foxx, who played catcher, managed a base hit while batting third in the lineup. It's also certain that Byrd knew of Foxx's accomplishments at the annual State of Maryland Olympiads for high school students.

Bruehl said of Foxx, "He was the greatest natural athlete I have ever seen." While attending Dickinson College at Carlisle, Pennsylvania, Bruehl had scrimmaged against Jim Thorpe, a student at Carlisle Indian School. In later years he claimed Foxx's natural abilities probably surpassed those of Thorpe. Given Thorpe's legendary accomplishments, Bruehl's compliments put Foxx in very fast company. Thorpe was declared the greatest all-around athlete and football player of the first half of the twentieth century by over 400 sportswriters and broadcasters.

Jim was not without his moments of mischief. Whether sneaking out of school early or tying a string to a pig's tail and pulling it, he was like any other boy. But he was generally well-behaved and gave no cause to worry for Mattie Foxx. Jim's chores on the farm and his year-round involvement in sports allowed little time for mischief. Just the same, given the opportunity, Foxx enjoyed cutting up with the other boys as much as anyone. Some of his most frequent companions were his classmate Leon Stack and his cousin Claude "Shine" Smith.

The church that the Foxxes attended had a measurable effect on Jim's general attitude about himself and the way he treated others and occasionally went to great lengths to make a point. On Sunday, July 9, 1922, Calvary Sunday school teacher Harry Jones took fifteen boys, including "James" Foxx, by auto to the Delaware Work House at Greenbank, Delaware, as guests of Warden Plummer. The *Observer* opined: "The boys were given a glimpse of prison life and saw evidence of what happens when a man goes wrong."

Jim continued his baseball exploits by playing town ball for Sudlersville during the summer of 1923, mostly as a catcher, batting third and fourth in the order. Alton Scott was one of Foxx's teammates on the Sudlersville town team, and some of the more hotly contested games were against the Galena and Massey clubs from Kent County. Again, Dell umpired many of the games, so Jim and his father must have replayed them during their conversations on the way home.

Meanwhile, Frank "Home Run" Baker, who had retired from the major leagues following the 1922 season, was managing and playing for the Trappe (Maryland) team in the Talbot County League and was making loud rumblings about the Eastern Shore League giving Easton, Maryland, a franchise for the 1924 season. An editorial at the time in the *Observer* strongly supported Baker's proposal.

Baker, originally named John Franklin Baker, was born in 1886 in Trappe, Maryland, an Eastern Shore town only nine miles from Easton, Maryland. His homer-hitting exploits in the dead ball era of the major leagues made him a legendary folk hero up and down the Eastern Shore and earned him his nickname. Baker entered the majors in 1908 with Connie Mack's (real name was Cornelius McGillicuddy) Philadelphia Athletics. He went on to lead the American League (AL) in home runs for four consecutive years while with the Athletics from 1911 through 1914, and led in runs batted in twice. His two key homers for the A's in the 1911 World Series against the New York Giants initially prompted his nickname.

Baker was the third baseman of Connie Mack's famed "$100,000 in-field," along with Stuffy McInnis at first base, Eddie Collins at second base, and Jack Barry at shortstop. Frank was no slouch with the glove, either, leading the AL third baseman in fielding three times.

After a salary dispute with the A's in 1914-15, at a time when the Federal League was competing with the AL and National League (NL) for major-league players, Frank chose to play semipro ball in 1915 for the Upland (Pennsylvania) club. Beginning in 1916, Frank played for the Yankees for parts of six seasons, except for 1920, when he announced his retirement from the major leagues following his first wife's death, so he could be with his two young daughters. Still, he played part time for the semipro Upland club that season. Commissioner Landis reinstated Baker for the 1921 season with the Yankees, but Frank retired as a player from the major leagues for the last time after the 1922 season.

The Talbot County League was formed in the spring of 1923, and thirteen games were scheduled for each of six teams. The county league selected a former star amateur baseball player from Towson, Maryland— the Reverend Thomas Donaldson, who was the rector at Christ Episcopal Church in Easton—to preside over the league, and he accepted. The league was designed strictly for amateur players, and when Frank Baker appeared on the playing field for the Trappe baseball club on June 27 in a game against St. Michael's, that club's manager Dawson protested. Baker wore his light gray Yankee road uniform with a bold, navy blue "New York" written across the front of his jersey. As it happened, Frank batted a poor 0 for 4, with two walks and one run scored in a 17-2 victory for Trappe.

Trappe went on to compile a league-leading 11-2 record, with Baker appearing in six of his club's games while batting .400. Hard-throwing Mildred Slaughter was Trappe's ace starting pitcher, filling that role in more than half the club's games and striking out from ten to twenty batters per game.

As a young teenager, Jim Foxx was not generally interested in girls, although he had several dates with schoolmate Ethyl "Shorty" Coleman, who had a crush on him. Jim engaged in a longer-term romance beginning in the summer of 1923. Helen Tarring Harrison met Jim Foxx that year at the Fourth of July Firemen's Carnival in Sudlersville. Helen was spending part of the summer with her grandparents in nearby Templeville, Maryland, when they decided to seek out the carnival for entertainment. Shortly after they arrived, they noticed a crowd over by one of the tents. There stood Jim, throwing baseballs at milk bottles and winning most of the prizes. Helen's aunt, Lola Benton from Sudlersville, introduced her to Jim. Helen said, "It was instant attraction."

Helen and Jim dated on and off for several years, although the two teenagers never went to school together. Claude Smith would drive Jim over to Templeville, where they would double date with Helen and her sister, Dorothy, sometimes going to the Centreville Opera House to watch the feature motion pictures of the week.

In October 1923, Sudlersville High School's soccer team began league play with two games against each of three teams: Centreville, Stevensville, and Tri-County. Again, Jim was one of the standouts. Although he was listed as the center forward for the team, Coach Rasin played him at various positions, including halfback and forward. Judging from Jim's position in a photograph of the team published in the *Observer*, Foxx was probably the captain of the team. He was seated by himself in the front row in the center, holding a soccer ball in his lap. The other ten players and Coach Rasin were all standing behind Foxx. Jim combined his excellent speed and superior strength to make an imposing presence on the field, whether dribbling the ball or battling opponents for it, and he had tremendous leg strength for booting the ball a long distance or for rapid speed over a short distance.

On October 26, Jim enabled Sudlersville to defeat archrival Centreville by scoring the only goal of the game from the halfback position just as time expired. Two weeks later, Sudlersville finished the soccer season with a 5-1 record and took the county championship.

Sudlersville continued its dominance of county sports early in the spring of 1924 by copping the high school basketball championship. Harry Rasin was again the team's coach. Jim was the team's captain, played center, and led his team in scoring. He was by far the most muscular of the five players on Sudlersville High's squad, as seen in a picture of the team in their tanktop basketball jerseys.

Winning the championship was made more significant because Sudlersville had only five players (Foxx, Claude Smith, Leon Stack, Marion Wallace, and Merrick Wilson) and had no home court. It played all of its games away from home. Even its practice time was limited, because the team could practice only if weather permitted. The lack of a reserve made it difficult for any player on the Sudlersville team who suffered an injury during a game.

Foxx decisively dominated each high school sport he played, whether it was baseball, basketball, volleyball, soccer, or track and field. There is no reason to doubt that had football been available, Jim would have made an excellent player.

Before the 1924 Queen Anne's County baseball season began, the nearby town of Easton was pursuing the right to establish a professional baseball team, and some heady local players began to daydream of playing a sport they loved and getting paid for it.

2

THE BAKER-MACK CONNECTION

Baseball fever came to the Eastern Shore town of Easton in 1924. In fact, as early as October 1923, plans were being made to bring professional baseball to Easton as an addition to the Eastern Shore League, a Class D level of competition.

The Eastern Shore League had begun in 1922 as a six-team league. Easton had applied for admission into the league for that inaugural year, but the request was denied because league officials felt the city was too far north of the central city of Salisbury, Maryland. Yet just two years later, Easton's chances looked promising.

The Eastern Shore League fielded eight teams when the 1923 season started, but three clubs (Milford and Laurel in Delaware and Pocomoke in Maryland) dropped out at one point or another so that the league placed Crisfield (Maryland) on an interim status for 1924 and would only restore it to the league if another franchise could be added. Easton was a prime candidate to field a new franchise for the 1924 season because of its population and, quite possibly, because Frank Baker kept plugging for it to receive membership. In early January 1924, the New York Yankees gave Baker his unconditional release so that he could take management of a club in Easton. For two years, Baker had been carried on the Yankees' retired list and had not been made a free agent in the event that he decided to return to the major leagues as an active player.

But Easton's chances weakened when Baker made known his salary demands. In early February, Frank was quoted as asking for 50 percent of the monthly club salary limit ($2,000 to be allotted to the manager *and all the players*) and for a percentage of the gate receipts.

Late in February 1924, an organizational meeting was held in the Talbot County Court House in Easton. Representatives from several towns in Kent County supported establishing a ball club in Easton because many residents could easily attend home games if a club were based there. The town of Chestertown bought stock in the club, and Denton, Ridgely, and Preston from other nearby counties also expressed support. The stock was to be nonassessable, but based on profit sharing. Prospective manager

Frank Baker stated, "No free passes will be issued. This is a good policy." The *Easton Star-Democrat* opined, "No better manager can be secured than Frank—for he knows the game well."

In 1924, Easton had an enthusiastic baseball population of over 3,400 with a larger proportion of well-to-do gentry than other towns on the Eastern Shore. It was the county seat of Talbot County and therefore the center for commerce and law. Talbot County was composed primarily of farmland, especially for grain crops, dairy cattle, and tomatoes, and it had its share of watermen, too. The *Star-Democrat* kept county readers abreast of all farming issues as well as trends in the productivity of local oyster and blue crab harvests, not to mention baseball.

On March 20, the league voted formally to admit Easton. Baker said it was impossible to field a winning club in Easton for the first season but he would do his best by offering every local player a chance to make good. Projected expenditures for the team included a $1,500 deposit with the league, $1,000 for the grandstand and bleachers, $1,000 for spring training expenses, $6,000 for salaries, and $4,500 for uniforms.

By the end of March, *The Sporting News* reported that Baker had lowered his salary demands to some unknown figure and would definitely manage the club and play some at third base. Because he had starred as a major leaguer and was born and raised on the Shore, Baker would prove to be a powerful drawing card as the season unfolded.

Easton merchants asked Reverend Thomas Donaldson to be president of the club. Donaldson loved athletic competition, especially baseball, and considered pursuing a career in professional baseball before turning to the ministry. He was an outfielder on the 1909 Towson Baseball Club in Baltimore County, which won the pennant in the six-team Suburban League. Reverend Donaldson had been in Easton for only two years at the time but had quickly gained a great amount of respect for the spiritual support he had provided to the community. He was well-known for his baseball-playing ability.

Now that the Easton ball club was an official member of the Eastern Shore League, preparation of a ballpark proceeded quickly, and Baker began constructing the team roster through tryouts and scouting trips. After the club's directors were elected on March 24 and an option was secured for a one-year lease for Federal Park, groups of box seats, each containing four fancy wooden chairs with slats on the back, were offered for $25 each chair for the season's forty home games. Federal Park was located near the civic center and courthouse.

As of April 23, Baker had signed eight players to contracts. Doctors, lawyers, merchants, preachers, and farmers began building the tall out-field fence (about twelve feet high) on April 30, signifying the community's strong, unified support for its new professional baseball team.

The *Star-Democrat* greatly expanded the length of its sports section, giving its readers extensive coverage of the Easton ball club and the Eastern Shore League. Narrative summaries and box scores for league games became the norm.

Jim Foxx was still primarily a catcher and batted fourth in the lineup for Sudlersville during the 1924 Queen Anne's County high school season, when his baseball playing took a major turn in direction. Dell and Mattie visited Frank Baker at his home in Trappe, probably in mid-April, and asked him to give their son James a tryout with his club. Baker consented, and near the end of April he watched as Foxx made his appearance. By then, Jim was about 5 feet, 11 inches tall and weighed about 170 pounds. Jim's batting power was especially impressive, but what set him apart from many other power hitters was his speed on the base paths and versatility in fielding several different positions.

Some accounts years later asserted that Jim intended to try out as a pitcher or third baseman, two positions he played very infrequently in high school and town baseball. Those same stories reported that he would try catching if Baker insisted, but he didn't know if he could manage the position or not. Foxx recounted nine years later that he told Baker, "I can play any position except shortstop. I don't like shortstop."

An interview with Baker several years after the 1924 tryout revealed that Foxx showed up for the tryout hoping to make the team as a third baseman or outfielder. When Frank asked Jim if he had played catcher in high school, Foxx told Frank he had. Baker told Foxx, "You are going to catch today, and if you make good, you are a catcher from now on."

Baker recognized instinctively that Jim Foxx had the makings of a star player in the major leagues. The *Observer* and the *Centreville Record* announced in their May 3 issues that "James Foxx had been signed by Baker to play for his Easton club several days earlier." Foxx was not scheduled to report to Baker for a preliminary workout to begin his spring training until May 16, so he was allowed to finish the 1924 high school season with Sudlersville.

Meanwhile, in April, Charles "Buck" Herzog, former NL infielder and speedster, had invited Alton Scott to a tryout with the Newark Bears of the Class AA International League (IL) at their training camp in High Point, North Carolina. If Buck knew about Scott from his pitching prowess in Queen Anne's County and nearby areas in 1923, he most certainly knew about Foxx. Jim's baseball exploits were as well-known as Scott's on the Eastern Shore at the time, and Herzog resided in nearby Caroline County (Maryland) in the off-season. Baker snatched Foxx right from under Herzog's nose and also signed Scott to play for the Easton club after he was released by the Bears.

Baker said that Scott's fastball had enough velocity to match that of major-league strikeout king Walter Johnson. Frank was an expert on the subject of Johnson's pitching ability and the speed of his fastball, having faced him numerous times during his career.

In late April, Sudlersville lost a 10-9 struggle to Centreville. Foxx was inserted as the team's pitcher at the beginning of the eighth inning, allowing no runs and striking out two batters. He collected three hits in four at bats, while playing catcher earlier in the contest.

In addition to playing high schools from Queen Anne's County, Sudlersville traveled to Wilmington, Delaware, on May 6. Wilmington High School defeated Sudlersville handily, 11-4, with Foxx getting one hit while playing center field, where he made six putouts and threw out two base runners from the outfield for two assists. Manager Rasin was correct in inserting Foxx in the primary outfield spot, since the hard-hitting Wilmington team kept the outfield busy.

With four wins and one loss, Sudlersville High entered the last game of the season just one game ahead of Centreville High (three wins and two losses) in the standings. Sudlersville's only loss to that point was the 10-9 game with Centreville and this last game, the grudge match to determine the County championship, was to be played May 9. The *Record* reported that the game was played at Church Hill, rather than Centreville. Despite Sudlersville's better team batting and pitching statistics, Centreville's bats exploded for a 16-10 victory over downhearted Sudlersville, with Foxx pitching the last several innings after Walraven and Walls allowed most of Centreville's runs and were knocked out of the pitcher's box. The final inning of the contest was not played due to darkness. Sudlersville's double loss to Centreville that season left the two teams as County co-champions, a circumstance somewhat less gloomy than the loss itself.

Foxx's potent bat overwhelmed league pitchers during the 1924 county baseball season. He easily led the league in batting, with a torrid .552 average, and was among the league's leaders in extra-base hits (9), hits (17), walks (6), and stolen bases (8) over the six-game schedule.

Jim was elected to the 1924 County All-Star baseball team, and his versatility was recognized when he was listed as playing "any position," by the *Observer* and "utility" by the *Record*—the only player listed as such on the roster. Also, Foxx was the first name mentioned on both newspapers' lists of the All-County team rosters, indicating his prominence in the high school baseball league. However, Jim couldn't participate as a member of the County All-Star team for its May-June schedule because of his contract with the Easton ball club.

Foxx also was unable to compete as a representative of Queen Anne's County in the Tenth Annual Maryland Olympiad on June 7 at Homewood

Field in Baltimore. Until his signing with Easton, the county had planned to enter him in the high jump and 100-yard-dash events.

Jim's last participation in county athletics was in the county track-and-field meet on May 14, two days before he reported to Frank Baker to begin spring training. Jim set county track-and-field records in both events he entered, winning the 100-yard dash in 10.6 seconds and the running high jump (senior unlimited class) with a mark of 5 feet, 6 inches.

Many years later, Jimmie recalled in an article, probably written by a ghostwriter for him for *Sport Magazine*, how he was contacted by Baker.

One morning, I walked down to the mail box and found a penny post card, written in pencil, addressed to me. It was from Frank (Home Run) Baker, who was starting out as manager of the Easton club of the Eastern Shore League. He invited me to come see him for a tryout. I'd never given much thought that I might be able to play pro ball, but I was excited.

If this account is accurate, then Baker probably sent the note to Jim as a formality after already having talked with his father and mother at his home in Trappe.

However, Foxx was suspicious when he read Baker's message on the card. "I thought someone was trying to needle me. I thought it was a couple of cut-ups around the general store in Sudlersville who sent it," Foxx said. But Jimmie noticed the postcard was postmarked in Trappe and figured no one would have gone that far to send a phony message back to Sudlersville. Foxx recalled:

I showed the card to my dad and he said, "Sure, let's go. It'll be an experience, anyway."

I went down to Easton with the idea that I was a third baseman and a pitcher. I'd done a good deal of pitching for the school team. But Baker didn't have any catchers and somebody steered him to me and he asked me if I could play catcher.

"I don't know, sir," I told him. "I'll be glad to try."

After the workout, Baker came up to me. "Did you bring your clothes along?" he asked.

I said, "No." He should have known better, anyway. I was only a farmboy and about all the clothes I had was the pair of overalls I had on. But I went home with dad, quit school (for the remainder of May and June) with the understanding I'd come back and finish up in the fall, and reported to Easton for the season.

The oddity about Jim's recollection of his meeting with Baker is the part that indicates that Jim didn't know if he could catch, but he'd try. Actually, Jim played catcher much more than any other position for his high school team and in summer town ball games, as verified in news accounts of the *Observer* and the *Record* from 1921 through 1924. Former teammates and high school classmates of Foxx remember him as an excellent catcher with a strong throwing arm. He pitched for his high school team only on rare occasions.

Several accounts of Foxx's early involvement with Baker state that Frank convinced Jimmie to bat right-handed instead of left-handed. These accounts seem to be wrong, because none of the people still living in the Sudlersville area in 1989-1992 who saw Jimmie play as a high school student could recall him ever batting left-handed. Besides, Baker, a left-handed batter, was well aware of the advantages, especially then, of batting left-handed. If Jim batted left-handed, why would Baker have tried to convince him to bat right-handed instead? Then again, there's the possibility that Foxx batted much better right-handed than left-handed and was simply experimenting as a switch-hitter at the time he was trying out for the Easton club.

Still, it is believed that Jimmie Foxx always was a right-handed batter. An article in the *Salisbury Times* in early July 1924 confirmed that Foxx batted and threw right-handed while playing for Easton.

A two-week training season began for the Easton club on May 14 at Community Park in preparation for the league's 80-game schedule (16 games against each of 5 teams). Sixteen rainy days in May thwarted completion of Federal Park and prevented proper conditioning of the team. Temperatures on the sunny days were normal, with highs in the 60s and 70s.

When Jim Foxx returned to Easton just before the regular season started, he reported to Reverend Donaldson at Christ Church rectory, as instructed by Baker. Donaldson answered the door and Foxx said, "I've come to play baseball, but I think I'm at the wrong place."

Donaldson paused, looked over the powerfully built Foxx, and said, "No, you've come to the right place," then promptly placed Jim in a boardinghouse in Easton where he could room during the baseball season.

The first mention of Jim Foxx as a player for the Easton club (nicknamed the Farmers) occurred in a May 24 issue of the *Star-Democrat*. The column, "Gossip of the Players," offered that "Fox [sic] is a young man in his teens, but he is good behind the bat [catching], his arm is strong, he is fast, and besides he can play infield. Many predict that he will be in the big leagues in two or three years time. He is said to be a hard hitter." Foxx's home-county newspaper, the *Observer*, spelled his last name correctly, whereas the *Star-Democrat* misspelled his last name for the entire season. This mistake would occur over and over again early in Jim's career.

Just as the Eastern Shore League season was beginning, the May 31 issue of the *Observer* gave its account of Baker's early impression of Foxx: "Foxx has been cracking the fences at Federal Park, and Baker is very much pleased over the way Jimmie Foxx lands on the horsehide." According to the *Star-Democrat* of the same day:

> [S. A.] Warren, [Charles] Bates, and Fox [sic] are fast runners. Each can run 100 yards in 10 seconds, and Fox holds the state record for the 220-yard run, he being merely a boy. Fox is the first catcher [starting catcher] of the club, but can also play outfield. Fox is another popular player. He throws well, is a good hitter, and every practice shows more and more his worth.

Foxx's salary with Easton is estimated to have been between $125 and $200 per month, or about $4.50 to $7.50 for each game.

Baker taught Foxx how to play third base and reinforced Jim's attitude toward umpires and a general clean style of playing. Foxx also paid close attention to Baker's method of batting, recalling several years later, "I tried to stride and swing at the same time the way Baker did."

Foxx's debut as a professional baseball player came on Decoration Day (May 30) against the defending league champion Dover club in Dover, Delaware. Before a crowd of over 3,000 fans, Baker's club fell short, 9-3. Foxx played catcher, batted eighth in the lineup, and drew mixed reviews from onlookers. He was charged with a passed ball in the bottom of the first that didn't figure in any runs scored by Dover. Jim was intentionally walked in the second inning in his first plate appearance, coming to bat with runners on second and third base, two outs, and the pitcher, McFadden, on deck to bat next. McFadden proved Dover's strategy was sound, fouling out to the catcher with the bases loaded. In the bottom of the third, Foxx made a nifty play in the field when he threw out a Dover base runner going from second to third on an attempted sacrifice bunt. Jim doubled to right-center in the eighth for his first base hit as a professional ballplayer, but was stranded there when manager Frank Baker fanned as a pinch hitter for the final out of the inning. Foxx had more trouble at catcher when he had another passed ball in the bottom of the eighth inning, although it again failed to lead to any runs by Dover. While Jim showed signs of the jitters, Baker knew the youngster had great potential and would keep him as a regular in the lineup throughout the season.

The next day, the same two clubs were scheduled to play each other in Easton's home opener. The grandstand at Federal Park seated more than 1,000 spectators at 40 cents a ticket. Bleacher seats were not yet finished because of frequent rain in May. Baker brought the finest light sandy loam, hauled from near his farm, for topsoil on the diamond at Federal Park.

On the day of Easton's home opener, many town merchants closed their shops so their clerks could attend, even though it was Saturday, normally the busiest day for sales. Fans came from nearby towns such as Chestertown, Centreville, Sudlersville, Church Hill, Preston, Denton, Trappe, Chapel, Cordova, and others. The game was heavily attended by folks from Queen Anne's County because three players hailed from there (Foxx, Scott, and Bob Brown) and were in the starting lineup for Easton.

Players left their respective boardinghouses, donned their new uniforms in the armory, and walked over to Federal Park for the pregame warmups. The band entertained the fans for more than an hour, beginning at 1:30 P.M. Exercises for the players began at 2:45 P.M. as the Easton club took the field in their white woolen flannels with purple pinstripes and a large block-lettered "E" on the front of the shirt, plus purple brimmed hats with pinstripes on the cap (no lettering was on the caps). Club President Rev. Donaldson, round-faced and with his proverbial dark-rimmed glasses, neatly tied bow tie, and close-cropped hair, raised the flag slowly in center field; Mayor Wrightson threw out the first ball. Box seat patrons peered through chicken-wire netting that protected them from injury from hard-hit foul tips. Fans that couldn't find a seat in the grandstand stood behind the ropes that reached far beyond third and first bases. Some fans saw the game for free, finding "seats" on firm ground; others climbed up the fence to the roof of the shed adjoining the grounds. Paid admission was 2,269 out of an estimated 2,500 spectators.

In the home opener, Foxx batted eighth and again played catcher. His battery mate was Scott, Jimmie's former high school opponent from nearby Church Hill and teammate on the 1923 County All-Star team. Scott's speedball was legendary among opposing batters, and he struck out thirteen Dover batsmen. Nevertheless, Easton's porous defense failed him miserably. He gave up six hits, three walks, and seven runs, all unearned. A high point occurred for the home crowd in the bottom of the seventh inning, when Foxx worked a three-and-two count from the Dover pitcher and then ignited Easton fans when he smashed a two-run homer over the left field fence. It was his first professional home run and likely one of the sweetest. The *Star-Democrat* likened Foxx's homer to a "Babe Ruth stunt." Not unexpectedly, he would be compared to Ruth many more times during his career.

A big carnival dance was held in Easton that evening from 8:00 P.M. to midnight to benefit the club. Most of the Easton players, including Foxx, probably attended. Some of the Dover club's players came to dance, and Bob Arthur's orchestra from Dover provided the music.

Although the fans kept coming to Federal Park in great numbers, with the guarantee of $75 per game to the visitor's club usually exceeded, the Farmers' first season was typical of any expansion team. Nearing the end of June, Dover was in first place with a 17-7 record and all other teams, except Easton, had a winning percentage of .500 or better. Easton was very much alone in last place, with only two victories in its first twenty-three games. However, the club's record and overall competitiveness improved thereafter.

Employees of the club dealt with the team's early woes in different ways. One of the vendors selling refreshments and snacks during the games hollered, "Coca-Cola and aspirin tablets," if Easton was behind in the score. When Easton reached 2-21, gatekeeper Dick Thomas released a black cat, "Sarah Louise," at the pitcher's box just before the start of the next game. She ran straight for the Easton dugout and into the hands of starting pitcher Scott, who proceeded to win the game. Because Easton won four of its next six games, a local newspaper suggested that fans "Send your black cats to Easton, Maryland. They will be welcome."

Foxx began hitting homers regularly in early July and slowly crept up the batting order from eighth to seventh to fourth and fifth. Baker kept Foxx in the middle of the batting order for the remainder of the season.

Foxx said Baker taught him the most basic rules of batting that season. Baker said things like, "Keep your eye on the ball," and "you don't realize it, but you make a pitcher's job just 50 percent easier than it would be if you forced him to pitch the way you want him to. . . . If you wait for the balls you want to hit instead of taking any old thing the pitchers want to give you, you would be hitting .350."

A July 11 report out of Easton said that Frank Baker was trying to coax manager Connie Mack into giving Foxx a chance to make the Philadelphia Athletics' club. "James Foxx is the most promising player I have ever seen," said Baker. Frank told reporters that Connie promised to come to Easton "and look Foxx over." As of July 13, Jimmie led Easton in batting, with 38 hits in 118 at bats for a .322 average.

No articles appeared in the *Star-Democrat* in 1924 claiming that Baker also told Yankees' manager Miller Huggins about how wise it would be to purchase the youngster's contract from Easton. Years later, many newspapers would assert that Baker had talked with Huggins before Foxx was purchased by a major-league club.

For the July 16 game, 400 to 500 friends of Foxx and Scott came to Federal Park for "Queen Anne's County Day" to see them start at catcher and pitcher. Unfortunately, Scott's pitching was off the mark and he was replaced by George Klemmick, a former pitching standout from Baltimore's Polytechnic High School. In the sixth inning, there was a call by Sam Meintzer, an Easton official, for all Queen Anne's County residents to stand up, and nearly half the spectators stood. Meanwhile, according to the *Observer,* Jimmie, batting fifth, slammed a triple and scored Easton's first run. In the ninth, "He pounded the horsehide over the left field fence for what some fans believed was the farthest hit ball so far this season." Dover defeated Easton, 10-8, but Foxx's slugging show surely satisfied many of the paying customers.

Scott had serious control problems for much of that season, forcing Baker to release him from the Farmers on July 17, the day after Queen Anne's County Day at Federal Park. Alton pitched for several more minor league and semipro teams during the next several years with some measure of success, but never got to the majors. Reflecting on his short career, Scott attributed his pitching success against Foxx when in high school to being able to locate pitches on the lower outside corner of the plate, especially his curveballs.

Easton's home games in July became a significant and frequent stopover for major league scouts who had caught wind of the hitting exploits of young Foxx. After playing in 46 games, slightly more than half of Easton's schedule, Jim had collected 50 hits in 162 at bats for a .309 batting average near the end of July. Oddly enough, Jack Dunn, of the Baltimore Orioles of the International League (IL), had not made any known attempts to purchase Foxx's contract. Dunn made a habit out of finding excellent major-league prospects and holding on to the players several years before selling their contracts to major-league clubs for huge sums. Some examples were Robert "Lefty" Grove, Jack Ogden, Max Bishop, and Joe Boley.

The scouting of Foxx culminated when Jimmie was sold to the Philadelphia Athletics on July 30 for roughly $2,000. Scout Mike Drennan of the Philadelphia club had been in Easton for several days looking over Foxx and Klemmick before a deal was closed for Foxx. Drennan, who had scouted and obtained Jimmy Dykes for the Athletics several years earlier, said he thought Foxx was the most promising prospect of all Eastern Shore League players. However, Baker made it a condition of the purchase that Jim finish the season with Easton before reporting for duty with Mr. Mack.

An article appeared in the *Philadelphia Inquirer* on July 31 about the Athletics' purchase of Foxx, correctly stated his age as sixteen, and noted the facts that he was an all-around athlete holding several state school records, that the purchase was negotiated on behalf of the A's by scout Mike Drennan, and that Foxx's native county was Queen Anne. The article mistakenly reported that Jimmie was born in Church Hill. *The Inquirer* considered Foxx to be the best catcher in the Eastern Shore League and a heavy slugger "having a number of home runs to his credit." His purchase was reported on the same day in the *Baltimore Sun* and the *Washington Post.*

Baker probably called Foxx aside to tell him the news of his "promotion" to the Athletics before the afternoon game with the Cambridge

Canners on July 30 in Easton. This was heady stuff for a sixteen-year-old, and Jimmie no doubt flashed his wide, toothy, dimpled grin before going out on the playing field and batting 0 for 3 in a loss to Cambridge. Foxx had other things on his mind that afternoon.

The Athletics barely beat the Giants to the punch in purchasing Foxx. The day after Jimmie was obtained by the A's, Baker was called by Howard "Nig" Berry, a scout for the New York Giants, with an inquiry about obtaining Foxx. Berry had been in Easton looking over Jimmie's performance but had not talked business with Frank, other than to say Foxx was being watched.

Berry's failure to relay his interest in Foxx to Baker while he was in Easton left the door wide open for Mike Drennan and the Athletics; otherwise a bidding contest for Foxx might well have been in the making. Berry had given one of the Easton players a message while he was in Easton, asking the player to tell Foxx to come to New York in the fall, following the end of the Eastern Shore League season.

Dell Foxx visited Frank Baker at his home a second time shortly after Baker sold Jim to Connie Mack. Dell was frustrated and accused Baker of having taken his boy from him. But after Frank explained the advantages Jim would gain in his baseball career under Mack's tutelage, Dell returned to Sudlersville in a lighter mood. Dell's dreams for his son's success in baseball were coming true—it's just that it was happening so fast, a lot faster than the average climb of a player through the minor leagues to the majors, and Dell had lost control of the situation.

The purchase of Foxx by the Athletics strengthened his role as a local hero and raised hopes of many Eastern Shore baseball fans that a successor to Frank Baker was in the making. If Foxx were to stick with the A's in the near future, fans could easily make the trip to Shibe Park to watch the powerful slugger in action. Events in August and September were enough to raise their hopes. The legend of Foxx's clutch hitting and his ability to star in important games continued to grow.

Upon learning of Foxx's scheduled move to Philadelphia, Easton fans expressed support mixed with disappointment. They had developed an early liking for Foxx and were sorry to see him leaving the team, but were proud that Baker's club had a role in Foxx's development. The *Star-Democrat* mentioned heavy interest by the ball club and fans in having a benefit game for Jim to show their appreciation of his outstanding play and raise some funds for a send-off. If such a game was played in August, it was on a Sunday or Monday open date, but a close reading of the *Star-Democrat* doesn't reveal a particular game when such benefits were raised, and the *Record* mentioned in its August 30 issue that Easton officials still planned such a benefit game for Foxx. If it occurred, it had to have been the game between Easton and the Wilkin club from Baltimore on September 3.

Baker's club split four games with four different opponents from August 2-8 during an oppressive heat wave. Temperatures during part of the week registered 100 or more. In various locations in Easton, nightfall brought little relief, and a breath of air was a rarity. Soda worker dispensers and ice cream dealers rescued Easton residents and ballplayers. Foxx didn't wilt, being accustomed to the heat and humidity of the Eastern Shore summer. He collected his customary number of base hits during the heat wave, as he often would during especially hot weather in the future. If anything, Foxx seemed to thrive in hot weather, compared to many ballplayers.

Jim was also recognized on several occasions during the season with Easton for his ability to hit home runs for distance. On August 13, Jim led Easton to a 4-2 victory over Salisbury when he homered over the center field fence at Federal Park with one on base. The ball passed over the "Fox Brothers" sign of the outfield wall and cleared it by at least ten feet. The *Star-Democrat* called it a "fearful smash."

Easton gained the honor of hosting the commissioner of baseball, Judge Kenesaw "Mountain" Landis, during his annual trek to the Eastern Shore to attend a league game. In the wake of the Black Sox scandal of 1919 and the weakening of the three-member ruling body of the major leagues, the National Commission, the appointment of Landis as the major leagues' first commissioner late in 1920 proved very timely for baseball. Landis became very popular and a well-respected hero figure to baseball fans. His stern ruling on various issues, especially game fixing and betting, quickly brought integrity back to the game. Later, the Judge's major character flaw was that he thwarted attempts by some major-league club owners, most notably in the 1940s, to sign on top Negro Leaguers to play with clubs in the major leagues, thereby greatly prolonging the color barrier in professional baseball.

On Saturday, August 15, a banner hung across telephone poles on Washington Street in Easton proclaiming, "Welcome Judge Landis—Aug. 15 Easton vs. Crisfield." Easton officials swelled with pride while Landis attended a luncheon sponsored by the Rotary Club. Afterward, he arrived at Federal Park to join Harry Rew, president of the Eastern Shore League, and J. Vincent Jamison, Jr., president of the Blue Ridge League (another Class D minor league) for the game between Easton and the Crisfield Crabbers.

When Landis entered Federal Park, the crowd of over 3,000 fans rose to greet him. The Judge shook hands with the players and managers from both teams, the greatest applause being reserved for Landis when he shook Baker's hands. Then Landis took his place on the pitcher's mound and threw a strike past an obliging Frank Baker before taking his seat in the grandstand behind the catcher to allow the game to begin.

Women were a prominent portion of the spectators rooting for the Easton Farmers at Federal Park, and "Judge Landis Day" was no different. Hanging over the railing from the first row of box seats, Frank Baker's daughter, Ottilie, and three other female friends rooted hard for a homer by Foxx and a victory by Baker's club.

The Farmers complied with the fans' wishes, riding the strong pitching of Klemmick and the batting of Foxx. In the first inning, Bobby Unglaub led off with a clean single; Henry Graff scored him with a double to right; Osgood walked; Foxx singled, scoring Graff; and Henry Pepper singled, scoring Osgood for a 3-0 lead. In the fifth inning, Easton scored its fourth and final run when Jimmie powered the ball over the left field fence for a homer. Landis exclaimed, "A dandy!" As Foxx crossed home plate, Landis said, "By jimminy, that's a beauty!" Jimmie had two hits in four at bats, with two runs batted in. Easton defeated Crisfield, 4-1.

The following day, Easton invaded Crisfield and again defeated the Crabbers, 10-7. Foxx continued his hot hitting with a single and another homer as the Farmers scored five runs in the eighth and ninth innings to overcome a 7-5 deficit.

Then on Sunday, August 17, the ball club celebrated its recent success when Baker and his wife hosted all the players at their farm in Trappe and Foxx and others indulged in swimming, boating, and "other sports." The main course that Mrs. Baker served was fried chicken, one of Foxx's favorites. The ballplayers thanked the Bakers profusely, promising Frank their very best efforts for the remainder of the season.

Given his young age and the fact that he lived in a boardinghouse in Easton, Foxx probably went to bed early most nights during the week. His only open date from baseball was usually Sunday, so he might have caught a ride home from Easton to Sudlersville on Saturday nights and returned to Easton on Sunday evening. It is not known if Jim had a girlfriend that summer, but being the handsome boy he was, with his polite and humble demeanor, and the adulation he received from the fans in Easton, he must have had many female admirers about his age.

Baker kept the Farmers busy by scheduling an exhibition game for August 18 against a semipro team, the Bearcats, with Alton Scott pitching for the visitors. Although Scott managed to strike out his former teammates thirteen times, he walked eight batters. Foxx hit Scott for a double and a triple in four at bats. It's possible that funds raised from this game were used in part as a send-off for Foxx.

Foxx starred again two days later in a road game against the league's Parksley (Virginia) club. The Farmers overcame a 6-3 lead in the seventh when Foxx batted with the bases loaded and smashed a long fly well over center fielder Mattis's head that bounded over the fence for a grand slam.

It was Jim's fourth homer in the last five league games, his best homer binge of the season.

The *Record* boasted about the young Sudlersville lad's improvement as a catcher on August 30 and published a large photograph of Foxx standing in his Easton Farmers' uniform.

> James Foxx, better known at Easton as "Our Jimmy" who has been purchased by Connie Mack's Athletics, is playing a wonderful game of ball. As the season draws to a close a great improvement is seen in his performance behind the bat. Few fly balls in his territory are missed. Some of the catches he makes are phenomenal.

The league's 1924 season ended on September 1 with Parksley clinching the pennant on that date. The Spuds, as the Parksley club was called in honor of the local crop of sweet potatoes, won both games of a doubleheader from Crisfield to edge out Cambridge by one game and Salisbury by two. Cambridge had won both of its games that day against Easton, while Salisbury lost twice to Dover. More impressive, the Spuds won their last nine games in a row to overcome Salisbury and Cambridge, so the Parksley club was red hot for the upcoming Five States Series. In spite of Foxx's star performance and Baker's presence as manager and part-time player, Easton finished dead last in the standings, with 23 wins and 57 losses. The club's composite pitching and fielding was especially subpar, compared to the rest of the league. They were the only team in the six-club league to finish with a losing record, and had at least twenty different players appearing in a Farmers' uniform. Still, the team was a financial success with a $4,000 surplus at season's end.

Foxx finished tenth in the league in batting for players with 150 or more at bats and played in 76 of Easton's 80 games. For much of the season, Foxx batted well above .300, but suffered a slump in early August and another brief slump for most of the last week of the regular season. Jim batted 0 for 7 in the final two games of the season in the doubleheader against Cambridge on September 1, dropping his average from .304 to a final mark of .296 (77 hits in 260 at bats). He collected 11 doubles, 2 triples, and 10 homers during the season. Runs batted in were not tabulated by the league's statisticians. Jim played most of his games at catcher and several at either center field, third base, or as a pinch hitter.

Baker batted .293 (27 hits in 93 at bats) with 5 homers to his credit as a part-time third baseman and pinch hitter while managing. At the age of thirty-eight, this was Frank's last season playing professional baseball.

After the regular season, Easton played in a couple of exhibition games. On September 2, the Farmers met the Talbot County All-Stars and won 11-3. Foxx, playing third base and batting fourth, batted 3 for 5 with two singles and a double. Then on September 3, Easton defeated the Wilkin Club of Baltimore, 9-1. Foxx, at the catcher's position again, batted fourth and hit one homer in three at bats. Jimmie was replaced late in the game by David Hickman because he had to catch a train for Parksley, Virginia, so he could arrive there in time for the beginning of the Five-States Series to play for the Spuds against the Martinsburg (West Virginia) Blue Sox.

Connie Mack had the option of requesting that Foxx report to him immediately following Easton's last game of the regular season on September 1, in keeping with the original agreement drawn up between the A's and Frank Baker. But Mack wisely consented to let Foxx play a couple of postseason exhibition games for Easton and in the Five States Series for Parksley, knowing the valuable experience he would gain.

One of the rules of the series was that the pennant-winning club from each league was allowed to pick two additional players for their squad from among other teams in their respective leagues. Parksley's manager, John "Poke" Whalen, had seen Foxx play entire games not only at catcher, but also at third base and center field during contests between the Spuds and Farmers, so he was well aware of the youngster's versatility at various fielding positions. Poke borrowed Foxx for the Spuds initially to play right field in place of Horace Moyer, who had a strained tendon, but Jim ended up playing more as the club's catcher during the series. On the eve of the series on September 3, Parksley's catcher Joe Tagg "was taken ill" and Foxx got the starting nod at catcher for the series opener while batting fifth in the lineup.

Foxx arrived in Parksley late on September 3 and was likely greeted by manager Whalen or another club official at the town's train station and shown his living quarters for the next couple of nights.

The series began on September 4 under a blue sky at Parksley, at 3:30 P.M., with a crowd estimated by the *Morning Sun* to be 1,479, swelling a town of only 600 to 700 residents. The *Peninsula Enterprise* guessed the crowd to be 1,500, "one of the largest crowds ever to see a baseball game on the Eastern Shore of Virginia." They began pouring into the ballpark before noon, and roads into town were jammed with both motor and horse-drawn vehicles. Foxx and Tom Glass donned Parksley's home uniforms with "SPUDS" in capital letters across the chest of their jerseys and the letter "P" on the front of their caps.

Eastern Shore League president Harry Rew made a short speech and introduced the Blue Ridge League president J. V. Jamison, Jr., who threw out the first pitch. Umpire Rudolph was picked to officiate on the bases, and umpire Derby was chosen to call balls and strikes. Derby announced the batteries: "Andrews and Woodring for Martinsburg and Hummer and Foxx for Parksley."

The Spuds routed the Martinsburg Blue Sox, 17-0, thanks largely to the pitching of Frank Hummer and the slugging of Foxx. The *Morning Baltimore Sun* reported, "Jimmy Fox [sic], catcher, loaned by Easton, had a field day at bat." Jimmie pushed six runs across the plate for Parksley, based on a first inning sacrifice fly, a two-run homer in the fourth inning, and a three-run homer in the fifth. Both of Foxx's homers were especially long drives over the center field fence, according to the *Enterprise*. Unlike the *Morning Sun* and the *Cambridge Daily Banner*, neither the *Enterprise* nor the *Accomack News* credited Foxx with a double; rather it was reported his base hit other than the two homers was a long single that hit the fence.

The *Baltimore Evening Sun* announced the purchase of George Klemmick by Connie Mack's A's on September 5 and published a photograph of Klemmick and Foxx entitled "Easton Battery Signed by Athletics." The photograph had Klemmick and Foxx standing in their Easton Farmers' uniforms, with Foxx in his catcher's garb. The caption misspelled Foxx's last name with one "x" and told readers that Frank Baker recommended the players to his former boss.

On September 5, Martinsburg's Charles "Lefty" Willis shut out the Spuds at Parksley on two hits. Foxx was hitless in two official at bats. The Blue Sox's 7-0 win over the Spuds evened the series at one game each.

It was a fortuitous meeting for Foxx and Willis, since the two youngsters would become teammates on the Athletics and roommates the following year. They remained lifelong friends.

The teams traveled to Easton for the third game on September 6. Fans began arriving at Federal Park in the morning, and the ticket window for grandstand seats was closed one hour before the 3:00 P.M. game time. Bleacher seats were filled earlier, and fans tugging and pushing to get onto the playing field in back of restraining ropes made a stampede for choice vantage points once the barriers were let down.

Foxx "met with a rousing reception when he came to bat in the first inning" and responded with a home run, leading Parksley to a 7-1 victory. Almost 3,000 fans stood at Federal Park to cheer for Jim as he rounded the bases. "The crowd went wild," according to the *Inquirer*. C. Edward Sparrow, sports editor of the *Morning Sun*, also told the story of the game:

> Eastonians came into their own as they saw their favorite, Jimmy Fox [sic], break up the game in the first inning. Jimmy made the longest drive ever seen in this park when he sent a ball 375 feet, the ball clearing the center field fence, near the flag pole. It was the first ball pitched [to Foxx] and cleared the fence with feet to spare. Mattis was on first base, and the stand shook as the Easton catcher who has been sold to Connie Mack's Athletics, touched home plate. The ovation lasted several minutes.

Foxx batted 2 for 4 in the game.

Amazingly, Foxx had homered in each of the five biggest games he appeared in during the 1924 season. Each time an unusual amount of hype or fanfare was associated with a game, Foxx starred at bat; Easton's home opener, Queen Anne's County Day, Judge Landis Day, the opener of the Five States Series, and the one game of the series played in Easton. He was not quite seventeen at the time. Considering that most professional baseball players don't accomplish their peak or career year in batting until between the ages of twenty-one and thirty-one, Jim was just skimming the surface of his potential.

Game four was played in Martinsburg, West Virginia, on September 8 and the Blue Sox evened the series again behind another complete-game victory for Willis, 11-4. Foxx solved Willis this time, however. Jimmie singled and homered in four at bats against Lefty.

Parksley turned the corner in the series on the following day in Martinsburg. Hummer again starred on the pitcher's mound with a complete game, an 8-2 victory on the strength of a five-run rally by the Spuds in the ninth inning. Foxx batted 1 for 4. During Foxx's short stay in Martinsburg, Connie Mack called and asked Jim to report to Shibe Park as soon as the Five States Series was over.

Parksley clinched the best-of-seven series on September 10 in Chambersburg, Pennsylvania, with a 6-3 win on the strength of Tom Glass's hurling and a 2-run single in the top of the ninth inning. Foxx batted 1 for 5. Overall, the Parksley club, with add-ons Foxx and Glass, won four out of six games from Martinsburg. Foxx's line score for the series was 9 base hits for 23 at bats, including 4 homers, a .391 batting average, and 22 total bases. He played five games at catcher and one game as the right fielder, and the *Enterprise* reminded its readers on the Eastern Shore of Virginia that Foxx was one outstanding member of the team, saying his "general all around work stood out prominently."

Players on the Spuds, including Foxx and Glass, received $132 each in bonus money for the winner's share in the series and were presented with miniature gold baseballs by the *Sun*. The team received the Ned Hanlon trophy to keep for one year and the Ban Johnson pennant.

Foxx appeared in another photograph in the *Baltimore Evening Sun* on September 10, this time with four other Marylanders (Klemmick, Eddie Rommel, Bill Lamar, and Max Bishop), all under contract with the A's. The Sudlersville "boy wonder" was now a statewide sports celebrity.

Mack must have been more anxious than ever to see Foxx in action upon hearing of his starring role in the Five States Series. Sportswriter Ed Sparrow offered that, "If Frank Baker had not sold Foxx earlier in the season, it's safe to say the Eastern Shore boy would have brought a much larger price following the Series."

After the Series ended, Jim was fitted for his first A's uniform and joined the Mackmen for the remainder of the 1924 season as a benchwarmer and understudy to Connie Mack, often sitting next to Mack in the dugout.

Mattie Foxx didn't like the idea of her son being bought and sold, but Dell Foxx saw it as a means to an end. Mattie's advice to Jim as he set out for Philadelphia was to do his best, be considerate of others, be honest and agreeable. Foxx was naturally easygoing, almost always grinning, honest, usually humble, and somewhat shy, given his age and limited exposure to people outside the Eastern Shore.

The first time that Dell was to meet Mr. Mack, he asked his brother-in-law, Elwood Coleman, to drive him up to Philadelphia in Elwood's car. Dell didn't like driving in the big city and Elwood gladly agreed to Dell's request. So Jim, Dell, Elwood, and Elwood's son, William (Winnie) Coleman, rode up to Philadelphia to meet Connie.

Winnie clearly recalled the moment.

Uncle Dell was awfully proud of Jim, you know, which he had a right to be. And they had an appointment to meet Conie [Connie] Mack out at Shibe Park. And we went and Mr. Mack was there, and he was glad to see us all. And Uncle Dell was there, too. He tickled me. Uncle Dell was talking for awhile and bragging on Jimmie, about how good he was, and everything, you know. And Mr. Mack says, "Well, Mr. Foxx, I'll tell ya, I've got some boys out there that can strike out your boy everytime he comes to bat!"

"Oh, no you can't! There ain't no way that can happen!" Dell said, standing and shouting.

First baseman Joe Hauser, who was with the Athletics when Foxx first arrived at Shibe Park, recalled his initial impressions of Jimmie as a hitter. "Foxx was a natural power hitter. He had those strong wrists and arms."

Foxx didn't appear in any of the A's regular season games in September but played in several exhibition games as catcher for Mack. In mid-September, it was rumored that the New York Giants bought Foxx from the Athletics for $12,000, but it was not true.

Jimmie made his debut in an exhibition game for Mack on September 12, in a 7-6 win over the Cincinnati Reds. He played the whole game at catcher, scored a run, and smacked a triple off veteran Eppa Rixey while hitting eighth in the batting order. Then, on September 28, he again played the whole game at catcher in an exhibition contest against "Lit" Brothers, a semipro team from the Philadelphia area. Foxx managed a double and a run scored in the Athletics' 4-2 victory.

During the Athletics' September road trip through Detroit, Chicago, and St. Louis, Jimmie saw Ty Cobb in action for the first time. But most likely, his biggest moment as a benchwarmer came when he had his first look at Babe Ruth in a season-ending series with the Yankees at Shibe Park.

By the time Jimmie Foxx joined the Athletics in September 1924, Connie Mack had been managing at the professional level for thirty-one years. In addition to managing the AL's franchise in Philadelphia for all twenty-four years of its existence, Mack managed the NL's Pittsburgh Pirates beginning late in the season in 1894 and all of 1895 and 1896. After being released by the Pirates, Mack was hired by the Western League's Milwaukee Brewers for the 1897 season at the urging of league president Ban Johnson. Mack continued as manager for Milwaukee in 1897-1900, the last year being the season the Western league changed its name to the AL. In 1901, the AL was officially recognized as a major league.

Mack's early tenure with the Athletics was one of the most successful in the AL. The A's won the AL pennant in 1902, but there was no World Series that year, the first being in 1903. In 1905 they won the AL flag again, only to lose to John McGraw's New York Giants in the World Series. The Mackmen rebounded with four more AL pennants in 1910, 1911, 1913, and 1914 and three World Series triumphs in 1910, 1911, and 1913.

Factions formed on the Athletics late in the 1914 season while the Federal League was forming and raiding players from the AL and NL. Mack lost many key players after 1914, with second baseman Eddie Collins going to the Chicago White Sox, Frank "Home Run" Baker retiring, and star pitchers Eddie Plank and Jack Coombs defecting to the Federal League.

From 1915 through 1921, the A's finished in last place in the AL every season. Then Mack finally found enough highly talented players over a short period of time from 1922-1924 to put the A's in a rebuilding phase.

The local pride in Foxx's baseball accomplishments was highlighted in an article, "Jimmy Foxx Has Had Benefit of Best Training," in the *Observer* on September 27. The article talked of the extensive role that Dell and Mattie Foxx had in Jim's upbringing and the development of his "splendid moral character." The *Observer* also attributed Jim's character in part to the teachings he received in Sunday school. The unnamed author of the article reminisced at length about Dell Foxx's baseball playing ability:

> No old-time county baseball fans need any introduction to Jimmy's father. Dell Foxx for many years was one of the best catchers the Eastern Shore ever produced. He too, had his chance to enter the big leagues, but he remained home. And many a time, a perfectly good ball game has been spoiled when he decided to give the horsehide a long distance ride over some remote outfield fence. Frequently the bleachers have groaned and the grandstand grown

when he came to the plate. There's no telling how many coins have
been chalked up to his able bat.

Apparently Jim inherited his ability to hit long-distance homers directly
from his father, and as was customary in the days of town ball, Dell was
showered with money by the spectators for some of his more spectacular
homers.

Jimmie Foxx's first season as a professional baseball player brought him
the attention he richly deserved, and Home Run Baker's early role in
Foxx's career was firmly established. Baker had tipped off Connie Mack
and Yankee manager Miller Huggins, probably in June, about the baseball
abilities of Foxx.

Had Easton not been awarded a minor league club for the 1924 season,
Jim probably would not have gained a tryout with any other Eastern Shore
League club that season or been purchased by a major-league club. Jimmie
didn't join the Easton Farmers until mid-May, right before the season-
opening date for all clubs, May 30, and no record exists of any other
professional club inviting Jim for tryouts in 1924. Although Jim was only
sixteen at the time, his physical development and batting skills were
advanced beyond his years. The Easton ball club was more likely than
others in the league to depend on local talent in constructing its team roster,
because Easton was added to the league just two months before the
beginning of the season. Therefore, establishment of the Easton club
provided early exposure of Jim to major-league scouts and proved timely
for him, allowing him to become one of the youngest men ever to appear
in a major-league baseball game.

3

AS A HITTER, HE'S A NATURAL

Jimmie Foxx returned to his studies at Sudlersville High in early October, after the A's 1924 season, in an attempt to keep his promise to his mother that he would return to school for his diploma in between baseball activities. His involvement in professional sports made him ineligible for fall soccer and basketball at Sudlersville High, but he was able to referee several soccer games. In the "Sudlersville Activities" section of the *High School Forum*, a newsletter of the Queen Anne's County schools, Sudlersville High welcomed Foxx back in the article, "Jimmy Foxx Comes Back."

We are delighted to have with us for the fall and winter, our own "Jimmie" Foxx, who has filled a very enviable position in the Eastern Shore League, as well as with the Philadelphia Athletics. He has made a record for himself and a reputation for S.H.S. We are very proud to claim him as a member of the class of '25 and wish him the very best of success for the coming year.

Jim didn't stay in school long. By December 1, he left school again, and the reason given on his school transcripts was "work." He must have suspected or known early that the A's were inviting him to spring training for the 1925 season.

Early in 1925, Foxx was playing basketball for the local Company "K" team sponsored by a local National Guard unit, but was notified by letter from Connie Mack before the middle of January that he could no longer play basketball or he'd be in violation of his contract with the A's. Company "K" appealed to Mack to reconsider his position and Connie firmly replied, "I could not conscientiously consent that James Foxx play basketball as this young man apparently has a bright future ahead of him in baseball and a fall on a hard floor might ruin his chances of realizing his ambition."

Jim received a contract from Mack in early February, accompanied by a letter inviting him to join the club's pitchers and other catchers for spring training a week earlier than the team's other players. The report date for pitchers and catchers was February 22, at the Mackmen's new training facility at Fort Myers, Florida.

On Monday, February 16, schoolmates and friends attended a send-off dinner for Foxx and former high school teammate Chris Wallace at Cox Memorial Hall in Sudlersville. Wallace was preparing for a tryout with the Easton Farmers in 1925, and Rev. Donaldson and Frank Baker were guest speakers. Baker gave a talk on "A Career in Baseball," and Foxx and Wallace responded enthusiastically to repeated toasts from the crowd.

The Athletics' first group left North Philadelphia by train the evening of February 20 and included Manager Mack, Cy Perkins, Mickey Cochrane, Stan Baumgartner, Freddy Heimach, Lefty Cline, Bing Miller, Al Simmons, Walter French, and team owner Thomas Shibe and his wife. Miller and Simmons rushed in together from their midwest homes by a genuine gold-plated automobile. Jim caught the train in Baltimore with Eddie Rommel and was joined by newcomers Lefty Grove, Al Stokes, Tom Glass, and Lefty Willis at Union Station in Washington, D.C.

Cochrane forgot his contract woes and after reconsidering his demand to receive part of the contract price from Portland, he reasoned that he had a good salary for a rookie, straight from Mack, without any extras. Because Cochrane decided to report, Foxx's potential playing time was reduced substantially.

Briefly interviewed at Union Station, Mack said he was expecting improvement in the club's position in 1925, in large part due to the additions of Grove, Bill Lamar, Max Bishop, Cochrane, and Foxx. This was probably the first time that Foxx met Grove and Cochrane. He had met Willis and Glass the previous autumn during the Five-State Series. A few weeks earlier, AL president Ban Johnson predicted that Mack's club should be well up in front in the standings when the season closes, also saying, "Bob Groves [sic] is the ace in the hole for the Mackmen."

Grove, about to turn twenty-five in March, was seven years older than Jim. Unlike Jim, he was already a seasoned veteran of professional baseball, having played five years in the minors, his first half-season with Martinsburg in the Blue Ridge League and the rest with Jack Dunn's Baltimore Orioles of the IL. Grove had so completely dominated the IL during his tenure there (109-36) that many observers then, and baseball historians since, believe that he could have starred as a pitcher in the major leagues during most, if not all, of the five-year period of 1920-1924.

Grove was born in the Western Maryland coal mining town of Lonaconing and probably had his own adjustment period to work out regarding city living after joining Baltimore in 1920, much the way Jim had to adjust to Philadelphia in 1924 and 1925. Connie Mack paid the hefty price of $106,000 to Jack Dunn in November 1924 for the contract rights to Grove.

More importantly, as spring training began in 1925, Cochrane had more experience than Foxx as catcher at the professional level, playing on the Dover club in the Eastern Shore League in 1923 and with Portland of the Pacific Coast League in 1924. Cochrane played under the name of Frank King while with Dover, in an attempt to retain his anonymity in case he wished to return to college and participate in intercollegiate athletics. For that same reason, he refused to have his photograph taken that season while in uniform with Dover.

Mickey played catcher and batted .322 to help lead Dover to the league pennant. One story claimed that Cochrane came to Dover as a second baseman and was converted later to catcher because the team lacked an adequate player at that position. In his early years of playing catcher, Cochrane was not at all sure it was the position for him, but perseverance and hard work paid off for Mickey as he sharpened his defensive skills to complement his offensive ability. On the other hand, the A's veteran catcher Ralph (Cy) Perkins was known primarily for his defensive abilities at catcher, rather than for hitting.

Mack reported that every Athletic had signed his 1925 contract by the middle of February, even though contracts were not mailed until February 1.

On Sunday, February 22, the Mackmen's train arrived in Fort Myers, where the city band, public dignitaries, and average citizens lined up to welcome the first thirteen Athletic players to arrive for spring training. The players let out a "whoop of joy" to be out of the train and visited a nearby hotel to satisfy hungry appetites. Following their meal, the players briefly visited the ballpark where they would be training, to inspect the grounds and clubhouse. Then they traveled by auto to Crescent Beach, on the Gulf of Mexico, to admire female sunbathers before training began in earnest. The team made camp at the Palms Hotel.

At the time, the A's camp in Fort Myers was farther south than any other "home" site holding a major-league club. Jimmy Isaminger told readers of *The Sporting News* that it was hot, not merely warm in this part of Florida during February, saying, "A man must dress as he does in Atlantic City, New Jersey, in August. Here, any overweight and out-of-condition A's shed extra pounds baking in the Florida sun."

The next day, Mack held a light workout for pitchers and catchers in the morning, beginning at 10:00 A.M. at Fort Myers, and warned them that it would be disastrous for any of them "to cut loose." The morning drill was little more than limbering-up exercises. Meanwhile, two outfielders who were early arrivals, Bing Miller, the "copper-colored" fellow, and Al Simmons, shagged flies for an hour or more. The morning drill was followed by a five-inning intrasquad game in the afternoon, with Foxx and Cochrane playing catcher for the two teams. Foxx made a headlong dive into the plate in the first inning, showing his youthful disregard for injury, the first of many times he did so during his first few seasons with Mack.

Simmons had batted .308 in his rookie season with the Athletics in 1924. Al started his professional career at the age of twenty with the Milwaukee Brewers of the American Association in 1922, but played most of that season with Aberdeen of the Dakota League, hitting a robust .365. Mack had Simmons scouted by former major league star Harry Davis while Al was playing for Aberdeen.

The following year, Al hit .360 in 144 games while with Shreveport of the Texas League under Mack's former catcher, Ira Thomas, and then hit .398 in 24 games for the Brewers to end the season.

Simmons had been advised by friends when he began his pursuit of a baseball career to change his last name, Szymanski, because of his Polish ancestry. Al was influenced one day by a sign he read over a hardware store and changed his last name to Simmons.

On Tuesday, Foxx warmed up Grove under a glaring hot sun and probably felt the sting of Lefty's fastball for the first time. Catching for Alton Scott on the Sudlersville town team, the Queen Anne's County All-Star team, and the Easton Farmers probably prepared Foxx for Grove's hard throws.

After a nine-inning tilt on February 25, Mack was so pleased with the progress of his players that he cancelled all afternoon workouts for the next couple of days until the second group of players, scheduled to leave Philadelphia the next day, arrived.

On February 28, Foxx's team, the Palms, named after the players' hotel, easily beat Cochrane's Royals, 13-5. The same day, Mack announced his plans to carry ten pitchers, six outfielders, six infielders, and his three catchers (including Foxx) on the regular season roster. The *Philadelphia Inquirer* noted on the next day, "Fox [sic] tips the scales at 180 and looks like a second Ray Schalk. He has the same snap-like throw that Schalk employed."

An article from *The Sporting News*, written March 2, gave an early report of rookies Foxx and Cochrane:

> It is plain that the Athletics are going to have a much faster catching staff than last year. Both Gordon Cochrane, the expensive Portland purchase, and Jimmy Fox [sic] late of the Easton, Maryland team of the Eastern Shore League, are streaks getting down to first or circling around the bases. Fox was timed circling the bases in 13.8 seconds last year (for comparison sake, Ty Cobb had been timed circling the bases at 13.5 seconds at age 22 in 1908). They are as fleet steppers as Wally Schang was in his prime. Both Cochrane and Fox hit the ball hard last week. It was Cochrane who made the first homer

of the training trip when he smote a boundary belt with the bases full (in an intrasquad game). The next day, Jimmy Fox smashed two home runs (also in an intrasquad game). Fox is perhaps the youngest player in the major leagues, Mack living up to his reputation of being a cradle robber. Fox lives on a farm near Sudlersville, Maryland, and celebrated his seventeenth birthday last October. He is 5 feet, 11 inches and weighs 176 pounds.

Oddly enough, not only had Cochrane and Foxx played in the Eastern Shore League in back-to-back seasons, but sportswriter Jimmy Isaminger claimed that Foxx, as a fifteen-year-old, saw Cochrane play for the Dover club in 1923. In fact, it seems quite likely that Dell and Jimmie saw the Dover club play that season against any number of league opponents, since Dover was only twenty miles from Sudlersville. If so, Dell measured his own son's baseball skills against those players already in this entry level of professional baseball and must have been churning inside with excitement. He was an excellent judge of baseball talent and had seen his son star for the Queen Anne's County All-Stars earlier that spring, so any time spent watching Eastern Shore League games convinced him that Jimmie was ready for professional baseball, or very nearly so.

Some reports indicate that in 1923 the Dover franchise of the Eastern Shore League offered Jim a contract to join the club, but Mattie said he was too young to play professional baseball. If Jim had such an offer that spring or summer, it's likely that scouts for Dover first saw Jim play baseball while he was on the Queen Anne's County All-Star club.

After a couple of hours of heavy work in both the preluncheon and afternoon drills on March 3, the Athletics "staggered around Dick Richard's drugstore (in Fort Myers) and let themselves down easily and gently in those comfortable sidewalk benches," according to *The Inquirer*. The whole first week of March was filled with daily intrasquad games between the "Regulars" and the "Yanigans," the Yanigans being the players, like Foxx, not expected to hold a spot in the starting lineup during the regular season.

Foxx hit an especially long drive in one of the earliest intrasquad games; several A's players said it would have landed in the center field bleachers in Shibe Park (more than 468 feet from home plate). Still, the Regulars beat the Yanigans soundly, 13-4, only to lose to Foxx's squad the next day by one run. Foxx "pocketed" three high foul flies while catching, despite a stiff wind on March 5.

Mack saw tremendous talent and natural ability in Foxx's hitting saying:

There is a great deal of power in that lad and I like him. He takes a free swing with the bat. There is no halting cut at the ball and he meets the sphere with every bit of force he possesses. Understand, Foxx needs plenty of experience before he will be a major league catcher, but he is one of the most promising men I have seen in years. He is very young and I think he will develop into a wonderful catcher. He is the youngest rookie in camp, is very sedate, and there is not a bit of braggadocio about him. He is well-liked by the veterans.

The A's spruced up that night for a dance with the local ladies at the Pythian Building in Fort Myers and were entertained by music by the "Florida Gaiters." Every Athletic was in the "hay" by 11:00 P.M., fulfilling an unwritten law of Manager Mack.

Foxx and Cochrane homered the next day against a semipro team and switched teams for the intrasquad game the following day, with neither player standing out in a pitcher's battle. That night, the town of Fort Myers roped off a square in the business section of town for a dance to be held in honor of the Mackmen and sprinkled cornmeal on the ground (perhaps to add noise or enhance traction for dancing). Every girl in town was invited to dance with the Athletics.

On Sunday, March 8, several players gathered around Ira Thomas to talk baseball and hear "old-time yarns" from the coach. Discussions eventually focused on great hitters, and "Shoeless" Joe Jackson's name was mentioned. According to Stan Baumgartner, writing for the *Inquirer* while also pitching for the Athletics, "All hands agreed that he was one of the greatest hitters in the game." The left-handed batsman had a .356 career batting average at the time of his banishment from organized ball by Judge Landis near the end of 1920 due to Joe's involvement in the 1919 Black Sox Scandal.

Baumgartner continued:

Young Fox [sic] spoke up and asked if Mr. Mack had not once had Jackson under his wing. Ira replied that he had, but had let him go to Savannah in the South Atlantic League. "Why, Ira?" queried the youngster.

Thomas replied, "It seems that Jackson was a very homesick youngster when he first came into the big show and several times took french leave from the club. And Mr. Mack, always keen to appreciate the feelings of a young man, took him back." But Ira failed to mention the excessive harassment that the illiterate Jackson received from his more educated teammates, maybe figuring that Joe should have been able to withstand the heavy needling.

Thomas said, "But one day Jackson, enroute to Chicago, stepped out on the railroad car platform for a breath of fresh air, saw a huge pile of milk cans standing at one end and said, 'Ira, I wish Connie would tie a can to me as big as that large milk can over yonder.'

Jackson then felt a sharp tap on his shoulder and turned to see Mr. Mack looking him in the face. Connie had enough of Joe's homesick blues. Mack said, "Joe, there is one large can over there marked 'Savannah.' Now you go in the car, get your stuff, and get the baggage agent to ship you along with it." Thus did Joe Jackson vanish from the legions of Mack.

If seventeen-year-old Foxx had any thoughts along the lines of being homesick, he probably kept them to himself after hearing Thomas' story about Jackson.

Foxx played catcher the last three games for the Regulars before the exhibition season with other major and minor league teams began on March 12. One of Foxx's best performances against another major-league club during the exhibition season was on March 13, when he drove home the tie-breaking runs with a triple against the Phillies with two outs in the seventh inning. Foxx batted 3 for 4 as a replacement for Perkins.

Isaminger praised Foxx's play again in *The Sporting News* on March 19: "Fox seems to be a natural receiver. His work behind the bat is remarkably smooth. Seldom does he drop a pitch, although he has caught every curver on Mack's big string."

Isaminger was especially impressed with Cochrane and Foxx, given the importance of the position in the daily lineup and the long history of good fielding catchers in the major leagues who were only average hitters. Catchers who were good fielders and also outstanding batters were among the biggest rarities in baseball, and Mack appeared to have two such players in the same spring training camp! The scribe reminded his readers:

A young catcher loses many a game for a club before he acquires the brains, poise, and skill to run the ball game. The young catcher is the biggest game in baseball and many are rejected before a jewel is found. The whole game revolves around them and it is seldom, very seldom that any rookie is able to break in and start to hit well, catch well and match wits with opponents who have been in the league for many years.

Foxx's photograph appeared on the front page of the March 19 issue of *The Sporting News,* the first time that Jim appeared in a national weekly publication and one of the earliest photos of him in an A's uniform. The picture's caption read, "Baby of the Major Leagues—Jimmy Fox [sic]."

In the final intrasquad game of that spring on March 24, Foxx drove in the winning run for the Kiwanis Club over the Rotary Club in the ninth inning.

Foxx and Babe Ruth became teammates for one day in an exhibition game on March 25 at Fort Myers. Mack had received permission from Yankee manager Huggins to borrow Ruth's services to play for the Athletics in a game against the minor-league Milwaukee Brewers, and the *Fort Myers News Press* declared it "Babe Ruth Day."

Watching baseball's idol bask in such heavy fanfare was an unforgettable experience for a youngster like Foxx. The town of Fort Myers was in a frenzy for Ruth's visit, much the way Easton reacted to Judge Landis' trip just six months earlier, all businesses being closed at noon.

Baseball's premier home-run slugger arrived by car instead of the announced method of train. While the welcoming committee anxiously searched an arriving train, Ruth was already resting at the Royal Palm Hotel and ordered a barber to come to his suite. After "priming himself," he walked to the Franklin Arms amid a cheering crowd to be the luncheon guest of the Kiwanis Club, where Connie Mack, Ira Thomas, and Stoney McLinn gushed with compliments about the Babe's baseball ability, his contribution to the sport, and his ability to hit long-distance homers.

Ruth then left for the ballpark, and 5,000 fans congregated there, hoping for a homer by the slugger. An overweight Ruth donned an Athletics' uniform and was hitless in four at bats. But the Babe pleased the crowd before and during the game with his presence on the field. It's claimed that he autographed six dozen baseballs. Foxx did not play in the game; Cochrane played the entire game at catcher.

Foxx traveled north with the team as a member of its opening-day roster. While an advance squad of Athletics traveled ahead to Philadelphia to prepare for the preseason City Series with the Phillies, Foxx stayed with the other half of the team that made stops in Richmond and Portsmouth (Virginia), to play minor-league clubs. He replaced Cochrane as catcher after the start of each game and homered in the game against Richmond on April 2.

Dell and Mattie Foxx, six-year-old Sammy Dell, Jr., and Alan Walls motored to Philadelphia on Saturday, April 4, to visit Jimmie just as he arrived from Florida for the beginning of the City Series.

New York Giants manager John McGraw had seen Foxx bat and play catcher only briefly in an exhibition game on March 17 at Sarasota, yet he had high praise for Foxx after seeing him, as indicated in a Philadelphia paper in a caption below a picture of Jimmie squatting in the catcher's position: "A diamond star—who will twinkle with the best in a year or so—is John McGraw's expert opinion of Jimmy Fox [sic], the seventeen-year-old catcher who made his bow as an Athletic this afternoon in a game with the Phils at their home park, the Baker Bowl." Several years later, Jim became one of only three or four batters ever to hit a homer over the left field fence and completely out of the Baker Bowl, despite playing there much less frequently than Phillie players or their NL opponents.

On April 7, on the very first play of the second game of the series, Joe Hauser broke his right kneecap after he turned and took several steps to cover first on a ground-ball play to infielder Chick Galloway. Mack immediately obtained Jimmy Poole, holdout first sacker of the PCL Portland club, to fill the vacancy at first base. Poole had led the PCL with 38 homers and a .353 batting average in 1924. Hauser, severely injured, would miss the entire season, but Foxx's lack of experience at that position prevented him from helping out with first base duties during the season.

Foxx didn't appear in the series until April 11 at the Baker Bowl, where he was pictured in the *Inquirer*, down on one knee, catcher's mask off, with his hair parted in the middle, waiting for Bill Lamar's late throw from the outfield in the bottom of the tenth.

Foxx played briefly in the A's exhibition game against the Orioles in Baltimore the following day, but rode the Mackmen's bench the remainder of the month for their final exhibition game and all of the team's regular season games in April.

Foxx got his first extended look at Shibe Park during the spring of the 1925 season. Shibe Park had opened its doors on April 12, 1909, as the first ballpark built completely of concrete and steel. The ballpark was named after Ben Shibe, the original majority owner of the Athletics in 1901 and a partner with A. J. Reach in the A. J. Reach Company, manufacturers of baseball equipment, especially baseballs for the American League. The tower behind home plate housed the front entrance turnstiles on the ground level, and above, Connie Mack's office at the corner of 21st and Lehigh Streets. Running parallel to Lehigh Avenue was the first base foul line, with the right field to center field wall aligned parallel to 20th Street, the center field to left field wall parallel to Somerset Avenue, and the third base foul line parallel to 21st Street.

In 1925, additional seating was put in Shibe Park when single-decked bleachers from the left field corner to mid-center field were double-decked and covered. The grandstand from the right field corner all the way around to home plate to the left field corner was already double-decked and covered, and no seats existed for fans beyond the right field wall. Of course, in those days, there were seats outside the park on the rooftops of houses on 20th Street facing home plate. The park's dimensions were 334 feet to the left field corner, 468 feet to deepest center field, and 331 feet to the right field corner. A 12-foot-high concrete wall stood behind the right fielder, and 8 feet of concrete topped with 4 feet of wire backed the left fielder.

Foxx watched his teammates from the bench for several weeks before his first major-league appearance in a regular season game on May 1 at Washington's Griffith Stadium. In the eighth inning, the Senators had a hefty lead over the A's when Mack decided to lift relief pitcher Grove for pinch hitter Foxx. On a two-and-two count, Jim singled off veteran Vean Gregg and proved his mettle under pressure. At seventeen and one-half, he was one of the youngest men ever to make his debut in the major leagues.

Jim appeared in games sporadically in May and June for Mack, mostly as a pinch hitter, and had his best chance early in the season to show his stuff when he played for the A's in an exhibition game against Villanova College in Philadelphia on June 7. Foxx cracked two singles in three at bats and the *Observer* boasted, "Sportswriters witnessing the contest expressed confidence that Foxx will prove out in big league ball."

During the middle of June, Jimmie suffered an arm injury from a practice pitch, a hard curve thrown by Lefty Grove. The arm was initially thought to be broken, but further examination proved otherwise, and the injury was only a temporary setback for Foxx.

In mid-June, the A's added catcher Charlie Berry from Lafayette College, and the youngster impressed Mack enough that it made it easier for him to send Foxx to Providence to give him more playing time over the next couple of months. Mack feared that Foxx would gain too much weight as a benchwarmer, and playing experience at the Double AA level would help sharpen his playing skills.

Before being sent to the Providence Grays of the IL on option in late June, Jim had appeared in only seven games for the A's. The *Observer* reported that the working agreement between Mack and Providence stated that Foxx could be recalled at any time, should a "break" occur in the playing of Cochrane or Perkins. Isaminger predicted in the *Sporting News* on July 2: "Fox [sic] is sure to return to the Macks and in a few years he will be one of the best receiving and batting catchers in the nation."

Jim attended graduation ceremonies for his classmates at Sudlersville High School on June 19. After all sixteen graduating seniors took their seats on stage, Jim walked in with the school principal, Anna Harrison, and other teachers and sat down with his classmates. Ms. Harrison handed out the diplomas and asked Jim to stand as she explained that he had foregone receiving his diploma for the time being to pursue a once-in-a-lifetime chance at a career in professional baseball. Foxx received a certificate of attendance and louder applause than any of the graduates.

Everyone in the school, whether a teacher or a classmate, was very proud of Jimmie at that point. "He was 'Our Jimmie'," recalled his classmate and cousin Mildred Barracliff.

Jim played along with other A's rookies in an 8-5 loss to Nazareth of the Bi-State League in Bethlehem, Pennsylvania, on June 22, the same date that an official announcement was made in Philadelphia that the A's were releasing him to Providence on an optional agreement. Foxx doubled in one official at bat against Nazareth, stole a base, and played part of the game at catcher.

Jim reported to manager Frank Shaughnessy and the Grays (often called the Clams by newspapers outside of Providence) as they were ending a four-game series with the Jersey City Skeeters on June 25 at Jersey City, New Jersey. The game between those two clubs that day was postponed, so Foxx and the rest of the Grays caught a 12:45 P.M. train for Baltimore for a four-game series with the Orioles. The Grays roomed at the Emerson Hotel in Baltimore, their regular "home" there, but the ballplayers were not easy to find, because the national convention of the Loyal Order of Moose was also being held in Baltimore and many members were staying at the Emerson. The players found the corridors so crowded that the easiest way to get in and out of the Emerson was through the back door.

The *Providence Journal* misspelled Jimmie's last name as "Fox" in its June 26 story and "Cox" in the story's subheadline and said:

> Foxx . . . made a fine record on that [Eastern Shore League] circuit last year, but there is no way of telling what he will do in Class AA company, although Connie Mack must have seen something worth while in the colt to have drafted him. He looks good in practice and will probably be given assignments now and then to help Lynn. . . .

C. Edward Sparrow, sports editor of the *Baltimore Morning Sun*, who was very familiar with Foxx's exploits at Easton, told his readers on June 25 that Foxx was turned over by Mack to Providence for further seasoning, rather than "warming the boards at Shibe Park," and he would be coming with the Clams for the four-game series with the Orioles beginning the next day.

Foxx, in his new Grays uniform, sat and watched the Grays battle the Orioles in single games two days in a row, without appearing in either game, but the *Sun* promised its readers that Foxx would appear in a game the following day at Oriole Park. A spike injury to catcher Bryd Lynn in the June 27 game made it necessary for Jim to play catcher in both games of a doubleheader against the Orioles on June 28.

Foxx managed two scratch singles in the doubleheader but wished he could have done better with the bat, because each time he stepped to the plate, "hundreds of fans cheered for the youngster," according to the *Morning Sun*. What impressed onlookers the most was that he threw out Oriole speedster Maurice "Comet" Archdeacon, trying to steal second. No other Oriole tried to steal off Foxx in the twin bill. His two singles came in five at bats while batting eighth in the order, facing the Orioles' hard-throwing right-hander George Earnshaw, who would be Jim's teammate just a few years later. Remarkably, Earnshaw pulled the "iron man trick" for pitchers that day, pitching two complete-game victories for the Orioles, a rare feat for pitchers in any league by the late 1920s. The second game was a seven-inning affair, which was customary in the IL at that time.

Two days later, in his next game for the Grays, Jim impressed the hometown fans in Kinsley Park at Providence, smacking two singles and a double in four at bats against the Orioles' Jack Ogden. In addition to Foxx's hitting exploits in that game, the *Providence Journal* said, "Fox [sic], the new catcher obtained from the Athletics caught the full game and gave a snappy exhibition behind the bat." As Dunn watched Foxx perform, he had to be wondering how he missed obtaining the youngster from Frank Baker.

The Grays had been the Newark (IL) club until the middle of May 1925, when the franchise moved to Providence because of the inability of Newark to upgrade its stadium. The Grays' new home was newly refurbished Kinsley Park by the Woonasquatucket River at Kinsley Avenue and Acorn Street.

Lynn returned as the starting catcher for the Grays after July 5, and Foxx played mostly as a substitute catcher, especially for the second game of some doubleheaders, through the third week of July. Shaughnessy felt that Lynn was a better handler of his team's pitchers. Lynn was twice Foxx's age and counted among his experience a five-year stint with the Chicago White Sox from 1916-20 as a backup catcher to Ray Schalk, a master at the position.

Jim caught very little for the Grays thereafter, playing mostly right field and a couple of games at center field and first base. It was a fortuitous move by Shaughnessy, whether it was his idea or that of Connie Mack, because Cochrane was continuing to improve at a rapid rate at catcher with the A's, so Foxx benefitted greatly from gaining experience at other positions. He also pinch hit frequently.

Jim had five hits (a double, triple, and three singles) in seven at bats in a doubleheader while playing mostly at first base on July 24 at Reading, Pennsylvania, convincing Shaughnessy of the extent of his batting ability. The hitting outburst forced the Grays' manager to move Foxx to third in the batting order for several games after that date and place him at various spots between first and sixth in the order for the remainder of the season.

On July 25, the *Providence Journal* mentioned that "Fox [sic] has a sore knee," but gave no further information on the origin or extent of the injury. The knee injury must have been minor, because two days later, Jim slugged a triple, two doubles, and a single in six at bats while playing right field for the Grays in a 15-7 victory over Jersey City.

Officials of the Providence ball club were impressed enough to want to purchase his contract. In July, the *Sporting News* reported, "Providence wanted to buy him [Foxx], but Connie Mack wouldn't let him go. He is an 18-year old boy—a big fellow and will no doubt be one of the great catchers of the game in a few years."

Foxx's only homer for the Grays came on August 21, against the Syracuse Stars at Syracuse. Jim opened the seventh inning and gave Providence a 3-1 lead when he homered over the right field fence off lefty Bill Hallahan, a future star pitcher for the St. Louis Cardinals.

Jim's worst injury while with the Grays occurred in the first game of a doubleheader against Syracuse on August 22. He walked to start the fourth inning but was tagged out when he tried to steal second base and slid over the bag, severely injuring his left shoulder. The next day, Jim visited Dr. Knight in Rochester, while accompanying the Grays there. The following day, he was carrying his left arm in a sling, the arm being so sore that he couldn't use it at all. Yet, just six days later, Jim appeared in both games of a doubleheader against the Bisons at Buffalo, playing catcher in the first game and center fielder in the second.

It was Foxx's final appearance in a Grays' uniform; Mack had sent orders for him to return to the A's by August 31. Jim celebrated by collecting three hits in seven at bats in the doubleheader, then remained overnight in Buffalo on August 30, because the Mackmen had a game scheduled with Buffalo the following day. Foxx didn't play for the A's against Buffalo on August 31, but he returned with the Mackmen on the train to Philadelphia that evening.

Foxx gained valuable experience at several positions during his stint with the Grays, proving that his assignment to the minor-league club was a wise move by Mack. He played in 41 games for Providence (17 at catcher), but missed 32 other games while with the club from June 26-August 30. Jim batted at a .327 (33 for 101) clip for manager Shaughnessy, quite impressive for someone not yet eighteen. Upon returning to the A's, Jim was noticeably lighter than earlier in the spring. His playing time at Providence served many purposes, and now that he was rejoining the A's, he would be part of his first pennant race.

As he returned to Philadelphia from Buffalo with his teammates, Jim read about the A's contending with the Senators for the AL pennant and the growing rift between Ruth and Yankees' manager Huggins.

Meanwhile, Queen Anne's County fans were hoping the "Sudlersville Flash" would be playing in the World Series. The Athletics entered their two-game series with the Senators on September 1 three and one-half games behind front-running Washington. Jimmie watched Walter Johnson pitch a complete-game win over the A's in the first game, followed by another loss to the Senators the next day. Jim didn't see action in either of the games against Washington, the two losses adding to a losing streak that now totaled eight games for the Mackmen at the worst time.

On September 6, Mack inserted Foxx as a pinch hitter for pitcher Walberg in the ninth inning against New York at Yankee Stadium with one out, Dykes on first, and the A's trailing by two runs. Jim slashed a pinch single to right, Perkins walked, and Bishop lined a single to right. Dykes scored on Max's base knock, but Jim choked the A's rally when he tried to score the tying run on the same hit, standing up, and was easily tagged out at the plate by catcher Benny Bengough. Many observers felt that a normal slide by Foxx would have resulted in an easy tally for the A's. Instead, he became the second out of the inning and Philadelphia came up one run short, 4-3. The *Inquirer*'s headline read, "Dumbness on Bases Costs 10th Straight," and the *New York Times* referred to Foxx as "a foolish boy."

On Labor Day, September 7, the *Observer*'s new player board on the front facing of its building in Centreville was used to rebroadcast the A's-Senators games. A Radiola Super-Heterodyne received play-by-play reports that were rebroadcast with a Magnavox amplifier and depicted on a player board with electrical flash signals. The player board had two rows of slides bearing the names of the players for both teams. The center of the player board had a miniature diamond with electric lights at each base and home plate to indicate which bases were occupied by base runners. Groups of lights also recorded balls and strikes and the number of outs in an inning.

Fans outside the *Observer* building in Centreville watched and listened intently on September 9, as Foxx started a five-run rally in the sixth inning to lead the A's past the Senators.

Then on Sunday, September 20, Foxx reinjured his left shoulder during a base-running contest before an exhibition game with Lit Brothers. Just as Foxx turned first base in a speed contest, his toe caught in the sack. He went spinning out into right field and fell heavily to the ground, landing on his weak left shoulder.

The *Observer* recalled that Philadelphia sportswriters gave Foxx a "terrific roasting" a couple of weeks earlier when he didn't slide into home, then stated that most sportswriters and fans did not know about Foxx's injury at Providence and Jimmie was trying to avoid another injury during the game at Yankee Stadium.

Foxx's injury was a big disappointment to Mack, because he had planned to use Jimmie in some of the remaining A's games. It ended Foxx's 1925 season, which otherwise might have been extended by some valuable playing time in an ambitious twenty-game barnstorming trip through Pennsylvania and New Jersey. Still, Mack believed that because of Foxx's youth and the long winter recess ahead, Jim would fully recover from the injury by spring training of 1926.

Although Jim played in only ten major-league games the entire season, at seventeen, he was the youngest player to see action in the majors that season—and quite possibly any season up to that time. He had six hits in nine at bats.

When Dell Foxx returned home from Easton after an operation for appendicitis in mid-February 1926, a small gathering of Jimmie's Sunday school class was held in honor of his upcoming departure for spring training. The Rev. R. S. Hodgson, pastor of Calvary Methodist Episcopal Church, and Mr. Harry Jones, teacher of the Sunday school class, gave short addresses to wish Jimmie good luck. Jimmie's hometown, always loyal, kept a watchful eye on him during his entire career.

Foxx caught the train in Baltimore in late February for spring training. Rommel, Grove, and Ike Powers climbed aboard with Jimmie; Mack, Gleason, and Cochrane had already boarded in Philadelphia.

When Foxx arrived at Fort Myers for spring training in 1926, he knew it would be an uphill battle to earn a spot on the roster, never mind a place in the regular lineup. He showed no signs of the dislocated shoulder injury from the previous fall, and Mack was satisfied with Jim's initial playing weight and that of Cochrane's. His salary for the season, if he stuck with the team, was reported to be $2,500.

Jimmy Isaminger said of Foxx as spring training was starting, "Fox [sic] can hit and run bases, as well as catch efficiently, and Mack thinks he is a second Cochrane. This Maryland youth is the kid of the outfit."

Manager Mack realized that Jimmie would have a hard time finding playing time as a catcher during the 1926 season, given the performance of Cochrane in 1925 and Perkins' defensive ability at catcher. So Mack had Foxx begin working at first base and the outfield during spring training. Sportswriter Stoney McLinn reported that Foxx's favorite position was actually first base. He had played several games at that position and many more games as an outfielder while with Providence the previous season. McLinn studied Jimmie closely:

Foxx has his eyes and ears open every minute. He has picked up some receiving tricks which make the job of catching such an easy one for Ralph Perkins. Frequently, he stands around first base when Joe Hauser and Jim Poole are playing that bag and getting instructions from Mack and Gleason. Now and again, he parks himself in the outfield and gets some tips from Simmons, Miller, Lamar, and other flychasers. Always he is listening, looking, and learning when lectures on batting are given. Foxx is fast and shifty. He is fearless. He has that athletic sense which made an all-around star of the quality of Jim Thorpe, the famous Indian. He swings the right-handed way and knocks a ball hard and on a line. Foxx is not an 18-year old lad who developed into a man suddenly. He insists that he weighed just as much and was just as tall when he was 13 years old, as he is today.

Foxx injured his ankle about mid-March in spring training, adding to a succession of injury woes beginning the previous August. The injury was variously referred to as a leg or ankle ailment. Mack was afraid to risk further injury to Foxx and restricted his activity to warming up the pitchers. This frustrated Mack, since he had hoped to put Foxx in as many exhibition games as possible. Now Jim was shelved effectively until the beginning of the regular season, and another valuable opportunity was lost for Mack to watch his young prospect in game situations, perhaps at different playing positions, outside the regular season.

In March 1926, for the first time, the *Sporting News* correctly spelled Foxx's last name. A story often told is that Foxx's last name was spelled with only one "x" by sportswriters until a scribe spotted a suitcase that Foxx was carrying with his name on it with two "x"s. The scribe reportedly asked Jim if he had added an "x" to his last name, and Foxx replied, in effect, "No, that's the way my parents spell it and my Grandpappy before that. So, I guess it belongs there."

Foxx earned a place on the Athletics' roster as they headed north for the preseason series with the Phillies, but he rode the bench while the A's and Phillies split four games in Philadelphia.

As the season unfolded, it was apparent that Mack was content to have Foxx remain with the club the entire season, despite his infrequent playing time. At eighteen, he was the youngest player to appear in a game in the AL in 1926. He usually played catcher to warm up relief pitchers and appeared in 26 games altogether, 9 as a pinch hitter, 1 as a starting catcher, 11 as a replacement at catcher, 3 as a starting outfielder, and 2 as a pinch runner. Foxx batted 11 for 33 for the season (rather than 10 for 32, as listed in the record books) and was still looking for his first major-league homer. He was 0 for 8 as pinch hitter, with 1 base on balls, and 11 for 25 when he was a position player.

After the A's traded Bing Miller to the St. Louis Browns on June 15, Mack chose Foxx to wear his outfielder's glove for the next three A's games. Jim played Bing's old right field position in all three contests, batting 2 for 5 in each of the first two games and 1 for 3 in the third game. Curiously, Mack then lifted Foxx from the lineup despite his lusty batting and replaced him with Walter French. Had Foxx been left in the lineup as the right fielder for several weeks, one wonders if he would have gained a regular spot in the starting lineup.

Foxx's name was still being misspelled by some sportswriters, and C. M. Gibbs of the *Morning Sun* dryly remarked on June 19:

> There seems to be something about the air in Philadelphia that makes the players become dissatisfied with the way the family name is spelt. First came Lefty Groves [sic], who this spring tried to amputate the "s" from his name, and now comes Jimmy Fox [sic], who has been made over from a catcher into an outfielder, and tries grafting another "x" on the end of his.

Jim caught in parts of three games for the A's at the end of July, impressing sportswriter Isaminger with a bare-handed catch of a foul pop. Foxx didn't play in August and September, when the Athletics, Senators, and Indians made a run at the Yankees after New York took a ten-game lead in mid-August. A's fans read from the August 1 edition of the *Inquirer*, "Don't be surprised if Jimmy Foxx catches the majority of games for the rest of the season after the team returns to Shibe Park. The 18-year old Marylander is booked for heavy duty."

As the A's road trip was about to end, on August 11 Doc Ebeling recommended that Jim return home to Philadelphia before the rest of the club, because he was suffering from stomach trouble. The ailment's exact nature is hard to discern from newspaper accounts, but it continued to nag at Jim and thwart any hopes of seeing action. As of August 31, Jim was still at home with his parents in Sudlersville and the A's had hired Harry O'Donnell of Port Richmond, Pennsylvania, to help warm up the pitchers for the rest of the season. The A's management seemed to believe that Foxx would be out of action for some time. Yet, just a few days later, the *Inquirer* said, on September 3, "Word has been received from catcher Jimmy Fox [sic] that he is on the mend and it is now believed that he will be able to join the team on its final western trip. He has been at his home in Sudlersville several weeks recovering from an illness."

Foxx traveled to Philadelphia and met with Mack on September 4 in hopes of returning to action with the A's, but Connie inexplicably decided not to take Jimmie on the club's road trip out west.

The A's won 21 and lost only 14 from August 15 through the end of the season. The Mackmen led the league in pitching with a 3.00 earned run average, but lacked the batting punch of the other contenders, especially the Yankees, who scored 170 more runs during the season. Still, the A's ended the season in third place, just six games behind New York, with only four more losses than the Yankees.

Foxx's strong showing at bat whenever given the opportunity suggested he deserved more playing time, especially on a team needing run production. Helen Tarring Harrison recalled that her father often complained, "Why isn't Mack playing Jimmie more often? He's a natural." But Jimmie, humble as he was at his young age, was not known to pressure Mack for more playing time.

Foxx traveled with teammate Lefty Willis to Lefty's hometown of Kearneysville, West Virginia, in early November for the hunting season, then brought Lefty back home with him to Sudlersville right before Thanksgiving, presumably to hunt for rabbit and quail. It's uncertain how Jim developed his interest in hunting, but it seems likely he hunted as a teenager in areas near his home with his father or uncles. Relatives and friends of Jimmie who were still alive in the 1990s in and around Sudlersville could not recall Dell and Jimmie hunting together, but Dell and Mattie planted the seed early in Jim's mind that hunting would be a hobby worth pursuing. A picture postcard typical of the early 1900s exists in which James Foxx, about six, is seated with a wide brim hat, holding a long gun on his lap reminiscent of the kind Daniel Boone would have used. The picture was probably taken either in Betterton (Maryland) or Tolchester Beach, because the background indicates the photograph was taken in an art studio.

Foxx and Willis sometimes roomed together on road trips, and Foxx introduced Lefty to Dorothy Tarring. Jim had been dating Dorothy's sister, Helen, for several years. Lefty eventually married Dorothy, representing an off-the-field home run for Foxx.

Foxx turned nineteen after the 1926 season in October, still a youngster in terms of major-league players. Boys of that age wearing a major-league uniform and playing in regular season games were a rarity, but Jim was more skilled than most. Dell and his friends kept encouraging him—to them, Jimmie was destined for stardom. It was only a matter of when.

4

OPPORTUNITY KNOCKS: THE NEXT RUTH?

In early 1927, Jimmie Foxx's All-Stars played several basketball games against other teams on the Eastern Shore, including several against Company E squad and Company K squad of the National Guard. Either Mack was no longer as heavy-handed about prohibiting Foxx's athletic activities outside of baseball or he simply didn't know about them.

A few hours after Jimmie signed a 1927 contract with the A's for a reported $3,000, he suffered cuts on his forehead when his automobile crashed in a head-on collision with Roy Godwin's automobile in a late-night fog on January 21 outside of Sudlersville. "Jim was on a date that evening with Polly Coleman, and the accident scared Roy Godwin half to death. But the automobiles were not traveling at a high rate of speed," recalled Foxx's cousin Winnie Coleman. Early reports out of Centreville the next morning indicated that Foxx incurred serious back injuries, but the early news proved to be false. The *Observer* assured its readers the following week, "Foxx's injuries in no way would interfere with his ballplaying ability."

The night before Foxx left Sudlersville for spring training, Jimmie's All-Stars tripped the Company K basketball team, 34-16. Foxx scored sixteen points to lead all scorers.

The following day, February 18, Mattie and nine-year-old Sammy Dell joined Jimmie on the train from Sudlersville to Philadelphia. There Jimmie caught a train carrying the first group of Athletics to Fort Myers.

The morning of the first session of training camp, Foxx was an early casualty when he was assigned to play shortstop during infield practice. Coach William "Kid" Gleason hit a hard grounder to Foxx. As he stooped to catch the ball, it took an unexpected hop and smacked him square in the eye. After first aid by Doc Ebeling, Foxx stayed on the field but suffered almost complete closure of his eye from swelling within a half hour.

Foxx began spring training at 164 pounds, compared to his 185 pounds at the end of the 1926 season. The *Observer* noted that he had kept himself in shape by playing basketball, hunting, ice skating, and presumably helping with farm work.

As in his first two spring training seasons, Jim saw little action when the A's played against other NL clubs, mostly the Cardinals, Braves, Giants, and Phillies. He was listed as a catcher on the club's early spring roster. Cochrane and Perkins did most of the catching in exhibition games; Poole, who had a mediocre season in 1926, and Edgar "Dudley" Branom shared first base duties during spring training. As the A's finished their exhibition season, Foxx played in four of the last seven games, playing the whole game against the Orioles while catching Grove for five innings, catching one whole game against the Phillies, and pinch hitting twice, once against the Phillies and once against the Newark Bears.

Rumors that Mack might trade Foxx to a club in the IL were dispelled in early April, when the A's released rookie Charlie Bates, who was listed as both a catcher and first baseman. Foxx was one of three catchers on the opening day roster for the A's.

Meanwhile, Ty Cobb had joined the A's for the 1927 season under a strange set of circumstances. He was lucky to be playing major league baseball at all. Cobb had resigned as a manager of the Tigers in November 1926 and told the press, "I have swung my last bat in a competitive baseball game." It was later found that AL president Ban Johnson told Cobb to resign rather than have Ban make an alleged game fixing-betting scandal public. Cobb, along with several other players including Tris Speaker, was accused of fixing a game late in the 1919 season. However, when the information was handed over from Johnson to Commissioner Landis as a "courtesy," Landis made the information public and conducted his own investigation. On January 27, 1927, Landis dismissed the fixing charges against Cobb and Speaker and didn't mention "betting regarding the case." The Tigers and Indians expressed no interest in welcoming Cobb and Speaker back, so they were made free agents with the right to negotiate with any team. Betting and game-fixing charges aside, Foxx would now watch the game's master batsman, Cobb, firsthand.

Simmons enjoyed Ty's tutelage, especially on batting. Cobb told Al to alter his stance depending on who was pitching, what kind of delivery the pitcher had, and any pitch location that the pitcher favored.

Foxx and his teammates witnessed an ugly rhubarb at Shibe Park on May 5 that stemmed from a poorly constructed rule regarding home runs versus foul balls. In the bottom of the eighth, Cobb led off with the A's trailing the Red Sox, 2-1. Ty socked a line shot down the right field line over the wall, sending the spectators into delirium. Umpire Emmett "Red" Ormsby shocked the crowd by signaling "foul" with his hands, sending the fans into a mad frenzy of bellows, boos, and catcalls. Jimmy Isaminger, writing for the *Inquirer* and *The Sporting News*, said the "ball was obviously fair" and Ormsby based his foul ruling on Section 1 of Rule 48, which stipulated that when a ball is batted out of the playing field an umpire must declare that it is fair or foul as it last looked in the umpire's views (even well after passing the top of the wall). Ormsby called it foul because he believed it veered foul after it left the park. Many observers called the rule absurd and claimed that umpires, almost without fail, ruled that a ball was fair or foul based on its location at the exact point when it passed over the outfield fence.

Cobb vigorously objected to Ormsby upon returning to the plate, intentionally or unintentionally bumped the umpire's shoulders, and was promptly ejected. Like throwing gasoline on a fire, the crowd now roared more disapproval. Simmons objected vociferously and was ejected by Ormsby. By now, police had to escort Ormsby off the field for his own safety. Following a review of Ormsby's report, AL President Ban Johnson suspended Cobb and Simmons, levied a $200 fine on each player, and the A's lost all three games that they played while their two batting stars were suspended.

Meanwhile, Cobb's hitting and all-around play for Mack were so sensational that he was an obvious inspiration to the other players. In addition to his heavy hitting, Ty stole home twice within the first month of the season. It was a clinic, an education for the A's players to watch Cobb in action, and although the magnitude of the benefits to Foxx is hard to know, he most certainly gained baseball insight from watching and listening to Ty.

Mack used Foxx very sparingly during April and May of the 1927 season. He appeared in three of the A's fifteen games in April, playing catcher for part of one game, as a pinch runner in another game, and as a pinch hitter in the third contest. Then in May, Jim played in part of six of the A's thirty games, finally appearing in action at Shibe Park for the first time that season on May 30. Again, he seemed to be the forgotten man on the roster, the odd man out, probably due to his age.

But on May 31, Jim made Mack stand up and take notice in a double-header that Connie otherwise preferred to forget. Foxx slammed his first major-league home run while pinch hitting against spitballer Urban Shocker of the Yankees at Shibe Park. Jimmie's homer came in his eighth at bat of the season in the second game of a doubleheader easily swept by New York, 10-3 and 18-5.

Shocker was thirty-seven before the end of the 1927 season, but won eighteen games and lost only six for New York. Abruptly following the season, he began a yearlong illness before dying of pneumonia and heart disease in September 1928.

A few days after Foxx's first major-league homer, Mack announced that he would play Jimmie at first base against left-handed pitchers. Foxx started at the first sack in four games on June 6, 8, 10, and 11, and smacked his second major-league homer on June 8. Some observers were quick to pronounce the experiment a success, Jimmy Isaminger saying:

> Foxx, still under the 20-year mark in age, has hit the ball hard and played excellently at the bag. Ever since joining the A's at 17, this wonderful youth has hit above the .300 mark, and when the A's were in their slump, the lean leader [Mack] simply had to provide a spot for him. So, he hit on the scheme of trying him at first base.

In the June 6 game, Foxx collected a key run-producing hit in a 4-1 win. On June 8, Jim was robbed of a triple by the Browns' outfielder Harry Rice but later countered with a homer into the upper deck of left field at Shibe Park. At this point, Isaminger told readers of *The Sporting News*: "He [Foxx] has the whole city at his feet, the fans demanding that Mack use him against the right-handed pitchers as well as the southpaws."

Then Mack made an ill-advised move. Rather than leave Sammy Hale out of the lineup when his shoulder mended, he returned Hale to third base and switched Dykes from third base to first base, fulltime. Foxx was benched. Dykes was hitting so well, as high as .390, that Connie couldn't remove him from the lineup; however, Mack should have kept Dykes at third and allowed Foxx to play at first. The fans were ready to see Foxx every day, and Jim seemed ready to handle major-league pitching.

The A's were out of the pennant race by early September, so Mack set his sights on finishing in second place to gain a share of World Series money for each of his players. The A's remained a distant second to the Yankees in August and September because New York maintained a record pace for an AL team's single season won-loss record.

Foxx finally got the break he needed when first baseman Dykes badly strained ligaments in his left leg in September. Jim became a starter at first base on September 12, and within the first week of playing time he impressed onlookers. Isaminger wrote, "this Maryland kid . . . has been covering first in dazzling fashion."

Foxx also flexed his batting muscles. On September 14, he beat the White Sox with a run-scoring single in the eleventh inning at Shibe Park. The following afternoon, he thrilled the hometown fans with a soaring homer, a 3-run blast off the White Sox's Ted Lyons that helped the A's win, 5-4. The homer went over the center field wall at Shibe Park, and Isaminger called it "a terrific homer—a lick of Ruthian might."

Beginning with the September 12 game, Foxx remained in the starting lineup for the rest of the season, playing 18 games at first base and two games at catcher. During that time, he batted 26 for 77 (a .338 batting average) with 16 runs batted in and 39 total bases. Foxx's potent batting performance continued to nag at Mack. Who should he drop from his lineup to make room for such a good hitter with outstanding promise? Foxx's versatility was paying off. His willingness to try new positions and ability to play them well kept opening opportunities for him to play and eventually crack the starting lineup.

After the Yankees swept the Pirates in four games in the World Series, Foxx received a healthy bonus. As a result of the A's finishing in second place in the AL, Foxx and each of his teammates received a little more than $1,000 from money from the Series. For the Sudlersville youngster, it was a sizable lump of cash added to his estimated salary of $3,000.

Jimmie Foxx had waited for a chance to make an impact on the outcome of an Athletics' pennant drive for three seasons. Each season offered Foxx more at bats than the season before. Jim gave steady performance at the plate but still had unknown potential as to his ability to play daily and adjust to the same pitchers after facing them several times in a season.

Again Jim spent the winter at his parents' home on the farm near Sudlersville. As spring training for 1928 approached, Jim kept in shape by playing basketball and taking long hikes while hunting for fowl and rabbits. Jimmie Foxx's "All-Stars of Sudlersville" played several local basketball teams from nearby counties, including the "headquarters" team of the Easton Armory. Jim impressed his old friends in Easton on January 5 by rallying his team from a halftime deficit to defeat Easton, 26-19. Foxx scored ten points in the contest.

A few days later, Jim initiated the purchase of a farmhouse and farmland known locally as "Wayside" or "Wayland" from Ed Gillespie. Ed's son, Tom, recalled that Jim and Dell Foxx came up to the porch of the farmhouse when Tom and Ed were both there. Dell and Jimmie asked Ed if they could step inside for a few minutes to talk business. Moments later, the three men emerged from the house and a deal had been struck. It was a satisfying moment for Dell, knowing that his son would own his own land and not be a tenant farmer if he took up farming after finishing professional baseball. The farm was located just outside of Sudlersville, about three miles west of the intersection of Main and Church Streets. An article in the *Observer* stated that the farm would be occupied by Foxx's parents sometime in 1929. The sale was finalized on July 28, 1928, when the deed was passed from Gillespie to Dell and Mattie Foxx. Jimmie paid a $3,000 down payment toward the $10,500 purchase price for the farmhouse and 172.5 acres of rich Eastern Shore farmland. Dell and Mattie would no longer be tenant farmers. Many years later, the small road adjacent to the farmland was named Dell Foxx Road.

A rare heavy snowfall covered Sudlersville late in January, and Dell Foxx and his neighbors, including Ben Wooleyhand, Thomas Smith, and Joe Clough, competed in horse-drawn sleigh races in town. School children stared out of Sudlersville High's windows until the races were over. Dell had gained plenty of experience handling horses from frequent driving in harness races.

On February 20, Jimmie, Ed Rommel, and Ike Powers boarded a train in Baltimore carrying the Athletics' first group bound for spring training. Mack announced one of the smallest spring training rosters ever, with only twenty-nine players. Cochrane, Perkins, and Foxx were listed as the team's catchers. Although twenty now, Foxx was still listed as the youngest player on the team. He was considered the team's third-string catcher. Jim had to wonder if he'd ever play full-time for the Athletics.

On the train trip southward, Foxx told his mates about his near brush with death just a week earlier. Jim recounted how he went to sleep at the wheel while driving at night along a road near Sudlersville, losing control of the car as it went into a ditch, snapped a telephone pole, and landed on its side. Though the front wheels were ripped off and the car engine was smashed, Jim escaped injury.

Joe Hauser was back in the fold with the A's after several seasons in the high minor leagues rehabilitating his right knee. If Hauser faltered, Dykes, Foxx, Ossie Orwoll, and even Speaker could replace Joe in the lineup at first.

After signing the nearly forty-year-old Tris Speaker in early February, Mack announced that he expected to use him at center, Simmons in left, and Miller in right field. Dykes and Foxx were mentioned as able replacements in the outfield, if necessary. Also, Mule Haas, a highly sought outfielder with excellent hitting and fielding ability, was purchased from the minor league Atlanta Crackers.

The *Observer* remained supportive of Jimmie's chances of cracking into Mack's regular lineup, reporting, "It is well known that Connie Mack is particularly fond of the Sudlersville lad. It is expected that he will have greater opportunities this season."

Mack signed Cobb to a new contract in early March, ensuring that Foxx would play alongside Cobb, Speaker, and Collins at the same time, though he would not see any of the three star players in their prime.

Connie's first look at Hauser's batting and fielding convinced him that Joe would be his first baseman. Hauser's right kneecap had recovered adequately from being broken in 1925 and had withstood 169 games with Kansas City the previous season.

The twenty-four-game preseason schedule announced by the Athletics included games only with NL and minor-league clubs. A rule in the junior circuit forbade preseason games between AL clubs so lopsided scores would not diminish early season attendance at AL ballparks. Strategies for financial solvency were always important; professional baseball was always first a business.

In early March, Mack was more puzzled than ever about how to get enough use out of Foxx's bat with a set lineup already in place. Connie's thoughts were made public when he said:

> I don't know what to do with Jimmy Foxx. That wallop of his that just went for three bases would have cleared the left field bleachers in Shibe Park, and anybody will admit, that's quite a drive. Jimmy can catch, play first or outfield and I just can't decide where to make use of his batting.

In the very first exhibition game of the season, Foxx made a rare start at catcher and responded with two hits in four at bats, including a homer against the Phils. Thereafter, he either caught about every third game, pinch hit, or sat out the game entirely.

In one of the last exhibition games for the A's before the preseason series in Philadelphia, Foxx singled, doubled, and homered twice against the Greensboro club of the Piedmont League at Greensboro, North Carolina. Then on April 1, Jimmie played the whole game at catcher for the A's against the minor-league Jersey City club, batted fifth, and had a sacrifice hit and a double. Mack only played Foxx in one of the five city series games against the Phillies. Foxx played the whole game at catcher for Mack against Dunn's Orioles on April 8.

Scouts must have been watching Foxx, because even before the season began, several flattering offers had been made to Mack for Foxx, but Connie rejected all of them. Foxx was still considered primarily the third-string catcher, but his potential was finally becoming appreciated in both major leagues.

Foxx was the bullpen catcher in games in which he didn't start, serving as chief of the new telephone in the bull pit when Connie called from the manager's bench to request that he warm up a new pitcher.

The Athletics' new uniform no longer had the white elephant, which was replaced on the jersey with a large old English "A." Two blue bands ringed on the socks instead of one, but the hat still had a blue bill with a white crown and several blue vertical stripes.

On opening day, April 11, the A's and Yankees played in cold intermittent rain with cold winds at Shibe Park before 25,000 fans. Jimmie replaced Cochrane early in the game due to an injury. Dell Foxx's loyalty to Jim and the A's paid off as he and four neighbors at Shibe Park whooped it up when Jimmie cracked a hard single against New York.

In his next game appearance on April 18, Jimmie smacked a three-run homer in a losing cause off the Senators' Tom Zachary. Mack planned early to give Foxx some playing time as catcher and third baseman, especially against left-handed pitchers. But strong starts by Joe Hauser and Sammy

Hale made it tough for Foxx, still a youngster by comparison, to break into the starting lineup. Hauser was hitting for power and Hale was hitting for a high average, staying among the league's leaders through May and early June.

Foxx homered while playing catcher on May 4 in a 10-5 victory over Detroit, but he did not see action again until May 13. A day later, Foxx pinch hit for Cochrane in the tenth inning and smacked a three-run homer into the left field bleachers at Shibe Park to defeat the Indians, 6-3. Some of the A's fans showed their approval for Jimmie's heavy clutch hitting by showering the field with their new straw hats.

After hitting a home run, Jimmie liked sitting next to Connie Mack upon returning to the dugout. On occasion, his mischievous teammates, being fully aware of Foxx's behavior, would sit squeezed closer than usual to Mack, but Foxx always managed to wedge himself between a player and Mr. Mack after hitting each of his homers.

Jimmie started the next two games at catcher and slammed three hits in both games. One of his extra-base hits on May 16, an especially fiercely hit line drive, hit the flagpole in center field, 468 feet from home plate. Jimmie continued to compete against formidable talent, however. By May 18, Hale was the second-leading hitter in the league with an average of .395.

A doubleheader between the A's and the Yankees at Shibe Park on May 24 attracted an overflow crowd estimated at 41,000 to 45,000, as the two teams split the two games. Foxx saw action only as a pinch hitter in the first game and did not appear at all in the second. The A's dropped to five and one-half games behind New York in the standings the following day, when they lost both ends of a second doubleheader to the Yankees at Shibe Park in front of another overflow crowd. Foxx batted 2 for 4, including two doubles while playing catcher in the first game, and did not play in the second game.

From May 27 through June 2, Jim appeared only once in a game. Then Foxx replaced Dykes at third base in the seventh inning of a game against the White Sox on June 3, the first time Mack had played Jimmie anywhere other than catcher during the 1928 season.

The game on June 3 proved pivotal for Foxx's career. When Jimmie stepped to the plate in the ninth with two outs and Hauser and Cochrane on first and second, he fought off Chicago's Tommy Thomas in a masterful at bat. Foxx socked Thomas' first pitch into the left field stands, but the ball landed foul by several feet. Then Jim smashed a long foul down the right field line. The redoubtable young slugger amazed Mack and other onlookers by belting Thomas' next pitch, a fastball over the inside corner of the plate, for a terrific line-shot home run into the lower deck of the left field stands. Despite Foxx's homer, the A's came up one run shy of Chicago, losing 6-5.

Foxx regarded the game as a key moment in his career. "I don't believe that I ever enjoyed anything more in baseball than getting a chance to play third base. I was so happy, maybe that's why I soaked that home run. I was certainly feeling good."

After playing one game each at third base, catcher, and as a pinch hitter, Jim began playing more regularly in the starting lineup beginning June 11. On that date, Simmons and Foxx hit successive homers in the eighth inning at Navin Field to defeat Detroit, 4-2. Foxx batted fifth and played third base.

On June 12, Jim split the index finger on his left hand during practice before the game but still played against the Tigers, slamming two hits, one of which won the game in the eighth inning. "I like playing third base," said Foxx. "But, every time I caught the ball yesterday [the day of the finger injury], it hurt like the deuce."

After one more start at third base, Jimmie started at first base and batted fifth in place of Hauser on June 14, due to Joe's ineffectiveness at the plate. Foxx's hitting binge continued, and his four hits in nine at bats in a doubleheader against the Yankees on June 20 prompted manager Miller Huggins to tell the story of how he missed signing Foxx.

> This kid has made the Philadelphia club. I sure like Foxx, as a hitter and as a first baseman. Connie will have a hard time dislodging this lad from the bag, as he is one of the finest natural hitters I have seen in years. Too bad I missed Foxx when he was in the Eastern Shore League. Frank Baker tipped me off to Foxx, who was only 16 years old at the time, but before we could rush a scout down there, Mack robbed him for next to nothing. Yes, Foxx is the real thing.

Imagine Foxx (3B), Gehrig (1B) and Ruth in the same lineup!

About the same time, Ruth was quoted as saying, "I like that Foxx kid's baseball playing. He has all the makings of a real star." The high quality of Foxx's play was becoming more obvious as the autograph hounds began seeking him out.

Jim continued to pressure Connie to make him an everyday player, especially based on his hitting early in the season. Foxx piled up a 15-game hitting streak from June 11-25 (23 hits in 59 at bats) and even adjusted his eating habits, remarking that "his huge daily order of griddle cakes had been eliminated on account of sultry weather, a sudden change from chilly breezes."

The Senators' Milt Gaston halted Jimmie's consecutive-game hitting streak on June 26 at Griffith Stadium. Gaston pitched often against Foxx during his eleven years in the AL for New York, St. Louis, Washington, Boston, and Chicago from 1924 through 1934 and recalled in 1990 that he was always told, " 'Don't throw him [Foxx] a high fastball'—so I mixed up my pitches and hoped for the best." After the June 26 game, Foxx had the second-best batting average in the AL at .383. Jimmie started at first base for the A's in every game from June 14-27, then was shuttled back and forth between first base, third base, and catcher before settling in for a long stretch at third base.

The A's, like their opponents, coped with extremely hot temperatures on the playing field about as best as they could. Doc Ebeling's mixture of sweet spirits of ammonia, water, and ice in a metal bucket was soaked into a towel and dabbed on the players' faces. All the players used the same bucket. The players liked the smell of the sweet spirits of ammonia.

The heat was such that sometimes the players changed their sweatshirts and woolen flannels several times during a game. The clubhouse errand boy would run the sweat-laden clothes into the room with the gas dryer, and the A's would put on dry clothes.

Many of the A's players, including Foxx, chewed tobacco to keep their throats from becoming dry from dust being kicked up from the infield during long periods of hot, dry weather.

Jimmie continued to travel down to Sudlersville on either Saturday evening or Sunday morning whenever he was in Philadelphia and the A's had an open date due to the blue laws that prohibited Sunday games in that city. During homestands, Foxx continued to board mostly with his Aunt Virginia Smith Spry, at 6725 Gratz Street in Philadelphia. Aunt Virginia lived in a stone row home with a garage in the basement with a back entrance to the house. Foxx liked everything she cooked for him, especially her fried chicken. Other players would often pick Jim up at Aunt Virginia's house to bring him to Shibe Park. Some of the players who frequently posted at Aunt Virginia's were Grove, Earnshaw, and Haas.

Jim never forgot Aunt Virginia's hospitality. Several times after the Depression first hit, when Jimmie was married, he came to visit his aunt and found that she was struggling so badly she had hocked her wedding ring at a local pawnshop. Each time, Foxx bought the ring back for Aunt Virginia.

She must have been a favorite with the entire Foxx and Smith families. Elwood and Mary Coleman, Dell and Mattie Foxx, and Jimmie's Uncle Charlie Smith often visited with Aunt Virginia during their trips to see Foxx play home games for the A's. They were usually waved through the press gate when they arrived at Shibe Park.

After their games of June 30, New York had a 50-16 record compared to the A's 39-28 log. The Yankees were threatening to blow open the AL pennant race the way they had in 1927.

Several days later, on July 5, big right-hander George Earnshaw, whom Mack had purchased from Jack Dunn on May 28, began to pay dividends. Earnshaw earned his first major-league win after several failures, a 5-0 complete-game victory over the Red Sox. Mack said, "George has a good fastball, curve, and change of pace. If he can turn wins in with regularity, and I know he will, and the other pitchers keep up with their hurling, I think we can shave down the lead Miller Huggins' team has amassed."

Mack was right. The Mackmen caught fire in July, winning 25 of 33 games while New York won only 20 of 35. Early in July, Foxx saw limited action again, playing catcher on a platoon basis with Cochrane and pinch hitting occasionally. He missed eight games entirely, despite his red-hot batting in June.

The Athletics won 17 of 18 games from July 17-August 2, allowing opponents only a total of 47 runs. Foxx celebrated his return to the starting lineup at third base when he smashed 20 hits in 40 at bats with 37 total bases from July 19-29. His overall average stood at .360 on July 29.

The 1928 season represented the peak of coverage of Foxx's exploits on a weekly basis in the *Observer*. Sports editor Vach Downes surely detected the degree of excitement and anticipation held by fellow residents in Foxx's native Queen Anne's County and acted accordingly by putting weekly updates about Jim and the A's in the *Observer*. But the *Observer's* coverage of Foxx's accomplishments was never as frequent or consistent in years that followed. This is peculiar, given the A's success over the next three-year period and Foxx's success over the longer haul.

Foxx's ability to hit long home runs became evident to a new extent on July 21 at Shibe Park. With Simmons on base in the fifth inning, Jim took a toehold, drew back his bat, and propelled a fastball from the Browns' Jack Ogden over the left field wall. Reports described it as a "record homer" for Shibe Park, not even touching the roof. The ball carried over the doubledecked stands, sailed across the street, struck the roof of a house, and bounded onto a second street. It was estimated the ball carried 467 feet to the roof of the house. Had the house not been there, it would have carried even farther before landing on the ground.

Some of the Athletics and Philadelphia sportswriters began saying, "He's going to be Babe Ruth's successor as a slugger. A kid who can pull the stunts Foxx has, before he is 21, is sure to be a famous ball player."

All hot streaks, whether by a player or a team, have to end, at least temporarily. Six unearned runs on August 3 enabled the Indians to overcome the Mackmen, 9-5. Two errors by Foxx at third, one fielding and one throwing, were largely responsible for the loss. When Foxx had a chance to atone for his errors with Cochrane and Simmons on base and the A's trailing by 3-0 in the eighth inning, his hard liner into right field was caught by a diving Homer Summa.

In early August, Mack held little hope for the A's catching the Yankees, despite the A's recent surge in victories. But Mack already was looking forward to 1929, saying:

> I can't call a year a failure that gives me four new players I can depend on and makes a 20-year old boy potentially the greatest star of the game. If the season brought me nothing except the development of Jimmy Foxx, I would still call it a success. Jimmy has borne out a prophecy I made the first time I saw him in action.

But the A's caught fire again quickly and stirred a major outbreak of pennant fever in Philadelphia for the remainder of the season. They continued to master AL opponents, especially from August 4-September 8, winning 23 games and losing only 10, while New York won 17 and lost 14.

In an interview published in the August 13 *Philadelphia Evening Bulletin*, Jim talked about the pressure of being in a pennant race:

> Playing baseball is hard work. And no one knows it more than the players. Right now, when we're only a few games back of first place, we are playing the hardest ball of the season. Our pitchers are bearing down from the first inning until the last out. Each one of the players would rather lose an eye than make a costly error. If each man was not in perfect condition, the strain would make him crack, sure enough. But we're going ahead, winning ball games and hoping we'll be in first place before the end of September.

Oddly, the interview was strewn with errors, saying that Foxx said he always played second base for the Sudlersville High School team (actually he almost always played catcher for the high school and town ball teams, as indicated by box scores in local newspapers); that he caught for the first time in his life when he played for Easton; and that he played for Easton more than one year beginning in 1921 (he played for the club only one season, 1924).

Even with the intensity of the pennant race, Mack retained scheduled exhibition games on Sundays that the A's were not slated to play an AL opponent, rather than cancel the game to give his club a rest. On September 2, the A's traveled to Cumberland, Maryland, to play the Cumberland Colts of the Middle Atlantic League. The *Cumberland Evening Times* reported that a record crowd overflowed the grandstand and bleachers to watch a 7-5 A's win. Foxx and Orwoll smacked solo homers early in the contest, but the highlight of the game for local fans was Grove's appearance in the eighth inning. More than a thousand fans came from nearby Lonaconing, Maryland, and they were not disappointed. After walking the first batter he faced, Grove fanned the next three Colt batters in a row, using only a fastball, while A's outfielders Speaker, Bush, and French moved just behind the infielders (a showoff trick similar to that used often by Satchel Paige).

Jim played 45 consecutive games at third base from July 19 to September 4, giving Mack his first extended look of Foxx at that position. It was Jim's longest stint at third base since beginning to play professional baseball in 1924. Foxx made 8 errors in 145 chances at third base during the 45-game string, for a .945 fielding average. If Foxx gained more experience at third base, he would likely continue to improve his fielding, especially on bunts and knowing where to play different batters.

A doubleheader win by Philadelphia over Boston on September 7, combined with the Yankees' two losses to the Senators, left the A's tied with New York. Then on September 8, the A's won another doubleheader from the Red Sox, while the Yankees won a single game from Washington, putting the A's a half-game ahead of New York. Fans and sportswriters alike were astounded that the A's had caught the Yankees, given New York's torrid start.

Foxx batted .306 from the August 4 through September 8. He returned to first base on September 7 and remained there for thirteen and one-half games before playing third base for the last six and one half games of the season. Now that Jim was established in the A's starting lineup, residents of the Eastern Shore of Maryland were assured of seeing Foxx in action if they made the trip to Philadelphia for a given home game. Occasionally the *Observer* even mentioned the names of people making the trip to Shibe Park to watch "Jimmy Foxx."

Foxx was interviewed late in season and listed three main objectives in his life:

> First of all, I want to see the Athletics win a pennant. Secondly, I want to be as good a ballplayer as my father was, and last, but I guess not least, I want to get married. My father has always been my staunchest supporter. He comes to most of the games and roots hard. Most of the folks down home tell me that I may be doing fine in the major leagues, but that my father would have been a greater star had he left the farm as a young man and gone away to play. I remember when I was a kid, when my father came to bat the outfielders used to drop to the edge of the park.

Indeed, Dell followed his son's baseball career very closely. He kept news clippings on Jim's achievements and even carved a wooden object to stand upright that was shaped perfectly so that a full-figure photograph of Jimmie about one-foot high could be pasted on the front of the wooden piece, giving the photo a three-dimensional look.

Foxx didn't mention Helen Heite's name (his future wife, not to be confused with Helen Tarring Harrison) in the interview when he said, "I want to get married," so that it's not known whether he was already courting Ms. Heite then.

A record crowd of more than 85,000 attended the doubleheader between the A's and Yankees on Sunday, September 9, at Yankee Stadium. American League president Ernest Barnard recognized the importance of the games in the league standings and assigned four umpires to officiate. Fans mailed in orders for game tickets from as far west as Chicago and as far south as Florida. Many fans from Philadelphia made the trip to root for the Mackmen, but to no avail.

The Yankees swept the two games, 5-0 and 7-3. Foxx received a bitter taste of failure when veteran George Pipgras struck him out with the bases loaded with two outs in the eighth inning of the first game with the A's trailing, 3-0. In the second game, the A's went ahead 3-1 in the top of the seventh on a two-run homer over the right field screen by Simmons, followed by a showering of straw hats on the field by fans of the Mackmen. After the Yankees tied the game in the bottom of the seventh, Meusel came to bat in the bottom of the eighth with the bases loaded and lifted a 3 and 2 offering from Rommel into the left field bleachers, clinching the game for New York. Yankee fans responded by "pelting the field with straw hats, Panama hats, and felt hats." Ruth gave Meusel a big bear hug as Bob crossed home plate. The Yankees chanted in the clubhouse, "the same old A's, the same old A's," and Ruth bragged, "we broke their hearts."

The Athletics and Yankees battled for first place throughout September, and the closeness of the final standings show how important every game was in deciding the pennant winner. The A's were not able to make up one of the games of the season series with the Red Sox, having played only 21 times against each other instead of the 22 scheduled games. Mack's club had beaten Boston a whopping 18 times in 21 games.

During the last scheduled series between the two clubs for the season on September 6, 7, and 8, a rained-out doubleheader on September 6 made it impossible for the two clubs to play a total of 22 times for the season, despite back-to-back doubleheaders on September 7 and 8. This meant that the A's would likely finish the season having played 153 games, compared to 154 for the Yankees. If only one-half game separated the clubs in the standings at the end of the season, the A's and Yankees could have the same amount of wins and the A's one less loss, making them the pennant winners; or the two clubs could have the same amount of losses and the Yankees would have one more win, making them the pennant winners. Some sportswriters questioned the fairness of such a system for deciding a pennant winner. They asserted that the two major leagues should require that when the first and second-place teams are in such a close pennant race, they reschedule all postponed games so they played the full schedule.

Even after the A's lost three out of four games to New York early in September, they crept to within one-half game of the Yankees several times later in the month, but the Yankees held tough. The latest the A's were just one-half game behind New York was after the games of September 16.

The A's made their final visit of the season to Detroit's Navin Field in late September for a three-game series. Even though Cobb had been out of the starting lineup since about mid-season, it seems odd that Mack never played Ty in any of the three games, even as a pinch hitter. Cobb had already made it known that he was very serious about retiring at the end of the season, and he certainly had plenty of incentive to perform well in front of his former fans. Cobb drew applause from the 10,000 paying customers as he warmed up in right field before the third game of the series, but Mack refused to use Ty as a pinch hitter late in the contest, even as Philadelphia rallied with single runs in the fifth, sixth, seventh, and eighth innings, but lost 5-4.

The Yankees finally clinched their third consecutive pennant in their third-to-last game of the season on September 28, with a victory over Detroit, even though the A's defeated the White Sox on the same day. It made for a bittersweet season for the Athletics and their fans.

Philadelphia ended the season just two and one-half games out of first place, with one of the best records ever compiled by a second-place team, 98 wins and 55 losses.

Most of the Athletics' games that Foxx missed in 1928 were in April (7 games) and May (16 games), and he was only a pinch hitter in six of the games he appeared in in May. Jim played in 118 of the 153 games played by Philadelphia, missing very few games in July, August, and September. He appeared in parts of 61 games at third base, 30 games at first base, and 20 games at catcher. Jim batted .328 and compiled a slugging average of .548 on the strength of 29 doubles, 10 triples, and 13 homers. He collected 131 hits in 400 at bats, coaxed 60 walks, drove home 79 runs, and struck out only 43 times. Had Foxx been used by Mack more often, earlier in the season, would the outcome of some games been different? He missed 23 games completely in April-May and had only one plate appearance as a pinch hitter in each of five other games in May.

By the end of the season, Mack knew he wanted Foxx's bat in the lineup every day, but he was still uncertain what position best suited Foxx while still helping the A's the most. Sportswriter John Kieran said, "If the Athletics keep Foxx at first base, they'll have to find a regular third baseman. If they shift Foxx to third, they'll have to get a regular first baseman."

A chief factor that hurt Philadelphia's pennant chances was the team's inability to beat New York in head-to-head matches. They won only 6 of their 22 games against the Yankees. Grove mirrored the team's frustrations with a lowly 1-6 record against the Yankees, while posting an amazing record of 23-2 against the rest of the league.

As the World Series was ending, another alibi surfaced to explain some of the A's troubles in overcoming New York. Gordon Mackay, sportswriter with the *Philadelphia Record,* blamed the A's second-place finish on the hatred western clubs in the American League held for Ty Cobb and Tris Speaker. Reports indicated that many players on the Tigers, Browns, and Indians made every attempt to prevent Ty and Tris from getting in one last World Series, knowing they both had planned on retiring. A Detroit writer put it this way:

> They [the Tigers] were keyed up to lick the Athletics and not even give them a thing. That's the reason they grabbed two of three games from Philadelphia in the late September series. They turned around and while they played to win, they just ran out their string against the Yankees.

A sportswriter from St. Louis added, "Put St. Louis in the same boat. I know they played their heads off to beat the Athletics and all the while they were sorry that Connie Mack wasn't going to get into the Series, for everybody thinks the world of Connie."

As a result of the Yankees' four-game sweep over the Cardinals in the 1928 World Series, the Athletics received over $31,000 in second-place money. The series revenues for Mack's club meant that Foxx received a healthy bonus of over $1,000.

In an October 1928 article in *Baseball Magazine,* author Tom Doerer lauded young Jimmie Foxx's wisdom in finances and investment decisions:

> The beckoning of the primrose roadways and the glitter and glare of white lights made no impression upon him. In the five years that he has been in baseball, Foxx has saved enough money to be the owner of a 200-acre dairy farm near Suydlersville [sic], Maryland. Foxx believes when he reaches 30 years of age, he'll have enough income earned from baseball to make him comfortable for the rest of his life.

"When I get home after baseball season, I never go any farther than to the railroad station with a truck-load of milk," Foxx said, sitting on the edge of a trunk in the Athletics' clubhouse smoking an old pipe.

Foxx said that he was impressed with many other major leaguers who had a regular habit of saving some of their earnings, and that he has followed their example. "When I invested in a farm it was an hereditary instinct. All of my people have been, and are farmers," Jimmie said. The article claimed that Foxx "likes to talk of his cows and his farm work as much as he does his love for the game."

"I sure like them both," Foxx said with a grin.

In fact, it was impressive that Foxx had saved enough money to buy a farm by 1928. He had not yet earned as much as $5,000 in a season, but he had lived at his Aunt Virginia's house during homestands during the baseball season and had lived at home with his parents during the off-season. He did not have the expenses of a married man yet, and Jimmie's reputation for enjoying night life would come later in his baseball career.

Fritz Maisel put together a team of white major- and minor-league All-Stars to play against a group of black baseball players made up of about one-half Baltimore Black Sox players and the rest from several other Negro League teams. Maisel's team included Dick Porter, Johnny Neun, Max Bishop, Lefty Grove, Eddie Rommel, Jack Ogden, and eventually, Jimmie Foxx. The Black Sox contributed Crush Holloway, Jesse Hubbard, Robert Clarke, and Laymon Yokeley. Other black players on the team were Luther Farrell and Dick Lundy from the Bacharach Giants and Oscar Charleston, Walter Cannady, and Frank Warfield from Hilldale.

Rommel led Maisel's club to an 8-5 win over the Negro League All-Stars on October 7 before 7,000 fans at Maryland Baseball Park in Baltimore. The following Sunday the Negro Leaguers won easily over Grove, collecting 11 hits and 7 walks off the A's left-hander. Then on October 21, Maisel inserted Foxx in his lineup for the first time, batting him cleanup and playing him at left field. Ogden pitched for Maisel and shut out the Negro Leaguers except for the first inning, when John Beckwith smashed a two-run homer. Beckwith had been borrowed from the Homestead Grays. Just one day shy of his twenty-first birthday, Foxx led off the second inning with a solo home run off Yokeley, and later in the game added a triple, but Yokeley held on for a 2-1 win.

Once again, with the season over, Foxx returned to Sudlersville to join his parents and brother for the winter.

Orioles' owner Jack Dunn died suddenly of a heart attack on October 22 at the age of fifty-six. This was a serious blow to Connie Mack's future ability to obtain top-notch major-league-level talent from a reliable source. Mack and Dunn had shuttled players back and forth from their respective clubs on a regular basis from 1910-28. Mack loaned Dunn $10,000 in the winter of 1909 to help Jack purchase the Orioles for $70,000. Over time, Dunn gave Mack first licks at purchasing his two greatest prospects—Babe Ruth and Lefty Grove. Connie erred in turning down the opportunity to purchase Ruth in 1914, but he did obtain Grove at a record price to be paid over ten annual payments.

Since players like Bishop, Boley, Grove, and Earnshaw starred for the IL Orioles for at least several years each at the Class AA playing level, they came to Mack at a much steeper price than a player like Foxx, who was comparatively unknown, having played just one season at the Class D level.

The day after Christmas, Jimmie and Helen Heite of Dover, Delaware, eloped and attended the annual Christmas dance at the Armory in Centreville, Maryland, where they announced that they were married earlier in the day. Many of their friends were there, especially those of Jimmie, and Margaret Stack (wife of Jimmie's high school friend, Leon) recalled the event many years later. The band played "Here Comes the Bride," and not long after, they were off to tell Helen's parents about it in Dover, Delaware. At least one report years later said they were married in Church Hill near Sudlersville; another report said they were married in Sudlersville. When they arrived at the home of Helen's parents, they told Mr. and Mrs. Charles Heite that they had eloped and spent the night there. It's uncertain where they lived for the next month and a half until spring training, but it seems likely that they stayed with Jim's or Helen's parents.

Helen had graduated from Dover High School in 1926 with a class of twenty-nine students. She was slim, with small shoulders, dark hair and eyes, and a pretty face. She was athletic in high school and enjoyed track and field and basketball. Jimmie and Helen may have met during the 1924 season, when Foxx played for Easton at Dover.

5

THE MACKMEN ARRIVE

Just a few days after Jimmie and Helen were married, the Mackmen had plenty of reasons to be optimistic about the coming baseball season. Spring training was little more than a month away, and the "Macks" had a roster loaded with talent and the confidence of having battled the Yankees the season before in a very close pennant race.

For the 1929 season, the Mackmen had three topflight outfielders in Simmons, Haas, and Miller, with Homer Summa in reserve. Speaker and Cobb had been released as free agents, and Walter French had announced his voluntary retirement. Mack also announced that Ossie Orwoll would no longer be used as a pitcher for the coming season but would instead play first base or outfield. Meanwhile, Simmons headed for Hot Springs, Arkansas, early in the year for hot baths to guard against a recurrence of rheumatism. Mack sorely needed Simmons in the lineup daily for the coming season; he had played in only 106 games in 1927 and 119 games in 1928.

Sportswriter Jimmy Isaminger was adamant about the need to have Foxx in the everyday lineup for the A's, given Jim's potent bat. "It is absolutely necessary to find a regular post for Jimmy Foxx, so if Dykes is chosen as third baseman, Foxx will be found at first." For the same reason, Isaminger believed that "the release of Joe Hauser to Milwaukee of the American Association was not a serious loss to Philadelphia's starting infield, because the A's had Foxx, Orwoll, and Dykes available for first base duty." Bishop would likely start at second base and Boley at shortstop. Isaminger speculated: "if Foxx covered first, then Dykes and Hale would share third base and Orwoll would be an outfield reserve. If Foxx were to start at third, then Orwoll would most likely start at first, and Dykes and Joe Hassler would be the infield reserves, with Dykes seeing more playing time."

Cochrane and Perkins were again selected as catchers. Isaminger revealed that Foxx was no longer likely to be used at catcher, even though he was listed at that position on the team roster in *The Sporting News* on

February 21. Because of Foxx's playing time at third and first base in 1928, Mack now considered Jimmie to be primarily an infielder.

The A's had one new strong pitching prospect, right-hander Bill Shores, and an excellent list of returnees: Quinn, Rommel, Earnshaw, and Ehmke were the right-handers; Grove, Walberg, and Yerkes were the left-handers. But new prospects were needed to provide insurance to Mack's strongest pitching staff since 1912-1914.

Still, the defending World Champion Yankees, winners of three straight pennants, had a formidable roster. The pitchers were expected to be Waite Hoyt, Herb Pennock, Wilcy Moore, Tom Zachary, Hank Johnson, Pipgras, Fred Heimach, Myles Thomas, Al Shealy, and three minor leaguers—Floyd Van Pelt, Gordon Rhodes, and Roy Sherid. Before the season began, Huggins had a high opinion of young Bill Dickey but said he would have to go far to replace Benny Bengough as the starting catcher. Returning infielders included Gehrig, Tony Lazzeri, Mark Koenig, Leo Durocher, and shortstop prospect, Lyn Lary, from the Pacific Coast League. Outfielders included Ruth, Meusel, and Earle Combs.

Jimmie and Helen arrived in Florida early in February for Helen's first visit south during spring training. This enabled Jim to take in some golf before the report date for the Athletics' players other than pitchers and catchers at Fort Myers. That same month, the newlyweds purchased the deed for the farm and land that Jimmie had "given" to Dell and Mattie the year before for the balance of the purchase price of about $7,000. Dell and Mattie remained as residents on the farm because Jimmie and Helen planned to live in Philadelphia year-round.

Foxx was now a proven major-league hitter and had shown indications of better than average power. Still, he had no set position in the lineup as spring training began and no assurance that he was an everyday player.

At about the same time that the pitchers and catchers reported to Fort Myers, Coach Gleason and a party of six players (Dykes, Simmons, Miller, Ehmke, Quinn, and Earnshaw) arrived at the Mackmen's camp from Hot Springs. Shortly after their arrival, many of the players traveled by bus to Miami to see the Young Stribling-Jack Sharkey boxing match.

Foxx started at third base the first three spring training games for the Athletics, batting fifth, while Orwoll played first base. In the third game, on March 9, Foxx was hit on his right arm by a scorching grounder in a game against the Cincinnati Reds in Miami. The next day, Connie placed Jimmie at first base to gain from Foxx's hitting while his throwing arm recovered. Jim played first base for three games, then Connie gave Orwoll another try at first base. Despite the fact that Mack and most managers were partial to left-handed first basemen, some Philadelphia scribes began hinting that Foxx just might be the best choice to play the position.

Foxx preferred playing third base, but Orwoll was falling shy of Mack's expectations for fielding at the initial sack. Foxx didn't play third base much in high school or in town ball games, but he may have developed an ambition to play that position while watching manager Frank Baker play third on a part-time basis for Easton in 1924. Both Kid Gleason and Ira Thomas believed that Foxx would become the most valuable third sacker in baseball if he played there every day.

On April 1, a story out of Jacksonville, Florida, where the A's were slated to play, reported that Mack was still uncertain about his infield lineup, especially at first base. Mack stated that Dykes' play at first base compared favorably with Foxx and Orwoll. But Foxx continued to hit well, and Simmons continued to struggle with rheumatism in his ankles, making Jimmie's bat even more valuable and necessary in the Athletics' lineup.

Foxx played in nine exhibition games as first baseman before the City Series in Philadelphia, hitting 12 for 37 and batting fifth. On April 5, in a game against the Braves in Richmond, he poled two homers, one leaving the stadium and reportedly landing in the James River. The two homers gave him a total of four in three games. He was making his strongest case yet to be in the daily lineup for the 1929 season.

Jimmie played all four games of the City Series at first base for the A's just before the season opener. Mack had finally found a position for Foxx and a spot in the regular lineup. The fact that Foxx played at first base for a very long stretch of games before Opening Day refutes a story often told that it was a complete surprise to Jimmie on the day of the regular season opener when Mack told him he would be playing first base "so he better go find a first baseman's mitt."

In early April, Mack again predicted greatness for Foxx if he kept his health. Meanwhile, the majority of a pennant poll for 1929 by the Baseball Writers Association picked the Yankees and Athletics to finish first and second in the AL and the Cubs and Giants to finish first and second in the NL. The poll showed 78 first-place and 20 second-place votes for the Yankees, and 17 first-place votes and 60 second-place votes for the A's, out of 104 writers.

As the regular season began, Boley's sore arm forced Mack to play Dykes at short and Hale at third base. As expected, Foxx opened at first base.

Shibe Park was a haven for the avid baseball fan in Philadelphia in 1929. The Athletics were coming off a stirring season in 1928 in which the close pennant race aroused local fans, and the fans had money to spend. The Depression was still six months away.

"Cigars, cigarettes, and all kinds of chewing candy," the hustlers used to holler in Shibe Park. When Foxx played for the Athletics at Shibe during 1929 and the 1930s, items served at the ballpark included Cokes, Schmidt's malt brews, Canada Dry ginger ale, orangeade, sarsaparilla, Byerle's orange juice, no beer, Vogt's lunch rolls (Onlee ham sandwiches) and frankfurters, Burke's lunch rolls, Freihofer's rolls, Crane's Philadelphia ice cream, Cracker Jacks, peanuts, Quinlan's butter pretzels and potato chips, and Goldenberg's peanut chews. The hustlers served fans at their seats; there were no concession stands underneath the grandstands. "In between games of a doubleheader, that's when the money was made," recalled Al Ruggieri, former employee of the Shibes.

Prime times for good turnouts at the ball yard were Opening Day, games with the Yankees and Senators, and doubleheaders on Memorial Day, the Fourth of July, and Labor Day. Nick Altrock and Al Schacht entertained the fans with their comedy-slapstick antics in between games of a doubleheader when the Senators came to town.

Box seats cost $1.25, grandstand seats were 75 cents, and bleachers cost 25 cents. The lack of variety of promotions and giveaways made it easy for a baseball fan to walk up to the ticket window the day of a game and purchase a ticket for a prime seat without planning ahead.

Bull and Eddie Kessler had a reputation for being two of the loudest fans anywhere in the country in the late 1920s and early 1930s. The Kessler brothers sold fruit from their horse-drawn cart in the streets of Philadelphia in the morning and posted for most of the A's home games, which usually started at 3:15 P.M. On one occasion, the Kessler brothers harassed Tiger shortstop Billy Rogell to the point that he jumped in the stands and began chasing them down before being restrained by police.

A short (5 foot, 2 inch), heavy-set (185 pounds) man operated a megaphone to announce the starting lineups and substitutions to the crowd during the game. Gamblers usually sat in a group of at least twenty-five down in the right field grandstand seats and bet on anything including the outcome of each at bat.

Third-base coach Eddie Collins was helpful to some of the A's batters because he could signal what pitch an opposing pitcher was going to throw. Collins studied the various grips a pitcher had before throwing and called out a signal to the batter. For example, he sometimes called out the batter's first name for a fastball and last name for a curveball. Foxx often used these signals, but Simmons showed no interest in Collins's help.

Foxx homered far into the left field bleachers of Griffith Stadium in the season opener on April 17 against the Senators. It was just the prelude to a season-long celebration of hitting by Foxx, now that he was in the A's starting lineup. He ended the month of April among the league's batting leaders with a .351 average and was batting sixth in the lineup.

Meanwhile, the Mackmen and New York split two early season two-game series in April, the first at Yankee Stadium and the second at Shibe Park. The second game at Shibe Park filled the ballpark beyond capacity, and fans crowded rooftops of the homes on 20th Street across from right field.

The Athletics took hold of the AL lead in May, winning eight consecutive games by May 23. It wasn't just the fact that they were winning, but that an aggressive, cocksure style was evolving. In their seventh straight victory, they came back from an 8-0 deficit in the second inning to beat the Senators 9-8. They also beat Washington in 13 of the first 14 contests between them.

The Athletics were now a well-oiled machine, a cohesive unit on the playing field with a diversity of personalities. The team had a good combination of take-charge players, practical jokers, and players that led the team by their performance without on-the-field antics. Foxx liked to needle his teammates and spit tobacco on their shoes. He did it with a grin, not a vengeance, and he led by his performance on the field, avoiding rhubarbs. Cochrane was an outspoken leader, a "firebrand," according to some sportswriters. He inspired the A's with his hustle and was often in the center of rhubarbs. "He would cajole, scold, and berate his pitchers, in turn," according to sportswriter Fred Lieb, but he seemed to get the best out of Grove, Earnshaw, and Walberg. He was "pugnacious" on the field but mild mannered when not in uniform. Cochrane wore well-tailored clothes and liked to play the saxophone. Following the 1928 season, he even went on the vaudeville circuit. Dykes was a champion needler and bench jockey who barked out encouragement to his teammates in his staccato voice. He liked playing cards and golf and smoking cigars. Grove was another fierce competitor. He had the worst temper on the team, throwing tantrums in the clubhouse after a hard-luck loss. Grove liked his cigars, too, and early in his career, he was known to stash a jug of moonshine under his bed. Rommel started out as a spitballer and was one of the first pitchers to successfully use the knuckleball. He said he threw at a batter only one time during his entire career—Ray Schalk. Schalk scored the winning run in the game, and Rommel never threw at another batter again.

Simmons hit the ball harder than anyone on the club except Foxx. Al loved to hit. He described each opposing pitcher as his mortal enemy. He was a good tipper, but not as generous as Foxx. Like Cochrane, Simmons didn't mind getting in a rhubarb. He roomed with Cobb in 1927 and 1928 and said he learned a lot about hitting from Ty. The association between the two men certainly did not lessen Simmons' desire to win. Simmons was an outstanding outfielder with a strong arm.

Connie Mack was a stern disciplinarian. He was "Mr. Mack" to his players. Only rarely did he lose his temper or hold a team meeting to try to derail a losing streak, but when he did, the A's were attentive. If he was frustrated about two teammates in an argument, he'd bark a crisp order to knock it off. He allowed bench jockeying, but only to a point. Always attired in civilian clothes, he wore a serious, firm expression and rarely cursed.

Beginning on April 30, Foxx never slipped below a batting average of .350 for the entire season. He was hitting for high average and power, and coaxing walks at a much greater rate than other batsmen close to him in the AL batting race. Jim was a team player and would continue to reach base at a high percentage rate (due to high batting averages and many walks) each season in his career.

At the same time, the A's became more set in the starting lineup with Bishop still the leadoff batter, Haas batting second, Cochrane third, Simmons cleanup, and Foxx fifth, followed by Miller, Hale, or Dykes, and Boley.

On May 24, Foxx crushed a pitch off the Senators for a 468-foot homer en route to a ninth straight win for the Athletics. Foxx was leading the league in batting almost daily at this point and strung together a 15-game hitting streak from May 18-31.

Near the end of May, Foxx stroked a long homer against the Red Sox's Danny MacFayden at Fenway Park, as recounted by Jimmy Isaminger in *The Sporting News:*

> Foxx's homer off MacFayden at Fenway Park last Wednesday was one of the longest ever seen at these grounds. The ball sailed high and dry over the left field wall and kept on traveling. It passed over a factory and dropped down on the Boston and Albany [railroad] tracks.

Because the A's as a team were so dominant early in the season and so many players on the club were playing so well, it wasn't until the June 6 issue of *The Sporting News* that Foxx received heavy coverage by Jimmy Isaminger. The Philadelphia scribe cited Jim's league-leading batting average and noted his ability to clout long-distance homers:

> The steady and spectacular blasts from Foxx's bat are making him a national figure in the fast set. Foxx is simply running away with the AL batting championship. At every park the A's visit, Foxx is establishing record hits that make the fans buzz. Resident fans can see only Jimmy as the successor to Babe Ruth.

After June 6, Foxx was batting a league-leading .406, followed by second-leading hitter Cochrane at .384 and fourth-leading hitter Simmons at .361. The Mackmen had still not lost two games in a row during the season.

Now that Foxx owned his own home, he and Helen frequently had house guests from Sudlersville and other nearby areas on weekends. His high school teammate and friend Leon Stack came to Philadelphia on occasion, as did his cousin Winnie Coleman, and probably his cousin Claude Smith. The close proximity of Foxx's home games in Philadelphia bolstered a heavy following and support from friends and family. He thrived on the adulation.

Philadelphia visited Yankee Stadium in late June with a seven and one-half game lead over New York to begin a five-game series. After a split of a doubleheader on June 21, an estimated 70,000 fans showed for the second doubleheader on June 22. A crowd of 3,500 fans lined up at the ticket windows outside the stadium as early as 9:30 A.M., and car license plates showed that fans came from many states. The gates opened at 10:25 A.M., although game one didn't start until 1:30 P.M. When the Mackmen took the field for practice, Philadelphia rooters bellowed loud and lusty cheers. In game one, Foxx poked a second inning two-run homer and shook hands with waiting base runner Simmons at home plate. Walberg went the distance in a 7-3 win, but Quinn lost a 4-3 decision to Pipgras in the nightcap in which each pitcher lasted till the end of the 14-inning struggle.

The next day, Foxx, Simmons, and Haas each homered as the Mackmen took the deciding game of the series behind Ehmke, 7-4. The win pushed the Athletics' league lead over the Yankees to eight and one-half games, and Foxx climbed back over the .400 batting mark.

Next the Athletics swept the Red Sox four straight at home before a three-game series with New York at Shibe Park. The Mackmen and Yankees proceeded to each win one game sandwiched around a rain out. The crowds again swelled Shibe Park beyond seating capacity. Some of the crowd estimates were as high as 35,000 to 40,000. The windup game, won by the Yankees on June 29, featured two homers by Ruth and an incident involving Gehrig. Lou chopped the legs from under Boley in the third inning to prevent Ruth from being doubled up at first base. The crowd responded by throwing papers and cushions at Gehrig as he approached the dugout at the end of the Yankee half of the inning. The fans booed him royally the rest of the game. Foxx's 3 for 3 performance at the plate raised his league-leading average to .410.

From July 9-27, Foxx had seven homers and 26 runs batted in during a 22-game hitting streak, but actually saw his average dip slightly from .403 to .392. The latest date that Foxx averaged .400 or higher in the season was on July 12, when his batting average rested at .400 after collecting three hits in five at bats in a doubleheader against the Browns.

Foxx's high batting average made him the major-league sensation at mid-season. As often happens with a young player on an extended hot streak, the press wondered, what were the limits of performance for this new phenom? Jimmie's childhood story, his upbringing on a farm in an atmosphere of wholesome, clean living appealed to sportswriters.

Foxx made his hometown proud when he appeared by himself on the cover of *Time Magazine*'s July 29 issue. The cover's headline read, "Philadelphia's Foxx—He joined the .400." In the magazine article, he described how his daily work as a young boy on the farm gave him his upper body strength and proudly recalled some of the tests that demonstrated that strength.

> I worked on a farm, and I'm glad of it. Farmer boys are stronger than city boys. When I was 12, I could cut corn all day, help in the wheat fields, swing 200-pound bags of phosphate off a platform into a wagon. We had games on the farm to test strength and grip. A fellow had to plant both feet in half a barrel of wheat and then pickup two bushels of wheat or corn and balance them on his shoulders. Another trick was to lift a 200-pound keg of nails without letting the keg touch your body. I could do that easily, but never realized it was helping me train for the big leagues.

The article in *Time* said that Foxx had a chest expansion of 6.5 inches and his favorite position was third base.

At about this time, Ed Bang of the *Cleveland News* related,

> Jimmy's secret of success at the plate is found in the fact he always waits for a good ball, or at least tries to. It makes no difference whether it is a curve, fastball, or slowball. Last year, Jimmy was regarded as a dead leftfield hitter, so the wise pitchers started to work on him this year. They dished him up nothing but balls on the outside.

Foxx responded quickly by belting the ball to all fields. Bang also reported that while Ruth often tended to hit high home runs, Foxx hit most of his balls as line drives. Bang said, "Time and again when one of Foxx's drives nears the outfield barrier, it's just beginning to rise."

Foxx pounded one of his longer homers on July 30, when he cleared the left field roof at Shibe Park off the Tigers' George Uhle. Lynn Doyle of the *Philadelphia Evening Bulletin* used some hyperbole to make the point that Foxx's homer off Uhle was hit for an extraordinary distance: "Jimmy Foxx started one to Canada—at least it was on its way to Hudson Bay when it cleared the left field roof." Not yet satisfied, Doyle went further: "An unconfirmed report says that Foxx's home run landed in an Eskimo's fish basket thirty-seven miles north of Moose Cat, Labrador."

The Mackmen refused to weaken in early August. In a warmup for the Yankees' visit to Philadelphia, the Athletics split doubleheaders with the Browns at Shibe Park on August 5 and 6. In the second twinbill, Foxx hit a homer in each game, giving him 26 for the season. Gehrig also had 26 at this point, and Ruth had a league-leading 27 homers, thanks to his two homers against the Senators on August 6. A gathering of 20,000 saw Foxx's 4 for 7 performance net him a .390 season average and a 14-point lead over Al Simmons, his closest pursuer.

Rookie pitcher Wes Ferrell of the Cleveland Indians, who was enroute to a 21-10 record in 1929, was interviewed by John Kieran in early August and had already formed a very high opinion of Foxx. Wes was especially impressed with Foxx's ability to slug high fastballs, which was not surprising, given Jimmie's unusual habit of swinging much higher than most sluggers when taking practice cuts:

> Ruth . . . was the greatest hitter I ever saw. Next to him I'd put Jimmy Foxx. I think Jimmy's a better hitter than Simmons. And Simmons has been around quite a while and Jimmy is just a kid [same age as Ferrell at the time—21]. Say, he hit a high ball off me for the longest homer I ever saw. I know he hits high ones but this was too high for anybody to hit. But he hit it and sometimes I think it's going yet.

The archrival Yankees came to Shibe Park for a doubleheader on August 7, eleven and one-half games behind Philadelphia. Ruth, Gehrig, and company were running out of time, and fans of the Mackmen knew it. Fourteen seasons had passed since the last pennant for Connie Mack.

An overflow record crowd posted for the Yankee-Athletic battle. Philadelphia police estimated the number of fans outside the park who couldn't get in was the largest in the club's history. All seats inside the stadium were filled an hour before the game, and as many as 10,000 more clogged the aisles, clung to steel girders underneath the grandstand, and even sat on top of the left field roof. Roughly 1,000 more fans stormed the low right field wall fortified with barbed wire, entering the park without paying.

The Yankees crushed Philadelphia 13-1 in the first game, but Earnshaw and Grove combined for a 4-2 victory in the nightcap. Yankee pitchers pitched around batting leader Foxx, who was 0 for 3 in the doubleheader. New York left Philadelphia the next day after a 6-4 victory over the Mackmen in the third game. Still, the Athletics held an almost insurmountable lead of ten and one-half games with a month and a half to play. The *New York Times* noted that much of the Yankee success in the series was due to Foxx being held to one hit in the three games.

Even on a day off from playing a major-league opponent, Foxx enjoyed the role of crowd pleaser. Jim's homer led the A's to a 3-2 exhibition game victory over the Toledo Mud Hens of the American Association at Toledo, Ohio, on August 9. His knack for standing out in exhibition games throughout his career enhanced his reputation as a clutch performer and slugger, made fans from smaller towns want to see him play, and gave fans memorable moments. Like Foxx, Ruth always enjoyed the attention given him by fans in minor-league cities, and on the same day that Foxx's homer defeated Toledo, Babe homered in a losing cause against Albany of the Eastern League in Albany, New York.

In late August, the Athletics sputtered, winning 7 and losing 8 during a 15-game road trip in the Midwest. It was their worst set of games thus far in the 1929 season. Then the A's split a two-game series with the Yankees on August 27-28, holding a 13-game lead in the standings.

Foxx was back at third base late in August because of injuries to veterans Hale and Dykes and again said he preferred the hot corner to first base. Hale was also having trouble catching foul flies from the third base position, and Dykes was battling charley horses. It was the first time Foxx played third base in 1929, playing part of the game on August 23 at third and seven out of the next eight games at that position before returning to first base. Jimmie had committed only four errors at first base all season up until the time of the temporary switch to third base.

Ruth, Gehrig, and company returned to Philadelphia for a three-game series beginning with a morning-afternoon doubleheader on Labor Day, September 2. Quinn bested Pipgras in the morning contest, 10-3. Philadelphia had to come from behind in the afternoon game to win 6-5 after New York rallied with four runs to take the lead in the sixth. On the following afternoon, Earnshaw became the first American League pitcher to notch his twentieth victory in an easy 10-2 win over New York, putting the A's fourteen and one-half games ahead of the Yankees. After the game, Huggins said, "The Athletics have the pennant nailed to the flagpole. It's impossible for us to overtake them now!"

Foxx retained a slim lead in the AL batting race over Lew Fonseca, Simmons, and Heinie Manush through September 12, the day he appeared in *The Sporting News* in an ad with Babe Ruth for "The Louisville Slugger," the bat used by all the leading batters in the AL. Under a batting-stance picture of Foxx, the ad said, "Foxx, Philadelphia—On top of the AL batting list this year stands Foxx, who wielded a wicked Louisville Slugger for the leading batting average of the league." Following the games of September 13, though, Jimmie relinquished the batting lead to teammate Al Simmons, .369 to .366, and never again headed the pack during the last two weeks of the season.

The A's clinched the pennant the next day, when Earnshaw shut out the White Sox at Shibe Park while the Yankees lost the first game of a double-header to the Browns. The clincher occurred with 15 games still left to play for the A's and 17 left for New York. Oddly, Foxx did not play in the A's pennant-winning game.

Foxx managed to reach base at a higher rate than any other AL player during 1929. His season-ending on-base percentage of .463 actually led the league, but such a statistic didn't become official until 1984. Jim finished fifth in batting average at .354, despite hitting only 12 for 65 in September. He finished fourth in homers (33), fifth in total bases (323), third in slugging percentage (.625), fourth in runs scored (123), and second in walks (103). Jim also drove home 117 runs.

The early pennant win by the Mackmen meant they had to wait to see who their World Series opponent would be from the tighter, undecided NL race. Upon learning of the A's accomplishment, the town of Sudlersville prepared for a reception and banquet for their hometown hero to closely follow the conclusion of the World Series. Connie Mack was also to be invited. The *Observer* declared,

As a result of Jimmy Foxx's spectacular exploits in organized baseball, Sudlersville today is one of the best advertised little towns in America. In newspapers, magazines, over the radio, and wherever news is printed, flashed, or cabled, Sudlersville's fame has been carried as the birthplace of the AL's new swat-king.

Before the regular season ended, Babe Ruth picked Foxx as the first baseman on his All-Star Big League Baseball Team, which was published for the eighth year in the *New York World*. This all-star team combined the best from both major leagues, so Foxx won out, in Ruth's eyes, over the likes of Gehrig and Bill Terry.

Foxx's midseason flirtation with a .400 batting mark, season-long quest for a batting title, and presence on a dominant pennant winner gained him quick recognition in his first season as an everyday starter. The constant presence of Foxx and Simmons in the lineup was a key difference between the 1928 and 1929 Athletics.

Foxx still enjoyed playing catcher the most, because of the variety of skills needed and the high degree of involvement in every pitch of a game. Not thinking of the long-term effects playing catcher could have on his career because of injuries, Foxx said near the end of the season in an interview in *Baseball Magazine*:

I'd rather catch behind the plate than do anything else. And I say that in full realization that catching is the hardest and least appreciated position on the diamond. It goes without saying that I'm not in Mickey's [Cochrane's] class. But I do think I would have made at least a fair catcher if I had been allowed to catch. With Mickey in the lineup there is simply no chance.

Jim also said that he preferred playing third base over first base. He enjoyed the challenge of more hard chances at third base.

Near the eve of the World Series, Jim had a new reason to celebrate. Foxx received an urgent call from Kent General Hospital in Dover, Delaware, on October 3, before the A's began practice at Shibe Park and immediately motored to Dover to see his wife and view his healthy, nine-pound newborn son. Helen and Jimmie, Jr., were "reported to be doing well" shortly after the boy was born. Helen's private nurse, Cordelia Radke, recalled that Jimmie, Jr., was the perfect image of his father the first few days after he was born. Helen was forced to be content to listen by radio in the hospital to the exploits of Jimmie and the Athletics in the Series. The proud father promised that he would hit at least one home run in the upcoming series in honor of Jimmie, Jr.

Listening to radio broadcasts of the World Series at home or watching re-creations of the games on magnetic scoreboards around the country had become very popular by the 1929 World Series. Foxx was pictured in an October 7 ad for Majestic radio receivers in the *Baltimore Evening Sun,* along with several other members of the A's. The ad advised, "Fans, don't miss a single game of this famous classic." Foxx added, "I get a real thrill every time I hear my Majestic. I can always depend upon it under any conditions. Take it from me, folks, this Majestic is the greatest radio of all."

Foxx was speaking from experience. Earlier in the season, a truck entered Shibe Park before the game and dealers for Majestic radios presented Helen and Jimmie with a new model radio that usually sold for well over $100.

Tickets for the World Series games at Shibe Park were becoming a tough buy in Philadelphia, and plenty of local fans from in and around Queen Anne's County were extremely eager for the fall classic to start. The *Observer* announced it would rebroadcast each Series game in front of its building in Centreville on the day the game occurred with the aid of its electric player board and a Magnavox electric rebroadcaster with large speakers. The *Observer* had performed this service seven years running, but now a local hero was adding extra excitement to the festivities—"Now batting, Jimmie Foxx!"

The Athletics arrived at Union Station in Chicago on October 7 in heavy overcoats, white dress shirts, ties, and fedoras. Foxx, Simmons, and several other stars were pictured in the *Chicago Tribune* as they stepped down onto the train station platform from their train.

Foxx, along with Charlie Root and both managers in the Series, were contracted by Universal Services to write daily stories, presumably with the help of a ghostwriter, beginning October 7. The articles appeared in the *Inquirer* and probably other newspapers.

In his first article on October 7 on the eve of the Series, Foxx predicted that the Cubs would have great difficulty in handling the slants of lefties Grove and Walberg, unlike earlier in the season, when the right-handed batters of that club handily beat left-handers often in the NL. Jim said that the Series would be over in five games at the most in favor of the A's, based on his club's overall strength in starting pitching, hitting, and having Cochrane, the major league's best catcher. Foxx had received many letters recently from fans asking, "How does it feel to be about ready to play in baseball's most important series? Jim's reply was: "Well, I can say this much, that if a few years ago, when I was playing in the Maryland sandlots, that anyone had said to me that in 1929 I would be playing in the World Series, I would have suggested that they ought to have their heads examined."

The first game of the World Series played to a packed house in Wrigley Field on October 8. Cubs' manager Joe McCarthy picked right-hander Charlie Root, a nineteen-game winner, to face the Athletics. Mack surprised all observers by choosing Howard Ehmke rather than the hard-throwing Grove or Earnshaw. For six innings Root and Ehmke kept the Mackmen and Cubs tied in a scoreless duel.

In the top of the seventh, Simmons led off with a liner to Hack Wilson, who made a diving catch. Foxx stepped up to the plate.

Foxx swung three bats to limber up, tapped the inside of both feet with his bat, and stepped into the batter's box. Jim wiggled his bat a little, then held the bat still, and did not have an open or closed stance. Jim held his bat behind his shoulder, holding even the tip of the bat slightly lower than the top of his shoulder, rather than sticking it up in the air above his head like many other major leaguers. He stood almost straight up, rather than bending his knees or body. His head was tilted ever so slightly toward home plate, and he had an excellent view of the pitcher as he stared out toward the pitcher's mound. Foxx typically had a bit of a hitch before he swung, but he could get away with it because his wrists and arms were so strong.

Jimmie took the first two pitches for called strikes. Then Root whipped a fast one that Foxx fouled back to the screen. Root offered another fastball that Foxx propelled over the head of Wilson beyond the center field wall for a home run, the first run of the game. By smacking the homer, Jim also kept his promise to hit one in honor of his newborn son, Jimmie, Jr. Fans watching the game being recreated on player boards in Philadelphia on the *Bulletin* magnetic scoreboard, in Baltimore in *Sun* Square, and in

Centreville at the *Observer* building cheered loudly in celebration of the "Sudlersville Flash."

Foxx said:

> I waited for Root to throw me a fastball in the seventh inning. He did, and I put every ounce of strength I had into my swing. I met the ball squarely, and as soon as it left the bat I knew that it would find a place among those center field bleachers. I got a lot of kick out of my baseball since I started playing for the Athletics, but the biggest thrill came as I jogged around the bases in the seventh inning with the first run of the Series. What a thrill that home run gave me!

The Athletics put the game on ice with two runs in the top of the ninth for a three-run lead and an eventual 3-1 win. Ehmke set a new Series record for strikeouts by a pitcher in a single game with thirteen, confusing the normally hard-hitting Cubs with his slow curve.

In his article in the *Inquirer* about the first Series game, Foxx said that the Cubs were dumbfounded by Mack's selection of Ehmke to start and even more dumbfounded by his dazzling curves and underhand motion. Foxx gave his own home run only two sentences in his article—the rest was Ehmke.

The second game of the Series was again at Wrigley Field, featuring Chicago's top winning pitcher, Pat Malone, pitted against Philadelphia's George Earnshaw. Cold winds whipped through the packed stadium. Grove and Earnshaw, among others, were seated on either side of Mack in the dugout, wrapped in heavy blankets.

As Cochrane stepped on the playing field at Wrigley before the second game, he played the role of fortune teller. The A's catcher peered around the ballpark and said, "A nice big park, but Jimmy Foxx can hit the ball off the lot in any direction. He will, too."

After two scoreless innings, the A's drew first blood. Malone retired Bishop and Haas, but Cochrane singled to right and Simmons walked. Foxx stepped into the batter's box. First baseman and captain Charlie Grimm walked over to the pitcher's mound to encourage Malone to bear down. Foxx took the first pitch, low and inside. He took another offering from Malone that was right down the middle of the plate for a called strike. Pat's next pitch was a fastball and Foxx ripped it over the left field wall for a 3-0 lead enroute to a 9-3 win over the Cubs. Earnshaw and Grove combined for thirteen strikeouts to equal the single-game mark set the day before.

Some reporters referred to Jim's homer in game two as a "wild-pitch homer," because most onlookers considered the pitch to be a bad one for most batters—a high fastball inside the plate. Many accounts noted that

Foxx referred to it as a waist high pitch. Foxx had a propensity for hitting high pitches better than most batters, and his practice swing often was aimed at a high imaginary pitch, with the end of his swing actually above his shoulders.

Back in Kent General Hospital in Dover, Helen Foxx "let out a cry of delight" when her husband smashed his homer in game two of the Series. After the game, Helen wired her congratulations to Jimmie. Helen told newsmen, "I am mighty proud of Jimmy!"

An article in the *Inquirer* had fun with the happy result of Foxx's homer in the second game of the Series, saying, "It is said down Sudlersville way that Jimmy's newborn son, upon hearing over the radio that his fence-busting dad hit another homer, gave a shout of glee and yelled 'Atta boy, dad.'"

The mother of Cubs' manager Joe McCarthy said of Foxx after game two, "My, that young man must be a great player."

Foxx said:

> I got my second big thrill out of the World Series today when I drove the ball among those fans perched in the seats outside that wall in the third inning. Maybe that pitch looked high and outside to the experts up in the press stand, but it was only waist high, and when I saw it coming, I took a real cut at it. I can't explain my feeling of joy as I jogged around the bases. All of the boys have played great baseball, and are sure now that we'll win.

Foxx had three hits in the game. In his first two Series games, he had taken the lead batting role in propelling his team to victory. His penchant for hitting home runs in the Series was reminiscent of his similar performance five years earlier in the Five States Series.

In his article that covered the second game of the Series, Foxx noted: "Having hit the best pitchers that the Cubs have to offer, it looks to me as though the result of the Series is a foregone conclusion. Our aim now is to take four straight."

In the following day's article in the *Inquirer*, just before game three, Foxx felt it was all over but the shouting. Jim said:

> The only thing we lacked if anything when the Series started was thorough confidence. Not that we didn't have confidence, but it must be remembered that none of our regular players had ever seen service in the World Series and it was felt in some quarters that we might "blow up."

John Kieran of the *New York Times* noted that nothing had happened in the first two games of the Series to change the opinion made by Eddie Collins for any reporters in earshot about twenty minutes before the first game of the Series at Wrigley Field, when he said, "Jimmy Foxx is the greatest young player he ever saw."

After a travel day on October 10, the Series switched to Philadelphia's Shibe Park on October 11 for games three, four, and five, if necessary.

Foxx's participation in the Series electrified his hometown and county. More than twenty people from Sudlersville, including Dell and Mattie Foxx and son Sammy Dell, motored back and forth to witness the Series games at Shibe Park. Many more witnessed re-creation of the games on the player board at the *Observer* Building in Centreville. Frank Baker and his wife and Frank's brother Norman came to Shibe Park from Trappe, Maryland, for the October 11 game.

Down 2-0 in the Series, it was crucial that the Cubs win game three. McCarthy held a team meeting before leaving the hotel, and a police escort ushered them to 21st and Lehigh Streets for the Shibe Park opener.

The stands were filled to capacity well before game time, ensuring that the windows and rooftops on the houses on 20th Street would also be filled to overflowing. Some estimates of the fans watching the Series games from 20th Street were as high as 3,000, paying from $7 to $25 per head. Owners of the houses on 20th Street allowed cameramen from Pathe News Newsreel Service, Fox Movietone News, and Universal News to film the A's home games of the Series from their windows or rooftops for as little as $20.

The A's Bing Miller knocked in the first run of the contest off Guy Bush in the last half of the fifth inning, but Rogers Hornsby and Kiki Cuyler rejuvenated the Cubs by breaking out of their two-game hitting funk, driving in three tallies in the top half of the sixth inning off Earnshaw. George was pitching on only two days' rest but recovered to hold Chicago scoreless for the remainder of the game, only to be outdone by Bush. Guy scattered nine hits by the Athletics for a 3-1 Cub victory as most of the Shibe Park faithful went home disappointed.

After the Cubs' victory in game three, a story passed around the Cubs' dressing room suggesting why Foxx was hitless after homering in each of the first two games. Former Cub hero Joe Tinker had scouted the Athletics hitters in their final series with the Yankees, only to be fooled on the strengths and weaknesses of Mack's batters. Connie found out about Tinker's fact-finding mission and instructed Foxx to hit low balls but intentionally miss high hard ones. McCarthy met an AL hurler on the train back from Chicago to Philadelphia after game two of the Series and received the real scoop on the strengths and weaknesses of Mack's batsmen.

A Cub victory in game four on Saturday at Shibe Park would knot the Series at two games apiece; an Athletic victory would give the Mackmen a strong 3-1 lead in the best-of-seven-games struggle. Frank Baker visited Foxx and the other A's in the dugout before the game. The "Old and New" home-run sluggers from Maryland posed for photographers, and pictures of the two men leaning on bats on the dugout steps appeared on many sports pages across the country. It's a certainty that the proud Baker offered encouragement to his former protege.

Root started for the Cubs against the ancient veteran, Jack Quinn, for the A's. Grimm opened the scoring with a two-out homer over the right field fence in the fourth. Then in the sixth, Chicago really opened fire. Consecutive singles by Hornsby, Wilson, Cuyler, and Riggs Stephenson forced Mack to bring Walberg to the pitcher's box. Grimm followed with a bunt single to Walberg that triggered a two-run throwing error by Rube to first, then Grimm scored on a sacrifice fly by catcher Zack Taylor. The Cubs scored five runs in the inning and added another in the first half of the seventh. As the Athletics came to bat in their half of the seventh inning, Chicago had an 8-0 lead and appeared a shoo-in to tie the Series at two games apiece.

Simmons led off the inning and ignited a spark of hope for the A's as the crowd stood to watch his smash of a one-and-one pitch from Root land on the left field roof. Foxx followed with a single to right, then successive singles by Miller (lost in the sun by Wilson), Dykes, and Boley continued the rally. After George Burns popped out batting for Rommel, Bishop singled and Art Nehf replaced Root in the pitcher's box.

Then the Athletics stumbled across the luck they needed to truly put the Cubs through their worst nightmare. Haas launched a fly to Wilson in center, who again lost the ball in the sun and allowed it to roll to the wall for a home run, scoring Boley and Bishop ahead of him. Cochrane walked, and Sheriff Blake replaced Nehf. The Macks continued the party, much to the delight of the crowd. Lights on the bases on player boards in Philadelphia, Baltimore, Centreville, and elsewhere resembled pinball machines.

McCarthy couldn't believe the show. Simmons singled and Foxx approached the plate. Foxx recalled ten years later, "There was, indeed, moisture on my hands and the back of my neck. 'Well, Foxx,' I said to myself, 'get in there [in the batter's box]. You either do or you don't [keep the rally going].' " Ball one. Strike one, called. Ball two, outside. Ball three, low. Strike two, called. Then Foxx took a deep breath, swung, and drove a single to center, scoring Cochrane with the tying run. After new Cub pitcher Malone hit Miller with a pitch, Dykes drove both Foxx and Miller home with a two-run double. When Foxx reached the bench, Mack said, "Nice work, boy. You got the big hit." The A's ten-run rally was a record for a World Series game, and the Mackmen maintained the 10-8 lead for their third win of the Series.

On Sunday, October 13, while the Athletics and Cubs observed blue laws in Philadelphia, Jimmie traveled to Kent General Hospital in Dover to visit Helen and Jimmie, Jr. Photographs of a grinning Jimmie with his wife and newborn son appeared in the sports pages of Philadelphia papers. By evening, Jimmie's mind was turning to game five and the Cubs.

Game five on October 14 generated feverish interest in Philadelphia. Shibe Park was filling to capacity early, as usual, and the rooftops and windows of the houses on 20th Street were bulging with onlookers. President Hoover and his wife traveled in a private railway car from Washington, D.C., and joined Mayor Mackey in box seats.

Despite the wrenching setback that the Cubs suffered the day before, McCarthy's team came ready to play. Pat Malone started against Ehmke.

The Cubs collected two runs in the fourth, and Mack inserted Walberg on the mound. Malone and Walberg matched goose eggs on the scoreboard from the fifth through the eighth innings. After a scoreless ninth for the Cubs, the A's had one last chance to clinch the Series before having to return to Wrigley Field.

Walter French fanned while batting for Walberg. Bishop poked an opposite field single by third to excite the crowd with the power-hitting part of the order due up. Haas smashed Malone's first pitch over the right field wall for a game-tying homer, and the A's players mobbed Mule and pounded his back. The din of the fans carried well out of the park as several Cubs joined Malone on the mound to try to calm him down. After Cochrane grounded out, Simmons doubled, and the crowd was on its feet as Foxx stepped to the plate. Malone wanted no part of Jimmie, walking him on four straight outside pitches. Now the A's fans were beside themselves. Miller stepped up and promptly doubled to center, scoring Simmons with the winning run for the game and the Series. As the ball headed safely into center field, even plate umpire Bill Klem "showed enthusiasm, kicking his right leg into the air."

The A's rushed onto the field. The *Evening Bulletin* reported, "They danced and whirled and finally surrounded Haas and Walberg, pushing them back and forth. . . . It was a war dance of pure joy." Even the normally unemotional Mack joined the team on the field.

Graham McNamee, announcer for the National Broadcasting Company, which was reaching a radio audience from coast to coast, bolted for the A's dugout as the game concluded and said to his listeners:

> This is Graham McNamee down under the stands again, a little
> bit out of breath, as we came down pretty fast. I am going to ask
> some of the boys if they won't say just a word to tell you how they

feel in regard to winning this series. The first boy is the greatest ball player in the country—everybody knows that—Jimmy Foxx, the great first baseman of the Athletics.

Foxx replied, "Hello, friends. I hope you got as big a thrill as we did. Quite a finish, I think." Simmons, Cochrane, Walberg, Miller, and Ehmke followed.

Mack had a regular season bargain with Foxx's salary, but Jimmie made up for some lost ground by being on the winner of the World Series. The payment for a full winner's share was $5,621, doubling Jimmie's regular season salary of $5,000. Jim and Helen were now ready to spend their first winter in the Philadelphia area.

A newspaper reporter asked several of the players what they would do with their Series cash winnings. Players responded, "establish a sanatorium for blind umps; ask my wife first; pay the mortgage on the old homestead." Foxx replied, "a brand new baby carriage!"

Immediately following the World Series, Foxx was reported to have visited Helen's parents' home near Dover and his parents and eleven-year-old brother, Sammy Dell, for several days.

Then Jim attended a banquet for the World Champions in Philadelphia on October 17. That evening, the City of Philadelphia toasted Mack and all his team members at the Penn Athletic Club. Over 1,600 baseball fans squeezed into the grand ballroom and listened as various city officials praised Mack and he in turn beamed as he recounted the A's season. Each team member received a gold wristwatch, and the entire crowd cheered a motion picture replay of the Series.

Right after the banquet, Foxx and Simmons traveled to Al's hometown of Milwaukee for the first game of their own barnstorming trip, with the bulk of the games on the west coast.

At times, the tour was intense in terms of distance traveled on successive days. Over a five-day period in California, Foxx and Simmons, accompanied by coach Ira Thomas, played against each other at Wrigley Field in Los Angeles on October 27, followed by another game at Sacramento on October 28, played as teammates against the Long Beach Shell Oilers at Long Beach Shell Park on October 29, and against a team of Negro Leaguers on October 31 in San Francisco. Foxx and Simmons both hit solo homers while opposing each other in the game at Wrigley Field, a 2-1 victory for Simmons. Between them, Foxx and Simmons belted the ball out of Wrigley Field about twenty-five times before the game in a homer-hitting exhibition. Foxx tripled and Simmons homered in a 6-5 victory over the Shell Oilers, both hits coming off Cubs hurler Pat Malone. Then, on October 31, Bullet Joe Rogan pitched a 10-3 victory for the Negro Leaguers over an All-Star team that featured Foxx and Simmons. Simmons was hitless, while Jimmie had two doubles and a single in three at bats. Foxx even pitched part of the game for his team.

Upon his return to Philadelphia, Simmons told reporters that he and Foxx "played to ten grand on their quick tour of the Pacific coast." It was split three ways between Simmons, Foxx, and Ira Thomas, who managed the expedition.

Foxx returned to Sudlersville on November 13 for a banquet and reception in his honor at Cox Memorial Hall. James Godwin from Easton paid Foxx a visit at his farm near Sudlersville early in the afternoon that day, and they had a lengthy talk. Foxx showed Godwin over 250 pieces of mail he hadn't opened yet that he presumed for the most part were from firms seeking his services that coming winter.

One newspaper article referred to Jim's hometown and surrounding area as the turkey, country ham, wild duck, and oyster belt of Maryland, reporting that two or three truckloads of turkeys were gathered for the feast. More than 250 people attended the dinner served by the ladies of the Calvary Methodist Episcopal Church at $2.50 a plate. Jimmie's parents, relatives, and friends—many of them former residents of Sudlersville—crowded the hall, and the Sudlersville Orchestra provided music.

Foxx had graduated in a short time from the uncertainty of whether he could make it in the major leagues to becoming one of the game's top batsmen, capable of competing for the league batting title and a member of baseball's world champions. All the A's players and coaches were invited: Umpire Bill McGowan, Frank Baker, Ira Thomas, Rube Walberg, Bing Miller, Al Simmons, Jimmy Dykes, Doc Ebeling, and Steve Pflueger (A's clubhouse manager) joined the festivities. Earle Mack came in place of his father, who had been ill since the Series.

After the crowd ate roast turkey and country ham with all the fixings, cake, and Gills ice cream, numerous testimonials praised Jimmie Foxx. Typical of Jimmie, he minimized credit for his own achievements. Each town was called to say a few words about Foxx, and the citizens of Sudlersville gave Jimmie a cedar chest. Baker spoke in praise of Jimmie, and Earle Mack told the story of "Jimmie Foxx's character." Foxx told how Connie Mack had trained, encouraged, and helped him to realize his potential. The crowd bellowed out a song, "Jimmie Boy! Our Jimmie Boy!" to the tune of "Maryland, My Maryland," singing:

> To-night we meet to welcome you.
> Jimmie Boy, Our Jimmie Boy
> You've stood the test and proven true
> Jimmie Boy, Our Jimmie Boy

You've brought renown to Sudlersville,
With love for you our bosoms fill
Where e'er you roam, we'll claim you still
  Jimmie Boy, Our Jimmie Boy

We're so glad to have you back,
  Jimmie Boy, Our Jimmie Boy
To greet the ward of Connie Mack,
  Jimmie Boy, Our Jimmie Boy

The papers boost you morn and night
You catch the ball—and "swat" it right
The base ball game is your delight
  Jimmie Boy, Our Jimmie Boy

The world is talking of your fame,
  Jimmie Boy, Our Jimmie Boy
The way you play the base ball game
  Jimmie Boy, Our Jimmie Boy

The radio adds to our fun,
Oh, yes, we listen, every one
And hear—"For Foxx, one more home run"
  Jimmie Boy, Our Jimmie Boy.

During Jim's visit home, he told friends that he had a contract to work for a sporting goods house for the winter in Philadelphia at a "splendid salary." He and Helen moved to Philadelphia the day after the testimonial banquet.

Jim and Helen often visited their folks in Delaware and the Eastern Shore of Maryland that winter. During Thanksgiving, they stayed with Dell, Mattie, and Sammy Dell on the farm that Jim and Helen owned on the outskirts of town. Then on December 6 he played basketball as part of an "all-star team" against the varsity of Washington College in Chestertown, Maryland.

6

ONE OF THE BEST BASEBALL TEAMS EVER

Shortly after Jimmie and Helen moved into their home on Hillcrest Avenue in Elkins Park, a suburb of Philadelphia, Bill Dooly of the *Philadelphia Record* interviewed them before they left for the 1930 spring training season at Fort Myers. This was the first time that Jimmie was bound for Fort Myers certain that he was an everyday player in the lineup for Connie Mack. Dooly exclaimed, "Today the experts pick Jimmy Foxx as the coming batting champion of the game."

Asked by Dooly when he first aspired to become a major-league ballplayer for his livelihood, Foxx replied, "I never thought of myself as playing in the big leagues when I was around home. You see, I had only seen one big league game in my life until I joined the A's in 1924."

Even after joining the A's in 1924, for most of September, Foxx did not "get the big league bug." Foxx said:

I finished the rest of the season with the A's but played only in a couple of exhibition games. So you see that even while I was in the big leagues then, I didn't really get in any big league action. I felt kind of dubious about baseball, sort of doubtful, the same way as when Frank Baker sent me word to try out for his club.

The excitement of traveling south, however, baking in the warm Florida sun during spring training, and getting paid to play baseball finally gave Foxx the "bug," the motivation and the hope to be a major-league player. Foxx recalled, "I'll tell you when I first got the big league bug. It was when I reported to Fort Myers in 1925. It felt so great to be playing ball at that time of year that I made up my mind this was where I wanted to stick."

As Jimmie, Helen, and Jimmie, Jr., were finishing their first winter in Philadelphia, Foxx admitted he had missed the outdoor life that he had always enjoyed around Sudlersville. He missed the farm work and the frequent hunting trips. "Here, all I've done is play a few rounds of golf and get in a little bowling," Foxx said.

Jimmie and Helen were geared to leave for Florida by auto in early February and spend several weeks in Fort Myers before the beginning of spring training on February 24. Along with the article written by Dooly, they were pictured outside their home taking Jimmie, Jr., for a stroll in a baby carriage, Helen in her winter coat, Jimmie in his warmup jacket with an Athletic's white elephant prominent across his chest.

Before Foxx made his trip to Florida, he looked up William Phillips of the A. J. Reach Company in Philadelphia for equipment. He picked a first baseman's glove to his liking and turned to Phillips, saying, "I better get a catcher's mitt, too." Then Foxx said, "Come to think of it, if anything happens to Jimmy Dykes, I might have to fill in at third, so give me a third sacker's glove, too."

On February 3, Jimmie and Helen arrived at Fort Myers and Jimmie immediately began golfing. Jim was the first of Mack's players to arrive at Fort Myers and was briefly interviewed by anxious sportswriters. "Sure we expect to repeat this year," said an exuberant Foxx. "At least, all the boys will do their best for Mr. Mack," he added.

During his travels on the golf links in February, Foxx met Ruth at the popular Jungle Country Club in St. Petersburg. A photograph of the two sluggers posing together in golf attire holding their clubs appeared in the *Inquirer*. The caption for the photo said in part: "Can they Hit? Well. Here are two chaps who give AL pitchers plenty to think about during a season's strife. . . . They like their home runs and they like their golf."

While Foxx prepared in Fort Myers for spring training, many of the other A's made Hot Springs, Arkansas, their first stop. Coach Gleason joined Jack Quinn, Bill Shores, Simmons, Dykes, Boley, Wally Schang, Miller, Walberg, and Cochrane. The hot thermal waters were a very important feature in the players' program for preparedness. The players also took long mountain hikes and golfed.

On February 26, Foxx worked out with his 42-ounce bat and "sledged the ball to all parts of the premises" at Fort Myers. Because there was no left field fence at the spring training site, Foxx's shots to that part of the field landed in the far-off pine trees for home runs. After a long batting session, Jim worked at shortstop and "made some showy stops, while he fairly burned the ball to Jim Keesey at first base."

The A's had the same daily routine in spring training from 1930-35, for the first seven days before exhibition games, according to infielder Edwin "Dib" Williams. Foxx and his teammates went to the ballpark about 10:00 A.M. by bus, ran around the perimeter of the field, took batting practice, infield practice, then went home to the hotel for an optional lunch. Then Mack's players and coaches returned to Terry Field by bus for afternoon practice, more batting practice, more infield practice, and sometimes an intrasquad game.

Sportswriter John Kieran from the *New York Times* visited the A's training camp in Fort Myers on March 3, and his report the following day typified Manager Mack's behavior: "Wearing a starched collar as a gesture of defiance of the scorching sun, Connie Mack was out at the fairgrounds here looking over his veterans and rookies. He carried a pad and pencil and wrote little notes down from time-to-time." Mack, ever the cautious leader, said he didn't expect a runaway in the AL pennant chase, and unlike many of his players other than Cochrane, he picked the Yankees as the A's chief competitor to win the AL flag. Mack said, "The Yankees, the Yankees, Ruth and Gehrig and Lazzeri and Combs; you've got to figure them for their main strength." Many of the A's players picked the Indians as their early choice of a team to give them their toughest battle. Kieran said the A's lineup appeared virtually set, with every starter returning to the World Championship club. Grove's middle finger, which was injured before the 1929 Series, was healed, and Cochrane said of Lefty's early offerings in spring practice, "You'd think he shot them out of a cannon."

In contrast to many veterans on major league clubs, Foxx made rookies feel welcome in spring training. For instance, Jimmie woke up Eric McNair and Dib Williams one spring evening in 1930 and cooked chicken and rice for them on a charcoal grill outside the hotel in Fort Myers at 11:00 P.M., listening to the rookies' stories about their lives in baseball while weaving some stories of his own.

A couple of days before the regular season started, sixty of sixty-five writers and sports editors polled by the Associated Press picked the A's to repeat their AL pennant-winning performance. The other five writers picked the Yankees for first place and the A's for second.

The Athletics made final preparations to defend their world championship with four games against the Phillies in the City Series in early April. Foxx smashed homers twice in two of the four games against the Phillies, showing he was ready to assault AL pitching during the 1930 season.

Dell, Mattie, and twelve-year-old Sammy Dell traveled to Philadelphia on April 5 to visit Jimmie and Helen and attend the opening game of the City Series at Shibe Park. Jimmie celebrated the presence of his family in the stands with a three-run homer and a two-run homer in the A's 13-1 victory over the Phils.

Dell usually didn't stay away from Shibe Park too long. When Mattie couldn't leave home for 3:00 P.M. afternoon games, Dell organized a trip with other men from town. Usually up to four men, each dressed in a suit, white shirt, tie, and dress hat, loaded up in a car next to the Sudlersville Bank in the center of town, leaving Sudlersville as early as 9:00 or 10:00 A.M. They usually sat on the third base side near the Athletics' dugout.

Dell let others do the actual driving. He was strictly a country driver, as he had been years earlier, when Elwood Coleman brought him and his son to Shibe Park the first time to meet Connie Mack. Long-time Sudlersville resident Bo Benton recalled:

> This was a shining time for this area because Mr. Foxx's son was playing for the Athletics and Dell had the privilege of getting tickets and anyone who had a car could drive to Philadelphia 80 miles up the road and was welcome to go along. Dell would share his hospitality by seeing that you got into the game without any problems, and meeting Jim after the game and probably going out to dinner, or whatever. This was a baseball-oriented community. It had been for years and years and years. And that desire to see someone from a local area be part of the American game was outstanding.

As Foxx's star began to rise on the major-league playing field, his generosity became obvious. Foxx was generous towards his parents, his brother, Helen's folks, and countless others. Tom Gillespie, who played high school soccer with Jimmie and later worked at the bank in Sudlersville, recalled that Jimmie would send a check to Dell and Mattie every week.

The Athletics' clubhouse errand boy, Al Ruggieri, recalled, "the generosity of the man. After all, it was the Depression, and you didn't forget things like that. He was the biggest tipper on the team. He'd pay 50 cents for a shoe shine and three dollars for a pot of spaghetti that probably cost 30 cents to make."

Every couple of weeks or so, when Foxx and Rommel were in the clubhouse, they'd say to Al, "Hey little man, how about asking your mother to make a pot of spaghetti for us for tomorrow?" The following day Al would carry an aluminum pot from his house catercorner to the left field corner of Shibe Park, over to the clubhouse. The sauce contained braciole made from thin slices of rump steak rubbed with sage, garlic, and Italian seasonings, rolled up with minced proscuitto ham inside, and held together by toothpicks.

The Athletics would gather around the pot in the clubhouse when Al brought it in, but Foxx and Rommel always got their fair share since they paid for the meal.

Foxx liked Apple chewing tobacco, a nickel a square block, Optimo cigars, Eagle silk shirts, and French Shriner shoes. Jimmie was enjoying the high-life—fancy clothing, an automobile, extra money to spend, and parties at Mr. Shibe's home after the Athletics' games. It's generally believed he was not saving much money at this time, unlike a few years earlier, when he bought the house and farmland near Sudlersville.

One of Foxx's favorite foods was Texas-hot weiners from Nick's, a Greek restaurant one block away from the ballpark at 22nd and Lehigh

Streets. The weiners were two for fifteen cents and were enormous, slapped onto an oval-shaped roll and topped with onions and mustard. Foxx and some of the other A's players, especially Simmons and Miller, enjoyed the weiners for lunch before a game or in between games of a doubleheader. Miller and Simmons would tip Ruggieri ten or fifteen cents a trip, and Foxx, as usual, weighed in as the heaviest tipper, usually giving Al a quarter.

Connie Mack had made bold predictions on several occasions about Jimmie's future in the major leagues, beginning with Foxx's first spring training camp in 1925, when he was only seventeen. And Foxx's season-long consistency in 1929 and play in the 1929 World Series raised more than a few eyebrows.

Foxx failed to hit a homer when the regular season started in April, but a series of games in early May 1930 spurred some new remarks from Mack:

> When Babe Ruth drifts out of the home run scene, there is a young Athletic player waiting to take his place. He is Jimmie Foxx, our first baseman, who has petrified Philadelphia baseball followers in recent days with a series of home runs that carried so far as to make open-mouthed spectators believe that it was an overt violation of Ruth's well-known copyright for distance. I can never recall in my career where five straight home runs [of such distance] were made by one player. Foxx has the greatest pair of arms in America.

Three of Jimmie's homers cleared the left field stands at Shibe Park, roof and all. A fourth homer hit the roof of the left field stands and bounced onto the adjoining street, and the fifth homer sailed over the scoreboard, which was several feet higher than the adjacent wall in right-center field.

Not only did Foxx hit the ball for greater distances than most batters, but some fans insisted that when he hit the ball solidly, it made a distinctive sound, a louder "crack." Clubhouse errand boy Al Ruggieri recalled that if his duties in the grandstand or out at the scoreboard in right field took his attention from the game, he still knew that certain distinctive loud cracking sound could only have been made by Jimmie Foxx. Upon hearing that sound and looking up, he always saw Foxx starting out of the batter's box to round the bases.

After hitting six homers in the first nine days of May, Foxx tripled in the winning run on May 10 against Cleveland, to keep the A's a half game ahead of the Senators. But couldn't lead his club to victory against Washington when the Senators beat the A's twice on May 16 and once on May 17 to take the league lead.

In back-to-back doubleheaders at Shibe Park on May 21 and 22, the A's swept the first two games while the Yankees took the second pair. In the first game of the May 21 doubleheader, Philadelphia overcame three homers by Ruth, by a score of 15-7. Babe had slugged three homers in a game twice previously, both times in World Series, once in 1926 and once in 1928. In the fifth inning, Foxx bounced the ball onto the left field roof, scoring Simmons and sending pitcher Charles "Red" Ruffing to the showers. It was a tough outing for Ruffing in one of his first starts for the Yankees since being acquired from the Red Sox on May 6, but the big right-hander would go on to win enough games for New York to win a spot in the Hall of Fame. Foxx and Ruffing had been opponents as far back as 1924, when Jimmie played for Easton and Red played for Dover as a pitcher and outfielder.

In the doubleheader of May 22, Ruth hit two homers in the first game and another in the second. Gehrig smashed three homers in the second game and drove home eight runs, to tie the AL record. Meanwhile, Foxx homered twice in the second game. Then, after an open date, the Yankees swept another doubleheader from the Mackmen on May 24. After the A's beat New York in a single game on May 25, Mack's club was in second place, four games behind league-leading Washington.

Foxx was replaced by Jim Keesey at first base late in the game on May 26 against Boston and missed the next game on May 27 against the Red Sox, due to a minor injury or the need for some rest while the Mackmen trailed the Senators by four games. A rained-out game on the following day gave Foxx the extra time he needed for recovery. Jim returned to the lineup on May 29 in time to tune up for a crucial early season series with the league leaders that began on Memorial Day.

The A's swept the Senators twice at Shibe Park on May 30 to cut Washington's lead to one game. Simmons and Foxx starred at bat. Foxx smacked three singles, two doubles, and a triple in seven at bats in the first game and two doubles in the second contest. In the first game, Simmons tied the score in the bottom of the ninth with a three-run homer and scored the winning run in the thirteenth, but wrenched his knee. Al's pinch hit grand slam put the A's ahead for good in the fifth inning of the second game. Foxx's homer started a four-run rally the next day, to enable the A's to overcome the Senators again and tie for the league lead. The A's won their fourth straight over Washington on June 1 to take the AL lead.

The AL pennant race developed into a four-team battle in early June among the Athletics, Senators, Yankees, and Indians. After the games of June 15, each team had 21 losses, with the A's barely holding first place with 34 wins, two more than the Indians, three more than the Senators, and four more than the Yankees.

Philadelphia won 12 out of 15 games from June 18 through the end of the month, to remain two games ahead of the Senators, who maintained their own hot streak. Foxx was a chief contributor to the Mackmen's hot streak, hitting 23 for 51 (.451 batting average) with eight homers and 22 rbi's.

A Sunday game in Detroit on June 29 between the A's and the Tigers ended in a near riot when the Tigers' rookie Jimmie Shevlin tried to score the tying run from third in the bottom of the ninth. Shevlin was called out on a close play, and police reserves had to escort umpire William Guthrie from the field for his own protection.

Foxx never was known to argue calls with umpires. During his high school career and his early days in the majors, Jimmie sat down on the playing field or first base during prolonged arguments of players or managers with an umpire. He couldn't wait for the argument to end so the game could resume. No account has been found of Foxx ever being ejected from a game.

Foxx ended June with a cumulative 22 homers and a .359 batting average. He and Al Simmons were rivaling Ruth and Gehrig as the best one-two punch in the league. Jimmie had one more hot streak from July 10-29 when he hit .446 (33 hits in 74 at bats) with 26 rbi's over a 19-game period.

The Athletics and White Sox struggled at Comiskey Park on September 18 before Philadelphia was able to wrestle a 14-10 victory from Chicago to clinch a second successive AL pennant. Chicago led 10-9 after six innings, only to watch the A's push five runs across the plate in the seventh. Mack had to call on Grove to hold the White Sox scoreless for the rest of the game, despite already having used Earnshaw, Mahaffey, and Walberg. Foxx had a triple and a homer with three runs batted in.

The A's best lineup in 1930 was similar to 1929, except that Sammy Hale was no longer with the team, Dykes played the bulk of the team's games at third base (123), and Boley played more games at shortstop (120) than the year before. Mack's favorite lineup featured: Bishop (2B), Haas (CF), Cochrane (C), Simmons (LF), Foxx (1B), Miller (RF), Dykes (3B), and Boley (SS).

Foxx played the entire 1930 regular season at first base. His batting average (.335) was slightly lower than in 1929, but he drove home 156 runs, third in the AL, and finished third in homers (37) behind Ruth (49) and Gehrig (41).

Foxx was an accomplished bunter, but he hardly ever bunted because of his outstanding hitting ability. He made 18 sacrifice hits in 1930, an increase over his 16 in 1929 and 12 in 1928. These numbers were actually a combination of sacrifice flies and sacrifice hits, and in Foxx's case the number largely resulted from sacrifice flies.

In 1931 he made only four sacrifice hits, all of the bunt variety, and in 1932 and 1933 he had no sacrifice hits. In 1931 a new rule counted sacrifice flies as a time at bat and no longer lumped them together with sacrifice hits. An article published in *The Sporting News* after the end of the 1931 season estimated that sluggers like Foxx lost ten to fifteen points off their final batting average because sacrifice flies were counted as a time at bat.

Simmons led the AL in batting at .381 and in runs scored, due largely to Foxx's clutch hitting. Al also finished fourth in homers (36) and second in runs batted in (165) behind Gehrig's league-leading total of 174.

Late in September, some baseball fans from Foxx's hometown and surrounding area began purchasing tickets for the Series games to be played at Shibe Park, while the *Observer* reminded its readers that all Series games except those on Sunday would be rebroadcast on the player board at the *Observer* building on Lawyer's Row in Centreville.

Helen Foxx was interviewed by the *Inquirer* just before the Series and remarked that she didn't miss home games very often. She was looking forward to seeing Jim in the Series, having missed the 1929 Series due to the birth of Jimmie, Jr. Helen enjoyed watching her husband play and often was in the company of Simmons' fiancee, Ms. Dottie Kuhn, at Shibe Park. Dottie and Helen often went horseback riding. Helen was asked whether she considered Jim to be handsome and she said that she didn't think of him that way, but she remarked how clean and wholesome he always was.

Two days before the beginning of the Series, the Cardinals arrived in Philadelphia. The Mackmen held an extended batting practice with their spitballer, Jack Quinn, doing most of the pitching, since the A's anticipated facing spitballer Burleigh Grimes in the opener. After the batting drill, the A's held a closed practice, and Commissioner Landis certified "physical arrangements for the Series satisfactory." No preopening game injuries were announced by Philadelphia, whereas the Cardinals' starting catcher, Jimmy Wilson, was still suffering from a sprained ankle and pitcher Syl Johnson continued to be bothered by a fractured rib.

Sportswriter Grantland Rice reported that proponents of a Series win by the Athletics pointed to the "pitching of Grove and Earnshaw, the managerial craft of Mack, the catching and spirit of Cochrane, and the assaulting powers of Simmons, Cochrane and Foxx." On the other hand, Rice said that those who favored the Cardinals pointed to "the recent momentum of the team, more [first-rate starting] pitchers in Bill Hallahan, Burleigh Grimes, Jesse Haines, and Flint Rhem, a harder-hitting lineup all the way through, greater all-around speed, and a better infield."

Frisch did not appear in the final Cardinal practice at Shibe Park the day before the Series opener because of a case of "lumbago." Reports quickly spread that the second-base star of several past Series would not be available for the opening game. Betting odds favored the Athletics 5-4 to win the Series.

In a chilling wind, President Hoover and about 33,000 fans filled Shibe Park to capacity, and the rooftops overflowed on 20th Street for game one on October 1. An estimated 10,000 predominantly Athletics' fans watched the game on the *Sun* player board near the Savings Bank of Baltimore. Fans who preferred radio accounts followed the broadcasts from NBC by Graham McNamee or listened to CBS.

The A's made only five hits off Grimes in the opener, but each went for extra bases and accounted for a run as Philadelphia easily handled St. Louis, 5-2. Although Foxx tripled and scored the A's first run in the second inning, Grimes struck him out swinging in the fourth and sixth innings. Foxx's strikeout in the sixth inning followed a run-scoring double by Dykes and an intentional pass to Simmons, who hollered at Grimes on his way to first base. Cochrane's solo homer in the eighth sent the partisan crowd into a frenzy as he circled the bases. Grove scattered nine hits and one walk in pitching a complete-game victory.

The Cardinals were angry at the "luck" of Grove and the A's after the first game and vowed to avenge the opening loss. "Lefty Grove! Hell!" said Frisch in disgust. "If that's the best they've got, we'll beat them. We'll beat Grove the next time," said Street. "Bill Hallahan is a better southpaw than Grove. He's faster and he has more stuff. Grimes will be back at them and we'll beat them. I tell you we'll win this series," said Street.

Meanwhile, Connie Mack sat behind his desk in his tower room at Shibe Park, leaned back, and touched his fingertips together while calmly reflecting on Grove's performance. "Grove was not worried at any time. You cannot worry Grove. He was good but not as good as I've seen him. He put them where he wanted them and when he wanted them. Only two or three balls really got away from him during the game."

Game two of the Series played before a full house at Shibe Park and pitted Earnshaw against Rhem. The Mackmen scored two runs in each of the first, third, and fourth innings, while St. Louis could muster only a single tally in the second off the home-run bat of George Watkins, the A's winning, 6-1. Foxx doubled Simmons home after Cochrane homered in the first and started a two-run third inning with a walk. Syl Johnson struck out Foxx in the seventh with Cochrane and Bishop on second and third with two out. After the game, manager Walter Johnson of the second-place Senators lamented that his pitching staff found no way to stop Cochrane, Simmons, and Foxx during the regular season. "They hit high and inside, low and outside, over the plate, and anything they can reach."

As the Mackmen arrived in St. Louis, no fear was expressed about Hallahan, especially from Cochrane, who was the special target of jockeying and had been dusted off the plate by both Grimes and Rhem while homering once in each of the previous two games. "Let 'em keep trying that snozzleball on me," remarked Cochrane, "and I'll belt a few more out of the park."

But Hallahan was the perfect cure for whatever ailed the Cardinals. He shut out the A's in game three, despite seven hits and five walks by Philadelphia. Taylor Douthit's homer leading off the bottom of the fourth off Walberg ignited the Cardinals and the home crowd. The Cards easily downed Philadelphia, 5-0.

St. Louis tied the Series at two games apiece in game four on October 6 when Haines held the A's to four hits and four walks in a 3-1 victory over Grove. During the top of the sixth inning, Foxx gave his best shot at starting an A's rally. After Cochrane flied out to outfielder Chick Hafey, Simmons walked on four pitches. Panic shot through the Cardinals' fans at Sportsman's Park when Foxx stepped to the plate and sliced one of Haines' pitches down the right field line, a booming shot that landed in the upper tier, only a few feet or yards foul of being a home run. A homer by Foxx would have knotted the score. Instead, Foxx was thrown out after hitting a high bounder to third, and Miller took a called third strike.

Game five was the pivotal point; whichever team lost would have to win both games in Philadelphia to win the Series. For eight innings, Grimes blanked the A's and Earnshaw (seven innings) and Grove (one inning) shut out the Cardinals. Then, in the top of the ninth, Cochrane opened with a walk, but Simmons was retired. The Sudlersville Slugger's batting turn came next.

Foxx said, "I felt I was going to break up the game with a home run. During batting practice, I hit three home runs in the stand, and before the battle started, I told Mickey Cochrane and several other ball players I would win the game with a big blow." Before grabbing his bat, Foxx yelled back to the players on the bench, "I'll bust up the game right now!" Jimmie caught one of Grimes' high, fast, curveballs and walloped it into the left-center field bleachers (the same spot as his homers in batting practice) as a stunned crowd at Sportsman's Park looked on. "When I saw that curve come whizzing at me, I swung. It was one of the greatest swings that ever left my shoulders," Foxx said.

Cardinal fans stared in shock as Jimmie rounded the bases. As he crossed the plate, he shook the hands of the batboy, who had a wide-open smile, looking up to Jim with pure admiration. Foxx then looked toward the box seats behind the Athletics' dugout, where Philadelphia rooters were seated, especially the players' wives. He noticed a lot of commotion and Eddie Collins told him moments later that the tension of the moment affected Eddie's wife so badly that she fainted "dead away" and had not revived in time to see Foxx cross the plate.

Connie Mack felt the drama of the moment too, saying, "My heart beat faster at that moment than it had all year. I knew from the sound of the 'crack' of the bat hitting the ball that it was a homer. I tried my best to keep calm, but inside I was burning up."

The A's celebrated on the bench during Foxx's home run-trot by throwing their bat pile around until it resembled a cyclone of wood. Their confidence was revived—they just knew they'd win the Series upon returning to Shibe Park.

In the clubhouse, coach Kid Gleason threw his arms around Foxx and then jabbed his ribs with his fist and shouted, "Boy, what a mean wallop that was!"

The Macks joined in a chorus of "We'll Tell the Cockeyed World."

While in the dressing room, Foxx said:

> I'm the happiest fellow in the world tonight. That drive I hit into the bleachers in the ninth inning was as welcome as a million dollars on Christmas morning. When I saw the ball sailing high in the air and among those bleacher fans, I was ready to do a dance, or a high dive in the Mississippi River.

Dykes said, "That's all there is, there isn't anymore. We'll beat them in Philadelphia."

In the other locker room, Grimes lamented, "It was a perfectly pitched ball. I struck Foxx out with the same pitch in the seventh. I didn't think he could hit that one, so I gave it to him again. It was just one of those things, that's all. He's a great hitter."

It was an especially suspenseful game for fans listening at home on radio—a scoreless tie until the ninth inning. Ted Husing described Foxx's game-winning shot on the Columbia network and Graham McNamee and Ford Frick on the NBC system.

The A's were a joyous lot of players as they packed their belongings to rush to their special train.

The story also goes that after Jimmie's game-winning homer in that important fifth game a judge was heading home to Kansas City from Sportsman's Park and was stopped by a passerby who yelled, "What was the score?" The judge, future U.S. President Harry Truman, said, "Jimmie Foxx 2, St. Louis 0."

Foxx's homer-hitting heroics inspired young boys across the country, much the way Babe Ruth's did. George Callahan, a fifteen-year-old boy in the Camden County (New Jersey) Tuberculosis Hospital, had been confined to a bed for three years. The highlight of his life was baseball, particularly rooting for the Philadelphia A's as they challenged St. Louis for the world championship. During each game, the hospital nurses propped George up in his cot with a pillow and gave him headphones so he could hear the World Series on radio. George said of Foxx's game-winning homer in the fifth Series contest, "I nearly died with joy when Jimmie Foxx knocked the ball into the bleachers. I had a hunch all day that either Cochrane, Simmons, or Foxx would knock a home run and Foxx came through. The victory made me feel like jumping."

A couple of days later, Jimmie visited George at the hospital after reading about his loyalty to the A's in the newspaper. George broke out into a wide smile when Foxx walked into his hospital room and handed George a baseball with all the A's signatures on it.

George cried out:

> Gee, it's Jimmie Foxx! Did you come all the way down here to see me? Gee, I'm happy. Wait till all the kids down in Gloucester hear about this! I'm as happy as when you made that home run in the ninth inning and broke up the fifth game. Sit down and tell me how you did it.

Foxx was visibly shaken as he shook George's hand and sat down beside him to chat.

As the Cardinals gathered at the North Philadelphia railroad station on October 7, the players threw their bags into a line of taxicabs while Athletics' fans blurted hoots and catcalls. One group sang, "Goodbye, St. Louis" over and over. The Athletics were greeted by a larger crowd and a band that played "Hail, the Conquering Hero Comes."

After a day off, the A's and the Cardinals squared off for the sixth game in Shibe Park before another packed crowd. Hallahan faced Earnshaw, who had only one day's rest. Earnshaw was up to the task, and so were Mack's batters. The A's scored seven runs on seven hits; St. Louis scored its lone tally in the ninth. Foxx doubled once and scored a run in three at bats and made an unassisted double play. Earnshaw had held St. Louis scoreless for twenty-two consecutive innings—from the third inning of the second game through seven innings of game four and eight innings of game six.

The Philadelphia Athletics were baseball's world champions for the second consecutive year. Mack slipped into the Athletics' dressing room following the Series clincher as announcer Graham McNamee pleaded for him to speak into a microphone. The A's let out a roar when they saw Mack. He walked down a lane and patted some of his aces—Earnshaw, Foxx, Cochrane, and Dykes. Mack then said to the A's, "You did what I asked you to. You are really a great team." The players yelled and cheered for Mack and themselves. McNamee briefly interviewed a host of the A's stars, including Foxx, Simmons, Cochrane, Grove, Earnshaw, and Bishop.

Friends or family listening in from back home enjoyed a rare thrill, listening to their heroes celebrate their most joyous moment.

Foxx and Simmons were again the top hitters for the A's in the Series, with Foxx batting .333 with 14 total bases and Simmons hitting .364 with 16 total bases. The winner's share for each Athletics player was $5,038.

Right after the World Series, the *Observer* reported that Queen Anne's County fans wondered whether Jimmie Foxx would remain with the A's in 1931. The Mackmen fans worried that Connie "would pluck a leaf from history's pages and break up his championship outfit as he did another great club in 1914." After all, the A's had declining attendance in 1930 compared to 1929 as the Depression began to set in, and salary demands of Connie's star players were likely to rise. Nevertheless, Mack said convincingly, "The machine will be kept intact for next season."

Fresh from the World Series victory, Foxx played a few rounds of golf on October 9, then left Philadelphia the following day with Earnshaw, Simmons, and trip organizer Ira Thomas for a six-to-eight-week barnstorming trip. The first stop was to be Toledo, followed by Milwaukee, then southward to stops in Illinois, Texas, Mississippi, and Louisiana.

On October 18, Foxx, Simmons, and Earnshaw visited a hospital in Quincy, Illinois, to see local townsman Bert Heidbreder, who had missed a World Series game between the A's and Cardinals in St. Louis because of an attack of appendicitis. Upon the arrival of the A's, Heidbreder immediately sat up for the first time in days. The next day he was allowed out of bed.

The next day, a game scheduled for the A's stars in Dallas, Texas, was cancelled because of rain, so they proceeded directly to Houston, Texas, for a game to be played under the "arcs" at Buffalo Stadium on Monday, October 20. Foxx, Simmons, Earnshaw, and Thomas appeared in Houston on Monday morning for a full day of festivities. At noon, the athletic committee of the Houston Chamber of Commerce hosted a luncheon in honor of the Series stars. Catcher Gus Mancuso and pitcher Dizzy Dean of the Cardinals also attended. Dean had just completed his first season of professional baseball, winning 17 and losing 8 games for the St. Joseph (Missouri) Saints, a minor-league club, then won 8 games and lost 2 for the minor-league Houston Buffaloes and pitched a shutout for the Cardinals over the Pittsburgh Pirates in his major-league debut on the last day of the regular season. The twenty-year-old Dean was sporting a black eye for the luncheon and game, saying he suffered it during a friendly tussle with his seventeen-year-old brother, Paul.

Foxx, Simmons, and Earnshaw were presented to the luncheon group by Thomas, who said Simmons should be included in any all-time list of baseball's greatest hitters and Earnshaw had been likened recently to Christy Mathewson. Thomas said of Foxx, "No player ever hit a ball farther than Jimmy Foxx, the baby of our ball club. He is the man picked to succeed Babe Ruth as the premier long-distance clouter of the game."

Then the A's trio and Thomas chatted with fans at the Texas Sporting Goods Store in town for about two hours. The A's posed for photographers on one knee in their coats and ties, each with a wide grin, holding a rifle, cocked and ready to fire, with town officials standing behind them.

Sports Editor Lloyd Gregory of the *Houston Post-Dispatch* rode with the A's into the surrounding countryside later in the afternoon and lamented in his column the next day, "they are among the greatest players in the game, and are modest and likeable chaps, but we must say, however, they are terrible singers."

Riding down the road, Earnshaw said that the balmy weather reminded him of Florida. For some reason, the A's players then broke into a chorus of "When It's Springtime in the Rockies." Gregory told his readers that he doubted the composer of the song would have recognized the rendition and said had the Cardinals, losers of the Series, heard it, they would have had their revenge.

About 2,500 fans came to Buffalo Stadium that evening, and Foxx and Simmons smacked two dozen baseballs over the fence before the game while members of the local "Knot Hole Gang" fought and scrambled for the souvenirs and the right to get their baseballs autographed. Foxx and Earnshaw played for Houston Gas and Fuel; Simmons and Dean played for Houston Lighting and Power. Dean pitched three innings, giving up two runs but striking out Foxx once and retiring Jimmie on a grounder in the other at bat. Foxx would get his revenge a couple of years later in spring training. Earnshaw pitched two innings and allowed two runs, during which Foxx was catcher before he switched to first base after Earnshaw quit the pitcher's box. Foxx was held hitless in three at bats, and Simmons smacked a double in three at bats. The A's left the game in the sixth inning to catch a train at 9:10 P.M. for Jackson, Mississippi.

On October 26, the *Times-Picayune* of New Orleans pictured Foxx and Simmons prominently on the sports pages, reminding fans of the game to be played that evening at Heinmann Park with other "leading ballplayers of minor league clubs of the section." As in many other games during the tour, long-distance clouting of Foxx and Simmons was featured before the game. Foxx's club easily beat Simmons' team, 7-2, with Jimmie doubling once off the scoreboard wall on one bounce in four at bats. Foxx and Simmons both pitched for their clubs in the last inning. Simmons blanked his opponents, while Foxx allowed one run and two hits.

Foxx, Simmons, Earnshaw, and Thomas arrived home in mid-November after their second successful postseason tour, in time to be with their families for the holidays. It would be the last tour that the three A's stars would make together.

7

MACK'S DYNASTY

Foxx was in his element when on a ballfield, a golf course, a farm field, or gunning for wild game. He devoted his early trips to Florida before spring training mostly to golf and sometimes to betting at the dog tracks. On January 22, 1931, Foxx scored the first eagle ever recorded at the sixteenth hole of the Fort Myers golf course. After a 300-yard drive, Jimmie sent a 71-yard mashie-niblick shot into the cup. Foxx's partner was Anthony "Dute" Harris, who had played as a part-time outfielder for the A's in 1930.

The A's and Cardinals faced off in an early three-game exhibition series on March 7-9, a grudge match from the 1930 World Series. Foxx homered in the opener, a 5-2 loss to St. Louis, and the clubs split the remaining two games. The two championship clubs played a fourth game on March 16 and again, the Cards were the victors, with both Hallahan and Dizzy Dean pitching well against the A's.

On March 8, Mack probably surprised no one when he told the press he'd be standing pat for the coming season. "I don't see how we could make any changes. The boys are all working hard. It's a pretty good club and I guess we have to stand on it." Simmons was a holdout, but Mack didn't seem worried. He felt that his infield reserves (Phil Todt, Eric McNair, Frank Higgins, and Dib Williams) were stronger than the year before, and the press noted that the main strength of the A's was built around the "big five"—Grove, Earnshaw, Cochrane, Foxx, and Simmons, all in their prime with an average age of twenty-eight.

Mack knew his club still had the talent, but he wondered how hard it would be to keep the A's focused and hustling. Mack said, "That third pennant is awfully hard to get. You see, when a team has won twice, the boys aren't stirred up by the excitement any more. They're used to winning. They may think they're trying just as hard as ever but they ease up unconsciously. They underrate the other fellows."

Mack didn't even have a sliding pit at training camp, saying that he looked for a lot of free swinging by batsmen throughout the league during the coming season, as in the past few campaigns. He said the new ball with the elevated stitching that might give pitchers a better grip wouldn't change strategies by managers very much. They'd still aim for the big innings, rather than one or two runs at a time.

One of the A's most loyal fans, inventor Thomas Edison, was on hand for an exhibition game on March 23 at Fort Myers. Edison had a vacation home there and over several years had watched the A's or invited the team to his home for dinner. Photographs of Edison, Mack, and the entire A's squad were taken on the front porch of his large house. On occasion, Edison would hold a bat and persuade Mack to lob a few pitches to him on the A's playing field. Edison was eighty-four and would die before the end of the year, leaving behind his legacy of inventing genius.

On March 27, reports released from Philadelphia indicated that the A's ownership was strongly considering moving the club to Camden, New Jersey, across the Delaware River. A year earlier, the A's owners expressed interest in playing Sunday games at Camden; now A's fans were faced with the threat of not seeing their club play in Shibe Park at all. It was said that the A's favorite site in Camden was within a fifteen-minute ride from the Delaware River Bridge and not as far away from central Philadelphia as Shibe Park. Such talk quickly subsided, and it's quite possible that the discussion was a bluff directed at the Pennsylvania State Legislature to get them to repeal the blue law prohibiting Sunday baseball.

The A's adopted uniform numbers for the 1931 season, but only for road games. Foxx wore uniform number three, as did Babe Ruth (the Yankees having worn uniform numbers since 1929). Unlike Ruth and some other players that wore number three, Jim didn't bat third in the order, but he did usually play first base, the position associated with number three for scoring games.

As the A's came north for the final leg of exhibition games before the regular 1931 season, the club struggled while losing three of four games to the much weaker Phillies and lost by a run to the Baltimore Orioles of the IL. Although homerless in the five-game span, Foxx slugged the ball hard for plenty of extra-base hits.

The April 5 game at Oriole Park in Baltimore was a reunion of sorts for some of the A's players and Joe Hauser of the Orioles. Former Orioles Boley, Bishop, and Grove all played for the A's in front of their former fans. Former Athletic Hauser had set a professional baseball record for homers in a season with sixty-three the previous season for minor league Baltimore and started the Orioles' scoring when he smacked a homer off former teammate Ed Rommel in the fourth inning.

Foxx had to enjoy watching Hauser trot around the bases after his homer. They had roomed together on road trips in 1928, and Hauser had fond memories of Foxx, even as a ninety-two-year old in 1991: "He was a good fella—Jimmie Foxx. A good, clean boy. He wasn't out looking for women. We would occasionally catch a show together. He wasn't out late at night at that point when we roomed together." (Foxx was twenty then.)

Hauser's 1925 knee injury seemed to end his career in the major leagues. His attempts to regain his hitting stroke in the majors failed in 1928 with the A's and 1929 with the Indians. Despite finding his homer swing again in the minors with 212 homers over a four-year period beginning in 1930, Joe never received more playing time in the majors.

Mack tried Foxx at third base during the City Series while starting veteran Phil Todt at first base. Todt had been the regular Red Sox first baseman from 1925-30, and Mack hoped to take advantage of Phil's penchant for extra-base hits. But Phil's bat was quiet during the preseason, and Mack penciled in Foxx at first base for the regular season opener with the Senators.

Simmons and Earnshaw finished their spring training at Hot Springs, Arkansas, and arrived in Philadelphia near the end of the first week of April. Simmons became the last player to sign a contract with Mack on April 9, for a reported $30,000 for one year. The crosstown Phillies had signed their star slugger Chuck Klein just four days earlier to a much lower contract of $15,000 per season for three years. Surely, Foxx made a mental note of these contract amounts for comparisons later.

The A's were favored to repeat as the AL pennant winners. Forty-one of 64 sports writers picked Mack's club to finish first; another 21 picked the A's to finish second. The Senators gained 16 first-place votes, 25 second-place votes, and 18 third-place votes.

Foxx's Sudlersville fans could hardly wait for the new season to begin. Anticipating another pennant for the A's and banner season for Foxx, baseball fans from the Eastern Shore were primed to follow their hero's exploits. Many traveled to Shibe Park; otherwise they listened to the A's on radio station WCAU from Philadelphia, with broadcaster Billy Dyer. In the Philadelphia area, Athletics fans followed the Mackmen from any of five city newspapers: *The Philadelphia Record*, the *Evening Bulletin*, *Public Ledger*, the *Inquirer*, and the *Daily News*, plus the *Post* and *Courier* from nearby Camden, New Jersey.

The A's and Senators opened the season on April 14 at Griffith Stadium in front of President Hoover and 35,000 fans, a large crowd, given the economic woes around the nation. Foxx, still tanned from spring training in the south, managed one single and one run batted in as the A's edged Washington, 5-3, in 11 innings. Then the A's and Foxx suffered an early season setback.

On April 15, Foxx badly twisted his knee at Griffith Stadium. As he rounded second base at a sprint effort from first to third in the fourth inning, the spikes of his right shoe caught in the bag, throwing him onto his left leg. Doc Ebeling was unable to determine the extent of the injury and sent Jimmie back to Philadelphia for treatment by Dr. J. B. Carnett at University Hospital. The day after the injury, Dr. Carnett determined that Foxx had torn ligaments on the outside of his left knee and they would not support him properly, other than for walking in gimpy manner.

Foxx missed the last two games of the opening road series with the Senators, a three-game series at Yankee Stadium (the Yankee home opener on April 19 against the A's drew about 80,000 fans), and the home opener with the Senators. Phil Todt filled in for Jimmie at first base, and the A's lost four of the six games that Foxx did not play as the starting first baseman.

On April 21, Foxx watched the Yankees tune up in batting practice for the second game of the three-game series at Yankee Stadium. Jim was in full uniform for the game, even though he was still waiting for his left knee to heal, and he assessed the Yankees and the Indians.

> Yes, they [Yankees] can hit, but what will they use for pitchers? They're uncertain in spots, these Yankees, and you can't win pennants that way. Look at Tony Lazzeri out there. How'll he go over a full season at third base? How about second base and Chapman's fielding? Look at left field. They've got two men out there. That's the club we have to beat? Nope, for me, I'll take Cleveland. They've got a hitting club. They've got pitching. They're young and tough. Cleveland will be dangerous every step of the way.

In pregame festivities for the home opener, the A's and Senators paraded to center field and stood at attention as the AL pennant and world's champion flag were unfurled. Then Commissioner Landis gave each member of the A's from the previous season a gold watch or a diamond ring, according to the individual's choice. A crowd of 25,000 braved cool weather and cloudy skies and were rewarded with a 5-1 A's win over the Senators on the strength of Grove's pitching.

Foxx appeared as a pinch hitter in the next two home contests against Washington and played a key role in both victories for the A's. On April 24, Jim batted for pitcher Leroy Mahaffey in the eighth inning, walked, and paved the way for his own pinch runner, McNair, to score an important run in the A's 5-run rally that gave them a 10-7 win over Washington. The next day, Foxx batted for Todt in the bottom of the ninth with the bases loaded and hit a long fly that scored Cochrane with the winning run.

The Mackmen didn't play April 26-29, and Jimmie returned to the starting lineup at first base on April 30. Foxx was slow in getting on track, with only three hits in his first 25 at bats through May 5. The knee must have started feeling better because, beginning on the following day, Foxx collected seven homers and 29 runs batted in the next 16 games, all victories for Philadelphia during a 17-game winning streak. The last three games of the win skein came at the expense of the Yankees, and the A's stood five games ahead of the Senators and six ahead of New York after the seventeenth consecutive win on May 25.

Near the end of June, a leg injury to Boley and chipped bones in the left ankle of Dib Williams forced Mack to switch Dykes to short, Foxx to third, and Todt to first. The low point of the Athletics' performance occurred when the Browns swept Philadelphia in four straight in St. Louis before Williams returned to the lineup and Dykes and Foxx returned to their normal positions.

In July, the Athletics acquired veteran hurler Waite Hoyt from the Tigers to support Grove, Walberg, and Earnshaw in the starting rotation. It was probably Mack's intent that Hoyt would fill the gap left by Jack Quinn, who didn't rejoin Philadelphia in 1931. Now the A's had both Rommel and Hoyt for part-time starting and relief pitching duty.

Hoyt's impact was immediate. He logged five wins and one loss in July. Three of the wins and the one loss occurred between July 15-30, when the A's won 17 out of 18 games.

Foxx reached the .300 batting mark for the first time in the 1931 season during the July 4 doubleheader with the Red Sox at Shibe Park. However, Foxx's batting average dipped below .300 on July 24 and he slumped badly through August 13, batting only .180 (11 for 61), dropping his overall average from .302 to .283. Thereafter, Foxx gained a measure of consistency. While not compiling the number of multihit games he did in 1929 and 1930, Foxx collected one or more hits in 22 of his next 26 games.

Simmons picked up the slack in late July and continued his pursuit of a second straight batting title. On July 25, Al replaced Ruth as the league leader in batting average.

When the Athletics returned to Shibe Park from a long road trip near the end of August, Mack hoped that Simmons, Haas, and Cochrane would all be ready to return to the lineup. Simmons called Connie from Milwaukee and said his infected left ankle needed a few more days to completely heal and he would report to Boston for the five-game series beginning September 4. Playing on the fact that Simmons had previously been named "Bucketfoot Al" for his follow-through stance that deposited his left foot toward third base, *The Sporting News* published a picture of Simmons with his foot in a real bucket as his mother, Agnes Szymanski, poured hot water over his left foot to fight a skin infection.

Haas was not ready to return to action, either. He had been out of the lineup since July 25 with a broken left wrist. Meanwhile, Cochrane, who had been given several days' rest due to fatigue, was ready to return.

Lefty Grove's heartbreaking 1-0 loss to the Browns on August 23 interrupted a remarkable winning string during the 1931 season. After winning the season opener on April 14 and losing his next start on April 18, despite allowing only two earned runs, he won his next eight decisions. Then, after a loss on June 5, Grove won eleven starts in a row, plus a win in relief, and four more starts in a row for sixteen consecutive wins before losing 1-0 on August 23. The only run of the game scored because of a misplay by outfielder Jim Moore, who was playing for the injured Al Simmons. Lefty proceeded to win his next six starts before losing his last game of the season on September 27 to the Yankees and finishing with a 31-4 record.

Although Foxx's salary was lower in 1931 than it might have been if not for the Depression, he was still living the good life compared to many others around the country, and he knew it. Jim was not usually a braggart when it came to his ballplaying abilities, but he loved to show off new material possessions, especially clothing and automobiles. The September 1 issue of *Studebaker News* featured a picture of Foxx next to his new auto, a free-wheeling President Brougham. Unlike his dad, Jim liked driving a car. Jim's onetime girlfriend Helen Harrison said, "Jim loved to show off a new auto!"

Foxx joined the injured list on September 9 when the Senators' outfielder Heinie Manush stepped on his right foot while running to first, bruising it so badly that Jimmie had to move about on crutches. The Athletics feared that Foxx had broken bones, in which case he would be lost to the team for the World Series, but x-rays proved otherwise.

The A's clinched the pennant on September 15 in their 142nd game, beating Cleveland 14-3 behind Eddie Rommel at Shibe Park. The A's win, combined with the Senator's loss to the Browns about an hour later, mathematically eliminated Washington. The pennant win occurred with twelve games still remaining on the A's schedule and thirteen on the Senators', showing the degree to which the Mackmen dominated the league that year. Had the pennant race been closer, attendance would have been better for the A's at home and even for some road games. Foxx's injury prevented him from playing in the decisive pennant-winning game, and for the second time in three years, he missed a pennant clincher. Mack turned his attention toward getting his team ready for the Series.

After missing eight games, Jimmie returned to the lineup for a doubleheader on September 19. Trainer Doc Ebeling was confident that none of Foxx's speed would be affected by the injury. But what about his batting? Jimmie collected only two hits in the doubleheader, but then hit homers in three consecutive games, including a pinch-hit grand slam. Overall, he batted 7 for 25 from the time he returned to the lineup until the end of the regular season, but he hit with power. Foxx was ready for the World Series, and his rapid and full comeback had an "exhilarating effect" on the Mackmen.

Jim's season-ending batting average was .291, a career low to that point. His batting statistics were lower than in the previous two years, in part due to his early and late season injuries. Foxx also mentioned, early in 1938, that he had had sinus problems in 1931, so that if they were severe enough they could have affected his batting. Still, he smashed thirty homers (three inside the park) and collected a very productive runs-batted-in total of 120.

Cochrane commented on Foxx's penchant to continue driving in runs despite his lower batting average.

The boys always seem to hit in the pinch. Look at Jimmy Foxx, hitting way down [in batting average] this year. They say he's in a slump, but you'll notice he's driven in almost as many runs as Al Simmons and they've been at bat about the same number of times.

Again Foxx showed his versatility. He played in 109 games at first base, but injuries to Mack's infielders made it necessary for Jim to play 23 games at third base and split another three games between third base and first. He also played one game in left field and pinch hit in three games.

Simmons appeared in only 128 games due to injury but still collected 200 base hits for a league-leading .390 batting average, his second batting title in a row. He usually coaxed about one-half to one-third the number of walks that Foxx did, and 1931 was no exception.

The World Series was a rematch of the Athletics and Gabby Street's Cardinals. Both teams finished well out in front of their second-place rivals, the Yankees and Giants.

For the third consecutive year, baseball fans from Sudlersville and the rest of Queen Anne's County had the option of seeing some of the games at nearby Shibe Park or watching a re-creation of all games other than on Sunday on the player board at the *Observer* building in Centreville, Maryland. Barbershops, sporting goods stores, and other public places were the focal points where fans in many medium-sized towns gathered and listened to the Series games on radio. The *Easton Journal* said that the games could be heard up and down the streets in Easton.

Several days before the first game of the Series, to be played at Shibe Park, the A's management sent letters by special delivery to 15,000 citizens in Philadelphia, instructing them to bring their money to the ballpark to purchase their tickets. The ticket holders were selected from more than 150,000 applicants.

The value of housetop privileges on the roofs of 20th Street homes adjoining Shibe Park was revealed in a court action late in September. Charles Morro bought one of the houses before the Series began, but the seller, Mrs. Catherine Sweeney, insisted that she wished to continue to occupy it long enough to reap the profit of $750 to $1,500 during the Series from paying customers using her rooftop to watch the games.

On September 26, the A's were installed as early 7-5 favorites, seeking an unprecedented third straight world championship. Grantland Rice gave the edge to the A's just before the Series, citing the batting eyes of Cochrane, Simmons, and Foxx and the fact that "there is only one Grove in baseball today, whatever happens to him the next few days."

When the Athletics arrived at the railroad station in St. Louis, the city's Mayor Victor Miller and a crowd of several hundred fans greeted them as they loaded into a caravan of automobiles. Grove attracted much of the attention as he walked down the platform puffing a cigar.

The first game of the Series, on October 1, featured Grove against the young, hard-throwing Paul Derringer for the Cardinals at Sportsman's Park. St. Louis scored twice off Grove in the bottom of the first. The A's answered back with four runs in the third, the last two on Foxx's single. Simmons' two-run homer in the bottom of the seventh completed the game's scoring. Grove lasted the whole game, despite giving up twelve hits.

Wild Bill Hallahan outpitched Earnshaw in game two of the Series, blanking the A's, 2-0. Center fielder Pepper Martin manufactured both Cardinal runs with daring base running. Hallahan was especially careful when pitching to Foxx. Jim led off three different innings by reaching base—a walk in the fifth, a single in the seventh, and a walk in the ninth—but to no avail.

Two days later, on Sunday, the A's and Cardinals both held two-hour drills at Shibe Park in preparation for game three of the Series on Monday. Ticket scalpers were getting $10 for $5.50 reserved seats.

Grimes, wearing a two-day growth of beard in the third game, pitched seven innings of no-hit ball before the A's threatened in the bottom of the eighth. After Foxx walked and Miller singled for the A's first hit of the game, two batters were retired before pinch-hitter Cramer lofted a high drive that was barely caught by Frisch as Foxx and Miller circled the bases. The Cardinals escaped with a 5-2 victory over the A's, who didn't score until the ninth inning on Simmons' two-run homer with two out. Foxx fanned for the final out, missing the final pitch "by two feet." The Cardinals again hit freely off Grove with twelve hits.

Street tabbed Syl Johnson, and Mack picked Earnshaw to pitch in game four at Shibe Park. Simmons' run-scoring double in the bottom of the first was the only tally of the game until the bottom of the sixth, when Foxx stepped to the plate to start the A's rally. Foxx rocketed one of Johnson's high fastballs over the left field roof for one of the longest-hit home runs in World Series history. Foxx's homer cleared the left field seats and roof (the left field wall measured 334 feet from home plate, and the seats towered at least 100 feet from the ground). Mack described Foxx's homer as the "longest hit I have ever seen in the World Series. I doubt if anyone but Babe Ruth ever hit one any farther." Then the A's scored one more run in the inning enroute to a 3-0 victory, to even the Series at two games apiece. Pepper Martin had the only two hits off Earnshaw.

Martin and Hallahan teamed up in game five on October 7 at Shibe Park to easily defeat the A's, 5-1. Martin rewarded Street's placing him in the cleanup spot in the batting order by driving in four of the Card's runs with two singles and a homer. The Card's victory put them within one win of unseating the A's as the world champs, with the final one or two games to be played in St. Louis.

The Cards arrived at the railroad station in St. Louis just after noon the following day. About 2,000 fans burst through the guard lines and swarmed Martin as he stepped out of the train and began to walk to the taxis. The Cards met at Sportsman's Park about 3:00 P.M. for some hitting and fielding practice, whereas the A's elected to take an early train and skip any practice at the Card's ballpark.

Mack chose to pitch Grove in the sixth game and rest Earnshaw an extra day, in hopes the Series would be extended by an A's victory. Grove responded with a complete-game 5-1 victory over St. Louis, striking out seven batters, walking one, and allowing only five hits. Foxx singled twice in four at bats and scored two runs.

Earnshaw and Grimes were chosen to face each other in the crucial final game. Grimes came within one out of a 4-0 shutout, only to have Philadelphia rally for two runs before Hallahan came in to relieve him and retire Bishop on a long fly to Martin for the final out. Two misjudged fly balls by Dib Williams in the first inning resulted in Texas Leaguer singles, a bad relay throw to home by Foxx, and a passed ball by Cochrane, all contributing to two runs by the Cards. It was one of the few times that the Mackmen had beaten themselves all season.

The loss of the seventh game made a difference in Series payoff of almost $1,500 less to each member of the A's. However, each team member, along with Mack, the coaches, and the trainer, received almost $3,000. When it was over, Simmons, Cochrane, and Grove left St. Louis for their barnstorming tour of the Orient.

As Mack stepped off the train in Philadelphia on Monday evening, a small crowd of a several hundred loyal fans greeted him at the station. Mack said:

> The Cards played better ball than we did, and that's why we lost. Our boys didn't click as they have in the past, but it's silly to say that they've slipped permanently. They all tried hard and I have nothing

but praise for them. It's over now and I'll start thinking about next year.

During the Depression, very little was wasted. The Athletics often sold their used uniforms at the end of each season. Several times Dib Williams bought the uniforms for an amateur team near his hometown in Greenbriar, Arkansas. Everybody always wanted Foxx's or Simmons' uniform. Several times, Foxx obtained some of the uniforms and gave them to the Sudlersville High baseball team.

Meanwhile, for three straight Saturdays beginning on September 26, the *Star-Democrat* heralded an upcoming appearance by Foxx and some of his teammates in Easton sometime after the end of the Series. Dell Foxx made the initial announcement on September 20. On October 1, Dell confirmed with Lee Seymour, manager of an Easton town team, that Jimmie would come to Easton around the middle of the month. The local newspaper reminded fans that Foxx was one of the few players ever to have hit a ball over the center field fence at Federal Park.

Jim told the press in Easton that he was particularly hopeful that Frank Baker would be able to attend the baseball exhibition. It would probably mark the first time Foxx was in a baseball uniform in Federal Park since he left Easton's minor-league club for Philadelphia seven years earlier. A quarter-page ad in the October 10 issue of the *Star-Democrat* proclaimed that Jimmy Foxx and his teammates would play the "Easton Club" on October 17—Admission $1.00.

Given all the hype before the game, coverage of the results was scant in the *Star-Democrat* and the *Journal*. Jimmie and some of the A's managed to defeat the Easton Club, 5-0, but no details were reported on Foxx's performance or the other A's who came with him. The crowd size was a disappointment—only 700—but the fans who came certainly enjoyed seeing Jimmie Foxx again.

Later on that winter, before the start of spring training in 1932, Whitey Whitt, former A's and Yankee outfielder, hosted a score of major leaguers and other baseball associates at his farm near Woodstown, New Jersey. The event appears to have been "for men only" and was featured in *The Sporting News* with a group picture that included Foxx, Bing Miller, Eddie Collins, Rube Walberg, Cochrane, Ruddy Van Ohl (business manager of the A's), Browns' outfielder Goose Goslin, John Quinn (Southern Association umpire), Eddie MacLaughlin (Pacific Coast League umpire), and sportswriter Jimmy Isaminger. Foxx was the youngest attendee, fending off remarks about his riding garb and his oversized sombrero. Some of the boys shot clay pigeons, others strummed ukes for background music, and the city slickers took a tour of Whitt's livestock. The main topic of conversation was baseball, according to Isaminger. Whitt's main entree was a steaming roast pig stuffed with sauerkraut and potatoes and "all the trimmings." Talk about Foxx in his element. It didn't get much better than this—a farm and baseball.

8

FOXX CHALLENGES RUTH

The Athletics entered the 1932 campaign seeking their fourth consecutive AL pennant. This feat had never been accomplished in the AL and only once in the NL, when the New York Giants won pennants from 1921 through 1924.

As the new year turned, Connie Mack banned the exhibition basketball excursions of Foxx, Dykes, Earnshaw, Haas, and Jim Peterson. Although their basketball tour started out as a way to pick up a little extra change, their status as three-time pennant winners attracted heavy bookings and finally prompted Mack to stop the tour and prevent injuries to his valuable "property."

Mack had a number of top stars under multiyear contracts through 1933, including Foxx, Cochrane, and Simmons. Simmons again received permission to limit his spring training to conditioning at Hot Springs, Arkansas, for 1932, and who could argue with the decision? In 1931, Simmons conditioned himself in Hot Springs, worked out with the Minneapolis Millers of the American Association, joined the A's when they traveled north, and won his second straight batting title.

Overall, this was a time of team unity. Various groups of players barnstormed together playing baseball or basketball, hunted for wild game, or attended various social functions. In mid-January, players from different clubs, including some of the Athletics living in the Philadelphia area, vied in a clay target shooting match in Bustleton, Pennsylvania, including Foxx, Collins, Cochrane, Walberg, Miller, Krausse, Doc Ebeling, Joe Bush, Goose Goslin, and Jimmy Wilson.

Jimmie, Helen, and Jimmie, Jr., motored to Fort Myers with Lew Krausse the first week in February. During the first week of spring training, Grove ended his contract holdout by signing for $25,000, about $8,000 or $9,000 more than Foxx. Walberg followed suit signing his contract, and Foxx, Cochrane, Dykes, and Krausse spent their first Sunday in Fort Myers baking in the sunshine on the golf links. Meanwhile, coach Gleason reported to the team that he was too ill to participate in early spring training.

Mack labelled Oscar Roettger, Ed Coleman, and Joe Bowman as three of his best-looking recruits "in years." Mack thought so highly of Roettger that he moved Foxx to third base and fifth in the batting order and Roettger to first base and fourth in the lineup as the exhibition season began. Mack said, "I know what Dykes can do. I know what Foxx can do." Coleman was a heavy hitter in the minors and impressed onlookers with his bat in spring training. Ed was making a bid to crack the Athletics' starting lineup as an outfielder. Bowman was a right-handed pitching prospect who Mack probably hoped would eventually replace the aging Rommel.

Meanwhile, some sportswriters labelled a set of four spring training games between the A's and the Cardinals the "Spring World Series." After the A's lost 6-5 on March 5, the Mackmen pulverized rookie Dizzy Dean the next day for six runs in the first inning, the only inning he pitched for St. Louis. The A's smacked four consecutive home runs off Dean, including one over the fence by Roettger and three inside-the-park jobs hit by Foxx, Cramer, and Ed Madjeski.

Earnshaw joined Simmons in Hot Springs to remedy his ills, while Cochrane remained out of action in a hospital in Lakeland, Florida, for much of spring training with an infected foot and was sent back to Philadelphia until the City Series against the Phillies.

Foxx received accolades from some Philadelphia scribes for his play at third base during the exhibition season. Meanwhile, Roettger's heavy hitting during the spring continued to confound Mack as to whether Foxx should start the season at first or third base.

A couple of players on each team were bound to lose playing status, because the major leagues decided to cut rosters to twenty-three players. The purpose was to help lower operating costs because of lower revenues from declining attendance during the Depression.

On April 3, the Professional Betting Commissioners picked the A's as a 6-5 choice to repeat as AL champions against the Yankees and, as a 9-5 choice to place first in the AL. The Associated Press pennant poll followed a few days later and posted 38 first-place votes for the A's, 28 for the Yankees, and only one for the Indians.

Foxx missed the opener of the City Series on April 2, but then played the entire game at first base for the A's in the last three games of the Series and two other exhibition games. Twice, Foxx homered in a game against the Phillies, but few people suspected the Ruthian-type season he was about to have.

In the season opener at Shibe Park, Coach Gleason left his sickbed, donned an old baseball shirt, and appeared at the opening festivities long enough to pat starter George Earnshaw on his shoulder, a ritual without which neither George nor Grove would think of taking the mound. Still, the Yankees pounded Earnshaw for 10 runs enroute to a 12-6 win. But Foxx again stood out, hitting the longest homer of the day, a shot beyond the wall in dead center field near the flagpole, meaning the blast went farther than 468 feet.

Jim began the season at first base and launched an early assault on Ruth's single-season homer record with four homers in the A's first five games. Then on April 21, Jim hit two triples in a game against the Yankees in spacious Yankee Stadium, both of which the *New York Times* claimed would have been homers in most other parks. On May 24, Jimmie hit a long fly in Yankee Stadium, "a fly to [Ben] Chapman close to the left field bleachers which would have been a homer in any other park in baseball." Still, it's a sure bet that Ruth lost many homers in Yankee Stadium, year after year, on long flies hit to parts of the outfield other than close to the foul pole in right field.

The "Maryland Broadback," as Foxx was now referred to by Philadelphia scribe Jimmy Isaminger, took an early lead in batting in the AL in late April and ended May in the same lofty spot with an average well over .400. Not only was he leading the league in batting average at this point, as he had in 1929, Jim was now the leading home-run hitter. Foxx was making so many headlines, he surpassed his All-Star teammates Grove, Simmons, and Cochrane in gaining the attention of the media and fans.

As usual, Foxx's batting performance was not affected by what fielding position he played. Over a 12-game stretch in late May, Foxx played at third base and hit seven homers. Cochrane marveled at Jimmie's homer-hitting ability late in May, giving his own comparison of Foxx to Ruth. "I think Foxx can hit as long a ball as any of them. That even goes for Ruth. Why, Jimmy knocked four over the left-center roof at our park. He certainly can golf them. How I'd hate to be a pitcher with Jimmy walking up to the plate."

Foxx always enjoyed meeting rookies, and he took a special interest in players hailing from his home state of Maryland. Louis "Bozey" Berger lettered in baseball and basketball at the University of Maryland, and when he came up to the majors for a short stint with the Indians in 1932, one of the first players he met was Jimmie Foxx. Berger recalled:

> Outfielder Dick Porter on the Indians was a few years older than Foxx and was born and raised in Princess Anne in Somerset County on the lower Eastern Shore of Maryland. Foxx and Porter were well acquainted and Porter said, "Jim, this is Curley Byrd's 'pet' from over at the University of Maryland."

Foxx didn't like the looks of Bozey's bat for one reason or another and gave him one of his own Louisville Sluggers. Although not known for his power hitting, Berger recalled, "I hit a few homers with that bat."

Meanwhile, the A's starting pitching was not up to its standards of the past three years. Mack bolstered his starting rotation when he purchased left-hander Tony Freitas on May 20 from Sacramento of the Pacific Coast League about two weeks after Tony pitched a no-hitter.

Foxx slugged 13 homers in May and drove home 37 runs, making a strong early season bid for Triple Crown honors in the AL with large leads in homers, runs batted in, and batting average.

On June 1, the largest crowd of the season (estimated at 31,000) filled Shibe Park beyond seating capacity to watch the Yankees battle the Athletics in a doubleheader. Bishop's two-run homer won the first game in the sixteenth inning, and Foxx's eighteenth homer of the season with one man on base in the seventh won the second game. Foxx's homer put him on a pace to hit about sixty-five over the entire season. As was often the case, Jim's homer was the longest of six homers hit in the game, this one landing on the roof of the left field stand.

Two days later, Gehrig stole the spotlight from Foxx, slugging four homers in his first four at bats at Shibe Park. He came close to hitting a fifth in his last at bat on a shot to deep center field, just a few steps from the outfield wall, but it was snared by Al Simmons. Lou's homer hitting paced New York to a 20-13 victory. Foxx hit his nineteenth homer in the ninth inning.

Foxx's early season batting was so torrid that as late as June 5 his batting average stood at .401. The only other time his average stood above .400 later in a season was 1929.

The Mackmen headed west on a road trip. As the Athletics slept in their hotel in Cleveland on June 7, an explosion from a fire in the Ellington Apartments and Hotel across the street awoke Foxx and some of his teammates in the middle of the night. Jimmie said the explosion threw him out of the bed. Foxx, Simmons, and Cochrane scurried to the scene and aided firemen in placing ladders and carrying persons to safety from the second and third floors of the burning building.

On June 13, Foxx faced the Tiger's righty hurler, Tommy Bridges, and slammed a ninth-inning three-run homer to clinch an A's victory over Detroit. The *Baltimore Morning Sun* said, "it was one of the longest hits ever seen at Navin Field." It was one of three homers Jim hit off Bridges for the season.

The next day, Grantland Rice told his readers, "Don't overlook the home-run war between Jimmy Foxx and Babe Ruth." Rice pointed out that although others might be in the homer chase, either Foxx or Ruth would be leading the American League when the season was finished. He marveled that, "Ruth is spotting his rival 14 years, a killing handicap for anyone but Ruth." That same day, Foxx homered twice against the Tigers to begin pulling away from the Babe, 25 homers to 21.

Jim had another near-miss of a homer on June 15 when he powered a long fly ball to the deepest part of center field beyond the flagpole at Sportman's Park. Browns' outfielder Fred Schulte caught the long smash with his back against the wall, 430 feet from home plate.

Manager Mack continued to schedule exhibition games to collect extra revenue on most days that the A's did not have a regularly scheduled league game. Many players—especially star players on various clubs—opposed such extra games, citing the need for rest and complaining about the risk of injury, but not Foxx. Fans in towns without a major league club were genuinely disappointed upon learning that star players would be a no-show. What a thrill it was to see Foxx or Ruth stepping in the batter's box, wielding a baseball bat, and powdering a ball or even striking out.

Jim homered in an exhibition game on June 15 in a 6-5 loss to Springfield (Illinois) of the Three-I League, having also homered a month earlier in a 12-8 A's win over Springfield (Massachusetts) of the Eastern League. Foxx took exhibition games seriously. He was a competitor and always had pride in his performance.

On June 19, Gordon Cobbledick of the *Cleveland Plain Dealer* offered several reasons why Foxx might be able to break Ruth's home-run record of 1927. He pointed out that Jimmie played half of his games in Shibe Park, where both the left and right field fences were inviting targets for home runs. On the other hand, Ruth played half of his games in Yankee Stadium, where the right field wall was a friendly distance from home plate but most of the outfield fence from the left field corner to center field commanded a long drive for the Babe to register a homer. Cobbledick asserted that this gave Foxx a good chance to maintain his early season homer pace. The writer also reported that Foxx altered his style of batting for this season to be much more aggressive. Rather than being strictly a guess hitter and waiting for fastballs as in the past, Mack and some of his other teammates urged Jimmie to "hit what he saw." Foxx was taking a cut at any kind of pitch that was over the plate—fastballs, curves, change of paces, or whatever. And, Foxx was hitting for a higher average (crowding the .400 mark) than in past seasons (except the first half of 1929), which Cobbledick thought gave Jimmie a better shot at breaking the homer mark because Foxx hit the ball hard (some players were saying harder than Ruth) and a certain percentage of his hits figured to go over the outfield fence.

Foxx's twenty-seventh homer of the season was a highlight of an 18-11 shellacking of the White Sox on June 20. Jim's blast off lefty Pat Caraway cleared the high wall in left center of Comiskey Park. *The Sporting News* described it as one of the two longest homers ever hit in Comiskey Park, the other being slammed by Foxx in 1931.

When the Mackmen visited New York on June 25, Foxx showcased his power-hitting abilities with one of the all-time longest homers in the history of Yankee Stadium. After Lefty Gomez walked Johnnie Heving and Simmons in the fourth inning, Foxx made the first hit of the game off Gomez, "a mighty drive into the upper tier of the left field grandstand, far out towards center field along its curve. Had the ball been hit several more feet towards center field, it would have left the ball park." Red Sox hurler Charlie Wagner recalled that for many years thereafter, two "Xs" were painted on the seat hit by Foxx's shot, and the seat remained that way until Yankee Stadium was renovated in the 1970s.

Foxx's power output remained red-hot in June, with twelve more homers. Fans around the country began to wonder if Foxx could overtake Babe Ruth's record of sixty homers in one season, and Philadelphia scribes were making daily mention of Jimmie's success or failure in adding to his home-run total. Two years earlier, the Chicago Cubs' Hack Wilson established a new NL home-run record with 56, but no one other than Ruth had ever collected 50 or more homers in a season in the AL.

Foxx was well ahead of Ruth's homer pace at the end of June with 29 homers, hitting his twenty-ninth on June 25, whereas in 1927 Ruth slugged his twenty-ninth on July 9. Of course, the trick to such comparisons was that Ruth collected a record 17 homers in September when he homered 60 times in 1927. Anyone challenging the Babe had better be far ahead of his pace heading into September. Jimmie continued to lead all AL batters, maintaining an average above .370 for most of June.

For the first time in his career, Foxx had a chance to surpass Ruth's single-season home-run record. Foxx had watched Ruth in the major league homer spotlight for seven seasons from 1925-31 and had been compared to the Babe often—the "right-handed Ruth" and the "successor to Ruth." Understandably, Ruth was one of Foxx's idols. Now Jim was fulfilling some of the predictions of the press and other players in the league. Despite Ruth's immense popularity among fans, he was carving out his own niche of followers. A lot of fans preferred Foxx—the underdog, the upstart, the quiet, humble type—compared to the boastful, established Ruth. Both men were gregarious and enjoyed the accolades heaped upon them.

An article in the *Baltimore Morning Sun* on July 2 hinted that Simmons might not be happy with the attention that Foxx was getting as the new favorite batsman of Philadelphia fans. "And so they are saying that Foxx and his batting mark with the ensuing capture of the spotlight has Simmons a-jitter with jealousy."

Foxx said he was swinging a lighter stick in 1932 than in previous years. Jim felt that the bat with slightly less total weight, a thinner handle, and more weight around the barrel enabled him to read pitches a fraction of a second longer and swing with more bat speed.

The A's trounced the Newark Bears (International League) on the last day of June in Atlantic City, New Jersey, in a benefit game for the Betty Bacharach Home for Crippled Children. Fans "yelled for action" from Foxx, but Jimmie couldn't muster a hit, let alone a homer, before being replaced in the seventh inning by Roettger at first. On the following day, Jimmie smashed a double and a triple to right field against the Senators at Shibe Park. Both clouts barely missed clearing the wall, hitting the very top but bounding back onto the playing field.

A biographical sketch of Foxx in the July 7 issue of *The Sporting News* summarized Jimmie's recent tape-measure homers around AL parks. The article credited Foxx as being the only player ever to hit a ball over the roof of the left field pavilion in Comiskey Park, the record for the longest drives over the left field double-tiered pavilion at Shibe Park, and some of the longest homers ever hit over the left field fences in Navin Field, Fenway Park, and Sportsman's Park.

The article asserted that Foxx spells his first name with an "IE" at the end for "autograph hounds," and added that "Foxx likes hunting, mild cigars, light-hued sports clothes, bowling and golf. He owns a 250-acre farm near the old home town of Sudlersville, Maryland, that may some day be his family homestead." Because Foxx was featured in "Daguerreotypes" of *The Sporting News*, France Laux, sports announcer for station KMOX in St. Louis, dramatized the Sudlersville Slugger's life story over the radio on July 7.

Foxx's teammates, especially Cochrane, called him "Ingagi" after the big ape in the movies. He regularly received a manicure and paid special attention to his appearance. Foxx was handsome. He had a charismatic, toothy grin and dimples, and was happy just about all the time he was in his element—around people, especially when it had to do with baseball. He had blue eyes you could see through, and his dark hair was slicked back and parted slightly to the left side. His legs were very strong, and his chest, shoulders, and arms were masses of muscles. None of it was from daily weight lifting, but some of it was obviously from his work on the farm as a boy.

Foxx was one of the first players to wear cut off sleeves in the summer to show off his biceps—a reminder to pitchers and infielders to pay attention. A lot of pitchers still alive in the early 1990s who pitched against Foxx recalled those cut off sleeves and bulging biceps. He was an imposing sight in the batter's box.

Jim enjoyed the night life. Even though it was the Prohibition Era, ballplayers found alcoholic beverages easy to come by. Joe Hauser roomed with Foxx on some road trips in 1928 and says Jim didn't drink alcoholic beverages then. But during the early days of Prohibition, Foxx visited regularly at owner Tom Shibe's house for parties after home games.

According to Foxx's cousin Winnie Coleman, the players felt obligated by their club owner's invitation to appear at his house for cocktails after home games. Winnie would go to Jim and Helen's home in Philadelphia in the summer and stay for two weeks or so. He attended each game played by Foxx and the A's when he visited, and had a great deal of pride in his cousin's accomplishments as a baseball player. "Some of them got to drinking right sharp at those parties at Mr. Shibe's house. And I believe that Jim was one of them, too," Winnie recalled. Sometimes Foxx went to bars with his friends at Havre de Grace on the Western Shore or Betterton on the Eastern Shore during Prohibition. The bars were only open because the local sheriff had a financial interest in them.

Jimmie, Helen, and Jimmie, Jr., were making their home at 474 Kenwood Road in Drexel Park, near Philadelphia. Louise Hollett served as a live-in nurse for two-and one-half-year-old Jimmie, Jr., and Naomi Hill served as a live-in cook. The house had ten rooms, two baths, and a small yard. Jim's parents visited them often in 1932 while attending the Athletics' games at Shibe Park; Helen's parents rarely visited.

Jimmie's mother's family was larger than Dell's clan and frequently came to Shibe Park. Bessie Foxx Staats, Dell's sister, her husband, Lewis, and their son, Lewis, watched Jim chase Ruth's record, too. Young Lewis recalled many years later the image of Dell taunting the A's opposing pitcher at Shibe Park when the hurler wouldn't pitch to Jimmie. Dell wanted that record as much as his son.

It was an exciting time for the Foxx household with Jimmie chasing Babe Ruth's home-run record. Whenever possible, Helen attended home games that season. Louise and Naomi listened to the radio daily while doing their chores to find out if Jimmie would hit any homers, and Helen clipped newspaper articles about her husband when she wasn't shopping for clothes or attending a game at Shibe Park.

Foxx was idolized by young boys aspiring to be ballplayers. Gil Dunn lived in Baltimore when Jimmie was peaking as a player for the Athletics and recalled, "I looked through the box scores every day and Jimmie Foxx never disappointed me."

George Jenkins lived in Wilmington, Delaware, at the time and remembered meeting Jimmie Foxx at Shibe Park when George was the impressionable age of ten, along with Jimmie's uncle, Benton Foxx, and George's dad. George, with his father and Uncle Benton, went to see one of the guards, and Uncle Benton said, "Could you go see if Jimmie Foxx can come out here?"

George recalled, "I'll never forget the sound—I could hear the loud clanking of spikes on concrete, steel spikes." George looked up and saw his baseball idol, and his heart beat faster. Jimmie's arms looked like steel cables. He was wearing short sleeves.

Jimmie said, "Uncle Benton, how are you?"

Benton said, "Well, Jim, we come up here to see you play ball, but we don't have a ticket. And I thought maybe if I see you, why, talk to you, why, you could manage to get us in to watch you play baseball. And this is Mr. Jenkins, and . . . "

"Who's this?" said Jimmie, referring to young George. He shook young George's hand, and George claimed he didn't wash his hands for six weeks.

Jimmie said, "You just wait here and I'll be right back." He came back with box seat tickets on the first base side and two ten-dollar bills.

George recalled, years later, "Foxx creamed one that day and it looked like an aspirin tablet leaving the ballpark."

Another fan of Foxx, Oscar Eddleton, wrote:

> For some reason the dominance of the Yankees did not appeal to me in the late '20s, so that when the A's came to the front in 1929, I adopted them as my team and Jimmie Foxx as my favorite player. He was sort of a counter-balance to Ruth and Gehrig. Here was a young slugger who could play on their level and match them for hitting home runs. I also admired his strength and the tremendous distance of his homers.

In his book, *Sports in America*, author James Michener recalled Foxx being his early idol. "I must have watched this huge, square-faced boy play a hundred games, always with distinction, and he remained my favorite, same age as I."

On July 8, Foxx finally connected for his thirtieth homer after a two-week wait. According to Jimmy Isaminger, "the Broadback waved his bat and inserted his pill in the top tier of the left field seats." The homer gave Foxx as many homers as he had in all of 1931, with 76 games left to play in the season. Jimmie would have to maintain his homer pace of the first half to hit 31 more homers and surpass Ruth's record.

Dib Williams claims that Foxx aspired to pitching in a major-league game and often limbered up before games by practicing with one of the club's catchers, especially Heving. "He liked to throw knucklers and spitters and experiment with those pitches. He had a very strong arm."

On Sundays, the A's often traveled to another city for a game due to the blue laws in Philadelphia. "Connie wouldn't bring every player on the roster, but always brought Jimmie Foxx," Williams recalled. "He'd especially leave a lot of pitchers behind."

On Sunday, July 10, Mack brought only two pitchers, Krausse and Rommel, along to League Park in Cleveland, where Rommel pitched batting practice. The Indians' hitters shelled Krausse, and he lasted only one inning. "I thought Jimmie was gonna get his chance to pitch, but when Mack motioned, it was for Rommel to come in and relief pitch," recalls Williams. Rommel remained in the game to the end, despite a slugfest lasting for eighteen innings. Foxx walloped three homers, drove in eight runs, and scored the winning run in an 18-17 victory. His first homer came off Clint Brown, and two were off Wes Ferrell.

Cleveland's shortstop, Johnny Burnett, collected nine hits in eleven at bats. The Athletics' win, coupled with two losses by the Yankees to the Browns, cut New York's lead over Philadelphia to just six games.

The next day, the two teams returned to Philadelphia for a double-header, where the Indians won both games. In the second game, Foxx faced Mel Harder and again propelled a ball high over the roof of the left field stands for his thirty-fourth homer. The ball landed on Somerset Street.

Four losses in a row to the Indians at home dropped the Mackmen to fourth place, nine and one-half games behind the Yankees.

Three days later, Jimmie socked another ball onto Somerset Street without touching the roof of the left field stands for a three-run homer, his thirty-fifth, to lead the Macks over the Tigers, 9-2. Then, on July 16, Foxx and Grove led the A's to another victory over the Tigers, 14-3, as Jimmie again cleared the left field roof with a homer, "a drive for which Foxx holds the copyright, for he has done it repeatedly this season," wrote the *Inquirer*.

Foxx capped his homer-hitting binge with two more the following day off Whitlow Wyatt, leading Philadelphia over Detroit 4-3. One of the homers again cleared the left field roof. Jim had smashed eight homers over a nine-game period.

On July 18, Foxx missed a bid for another homer against the Browns when "a strong wind robbed him of number 39 in the first inning. You could actually see the wind holding the ball back and it fell in Goslin's glove," according to the *Inquirer*.

The following day, Foxx smote a wicked line drive that hit the top of the center field wall in Shibe Park and took a long bound in the direction of the right field scoreboard. Jimmie rounded the bases for an inside-the-park home run without a play at the plate. His thirty-ninth homer put him thirty-two days ahead of Ruth's 1927 pace.

Foxx smashed another tape-measure homer on July 23 off the Senators' right-hander Dick Coffman, this time into the center field bleachers of Griffith Stadium.

The next day, Foxx was the feature of an article in the *Inquirer* entitled, "Babe Ruth's Home Run Record Endangered as Foxx Continues Slugging Spree," in which Mack recalled:

As soon as I saw Foxx take his stance at the plate [for the first time] I felt sure he was going to be a great hitter. The remarkable point of Foxx's homers this year has been their "carry." He hits them as if they were shot out of a gun and the majority of them steam out of the park.

That same day, Foxx was cheered by a big crowd at Yankee Stadium every time he stepped up to the plate, but Gomez neutralized Foxx, who was hitless, and the Yankee lefty outclassed Grove, 9-3.

On the following day, the A's managed a victory over the Yankees despite Foxx's being walked four times. It was a costly win for the A's because Roger "Doc" Cramer suffered a broken collarbone when he fell hard on his left shoulder fielding Joe Sewell's hit in the sixth inning. Freitas was still walking on crutches from a foot injury from a week earlier, Bishop had been lost to the team for three weeks due to a dislocated right shoulder, and Coleman was lost to the team for the season due to a broken left ankle suffered in Cleveland in June. Pennant hopes were fading for the Mackmen.

Foxx continued to challenge Ruth's home-run record with his forty-first homer in Navin Field on July 27 against Detroit, keeping him thirty-one days ahead of Ruth's pace of 1927.

Freitas recalled, "I don't know how the fans around the league felt about Mr. Foxx, but the Philadelphia fans along with the ballplayers were pulling for him all the way to beat Ruth's record."

The following day, Jimmie held a slim lead in the batting race with a .360 batting average, compared to .357 for Dale Alexander and .346 for Heinie Manush. In 101 games played, Foxx had 139 hits in 386 at bats, while Alexander had 61 hits in 171 at bats in only 64 games played.

Detroit had traded Alexander and Roy Johnson to the Red Sox for Earl Webb on June 12. Until then, Alexander had been used only as a part-time player by the Tigers, batting 4 for 16 in 23 games.

Between July 27-August 20, Foxx hit only two homers. Years later, Jimmie recalled that he chipped a bone in his left wrist sliding into second base to break up a double play during this time and this injury hampered his power-hitting ability.

On July 30, "Evacuation Day" for League Park, home of the Indians since 1901, Philadelphia defeated Cleveland, 7-2. A bugler arose in the stands following the final out and sounded taps while the spectators, A's, and Indians stood with heads bowed, caps removed. A few sentimental tears were shed among the crowd.

The next day, the Athletics and Indians dedicated Cleveland's new, spacious Municipal Stadium before more than 80,000 fans, where Lefty Grove pitched the Macks to a 1-0 victory. Foxx couldn't tally a homer in the spacious new park and was still at forty-one homers. The outfield fence in Municipal Stadium was only 322 feet from home plate along the foul lines, but was 435 feet to the power alleys and 470 feet to deepest center field, while League Park was 370 feet along the left field line, 467 feet to the deepest corner just left of center field, but only 290 feet to the right field corner.

Jim collected his forty-second homer on August 5, a clout into the center field bleachers of Sportsman's Park; he was still twenty-three days ahead of Ruth. But sportswriters varied on his chances to break the record. Shirley Povich wrote in an August 10 article in the *Washington Post*, "The Philadelphia slugger must maintain better than his present average if he is to eclipse Ruth's record. If Foxx fails in his quest for Ruth's record by two or three homers, he may be able to blame his failure on the fact the Indians moved into their new home."

Isaminger published an interview with Foxx just two days later in the *Inquirer*, with Foxx saying:

> I don't want to make any predictions, but I think I'm equal to smashing 19 more homers during the remaining games of the season, providing I am not hurt [the injured wrist was not mentioned so that it may not have occurred yet]. I hope to cop a few in Boston and make up for my western delinquency.

Jim, called "Muscles" by the Athletic players, had managed only two homers in twelve games of the western road trip. Isaminger blamed adverse winds for Foxx not getting three or four more homers on the trip.

Foxx was homerless in a single game and a doubleheader at Boston on August 12 and 13 but hit safely twice in each game of the twinbill on August 13, despite having a tooth removed that morning. The following day, Foxx hit a long homer over the center field wall in Fenway Park in the third inning of the first game of another doubleheader. He barely missed another in the first game when his first-inning triple struck the right field wall only one foot from the top.

After five homerless games, Jim regained his home-run stroke and drove a ball into the upper deck of left-center during the A's 6-4 loss to the White Sox at Shibe Park in the first game of a doubleheader on August 20.

A minor homer slump for Jim in August was halted at the insistence of his wife, Helen, while she was confined to a hospital bed in St. Joseph's Hospital in Philadelphia. During a homestand, Jim was visiting Helen every day after the games, bringing her books and flowers, but Helen said, "He kept forgetting to bring reports of home run drives, so I told him to get busy and make some home runs." Foxx responded to his wife's orders with three homers in a week.

In a picture with several of his teammates about this time on the front cover of the *Inquirer*, Foxx was the only player with short sleeves. Jim often wore his sleeves clipped to the shoulders because he claimed to have greater freedom of arm movement for extra batting power.

Foxx started another mini-homer spree with homers in three consecutive games at Shibe Park on August 24, 25, and 26. The homer on August 25 cleared the left field roof to become another souvenir on Somerset Street.

Foxx's forty-eighth homer on August 30 clinched a 6-4 victory over Detroit for Grove's twenty-first win of the season. This shot cleared the right field barrier at Shibe Park with many feet to spare and landed on the roof of a dwelling on 20th Street. Since Foxx's forty-eighth homer came in the A's 130th game, he needed to hit a homer in every other game for the rest of the season (12 homers in 24 games) to tie Ruth. Foxx's lower homer production (7) in August meant he had to hit 12 homers in September to tie Ruth and 13 to set a new record. He had already hit 12 homers in one month twice and 13 homers in a month once during the season.

In early September, *The Sporting News* reported that Dale Alexander had forged ahead of Jimmie Foxx in the race for the batting championship. With Alexander having played in 104 games through September 4, the most games he could appear in by the end of the season was 120, whereas Foxx was on track to play 154 games, especially if his pursuit of Ruth went all the way to the wire.

The Sporting News noted, "It has been the position of the league statisticians and league presidents for some time that a player taking part in two-thirds of the regular schedule of games shall be accorded consideration in the batting award. . . . " But what if a given player was a pinch hitter in a lot of those games?

On September 6, Charles Durning, former Phillies' outfielder, announced through the *Salisbury Times* that Foxx and Cochrane would be heading a team of major-league All-Stars to play an exhibition game in Salisbury, Maryland, on September 26, the day after the end of the regular season. Other A's players who were expected to be in the visitors' lineup included Max Bishop, Bing Miller, Lew Krausse, and Eddie Madjeski. Also slated for the visitors' lineup was Denny Sothern, former pitcher for Salisbury of the Eastern Shore League and outfielder for the Phillies and Dodgers. An advance ticket sale at hotels, newsstands, and drug and cigar stores in various towns along the Eastern Shore made the pasteboards available to fans of Jimmie Foxx all over the "sho'." Anytime Foxx returned to the Shore to play baseball, it was big news, and his rise in stature as the top major-league player in the 1932 season made him an even bigger attraction for this game. The *Salisbury Times* referred to him as the 1932 AL Sultan of Swat, an indisputable claim.

Bill Dooly pointed out in a September 15 article in *The Sporting News* that Foxx, being right-handed, did not have the benefit of any short fences. "Nowhere in the league can one hit a cheap homer to left." Actually, the outfield fence at Fenway Park—in the left field corner—was just a bit closer (7 feet) to home plate than the right field corner in 1932. But the outfield corners in right field were closer to home plate than the left field corners that season for Sportsman's Park (41 feet), Griffith Stadium (87 feet), League Park (84 feet), Yankee Stadium (5 feet), and Shibe Park (3 feet). The greater differences in several AL parks heavily favored left-handed power hitters over right-handed sluggers. Comiskey Park in Chicago was the only AL park with equal distances in all fields.

Dooly went a step further in his rationalization for Foxx possibly falling short of Ruth's record. He suggested that when Ruth hit his seventeen homers in September 1927, "in many cases, the hurlers tossed fat ones down the slot just to see how far the Babe would drive them. But the same gentlemen have yet to throw down there to learn how far Foxx may slap it." Dooly didn't reveal the source of his information or, if he was only speculating, he didn't give a reason.

Foxx didn't seem rattled or the least bit nervous about chasing Ruth's record, even while playing against the reigning homer champion. The Yankees arrived at Shibe Park on September 21, and Foxx had only five games left in which to catch Ruth, almost a hopeless task.

It's a sure bet Ruth was not rooting for Foxx that afternoon. The Babe had plenty of pride in his homer-hitting feats, especially his major league single-season homer mark. Ruth had set and reset the single-season homer mark four times from 1919-27, with totals of 29, 54, 59, and 60. After smacking his sixtieth homer in the final Yankees' game of 1927, Ruth shouted triumphantly in the locker room, "60, count 'em, 60! Let's see some other son-of-a-bitch match that!"

Only five seasons had passed since Ruth's accomplishment, and Foxx was indeed challenging Ruth's mark. Ruth was now thirty-seven, well past his prime and aware that he could not improve his single-season homer mark. He watched as Foxx socked his fifty-fourth homer off the Yankees' hard-throwing Red Ruffing at Shibe Park on September 21. Only 7,000 fans were on hand with the pennant already clinched by New York, and Ruth must have wondered, "Even if this young fellow Foxx doesn't break my record this year, isn't it just a matter of time before he does?"

On September 22, Foxx further threatened Ruth's mark. Jimmie slugged two more homers against the Yankees to tie Hack Wilson for the major-league record for right-handed batters set two years earlier. John Nolan described Foxx's first homer of the day in the *Evening Bulletin*:

> The bases were jammed in the third and Gomez who had beaten the A's seven times this season was serving on the mound. Gomez got two strikes on Foxx after first driving him back with a swift pitch around the shins. Jimmy braced himself at the plate, took a grip and

swung from far in the rear. He guessed it would be an outside pitch and his full power was behind the drive that sent the ball zooming over the right field wall just south of the scoreboard.

The fans gave a thunderous ovation for Foxx's grand slam as Ruth, the Yankees, and A's watched him round the bases. Jim added to his lusty homer total by hitting number fifty-six in the seventh inning off relief specialist Wilcy (Cy) Moore.

Although Ruth, still recovering from a recent illness, watched Foxx hit his fifty-fifth homer, he was already on his way back to New York by train by the time Foxx hit his fifty-sixth later in the same game. That day the *New York Herald Tribune* called Foxx "the pretender to Ruth's home-run crown."

On September 23, Frank Baker said, "You are looking at a young man out there who is going to out-Ruth Ruth one of these days," referring to Jimmie Foxx. An article opined that with only three games left to play (after September 22) it seemed unlikely Foxx would break Ruth's record. "I'll grant you that," said Baker, "but the mere fact that he came so close as he did this year is indicative of what you can expect of him in years to come."

Baker was no stranger to Ruth. In one of the two years that Baker and Ruth were teammates, Baker saw Ruth hit fifty-nine homers in 1921, adding credibility to Baker's prediction.

On September 23, Foxx crept within one point of recapturing the batting lead from Alexander, but failed to hit a homer.

Then on September 24, Jimmie hit his fifty-seventh homer off the Senators' Bill McAfee at Shibe Park. It was another grand slam in his next-to-last game of the season and set a new single-season major league record for home runs by a right-handed batter.

Following the game, Foxx was in a "half-study," gazing at his locker, putting on his clothes as he was interviewed by Cy Peterman of the *Evening Bulletin.*

Peterman: "Well, Jimmy, a big year . . . "

Foxx: "The biggest I ever had in my life," he smiled back happily.

Peterman: "Any regrets now that you look back on the season, a drive here or there that may have gone in [over the fence for a homer]?"

Foxx shook his head. "I got my share," he said simply. "I might have done better here and there along the line, but there's satisfaction to know I was trying."

Foxx realized that the chances of hitting two or three homers in his last game the next day were remote, at best.

The following day, Foxx slugged his fifty-eighth homer in the last game of the season at Griffith Stadium. It was the A's only run, and it came off Alvin Crowder, the league's winningest pitcher. Thus Foxx added to his single-season major-league record for right-handed sluggers.

Jimmie ended the season just three points below Boston's Alexander in the AL batting race with an average of .364, preventing him from winning the Triple Crown for leadership in homers, runs batted in, and batting average. On September 26, the day after the regular season, Irvin Howe, official AL statistician, checked and double-checked his record books and concluded that Dale Alexander was the AL batting champion "by 32 thousandths of a percent" (.3673 to .3641) over Foxx. An Associated Press story reported that Howe had never been wrong in naming a batting champion in his twenty-two years as the league's statistician. The article also asserted that "there is no hard and fast rule" in the number of games a player must compete in to be eligible for the batting title, but Howe fixes it at a 100 or more games. So, for diehard fans of Foxx, a slim chance remained that a final check of all box scores, once official, would indicate Foxx was the batting champion.

While sportswriters and officials debated who was the regular season AL batting champion, Foxx and Cochrane arrived by airplane at Hebron Airport near Salisbury on September 26, just before noon. A 2:00 P.M. starting time for their game in Salisbury left little time for Jimmie and Mickey to banter with anyone. Although Bishop, Miller, Krausse, Madjeski, and Sothern did not show for the game, Foxx's team featured Cochrane at catcher, Jack Ogden in right field, and Rube Walberg and Red Sox rookie Ed Carroll as pitchers. The biggest name on the local Salisbury club was Dick Porter.

Foxx had an uncanny knack for pleasing his fans on the Shore. In his first at bat, he thrilled the crowd, clubbing a long homer over the center field wall with Cochrane on base in the first inning. Jim had three hits in four at bats and pitched the eighth and ninth innings, giving up two runs in his team's 13-4 win. Ever the showman, Foxx played at first base, catcher, and pitcher.

Almost immediately following the game, Jimmie and Mickey left Hebron Airport by plane for Philadelphia, meeting their wives before catching a train there for Chicago that evening, presumably to attend the Yankee-Cubs World Series games to be played at Wrigley Field.

The day after the regular season ended, Alexander's record was official through September 20 and Foxx's was official through September 16. Unfortunately for Foxx, Howe checked official records for the remainder of the season for Foxx and Alexander as they became available in October and confirmed that Alexander was the winner of the batting title by the same margin indicated on September 26.

Years later, Foxx was interviewed during his retirement and insisted he was more interested in winning the AL batting title in 1932 than in breaking Ruth's single-season homer record. Foxx felt little remorse. He had produced some of the best hitting statistics ever combined by a batter in one season, yet he barely fell short of two lofty goals—the batting title and Ruth's homer mark. Alexander had 392 at bats, 61 bases on balls, and 1 hit by a pitch for 454 plate appearances. He would not have qualified for the batting championship for most years after 1945. Before 1945, a player simply had to appear in 100 games; from 1945-56, he had to have 400 or more at bats; and beginning in 1957, he had to have a total of at least 3.1 plate appearances for every scheduled game (477 appearances for a 154-game schedule and 502 appearances for a 162-game schedule).

On September 26, the *Sporting News* announced that Foxx was chosen as the Most Valuable Player for the American League. He outdistanced Gehrig by 56-47 points. The strength of Gehrig's point total relied partly on the fact he was on a pennant winner.

But Foxx would have gladly traded the award for another pennant for the A's. The Yankees gained an early lead over the Mackmen in 1932, playing the toughest part of their schedule early and never giving much ground to Philadelphia during the season. New York was bolstered by Gomez's 24 wins, an 18-7 season by Ruffing, a comeback by Pipgras (16-9), and right-hander Johnny Allen's sensational rookie season (17-4). Ruth, Gehrig, Combs, Lazzeri, Dickey, and Chapman contributed heavily to the Yankees' .286 team batting average and 160-homer attack.

Meanwhile, the A's received heavy pitching support from Grove (25-10), Earnshaw (19-13), and Walberg (17-10), but the big three for the A's won eleven fewer games and lost ten more games in 1932 than in 1931. Freitas made up for the loss of Hoyt, but Mahaffey had an off year and Rommel was not able to contribute as much as he had in 1931. The big difference for the A's was that they allowed an average of one more earned run per game in 1932 than in 1931. The Mackmen actually scored 123 more runs during the 1932 season and led the AL in homers with 172 and batting with a .290 mark.

Despite a star-studded lineup and a second-place finish, revenues for the Athletics continued to plummet from 1931-32, and Mack began the painful process of selling some of his most coveted property to try to keep the franchise financially solvent. On September 28, Athletic players and fans were saddened to read that Simmons, Dykes, and Haas had been sold to the White Sox for a reported total amount varying from $100,000-$150,000. Simmons had led the league in batting in 1930 and 1931 and had batted a cumulative .358 for the Athletics from 1924-32.

Although Simmons' average had fallen off to .323 in 1932, he still managed to finish in a tie for second in the league in runs batted in with

151. But the *New York Times* reported: "Rumors had been current during the summer that Simmons was playing his last season with the Athletics."

Some fans in Philadelphia felt that Simmons' performance suffered because of "the praise heaped on Jimmie Foxx, his successor for premier batting honors in this city and the new idol of the Athletic followers."

Foxx led the league in homers, runs batted in, total bases (438), slugging percentage (.749), and runs scored (151). He played in all the Athletics' games, 141 at first base and 13 at third base.

Foxx hit 13 homers off left-handers and 45 off right-handers during the season; he hit 31 homers at Shibe Park and 27 during road trips. Since most pitchers in the league were right-handed, Foxx had to face a larger proportion of hurlers that threw their curveballs on the outside of the plate, compared to left-handed batters like Ruth and Gehrig.

Foxx batted fifth in the order almost every game of the season, as he had done for most of the previous three seasons for Mack. He probably had fifteen to thirty less plate appearances during the season than he would have had if he had batted third or fourth in the order.

On the eve of the World Series, Lefty Gomez was still smarting from some of Foxx's homers off him during the regular season. "I've developed a deep-rooted hatred for Foxx. He hit two of the longest home runs I've ever seen—and they were both off me. Facing the Cubs—if I face them—will be a vacation after battling with that assassin."

While Foxx and Cochrane and their wives were still in Chicago for the World Series, the *Los Angeles Times* touted the upcoming appearance of Jimmie, Mickey, NL batting champion Frank (Lefty) O'Doul, and others who were to appear at Wrigley Field in Los Angeles for an exhibition game against an "All-Stars" aggregation from the Hollywood and Los Angeles clubs of the Pacific Coast League.

The Yankees completed a four-game sweep of the Chicago Cubs on October 2, and series shares were announced for other first division clubs in the AL and NL the following day. Because the A's were slated to receive close to $30,000, Foxx knew as early as October 3 that he had another $1,000 in earnings.

The Foxxes and Cochranes arrived at Grand Central Airport in Glendale on the evening of October 3. The full contingent of major-league players arrived in time for the October 4 game and included Jimmy Reese (2b), George Puccinelli (lf), Wally Berger (cf), Johnny Vergez (3b), Gordon Slade (ss), and pitchers Ted Lyons and Fay Thomas. O'Doul and Berger were former Pacific Coast leaguers, adding to the interest of local fans. Before the night contest, O'Doul and former major-league outfielder Arnold "Jigger" Statz offered their slants from the pitching mound to Foxx, who local scribes said was "bigger, broader, and better than three years earlier." Jimmie powdered batting practice pitches "to all fields and jolted a few over the left and center field walls."

But the major leaguers found night baseball and the pitching of Hal Stitzel from the Los Angeles Angels and former major leaguer Tom Sheehan not to their liking, losing, 7-1. Jim was hitless in the game, to the disappointment of the fans, and the *Los Angeles Times* wondered sarcastically if the Los Angeles area really wanted a major-league franchise, after all.

The next morning Foxx and Cochrane and their wives arrived at the Oakland Airport from Los Angeles as the ocean liner *Maui* was set to leave San Francisco for Honolulu. A small airplane was pressed into service to carry the two couples from Oakland to San Francisco. The short airplane flight was followed by a taxicab ride to the boat's gangplank, which was being drawn up as Foxx and Cochrane arrived.

In mid-October, the Baseball Writers' Association picked Foxx as the AL's Most Valuable Player over Gehrig by a 75-55 count. Indeed, his assault on Ruth's single-season home-run record and near Triple Crown season made him the deserving winner of the award.

After the two-game set in Honolulu on October 9 and 11, Herb Hunter, O'Doul, Lyons, and Moe Berg continued on to Japan to coach several university teams there, while Foxx and the rest of the players returned home. Shortly after returning to Philadelphia, Foxx was back to one of his other favorite pastimes. Jim hosted Eddie Collins, Bing Miller, Doc Cramer, and Lew Krausse at his parents' farm in Sudlersville late in November in between "treks in the woods," probably hunting for squirrel and game birds. Jim was ever the "social animal," enjoying the company of ballplayers. At the same time, Dick Porter entertained hunters Joe Boley, Max Bishop, Joe Vosmik, and Johnny Burnett at his lodge at nearby Princess Anne.

Near the end of 1932, Fred Lieb wrote an article in *The Sporting News* that in part revisited Foxx's accomplishments of the past season, especially his fifty-eight homers. Lieb, like many other sportswriters and fans, was still in awe of Jim's challenge of Ruth's record. Fred marveled, "I did not believe the present generation of fans would live to see Ruth's mark threatened."

Foxx offered an interesting alibi for not breaking Ruth's record in Lieb's article. Jim pointed out that had the wire fence (21.5 feet high) not been erected on top of the 11.5-foot high concrete wall in front of the right field pavilion in Sportsman's Park in 1929, he would have passed Ruth's record by four homers. Foxx claimed he hit six balls against that screen in 1932 that would have been homers in 1927.

Still, several questions can be asked on Ruth's behalf. How many long fly outs by Ruth in 1927, or even in the season he hit fifty-nine homers, fell just shy of going over the fence, especially in the spacious power alleys of Yankee Stadium?

There is no doubt, however, that Foxx had managed to set himself above every other former and current home-run slugger of his time by amassing such a high single-season homer total—second only to Babe Ruth. It ensured that the comparisons between Foxx and Ruth would continue. Although Jim occasionally felt pressure from the expectations of fans and the press, he still loved playing the game.

9

FOXX AT THE TOP OF HIS GAME

Foxx's outstanding 1932 season triggered continued speculation in *The Sporting News* about his chances of breaking Babe Ruth's single-season home-run mark. But hot-stove-league discussions on this and other matters were interrupted on January 2 with news that Kid Gleason had succumbed to heart disease after a lengthy illness.

Gleason had managed the Chicago White Sox from 1919 through 1923. The Kid watched his heavily favored team lose the 1919 World Series to the Cincinnati Reds with more than a little bit of suspicion and then lost eight key players accused of throwing that Series in the final week of the 1920 pennant chase, which enabled the Indians to edge out the White Sox for the AL flag. The Kid had joined the Athletics in 1926 and stayed with them through 1931, resigning from the club before the 1932 season due to health problems. He was extremely well liked by the players. Foxx enjoyed a pregame fielding drill with Gleason in which the Kid would hit hard one-hoppers that Foxx would snare and then rifle to third to nip an imaginary runner.

The Athletics' management and fans had reason to be concerned about the Mackmen's chances to rebound in 1933. The sale of Simmons, Haas, and Dykes to Chicago would probably weaken a team already facing question marks about the pitching staff. Several outstanding rookie prospects who starred with Portland of the Pacific Coast League in 1932 were being invited to spring training by Mack. They included infielder Mike Higgins and outfielders Lou Finney and Bob Johnson.

Connie Mack blamed the old blue laws in Philadelphia for the failure of the team to finish out of the red in 1932. He maintained that Sunday ball games would have provided the difference in revenue needed to avoid selling Simmons, Haas, and Dykes to the White Sox. Still, the Pennsylvania legislature wouldn't budge. Other major-league cities except Pittsburgh had already approved baseball on Sunday. In fact, Chicago, Cincinnati, and St. Louis permitted Sunday baseball as early as 1902. Cleveland, Detroit, and Washington, D.C., legalized Sunday baseball by 1918, with New York following suit in 1919 and Boston in 1929.

Some sportswriters and other observers, including Babe Ruth, claimed that the loss of Simmons from the A's lineup would remove considerable protection for Jimmie Foxx, resulting in a substantial increase in walks and less homers for the A's slugger in the coming season. Was the Babe a little worried about this young upstart beating his home-run record?

Foxx claimed he was not worried about the loss of Simmons, at least in terms of its effects on the frequency that pitchers would walk him. He felt that just about any replacement for Al would be less prolific at reaching base, especially with doubles and triples, so he would receive fewer intentional walks. Foxx reasoned that without Simmons, first base would be left open with men in scoring position less often when he batted. Sportswriter Stoney McLinn agreed. He said that Foxx would probably receive less bases on balls without Simmons in the lineup because first base would be left open with a man on second or third base less often.

But one thing was certain—the Mackmen as a team would miss Al's lusty bat. He had averaged 150 runs batted in per season from 1929-32. Quite possibly, Jim's runs batted in count would decrease.

Meanwhile, power-hitting Bob Johnson was the chief hope as a replacement for Simmons in producing runs along with Foxx. Many of the Athletics warmed up before a game mostly through running, but Foxx and Johnson liked to wrestle each other standing up, to limber up.

While Earnshaw was predicting that the Yankees would have the pennant sewed up by July 4, Grove and Foxx remained positive and forecasted that "the A's will be in the fight to the finish, in the thick of things." Both Grove and Foxx were weary of the Senators as the dark horse of the league.

Just before they left for Florida, Foxx and most of the Athletics were among the 500 attendees at a farewell testimonial banquet at the Penn Athletic Club of Philadelphia to send off Jimmy Dykes to Chicago. Among the attendees was Mike Drennan, still scouting for the A's as he did in 1917, when he obtained Dykes, and 1924, when he purchased Foxx from Frank Baker.

Foxx, Cochrane, Krausse, and Grove motored to Florida early in February to catch a few rounds of golf before spring training began. The attitude of baseball players had changed since Cobb had retired. Many top batsmen, including Foxx, Ruth, Gehrig, and Klein, were ardent golfers. Cobb had preached "that the stance and swing of the two sports were so different that a batsman would be ruined by serious work on the links."

The Mackmen had their first workout at Terry Field in Ft. Myers on March 1 with both a morning and afternoon session. Within a few days, the Regulars and Yannigans were scrimmaging almost daily. On March 9, Foxx, playing for the Regulars, walloped an eye-opening long-distance shot off Merritt "Sugar" Cain, a four bagger over the center field wall behind the signboard at Terry Field. Longtime onlookers described the homer as the longest hit in the nine-year history of the ball field, and the *Fort Myers News Press* noted the ball traveled 500 feet. The center field wall itself was painted dark green to provide a good "hitter's background" for seeing baseballs leave the pitcher's hand. The center field wall looks from pictures to have been 12-15 feet high, so Foxx's homer had to go over that barrier and another 50 feet beyond the base of the wall.

Foxx entered spring training feeling good about his chances for breaking Ruth's single-season homer mark. A picture of Foxx smiling in his warmup jacket while sitting on the bench in the dugout at Fort Myers appeared in the March 14 issue of the *Philadelphia Inquirer* and was titled, "Maybe It Will be 61." The caption below the picture noted: ". . . that Foxx's feat of 58 homers the previous season greatly inspired 'Sir James' and he feels confident he can whack the apple hard enough to get 61 4-ply [4-base] blasts before brown October comes and chases the players off the diamonds."

Foxx's home run and runs batted in production in 1932 gained him wide coverage in baseball periodicals. He appeared on the front covers of the February 1933 issue of *Baseball Magazine, The Sporting News* Record Book of 1933, and the *Famous Slugger Yearbook of 1933* published by Hillerich and Bradsby.

On March 16, an Associated Press photo captured Foxx and Chuck Klein posing in the right-handed and left-handed batter's boxes, respectively, at the Phillies' spring training field in Winter Haven, Florida. The picture was entitled, "Home-Run Kings Prepare for Coming Season." While Foxx had led the AL in homers in 1932, Klein tied Mel Ott for the NL lead that season and led his league in homers, outright, in 1929 and 1931. Foxx and Klein had battled annually from 1929-32 for home-run honors in Philadelphia (with some occasional competition from Simmons), much the way Jimmie and Gehrig competed annually for bragging rights as the top first baseman in the AL. During that four-year span, Foxx smacked 158 homers and Klein hit 162. In 1932, both Klein and Foxx had been named MVP, Klein in the NL and Foxx in the AL. They were the chief box office attractions for their respective teams.

Foxx hit consistently in spring training exhibition games during 1933. In one game against the Montreal club of the IL, he thrilled spectators in Orlando, Florida, with two "huge homers that traveled far from the plate."

On March 19 in Tampa, what looked like an easy grounder from the Reds' first baseman Jim Bottomley's bat took a bad hop and bruised Foxx's left shoulder for a double. Jim was removed from the game in the fourth inning. When Foxx climbed into the team bus that night, his arm was limp with intense pain.

Foxx sat out the scrimmage between the A's and The House of David the next day at Terry Field and worked out only for a moment the following day. Doc Ebeling asserted that he wouldn't return to first base for another five days or so.

Foxx unexpectedly returned to the lineup the very next day, on March 22. He didn't like missing games, not even in spring training. Jimmie pleaded with Mack to put him in the lineup, even though he could not swing a bat properly. "I might not hit so much as a foul, but I need the work." Mack complied and Foxx singled, doubled, and tripled, driving in three runs to pace the A's over the Reds, 7-6 at Fort Myers.

Jim suffered a spike wound on his left shin inflicted by the Cardinals' catcher, Jimmy Wilson, on a play at the plate on March 27. He, Eric McNair, and Ed Coleman received permission to leave camp early and head north for Philadelphia, despite two remaining games scheduled with the Dodgers in Florida. Mack figured, probably with the advice of Doc Ebeling, that Foxx needed a few days away from baseball action.

Jim visited his family and friends in Sudlersville and Crumpton on his way north on March 30, arriving in Philadelphia in time for the beginning of the annual City Series between the A's and Phillies.

Foxx's leg benefitted from a few days rest, because he was able to play in all four games of the Series, batting 6 for 16 with six runs batted in. He then played against the Newark Bears of the IL on April 9, but missed the final exhibition game the next day against the Dodgers at Ebbets Field.

On April 11, Foxx was again treated for swelling of the spike wound on his left shin. The infection caused him to miss the season opener for the A's, a road game in Washington the following day (which was Joe Cronin's managerial debut with the Senators and a 4-1 victory over the A's). Foxx joined the lineup the following day, but the Macks lost again, 11-4. Jim said, "This latest daub on my leg will make it necessary to do some real home run hitting, and then I can walk around the diamond." Grove salvaged the final game of the series for the A's, 8-1.

When Jim played for the A's against the Yankees in New York on April 15, "his left leg was still heavily encased in a bandage." Although Foxx and Ruth were opponents, they certainly admired each other's accomplishments and even traded bats on occasion, as they did during the first series of the season between the A's and Yankees. During batting practice, Ruth and Gehrig watched the A's while Ruth held a yellow bat in his hands.

"Just swapped with Foxx," Ruth said. "He says he has had this [bat] home for two years, but it looks as if it was going to crack on me."

Foxx came to the plate and hit two in the left field stands in Yankee Stadium, and then one on the running track.

"Better keep that stick," bellowed the Babe. "Throw the other one back."

Foxx grinned at Ruth, picked up a bat, and tossed it toward the Yankee's dugout. The Babe had given him the choice of two of his own sticks.

As the season began, *The Sporting News* announced that "beer, long barred in polite society was back again." It was expected that the only parks that wouldn't be selling beer for the 1933 season were Philadelphia (both teams), Pittsburgh, and Washington. There would be no beer and no Sunday games for the Shibe Park faithful.

In the A's home opener on April 20, Foxx smashed two homers off the Senators' Walter Stewart, the first landing on the roof of the left field pavilion and the second clearing the roof.

Meanwhile, a new twenty-foot screen was connected to the left field fence in Navin Field. The Athletics called this the "Jimmie Foxx spite fence." Foxx had hit nine homers in Navin Field in 1932, making it his favorite target on the road.

Late in April, *The Sporting News* was either making reference to an actual injury that Jimmie inflicted on a third baseman while he was batting or the general fear he created for third basemen around the American League. "That third baseman down South [spring training] who played 'in' for Jimmie Foxx's bunt is now able to walk from the porch to the front gate."

Everybody agreed that Foxx consistently hit the ball very hard. Ken Keltner, third baseman for the Indians in the late 1930s and early 1940s, said, "I played Jimmie deep and close to the third base line." Rusty Peters, former part-time AL third baseman and utility infielder in the late 1930s for the Athletics and the 1940s for the Indians, said, "Foxx could cripple a third baseman, as hard as he could hit." Former Tiger shortstop Billy Rogell says of Foxx, "I admired his power. He undressed me more than once with his hard-hit balls, one hop in front of me—nothing I could do with the ball. I was completely handcuffed."

Vern Kennedy recalled that Foxx hit the ball so hard back to southpaw Emil Bildilli that Emil's glove was knocked completely off his hand as Jimmie trotted down to first base, chuckling all the way.

Foxx led the Athletics in a 16-10 win over the Red Sox at Fenway Park on April 24, driving in seven runs, batting 5 for 5 with three singles, a double, and a homer. His homer off Paul Andrews was a rare opposite field hit. Through the month of April only Grove pitched effectively for Mack. Walberg, Earnshaw, and Freitas had very little success, which explains the A's 6-9 record for the month.

It wasn't long after Jim's "Ruth-like" homer season of 1932 that someone capitalized on his rising popularity by choosing him to give expert advice on batting. Late in May, *The Sporting News* announced that Foxx was the author of a book, *How I Bat*, published by the Courier-Citizen Company and edited by Bill Cunningham of the *Boston Post* and George C. Carens, Austen R. Lake, and A. Linde Fowler of the *Boston Transcript* for "Bill

Cunningham's Sports Series." For fifteen cents, boys could buy a copy of Foxx's instructional booklet loaded with pointers for better hitting, advice he had received from various other major leaguers, and events earlier in his career that influenced his development as a batter.

Whereas Jim recalled in a 1929 *Time* magazine article how he developed his upper-body strength from various chores on the farm, he discussed the origin of his strong wrists and their importance in hitting in *How I Bat*.

> When I was a little lad part of my job around the family farm at Sudlersville, Maryland, was to help milk our herd of cows. And from the time my chubby fists were large enough to perform the trick, and my knees strong enough to hold a 2-gallon pail, I sat under the stern end of our cows and milked until my wrists were sore and my fingers stiff. Then, of course, there was plowing to be done in the Spring and Fall so that, hired help being scarce, I took my turn with that, too. I can now drive a baseball so much farther than the average distance and that is why I have stated that I believe a strong pair of wrists is the most important factor in batting.

Foxx emphasized ten of the "fine points in batting" in his book.

1. Pick out the type and weight of bat that best suits your needs
2. Discover the spot in the batter's box which will allow you to cover the plate, both inside and out
3. Study your batting stride to see whether your style of swing requires a long step, a short one, or no step at all
4. Don't bring your bat too far back before you start to swing
5. Follow through and give the last part of your swing all the room it needs
6. Watch the ball from the moment it leaves the pitcher's hand until the time the bat makes contact
7. Relax, so that your muscles are loose from your ankles to your shoulders
8. Watch the shifting of fielders to get a hint on location of the next pitch
9. Be quick getting out of the batter's box after you hit the ball
10. Hit the ball "out in front" at the top of your swing.

It's unknown how many boys were influenced by Foxx's book and how wide a circulation it received. But Jim was at the peak of his popularity, having replaced Ruth as the AL homer king and coming so close to setting a new single-season homer record. Many boys, especially those living in major-league cities, probably bought a copy.

On May 26, Foxx scored the lone run in a defeat at the hands of Lynn "Schoolboy" Rowe, but twisted his knee while eluding Tiger catcher Ray

Hayworth at the plate. He left the game after only one plate appearance and missed the next two games for the Athletics.

Hayworth played briefly for the Tigers in 1926 and 1929 and stayed with Detroit from 1930-37, playing eight games with that club in 1938. Ray saw Foxx play often and recalled that

> Jimmie had been wearing us out in one game when I told Tiger pitcher Vic Sorrell to try a changeup since we hadn't used that pitch. Foxx smacked the changeup beyond the flagpole in center field in Navin Field about a dozen rows back. We never offered Foxx a changeup again. Jimmie Foxx was always very friendly, very likeable, never kicked up any dust, just went about his work. Jimmie whistled a little ditty or hummed a tune as he came to the plate before he stepped into the batter's box. I guess he just did that to relax a little bit before he began batting, and I think it worked.

When Foxx returned to the A's lineup on May 30 for a doubleheader, the injury may have still bothered him. Jim went 0 for 8 against Boston.

At the same time, Earnshaw was no longer the dependable right-handed ace he had been in 1929-31, and his decline in performance was blamed partially on lack of conditioning. His troubles with Mack culminated in a $500 fine and ten-day suspension beginning on June 3 "for reporting to the ball park today in no condition to play." A few days later, George publicly declared that Mack "did exactly right" and began to work himself back in shape, but he never regained his championship form, although he was only thirty-three.

Jim batted only 2 for 13 against New York in a four-game series at Yankee Stadium during the first week in June, striking out eight times as the A's lost all four games. Still, Foxx managed to shine, albeit only in batting practice, according to the *Inquirer*: "In batting practice, Jimmy Foxx hit a ball to the tenth row of the far-off left field bleachers. This was never done in a game and not even in practice before."

Jim was ready to avenge his poor showing at the plate less than a week later as the Yankees arrived in Philadelphia for another four-game set beginning on June 8. The first game of the series was played in record high-temperatures in the upper 90s. Jim flexed his biceps and gunned down one of his favorite victims, smacking three consecutive homers off Lefty Gomez in his first three trips to the plate. While he was a difficult hurler for most AL batters to solve, Gomez often was easy pickings for Foxx. Following his homers in the second, fourth, and fifth innings, Jim failed in his final two plate appearances to reach reliever Wilcy Moore for a record-tying fourth homer in one game. Moore retired Jim on a grounder in the seventh and walked him in the eighth.

Combined with the homer that he had hit the previous day in his last official at bat against the Senators, Foxx tied the major-league record of four consecutive home runs in four consecutive at bats. Jimmie's 5 runs batted in in the first game of the A's-Yankees series gave him 10 rbi's in his last two games.

Jimmie's home-run display on June 8 overshadowed single homers by Ruth and Gehrig and enabled the A's to beat the Yankees, 14-10. It was the Macks' first victory over New York in 1933 after eight straight defeats. The record heat wave continued as Foxx homered once the following day, giving him five home runs in three consecutive games, but the A's lost to New York, 7-6. The heat was so overwhelming that A's starter Jim Peterson collapsed after throwing just four pitches and Yankees' starter Walter Brown passed out in the dugout after the fifth inning.

The Athletics declared the next day, June 10, "Jimmie Foxx Day" at Shibe Park. A crowd of 33,000-35,000 tolerated the persistent heat wave to witness heavy hitting by the Yankees and Athletics in a doubleheader. Ruth threatened to steal the show from Foxx with two homers off Grove in the opener, but Philadelphia won, 9-5.

Both teams were called out onto the playing field between games of the doubleheader to line up along the foul lines while Foxx was honored at home plate. Eddie Pollock, President of the Philadelphia chapter of the Baseball Writers' Association, presented a chest of silver to Jimmie in recognition of his 1932 AL Most Valuable Player award.

Jim had often grabbed the spotlight in games that were important to his club or had personal significance. He showcased his slugging in the second game of the doubleheader by smacking a homer in an 8-7 victory by the A's. The home crowd had visitors from Sudlersville, and his performance and receipt of the MVP award made his towns folk beam with pride and admiration as they left the ball park and returned home to tell others about their native son.

Foxx reignited with another power surge a couple of weeks later, just before the first All-Star game ever to be played, hitting single homers in four successive games, June 27-30. Then, after two homerless games, he again defied record-high temperatures in a doubleheader against St. Louis on July 2, where he exploded for four more homers. The doubleheader at Sportsman's Park was played in temperatures exceeding 100 degrees, but no matter to Foxx. Jimmie smacked two homers in the first game and then impressed all onlookers with two more homers, a double, and a triple in the second game, for 21 total bases in the doubleheader. Both the double and triple were said to carry more than 400 feet on the fly before striking the outfield fence. Foxx had come ever so close to an unprecedented six home runs in a doubleheader. In the 6-game series with the Browns at St.

Louis, Foxx had 6 singles, 4 doubles, 1 triple, and 6 homers, for 41 total bases in 26 at bats.

The *Chicago Tribune* conducted a fan poll for the All-Star team selections, and voters had the difficult choice of Lou Gehrig vs. Jimmie Foxx for AL starting first baseman. Jimmie's dominance over all batters in the AL in 1932 was not enough to overtake Gehrig's reputation which was built over a longer period of time. As of the first week of June, Gehrig and Foxx had almost identical 1933 season records for home runs, runs batted in, and batting average. Foxx only began to overshadow Gehrig in various batting statistics after many of the All-Star ballots were already cast.

Gehrig received the honor of starting at first for the AL, receiving 312,680 votes compared to 127,104 votes for Foxx. Many fans voted for Foxx as the starting third baseman; Jim finished with 142,418 votes, compared to 207,992 for Jimmy Dykes. Foxx had not played in any 1933 games at third base up to the date of the All-Star game, but had played in 13 games at that position in 1932. He even received 891 votes for second base and 1,095 for an outfield position, the only player to receive that many votes at four different positions.

Oddly, AL Manager Connie Mack never put Foxx in the game. *The Sporting News* reported, "Most of the 49,000 fans at Comiskey Park were disappointed because Jimmie Foxx didn't get into the game and they gave Lou Gehrig the razzberry in the fifth inning when he dropped Dick Bartell's easy foul." Mack later explained, "I made no changes in the team because I did not believe in breaking up a winning combination." Foxx had to be extremely disappointed. If not deserving of the starting role, Jimmie should have at least appeared in the game as a batter at some point.

Entering the second half of the season following the All-Star break, both Foxx and Cronin trailed Simmons in the batting race by two points, .368 to .366. Foxx had a 19-game hitting streak from June 24 through the first game of July 10, raising his average from .325 to .367. Jimmie led the league in batting through much of July, with Cronin and Simmons in close pursuit, only to have Simmons retake the lead late in July.

Foxx and Grove teamed up on August 3, when Jimmie homered off Johnny Allen and Lefty blanked the Yankees, ending a string of 308 consecutive games in which New York scored at least one run. On August 11, Jimmie took over the batting lead for the rest of the season. His consistently high batting average between July 2 and the end of the season was remarkable, never going below .351 or higher than .373.

Simmons, whose average dipped more than 40 points during the last two months of the season, declared, "I won't play in Chicago again in 1934. I can't hit well in Comiskey Park." He was bothered mostly by the reduction in home runs he had hit, from 35 in 1932 to 14 in 1933.

Jimmie continued his hot hitting against the Yankees on August 12, in the first game of doubleheader, homering in the eighth inning and then pushing across the winning runs in the tenth inning with a two-run homer.

Two days later, Jimmie had one of his best games ever. He hit for the cycle off the offerings of Willis Hudlin and Belve Bean of the Indians in Cleveland Stadium and set a new American League record for runs batted in with nine in a nine-inning game. Hudlin says:

> My pitching pattern against Jim was mostly sinkerballs, my specialty. Not only did you have to power the ball as a batter, but you gotta raise a sinkerball pitch "up" to hit a homer. Foxx had "Popeye" arms. He had God-given power and a quick bat. He could hit a ball out of any park.

Jim drove home two runs in the first inning of the August 14 game with a triple off Hudlin, four runs in the second with a grand slam, one run in the fourth with a double, and two more in the sixth with a single. Mercifully for the Indians, in his last at bat he struck out swinging. According to *The Sporting News*, "Letters poured in to Foxx from all parts of the country. One Foxx fan told him that he had named his new baby after him." Foxx led the AL in batting after the game, with a .362 average and an 11-point lead over former teammate Al Simmons.

Meanwhile, fans and sportswriters wondered if Foxx would ever be able to break Ruth's single-season homer record. His homer pace for this season was slower than when he slugged fifty-eight home runs, but there would be other seasons, and Foxx was still in his prime, not quite twenty-six. Dick Farrington of the *St. Louis Times* wrote in his column, "Fanning with Farrington," in *The Sporting News*:

> This year he [Foxx] is again leading (in homers), but there is hardly any chance that he will reach his 1932 high. Nor is it at all likely that he ever will remove Ruth's high of 60. Conditions always have been less favorable for a right-handed batter than a southpaw swinger in batting home runs. This is due to the less neighborly walls in left field [in some AL parks]. There is the added consideration that Jimmy does not get the breaks that the "Bam" [Ruth] used to. He doesn't have quite the appeal to the boys that Ruth has always had and they are continuously bearing down on him.

It's simply unknown whether Ruth or Foxx occasionally received a purposeful fat pitch from an opponent late in the season or in a one-sided game, but Farrington was not the only writer to suggest that Ruth had the upper hand over Foxx in gift pitches from opposing pitchers.

The 1902 Sudlersville "Town" team. Jimmie Foxx's dad, Dell, is in the second row from the top, at the far right. Dell was the team's rightfielder. (*Courtesy Sudlersville Memorial Library*)

The Foxx family about 1911 or 1912. Mattie, Dell, and James (age 4 or 5). (*Courtesy Sudlersville Memorial Library*)

Taken in 1919 or 1920, this photo shows Jimmie Foxx (12 or 13) with his brother Sammy Dell, Jr. (*Courtesy Sudlersville Memorial Library*)

1923 Sudlersville High School soccer team. Team captain James "Jimmie" Foxx is crouched in front. (*Courtesy Sudlersville Memorial Library*)

The Foxx family at the "Foxx Farm," probably November 1933. Top row (l. to r.) Helen, Sammy Dell, Jr., and Jimmie. Seated: Dell Foxx holding Jimmie, Jr., and Mattie. (*Courtesy Nanci Foxx Canaday*)

Mattie Smith Foxx and her son James "Jimmie" Emory Foxx (about eight or nine years old) of Sudlersville. (*Courtesy Sudlersville Memorial Library*)

The 1921 or 1922 Sudlersville "Town" team. Front row (l. to r.) Sam Blades, Harrington Knotts, and Jimmie Foxx. Second row (l. to r.) Ralph Jones, Wallace Ross, Stanley Atkinson, Frank Coleman. Back row (l. to r.) Ralph Walls, Price Johnson, Paul Bostic, Kenneth Knotts, Chris Wallace, and Olin Smith (Jimmie's uncle). (*Courtesy Ellen Ross Johnson Coleman*)

Easton Farmers Baseball Club (Eastern Shore League) 1924. Frank "Home Run" Baker is seated in the center of the center row, and Jimmie Foxx is standing behind him in the center of the back row. (*Courtesy of the Collection of H. Robins Hollyday at the Talbot County Historical Society and the Sudlersville Train Museum*)

Jimmie Foxx and Dorothy Anderson Foxx on their wedding day in June 1943. (*Courtesy Nanci Foxx Canaday*)

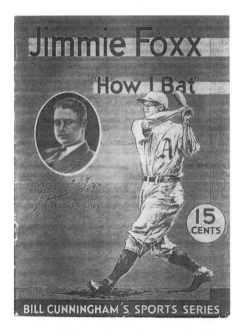

The cover of Jimmie Foxx's 1933 book: *How I Bat*.

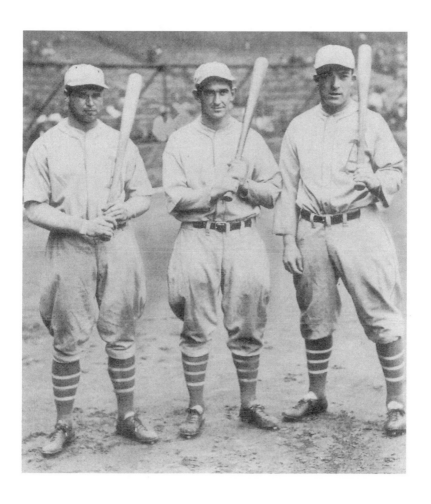

Powerful batting trio of the Philadelphia A's from 1928 to 1932. Jimmie Foxx (l.), Mickey Cochrane (c.), and Al Simmons. (*Courtesy National Baseball Library, Cooperstown, NY*)

Babe Ruth and Jimmie Foxx, probably taken in 1934. Foxx autographed the photo. (*Courtesy Babe Ruth Museum*)

After a thirteen-game homerless streak from August 19-29, Foxx hit seven homers in a week in the beginning of September, to clinch his second straight AL homer title. The seven homers gave him a lead of 44-28 over Ruth, his nearest competitor.

On September 6, Jimmie hit one of the longest homers ever seen in Shibe Park when he rocketed a pitch from Mel Harder onto the roof of the center field pavilion in the second inning. Harder says:

> My two main pitches were my sinkerball and curveball. Jimmie had strong arms and wrists, which provided good snap in his swing [a quick bat]. My approach to Foxx was, don't throw a ball down the middle. I tried to keep his timing off, by mixing the speed of my pitches and I kept the ball inside or outside, trying to hit the corners.

In late August and early September, rumors abounded that Connie Mack might sell or trade Foxx at the end of the season, given the further decline in attendance at Shibe Park. But on September 9, the *Easton Star Democrat* announced that Mack definitely set such rumors to rest: "I am sick and tired of denying such reports, and am going to take this opportunity to decline them without foundation. You may further state that both Foxx and Cochrane will not play with any club other than the A's next season."

When Foxx and Cochrane were asked about the situation following Mack's statements, both agreed they were very well satisfied to know exactly where they stood.

The Athletics ended the season deep in third place, seventeen and one-half games behind front-running Washington. All the while, the Depression had tied the noose tighter around the pocketbook of Mack and the Shibes. Paid attendance declined from 405,000-297,100; the Mackmen were in the red again.

Nevertheless, Foxx captured the AL Triple Crown with a league-leading 48 homers, 163 runs batted in, and a .356 batting average for his second successive Most Valuable Player award. He also led the AL in total bases, slugging percentage, and on-base percentage.

Foxx had now taken a firmer grip on the major league home-run hitting crown, wresting it away from the aging Ruth over the course of two prolific seasons for slugging homers, averaging fifty-three per season for the two years, a pace only surpassed by Ruth in his prime.

Sportswriters from New York were not happy to see Ruth finally falling from the top of the homer-hitting list, and John Kieran minimized Foxx's overhaul of the Babe on September 12 in the *New York Times:* "Jimmy Foxx has been walloping a lot of homers, but, strange to say, those things don't seem to count any more since the Babe sighed and began to sit out some of the afternoon parties [Yankee games]."

Out of a possible 80 points in the MVP voting, Jimmie received 74. One member of the Baseball Writers Association from each AL city voted. Joe Cronin, the Washington shortstop and player-manager who was runner-up in the MVP balloting, said, "Jimmie is the greatest all-around player in the game today."

As Foxx predicted, he walked less times in 1933 without Simmons in the lineup, and the "Jimmie Foxx spite fence" in Navin Field worked. He hit only two homers in Navin Field in 1933, compared to nine the previous year, which made up for most of the difference in his homer totals between the two seasons.

Beginning on October 3, Jimmie headed on a barnstorming tour that took him through Pennsylvania, Delaware, and Maryland. On October 11, Foxx and a group of American Leaguers went to Salisbury, Maryland, to play a team of local men picked from the Delmarva peninsula. The game was originally scheduled for October 6, but Foxx "accepted an offer to do some special reporting" during the World Series between the Giants and Senators.

Foxx delighted a crowd of about 1,000 fans in Salisbury when he smashed two homers in a 10-0 victory for the American Leaguers. One homer left the park over the right field wall and the other soared over the left field fence, leaving Henry's Park near the scoreboard, the first time the feat had been accomplished in that section of the park. Earl Averill, Max Bishop, and Cochrane also homered. Joe Vosmik umpired, and Clint Brown, Walberg, and Foxx pitched for the American Leaguers. Foxx also played third base. More than twenty local players saw action for the Eastern Shore All-Stars opposing the American Leaguers.

Meanwhile, Frank Baker, now an officer of the Trappe Fire Department, was organizing two fund-raiser games to be played in Easton for the benefit of his organization. Frank hoped Foxx would be able to play, knowing that Jim's appearance would swell the attendance at Federal Park, but Jim wired Frank at the last minute, sending his regrets that he would be unable to make it due to previous engagements elsewhere. Baker also attempted to bring Grove, Cochrane, and Porter to Easton for the games without any success.

Baker convinced Jimmie's fifteen-year-old brother, Sammy Dell, Jr., to pitch one of the two games for Frank's "All-Stars" against a strong local Easton club, but Baker's club came up short in both the Saturday and Sunday contests on October 13 and 14. Sammy pitched on October 14, but was shellacked soundly. Baker, now forty-seven, played third base for his own club and hit the ball hard, although not for distance, and Foxx's former teammates from the 1924 Easton club, George Klemmick, Mildred Slaughter, and Tony Chaconas, also played for Baker.

Not long after the game in Salisbury, Foxx's left foot began to bother him again. Jimmie went hitless in an exhibition game at Milford, Delaware, on October 17, batting against major-league pitchers Lew Krausse and Bill Dietrich, but homered in a losing cause in a game in Federalsburg, Maryland, on October 18. Jimmie pitched the last inning of the game at Federalsburg and received credit for the loss while aggravating an injury he originally received when he fouled a ball off his left foot in an exhibition game in Baltimore right after the World Series. A bone in his left foot was fractured, according to x-rays taken on October 19, prompting Foxx to abandon his ballplaying for the rest of the season.

But Jim found it difficult to sit and rest very long around the "Foxx Farm" being lived in by Dell, Mattie, and Sammy Dell, Jr. The day after the x-rays were taken, Jim walked down Commerce Street in Centreville with a cane, drawing a crowd of onlookers. Virtually everyone recognized Jim, and many called out to him. Plenty of handshaking occurred, according to the local county newspaper. Then, after a quick stop in the Sunset Pharmacy at Commerce and Water Streets around noon, where he often sipped a milkshake, Foxx commented to a reporter about the blue laws in Philadelphia and their effect on the A's finances and the makeup of the team roster, "If Sunday baseball was legalized in Pennsylvania then Connie might not have to trade any players to make ends meet."

Jim was prevented from playing in the local baseball game between Centreville and nearby Queenstown (Maryland) that day because of his injury, so he called balls and strikes while Dell umpired the bases. After the game, Jim spent several more days on his parents' farm in Sudlersville before traveling home to be with Helen and Jimmie, Jr., in Atlantic City.

A few days later, Foxx's teammate Bill Dietrich had another theory on how Foxx broke his foot. Dietrich recalls:

> Some two weeks before the season closed, Jim broke his toe while the team was out west. He was sitting on the bed in his hotel room with his legs hanging over the side. One of the other boys started to jump on the bed—but missed. He went right over Jimmy and fell on the outstretched foot. The impact broke the big toe, but Foxx didn't know it until some time later, when it bothered him so much that he had it x-rayed.

Although Jim did benefit occasionally from payoffs in the hundreds of dollars for playing in a single exhibition game, he didn't always play for money. During the early 1930s, Jim often organized pickup games at Washington College at Chestertown, Maryland, on his way north to Philadelphia after spring training or on his way south for a visit to his parents' farm after the regular season. He'd gather men he had played with and against in high school and play against the varsity baseball team of Washington College. Not many people knew about these pickup games ahead of time, so the size of the groups watching them was often small— testimony that Foxx wasn't always looking for a crowd or adoration from fans. Jim enjoyed playing the game for fun and considered helping developing talent to be important, too.

"Jim loved playing pitcher. He helped players with their problems if they asked for his advice," recalled Paul Bruehl, John Bruehl's son. Jim often asked Paul to catch when he pitched.

Foxx's home-run hitting was lusty enough in 1932 and 1933 that some speculation was being offered about his ability not only to break Ruth's single-season homer record but also the Babe's lifetime homer total of 683 as of the end of 1933. Sam Murphy of the *New York Sun* wrote, "If any man does surpass the achievements of Ruth, it will be Foxx."

On November 7, Sudlersville's Community Betterment Club celebrated Foxx's receipt of a second successive AL MVP award with Jimmie, his family, friends, and teammates on hand for a banquet and festivities. A large crowd gathered in Cox Memorial Hall in Sudlersville by 6:30 P.M. to pay tribute to Foxx. The first floor of the hall filled with well-wishers. Mack and Doc Ebeling arrived at about 7:00 P.M. to spearhead a migration of the crowd to the banquet hall on the second floor.

The occasion gave everyone a chance to escape the daily woes of the Great Depression. It seemed cities were especially hard-hit. While rural families still had to be prudent when spending money, at least farmers usually were able to put food on the table. The A's and many other major-league clubs struggled as attendance continued to decline. Many fans simply couldn't afford the price of admission because of the Depression, especially those who were unemployed. The high payroll of the A's, compared to many other major-league clubs, increased Mack's financial worries. But for one night, such problems were set aside while Foxx's family, friends, and teammates celebrated his rise to stardom as a major-league slugger.

After a meal of Maryland turkey, Virginia ham, vegetables, sweet potatoes, biscuits, ice cream, and cake, the program began with an invocation and speeches. Mayor Wallace Woodford of Dover, Delaware, and Maryland State Senator Dudley Roe praised Jimmie for his continued modesty while gaining baseball's honors. Senator Roe reviewed the days when Jimmie's father, Dell, played as a "local ball player in outstanding fashion," and attributed much of Jimmie's success to the atmosphere in which he grew up.

Anna Harrison, the principal of Sudlersville High, made a short speech about Jim. She said, "If the kids got in an argument over whether a runner was safe or out, the boys would respect what Jimmie said. He was known for his honesty."

Referring to Jimmie as "my boy," Connie Mack expressed the opinion that no one in baseball, not even Babe Ruth, could drive a ball with so little effort. Mack pointed out that Foxx could have broken Ruth's single-season record of 60 homers except for his high interest in achieving success for the team in 1932, rather than concentrating on individual records. Connie predicted that Jimmie would break Ruth's record. After all, Jimmie was only twenty-six. William Grose, Associate Editor for the *Queen Anne's Record*, said that if Foxx did break Ruth's home-run mark, Cox Memorial Hall would not be able to hold the crowd that would turn out to welcome the return of a hero.

To the tune of "Jingle Bells," the crowd sang, "Jimmy Foxx, Jimmy Foxx, is our home town boy; he can hit the ball so hard, it fills our heart with joy. . . ." As the tables were being cleared, autograph seekers got signatures on baseballs, a shoe, and "Maryland beat biscuits," which were about the size and shape of billiard balls, from Foxx, Mack, Mickey Cochrane, Rube Walberg, Mule Haas, Bing Miller, Frank Baker, and Bill McGowan. Jimmie Foxx was undeniably the "Pride of Sudlersville."

Some of the A's players stayed overnight at Frank Tarbutton's mother's house in Sudlersville. The large house had four rooms upstairs that could hold two or three people each. On different occasions, Cochrane, Earnshaw, Grove, Miller, Simmons, Ebeling, Bishop, Boley, Dykes, Haas, and Cramer hunted with Jimmie, staying overnight at the Tarbutton's home. The men ate breakfast and dinner there and often gave all or parts of their uniforms from the season just completed to the townsfolk.

The sad state of finances of the Athletics was obvious on December 12, when Connie Mack unloaded almost every star left on the team from the 1929-31 pennant winners, except for Foxx. The player deals were blamed on financial pressure forced on Mack and the Shibes by Philadelphia bankers. Mack traded Grove, Bishop, and Walberg to the Red Sox for pitcher Bob Kline and infielder Rabbit Warstler and $125,000. Then Mack acted contrary to his assertion in September that Cochrane would be with the A's in 1934, trading Mickey to the Tigers for Johnny Pasek and $100,000, followed by a trade of Earnshaw and Pasek from the A's to the White Sox for catcher Charlie Berry and $20,000. Tiger owner Frank Navin intended that Cochrane would be player-manager for Detroit.

In one day, Mack had disassembled the guts of a championship team, and Foxx couldn't help but feel a little lonely on December 13. Many of these men had been his teammates since his first spring training in 1925.

Foxx was the only regular left on the A's after the December 12 transactions, and Mack was faced with rebuilding the club from scratch around Foxx.

Sunday baseball finally became legal in Philadelphia and Pittsburgh through approval by local referenda in November 1933, but the law, long-sought by Connie Mack, was too little, too late, for him to retain the bulk of proven veterans from his pennant years. The Athletics' coffers were too far in the red and had gained too little revenue during the early years of the Depression.

Grove reportedly went into Yawkey's office shortly after reporting to the Red Sox. Tom pulled out a blank check, handed it to Lefty, and said, "Fill it out for whatever you think is appropriate." Grove penned in a figure of $33,000.

The *Boston Globe* reported on December 18 that a controversy was anticipated between Jimmie Foxx and Connie Mack on Foxx's salary for the upcoming season. According to Marshall Hunt, of the *New York Daily News*, "Encouraged by the possibility that there will be a loud salary argument between James Emory Foxx and Connie Mack, Tom Yawkey is ready to buy the rugged infielder and home-run manufacturer for $75,000." Hunt speculated that Yawkey would not get a chance to buy Foxx. If there had been a possibility of doing so, Hunt figured that Foxx would have been made available to Yawkey and purchased before obtaining Grove, Walberg, and Bishop. Hunt also reported that Mack told Eddie Collins more than a month ago that Foxx was one of five or six players he would not sell.

Foxx announced on New Year's Eve that he'd be traveling south to Miami the first week in 1934. He said, "There is nothing like getting off to an early start in training. I've got a tough job ahead of me keeping up last season's pace and what everybody expects from me. But I'll keep trying, you can rest assured."

10

A HOLDOUT AND A BEANING

Because Foxx had completely dominated the AL in 1932 and 1933, many observers were now calling him the best hitter in baseball—no small compliment, given the likes of Gehrig, Simmons, and the Phillies' Chuck Klein. New York sportswriter Dan Daniel listed his top ten players in baseball on January 3, 1934, with Carl Hubbell ranked at the top of the list and Jimmie Foxx second. Surprisingly, he still rated the aging Ruth as high as third, noting, "The Ruth of 1934 is not the Ruth of 60 homers in 1927. Foxx perhaps has yet to achieve his prime." Daniel rated Gehrig ninth on the list.

At the same time, Ruth predicted that he'd play in about 100 games in the coming season, realizing his playing career was well past its peak. Daniel said that when Ruth was asked about the possibility of Jimmie Foxx or anybody else beating his home-run record, Ruth said, "Nobody will ever hit 60 home runs again." Ruth gave no reasons for his conclusion. More than anything, he probably realized that he would never hit that many homers in a season again.

Foxx's growing popularity also landed his portrait and autograph on Wheaties boxes, making him one of the first athletes to be so honored, but the money paid for such promotions was meager. Former Athletics' pitcher Howard Ehmke lined up his old teammates Foxx, Simmons, Cochrane, Grove, and Earnshaw for a Wheaties promotion for which they each received $100.

Similarly, Foxx received a set of golf clubs from Hillerich and Bradsby in exchange for the right to put his autograph on some of their bats. Although the money value of the clubs wasn't anything comparable to the monies paid today's athletes for promotions of commercial products, Foxx was happy to receive them in support of one his favorite hobbies.

As of 1933, Foxx and other major leaguers began being featured more regularly on baseball trading cards, because bubble gum companies took an active interest in promoting sales of their products, much the way tobacco companies had earlier in the 1900s. It's hard to determine if Foxx and others were paid even nominal fees by the chewing gum companies, but young boys across the country now had an item they could carry, hold, and examine with pictures of their favorite players and some of their playing statistics. Goudey Gum Company and DeLong Gum Company, both located in Boston, produced trading cards in 1933, and Goudey produced cards in most other years in the 1930s, but not annually over an extended period of time. Gum, Inc. of Philadelphia, makers of "Blony" super bubble gum, made trading cards in 1940 and 1941 with Foxx appearing in both editions.

Much like their previous years, Jimmie, Helen, and Jimmie, Jr., began motoring from New Jersey to Miami on January 5, 1934. Right before they left, Jim brimmed with optimism, telling reporters, "that if I'm in condition, I'll pole 65 homers."

Soon after, in the second week of January, Mack announced his early choices for his 1934 starting lineup:

> We'll have Jimmie Foxx at first, Dib Williams at second, Eric McNair at short and Pinky Higgins at third. So much for the infield. Now the outfield. Big Ed Coleman will be in the outfield. No question about that. I look for him to be the Coleman he was at the start of 1932 with the leg he broke that season no longer handicapping him. If Coleman doesn't develop, I have Lou Finney, Bing Miller and newcomer Radcliffe for right field. My principal worries are with my pitching and catching departments. Yet, I think my young hurlers are better than they are rated. If I can land a catcher who will help, I will get him. But don't forget I have Charlie Berry, Eddie Madjeski, and Frank Hayes.

On January 27, Foxx announced from Miami that he had not yet received a contract from the A's for the 1934 season. His three-year contract had expired at the end of the previous season, and he had not heard from the A's since then on the issue of contracts. Foxx said, "Sure, I am expecting more money. I am not chesty about it but I believe my work last season warrants a mighty good raise. Don't worry, I am in top condition. I finished last season weighing 184 and right now I tip the scales at 181 without any spring cavorting." Foxx and his wife had been resting several weeks in Miami and were about ready to leave for the dog track, "his long suit" at the time of the interview.

A couple of weeks later, Foxx revealed that he had received a contract with a proposed pay cut. He had just had two of the most outstanding seasons ever put together by a major leaguer, but Mack was facing serious financial problems with his club. Foxx said he would not sign the contract at the terms offered to him.

I don't want to be classed as a holdout just yet, or of staging an
argument with club owners, but I don't deserve a cut and I feel badly
about the whole thing. My three-year contract which expired last fall
was $50,000 for three years. Now the Philadelphia bosses mail me a
contract calling for more than a 30% cut, despite my hitting that led
the league. I don't see why I should take a pay cut of any kind. I am
most certainly not going to accept it. I'm sending it back this morning.

Joe Williams asserted in the *New York World Telegram* that three or four
clubs in the league—the Yankees, White Sox, Red Sox, and possibly the
Indians—would take over Foxx's contract with enthusiasm and pay him
what he thinks he deserves, roughly $25,000 annually—"but baseball is a
tight monopoly."

By February 20, Foxx, still in Miami, was growing impatient and
becoming more bitter about the contract offer, especially when the salary
was compared with salaries offered other stars in the major leagues.

I don't want to quit baseball. I want to play. But I have one offer
of $10,000 to take charge of a boys' camp up north for a year. I've got
a 200-acre farm down in Sudlersville, where tending to business I
can make as much a year as the Athletics are offering me. Babe Ruth
gets $35,000 this year and he hopes to play in 100 games for that.
Last season the Babe hit just .300. Lou Gehrig gets $25,000 this
season, I've been told, and he hit .335 or thereabouts. Chuck Klein,
plenty of a hitter, is going to draw $22,500 from the Cubs. And I'm
to get $11,000 for hitting .356? Of course, I only hit 48 home runs last
year, so what can I expect?

Two days later, Foxx said he would not accept the cut offered him by
Mack but would demand a raise over the salary he had received the last
three years. Foxx pointed out that players like Jimmy Dykes, who was
thirty-seven and past his prime, would receive a greater salary than Foxx
would if he accepted Mack's terms. Some reporters speculated that he was
seeking a $30,000 salary. On the same day, Foxx said he had been asked to
report to Fort Myers when training started March 1, even though he was
unsigned by the A's. Jimmie said he intended to go to Fort Myers for a
conference with Mr. Mack the day after the heavyweight championship
between Primo Carnera and Tommy Loughran.

On February 24 the *Philadelphia Inquirer* reported that Ray Fabiani, a
wrestling promoter, had telegraphed Foxx an offer for $30,000 a year for
three years to turn wrestler.

Foxx stole the show at a workout for the Giants in Miami Beach on February 27 when he got into his familiar uniform and had his first practice session. On March 5, Foxx reiterated from Miami that he would not accept Mack's compromise offer of $15,000 for the season with a bonus rider calling for increases in his salary with higher attendance at Shibe Park. Jimmie demanded a one-year contract of $25,000. Meanwhile, that same day, Jim was a spectator at the international four-ball matches at the Miami Country Club, then worked out with a dozen or so players, mostly minor leaguers, who were awaiting calls to report to spring training.

Foxx agreed to terms with manager Mack in Miami Beach on March 9, after the two conferred for a while before an exhibition game between the A's and the New York Giants. The *New York Times* stated that "it was generally accepted" that Foxx signed a one-year contract and would receive $20,000 for the 1934 season, representing an increase of $3,333 over the previous year. Other press reports speculated that Foxx signed for $18,000 and attendance bonuses existed in Jimmie's contract for $22,000, if total attendance reached 600,000 or more fans at Shibe Park and $25,000 if the club attracted a million or more fans at home. With the country deep in the Depression and the A's having attracted only 260,000 fans in 1933, it seemed very unlikely that Foxx would achieve any bonuses in 1934. Besides, two longtime favorites of the Athletics' fans, Cochrane and Grove, were no longer with the team.

Whatever the exact terms of the one-year contract, the ordeal of being a holdout seemed to dampen Foxx's enthusiasm somewhat. Usually Jim was anxious to play every inning of every spring game. Now some fans and scribes described him as listless at times or just "going through the motions." Jimmie sat through most of the game between the A's and Giants on March 9, not putting on his uniform. He had been part of "light workouts" the past two weeks, and it was announced he would play for the A's within the next few days. Two days later, Jimmie played for the A's for the first time in 1934 in an exhibition game against the Giants at Miami Beach. The game was played despite temperatures not much above freezing, and Foxx had to face lefty ace Carl Hubbell. In two innings pitched, Hubbell gave up only one hit, an infield single by Foxx. It was Jim's only hit of the game.

Foxx's low salaries from 1930-35 stemmed from several reasons. By the time Jimmie had his first superstar-caliber season in 1929, Grove had four and Cochrane and Simmons each had five superstar seasons, making them more established stars than Foxx. Attendance also increased at Shibe Park from 1925-29, giving impetus to Grove, Cochrane, and Simmons to dig deep into Mack's pocketbook. When the Depression hit Philadelphia and caused declining attendance—even while the A's were pennant winners—a young upstart such as Foxx was less likely to catch up to the salaries of his already famous teammates. Many fans were not likely to be sympathetic towards Foxx's contract woes because of their own plight in coping with the Depression.

Mack couldn't cut the salaries of Grove and Cochrane for 1932 and 1933, or Simmons for 1932, because they continued to perform as superstars each season. Jimmie's two-year reign as the league's most valuable player in 1932 and 1933 came at the worst time for making a strong positive impact on his annual earnings. Drastically low attendance for the A's in 1931 and again in 1932 made it virtually impossible for Mack to reward Jimmie with big salary increases for 1932 and 1933. After Simmons was sold in late 1932 and Grove and Cochrane were sold late in 1933, Mack's revenues were so low that the money gained from the sales presumably was unavailable for any salary increases for Foxx in 1933 and 1934. The revenue gained from player sales was probably necessary just to keep the club in operation.

Mack conducted spring training in 1934 much the way he had during the A's championship years. There were usually morning and afternoon workouts. The players often stayed at the clubhouse and had a sandwich for lunch. The morning workout often had batting and fielding drills, while the afternoon sessions frequently included an intrasquad game. The A's gave the players laundry money and provided for their meals at the hotel.

Jim and his teammates met Babe Didrikson in spring training when she visited several baseball camps in between practicing her golf game. Didrikson had starred in high school basketball and track and field, and then set women's records in the javelin throw and 80-meter hurdle at the Los Angeles Olympics two years earlier. Now she was practicing golf in anticipation of turning professional, and Mack inserted her as the starting pitcher for the A's in a March 20 game against the Brooklyn Dodgers at Fort Myers. Didrikson, who had been taking lessons from the Cardinals' Burleigh Grimes, among others, was described as having a graceful, easy delivery. Although she induced two swinging strikes from each of the first two Dodger batters, she struggled in her only inning of pitching, walking lead-off batter Danny Taylor and nicking hard-hitting Johnny Frederick with a pitch. The A's infield saved her when the next batter, Joe Stripp, lined a shot to second baseman Dib Williams, who relayed to shortstop Warstler to Foxx for a triple play.

Near the end of March, *New York Times* writer John Kieran caught Mack in a cheerful, optimistic mood, looking forward to the prospects for the upcoming season. John and Connie talked at the Boston Braves' training camp in St. Petersburg, Florida, as the A's played the Braves two days in a row. While Connie remained confident in his infield and outfield aggregations, he was very concerned about his pitching staff's ability to keep the A's opponents' in check. Kieran said Mack, "chuckled and chirped in that high, thin, wispy voice of his," discussing his team and others. Mack repeatedly used terms like, "by George," "goodness gracious, yes," and "gosh sakes," during the conversation. Connie was concerned about the lack of a left-handed pitcher and had difficulty naming his top four starting pitchers. He desperately needed a left-hander, preferably of the quality of one of his previous portsiders, Rube Waddell, Eddie Plank, or Lefty Grove, and said Grove would be missed. Connie named his two best starters as Mahaffey and "Sugar" Cain, with the other two starters likely coming from rookies Johnny Marcum, Bill Dietrich, Joe Cascarella, or Tim McKeithan.

Foxx seemed to have forgotten his holdout woes by the time opening day came on April 17, when the Yankees visited at Shibe Park. Jim exchanged pleasantries with the Babe and probably Gehrig. Foxx, aiming for his third consecutive home-run crown, posed with Ruth for photographers before the seasonal opener. The A's edged the Yankees that day, 6-5, but lost the following day, even though Foxx hit two homers.

Jim started slow for the A's, batting less than .300 during April, and it soon became obvious that the regular season would be a bust for the Athletics. The highlight of the A's season probably occurred on May 10, when the Athletics tied the Senators for second place with a win over Detroit, even though their pitching was faltering further than in the 1933 season.

After his slow start in April, Jim had a hot streak in mid-May, batting 17 for 35 from May 11-23. On May 18, Foxx smashed a towering home run in the sixth inning into the center field bleachers at Comiskey Park, the first homer hit there since the bleachers were constructed in 1927. The distance from the plate to the bleachers was 436 feet, but the ball landed in the seventh row, for an estimated distance of 455 feet. Foxx remarked, "I thought it was about time those fans in the bleachers were getting a break. Someone ought to hit a ball there at least once a year. It's queer, but once or twice a year, Ted Lyons tries to sneak a high fast one by me with the result I generally hit it out of the lot."

Foxx was a good friend of Lyons and Ted's roommate, Vern Kennedy. Kennedy recalled that Jimmie frequently visited the White Sox dressing room after games with Chicago and that Ted and Jimmie always ended up in a wrestling match. Kennedy believed Lyons was the stronger of the two.

American League All-Star manager, Joe Cronin, received considerable criticism from fans and National Leaguers when he decided to start Foxx instead of Jimmy Dykes at third base. Foxx finished a distant second to Gehrig in the fan votes for the first base position, 33,890 to 2,151, and Dykes and Mike Higgins were the top two vote getters for the third base position. Gehrig was in the process of putting together one of his very best seasons, while Jim's batting production was not up to par with his 1932 and 1933 numbers for homers, rbi's, and average.

Dan Daniel pointed out that Foxx didn't even appear in the first All-Star game as a pinch hitter, despite being the player of the year in 1932. Daniel sided with Cronin's decision to select Foxx as the team's starting third baseman, even though he hadn't played at that position for several seasons. While Mack and many of the other A's players traveled to his hometown, North Brookfield, Massachusetts, for an exhibition game, Jim made his way to New York for the July 10 All-Star game at the Polo Grounds. Cronin put Foxx fifth in the AL batting order behind Gehringer (2B), Manush (LF), Ruth (RF), and Gehrig (1B), and ahead of Simmons (CF), Cronin (SS), Dickey (C), and Gomez (P). Observers estimated that the fans at the Polo Grounds were equally divided between AL and NL supporters. Hubbell took control of the game early by striking out Ruth on four pitches, Gehrig on six, and Foxx on five in the top of the first inning, all with two runners on base. Jim struck out with runners on second and third.

But the AL recovered to win by two runs after trailing early in the game, and Foxx had one of his best All-Star games, batting 2 for 5 (a single and a double) with one run batted in, while playing flawlessly in the field. Cronin said, "Foxx played a smart all-around game."

Jack Wilson, a hard-throwing right-hander who pitched for the Red Sox from 1935-41, actually came up as a rookie with the Athletics in 1934 for several games. Wilson recalled that, "Foxx was the first guy in the clubhouse to come over and meet me or any other new guy on the club. Not many of the veteran ballplayers were like that."

Foxx's bat really heated up in July. He smacked 13 homers, but only had 23 runs batted in. The opposing pitchers tried pitching around him in the order, walking him 28 times. He batted 36 for 95 for a .379 average. On July 28, Jimmie's two homers in a doubleheader against New York at Shibe Park brought him even with Ruth's homer pace in 1927. Ruth had hit his thirty-fourth homer on July 28, 1927, off Walter Stewart. The two homers gave Foxx the AL lead, 34 to 30 over Gehrig, but then Jimmie's homer pace slowed for the rest of the season.

Foxx's homer in the seventh inning of the second game off New York's Jimmy DeShong ruined a no-hit bid by the Yankee hurler while knotting the score at 1-1. Ruth's bases-loaded walk later in the game salvaged a 2-1 win for DeShong. Then, just ten days later, Foxx broke up another no-hit bid by a Yankee hurler on August 7, when he managed a fluke double off Lefty Gomez that was the only hit by the Athletics in the game. Lefty Grove, in a Red Sox uniform, faced his former mates for the first time on August 8 in Philadelphia, in relief for Wes Ferrell, and defeated the A's. Foxx batted 2 for 5, with a homer and 4 runs batted in.

In August, *Baseball Magazine* published an article in which editor Frank C. Lane presumably interviewed Jim as he described the "secrets of his slugging power." The article reminded fans that Foxx was the last survivor of the Athletic teams that were so dominant just a few years earlier, "but there was one player with whose services he [Mack] would not part for any consideration—Jimmy Foxx." Foxx repeated some of the advice in this article that he had given in *How I Bat*. In the article, Jim and Lane also compared Foxx's batting techniques with that of Ruth.

Ruth's power was attributed to his combination of height, weight, strength, hard cut at the ball, and excellent batting eye. Foxx, who was three inches shorter and thirty to forty pounds lighter, also had excellent batting power from strength and an excellent batting eye, plus the all-important balance.

Lane compared Ruth and Foxx's relative ability to hit homers for frequency and distance:

> For his [Foxx] is the distinction of hitting nearly, if not quite as hard, as the Herculean Babe himself, and his is the distinction of driving out homers with quite as much abandon as Babe was wont to show in his palmiest prime. . . . Jimmy Foxx is, in every way, a worthy rival of the immortal Ruth himself . . . On more than one major league diamond the longest hit is not a trophy of Babe Ruth's. That hit was made by Jimmy Foxx. . . . Babe's specialty, the thing that made him famous, is Foxx's specialty also, the ability to hit a ball harder than any other player.

Foxx said that the basis for hitting success started with the batter's legs. The legs needed to be strong, and that was Ruth's biggest weakness at this point in his career, "his legs are going back on him." Foxx said that many batters swing so hard that they completely lose their balance after the swing. Foxx said that he never does that; he stands firmly on his feet. He added that a firm toe hold is important to batting strength. Foxx stood flat-footed, whereas Ruth held his feet close together and strode more with his swing.

As for batting slumps, the first thing Jim focused on during a hitting slump was his feet: "I'll find that I've unconsciously shifted a little, that I'm not standing just right, and that's one important reason I am not hitting. I try to correct that fault and soon get back into my stride."

Foxx earnestly believed that "Batting strength is in the fingers, wrists, and forearms. Shoulders and body are merely incidental. They look impressive, but they are secondary, at best. In my youth I developed strong fingers and wrists from milking cows." Foxx also mentioned it is important to follow through with your swing rather than stop the swing when the bat meets the ball. He said a lot of "arm hitters," like himself, don't follow through, but he does, although not to the extent that Ruth does.

Foxx viewed strength as being most important at the precise moment when the bat meets the ball. That is the only time the bat should be gripped hard. He said that timing is very important and that it is a matter of the batting eye and balance.

Foxx asserted that the choice of bat is also important for power hitting. He said that when he first came to the majors he used a 42-ounce bat. He had since cut it down to 40 and then to 38 ounces. In fact, during the last couple of seasons, he had been using a 36-ounce bat. "It's the snap and velocity which drive the ball."

While vacationing for a few days in Nashville, Tennessee, Yankee's owner Colonel Jacob Ruppert paid Jimmie Foxx some high compliments. According to the August 17 *Nashville Banner*, Ruppert said that Foxx is the only player in the AL who would "qualify as a successor to Babe Ruth as a drawing card and as a hitter."

A *Banner* reporter asked, "Are you in the market for Foxx if Connie Mack is willing to sell for a reasonable amount?"

Ruppert replied, "Absolutely. And I will pay him as much for Foxx, I believe, as any club in baseball. He would be sort of a new Ruth to the Yankees."

The same day as Ruppert's interview, Jimmie slugged his thirty-eighth homer in the second game of a doubleheader and passed Gehrig by one for the AL and major-league leadership.

On August 29, Lynn "Schoolboy" Rowe of the Tigers sought his seventeenth straight victory of the season at Shibe Park, having already tied the AL record of consecutive wins held by Walter Johnson, "Smokey" Joe Wood, and Lefty Grove. The largest crowd for a regular season game at Shibe Park to that point in the ballyard's history (33,318) crammed the stands and saw the A's reach Rowe for ten runs and twelve hits in six and two-thirds innings. It was Rowe's worst outing of the year, and Foxx contributed two hits in five at bats. Fans at Shibe Park gave Rowe a five-minute standing ovation as he walked off the field, head bowed down, and sat in the dugout.

About the same time, H. G. Salsinger, editor of the *Detroit News*, predicted that the A's would sell Foxx to the Red Sox during the winter. Other rumors had Foxx going to the Yankees, presumably as their new third baseman, in exchange for George McQuinn.

Despite Foxx's consistent hitting, Gehrig maintained a hotter pace. By September 7, Gehrig led Foxx in the AL homer derby, 43-41, and pulled further ahead when Foxx had a twelve-game homer drought that eventually gave Lou the homer crown over Jimmie, 49 to 44.

When Mack pulled Higgins from the lineup in early September due to an injured thumb, Foxx was inserted at third base while Finney played first. Isaminger wrote, "Foxx showed he was a real third baseman by making thrilling plays . . . Boston, New York, and Detroit players marveled at his work."

About the middle of September, Isaminger reported in *The Sporting News* that Mack had purchased first baseman Alex Hooks from Tulsa, spurring new rumors that Foxx would be traded, also given Finney's hot bat recently. Mack told Isaminger that despite any rumors, Foxx was not for sale and the slugger would be with the A's in 1935.

Jimmie's batting average dipped from .348 to .335 when he batted only 5 for 32 from September 8-17. His final average for the year was .334. He led the league with 111 bases on balls and drove home 130 runs while playing in 150 of the A's 153 games, 140 at first base, 9 at third base, and 1 as a pinch hitter.

Mack quelled trade rumors when on October 1 he signed Foxx to a three-year contract through the 1937 season. The salary amount was not revealed, but it was believed to be close to the same amount paid to Foxx in 1934. Mack announced that Foxx was expected to be the regular catcher for the A's and their team captain in 1935.

Isaminger had followed Foxx from the beginning of his career with the A's in September 1924, so he was an expert on Jim's skills and abilities, any weaknesses he had, progress he had made over the years in playing various positions, and his playing statistics. The famous sportswriter said he believed that had Cochrane not joined the A's the same time as Foxx, the Maryland Broadback would have been an outstanding receiver. But playing catcher is often thought to shorten the number of years played and the number of outstanding years with the bat, so the fact that Cochrane beat out Foxx as the starting catcher beginning with their first spring training in 1925 may have been a blessing in disguise for Jimmie.

Isaminger asked the same question many of his readers had also been asking:

> Can he [Foxx] come back and catch after playing nine years at other positions [and not having played catcher in a regular season game since 1928]? The answer to this is that Foxx practiced behind the bat nearly all season [in 1934] and was ready to get in at any time. He showed that he could throw swiftly and accurately, while his judgement of foul tips was never questioned.

The A's continued to slide in the standings, ending the season with a fifth-place finish and 68-82 record. Other than Foxx, bright spots in the lineup were shortstop McNair (.280 average with 17 homers and 82 rbi's), Higgins (.330 average, 16 homers and 90 rbi's), Johnson (.307 average, 34 homers and 92 rbi's), and Cramer (202 hits and a .311 average). Johnny Marcum had the only winning record among Mack's starting pitchers,

14-11. The staff's earned run average (5.01) was the second highest in the league, while Earnshaw went 14-11 for last-place Chicago and Grove struggled to an 8-8 record for the Red Sox due to arm problems.

Grove wasn't the workhorse in 1934 that he had been in previous seasons. He pitched in only 109 innings and didn't pitch at all in April, nor from June-July 2 and from July 4-23.

Grove's arm had been through quite a workout. He had logged 1,184 innings pitched over four and one-half seasons with the Baltimore Orioles from 1920-24 and 2,400 innings from 1925-33 with the Athletics. He also threw a lot of pitches in those innings. Grove led the IL in strikeouts all four of his full seasons with Baltimore and led the league in bases on balls in three of those seasons. He averaged almost a strikeout per inning with Baltimore. Lefty's rate of walks and strikeouts per nine-inning game was lower for the A's than when pitching for Baltimore, but he still led the AL in walks once and in strikeouts seven consecutive times from 1925-31.

Immediately after the regular season, Earle Mack led a team of AL All-Stars, including Foxx, on a barnstorming trip through the Midwest and Northwest. Other teammates on the tour included Heinie Manush, Luke Sewell, Earl Whitehill, Ted Lyons, Red Kress, Pinky Higgins, Marty Hopkins, Bruce Campbell, and Doc Cramer. Upon their arrival in Vancouver, British Columbia, only a few of Earle Mack's All-Stars were to join Connie Mack before leaving on an historical journey to play baseball in the Orient. Earle Mack's club lost the first game of the trip to the Minneapolis Millers of the American Association, 5-4 on October 3, and defeated a team of All-Stars from the Northern League at Grand Forks (North Dakota), 5-1 on October 4. Foxx missed those first two games, detained at home for unknown reasons. Jim first appeared with Mack's club in a series of games played in North Dakota beginning on October 5, losing to a club from Valley City, augmented by players from Jamestown, 6-5. Foxx pitched the final three innings, hurling no-hit ball. Then the All-Stars lost to a combined semipro club from Bismarck, Jamestown, and Valley City, 11-3, and Jamestown 11-0.

Foxx was seriously beaned on the left side of his head by Lefty Brown of the North Dakota All-Stars in a game at Winnipeg (Manitoba) on October 9. Initial reports indicated a slight fracture or mild concussion, much to the concern of Connie Mack. Jimmie wired Connie Mack from the hospital that he was alright the day after the beaning, then proceeded westward to catch up with the All-Stars.

But fans of the slugger were worried again when he missed an exhibition game on October 15 at Spokane, Washington, complaining that he had dizzy spells and felt like sleeping all the time. Speculation grew that Foxx's career as a major leaguer was over. Herb Hunter, advance agent for the AL

All-Star team said, "There is no chance for him to play here, and he may never don a uniform again."

The very next day, Foxx said, "I probably won't be in uniform here or in Seattle, but I plan to go to the Orient with the team." Foxx told listeners that he had not consulted a doctor since leaving Winnipeg, but was told by the doctor there that all he needed was rest. Earle Mack, the club's manager, agreed, indicating that "Foxx is all right. He'll be playing in a few days."

Dr. William Rogers, Foxx's doctor in Winnipeg, was surprised to hear of the reports from Spokane that suggested Foxx might never play baseball again. Rogers indicated that an examination showed Foxx suffered a mild concussion but had no fracture, although there was an apparent small break at the top of the skull which he received six years earlier. The earlier damage to Foxx's skull may have occurred when he injured his head in an auto accident near Sudlersville before spring training in 1927.

When the touring All-Stars left Vancouver for the Far East, Foxx and his wife accompanied them after convincing Connie Mack that he was sufficiently recovered. Most of the players brought their wives with the team, including Foxx, Ruth, Gehrig, Bing Miller, Clint Brown, Lefty Gomez, Earl Whitehill, Moe Berg, Frank Hayes, Earl Averill, Eric McNair, Frank O'Doul, Joe Cascarella, Charlie Gehringer, and Harold Warstler. Ruth was the player-manager, and Hayes was a replacement for Charlie Berry, who had recently had his appendix removed. The tour group included more than thirty people. Some of the nonplayers were Doc Ebeling, umpire (and former A's pitcher) John Quinn, J. A. Hillerich, president of Hillerich and Bradsby Company, and Stuart Bell, sportswriter for the *Cleveland Press*. The team's uniform sported a shield of the USA inside a circle on the left side of the chest, around which was "All Americans" in block letters.

According to Dib Williams, "Foxx, Ruth, and Gehrig were guaranteed $10,000 each for making the trip and were allowed to bring their wives. Most of the other players were not paid nearly so much."

The All-Stars' first stop was at Honolulu, Hawaii, where the entire touring group was draped in leis and photographed by Jimmy Wilson of the *Honolulu Advertiser* for *The Sporting News*. The team stayed for several days, played a couple of exhibition games, then headed for Japan on the *Empress of Japan*.

Japan was mobilizing for war and was a serious threat to its neighbors at the time. The country's leaders resented pressure from U.S. politicians to back off from aggressive military behavior, and the resultant paranoia made it very difficult for U.S. tourists to take photographs during the trip. Still, the players and their wives were able to tour the country with relative ease. Some of the players, including Foxx, enjoyed a trip to a geisha house.

Upon their arrival in Japan on November 2, the American All-Stars paraded through the Ginza (Tokyo's Broadway) in front of 100,000 Japanese, many of them avid baseball fans. The Babe was by far the main attraction. The American All-Stars were undefeated during their one-month tour of Japan, with Ruth, Foxx, and Gehrig dominating the homer hitting. Even at his advanced age, Ruth out-homered Foxx and Gehrig, who were much younger and in far better condition.

Charlie Gehringer recalled that, "Jimmie was the most powerful right-handed hitter during my entire career. I took a trip to Japan in the '30s [1934] with him and he hit a home run out of Tokyo Stadium that had to be the longest in history."

Some observers of the home run belted by Foxx at Tokyo Stadium claimed that the ball traveled over 600 feet. As the ball left the stadium, Ruth and Gehrig shook their heads in disbelief from the dugout. They agreed no man should be able to smack a baseball that far.

Jim took advantage of the trip to the Orient to overcome the beaning incident by stepping into the batter's box over and over again, rather than mulling it over for three months before spring training. His lusty homer hitting on the tour indicated that he had no ill effects from the beaning nor any serious anxiety about batting.

Ruth, Mack, Foxx, and most of the other All-Stars were featured in a trans-Pacific radio telecast from Japan to the United States by the National Broadcasting Company on November 9. The players shared some of their experiences in Japan and were generally impressed with the progress in the quality of play of their Japanese opponents. Foxx showed off his versatility on November 17, when he played all nine positions, starting at third base and ending the game as pitcher in a 15-6 victory over the Nippon All-Stars in Tokyo. Mack played Jim at catcher in many of the games in preparation for the 1935 season.

The steady decline of the Athletics over the previous three-year period required drastic measures from manager Mack to try to revitalize the A's as the 1935 season approached. The pitching staff, which finished seventh in earned run average in 1934, required substantial improvement, especially in the starting rotation. With morale low, the team was hoping for a comeback from Roy Mahaffey or steady improvement from Marcum, Benton, and Dietrich, and more batting punch, especially from the catcher's slot.

Fresh from his tour of the Orient, Jimmie dispelled rumors in early January that Babe Ruth would be joining the A's in 1935. "He wants to manage a team," Foxx said. "And I have an idea that if he doesn't hook on as a manager he may stay out of the game. Also, I don't think he could play because of his playing weight."

Jimmie, Helen, and their son visited Dell, Mattie, and Sammy Dell the second week in January to recap the trip through Japan and deliver their gifts for the family. Jimmie brought home a dozen silk shirts from Japan, but had only two when he arrived in Sudlersville and gave one to Sammy Dell. A friend admired the shirt so much that Jimmie gave him the remaining shirt, leaving none for himself, another example of Foxx's generous, unselfish nature.

Jim also visited Sudlersville High School. He spoke in front of all the students in the assembly room and advised them of the importance of staying in school and receiving their diplomas. Jimmie mentioned that it was not China we should fear the most, in terms of an Asian country threatening world peace. Rather, we should be watchful of Japan.

That same weekend, Jimmie squeezed in a hunting trip at a lodge across from Box Iron in Worcester County, Maryland, on the lower Eastern Shore, probably hunting for rabbits and waterfowl.

11

FOXX RETURNS TO CATCHER AND THE BIG TRADE

In mid-January, opinions started appearing on sports pages regarding the wisdom, or the lack thereof, of Foxx being switched to the catcher's position. Columnist Joe Williams opined:

> Personally, I regard it as the most drastic baseball experiment ever tried in my time. I know as you do, he came to the Athletics as a catcher, but in the big league circles he is not known as a catcher, he is known as a first baseman. For one thing, there is the element of danger. A foul tip breaking a finger can send Foxx, a .350 hitter, to the bench at least two months. Among others, Mr. [Ed] Barrow who knows baseball thinks it's a stupid move, mainly because of the danger element.

In an interesting sidelight, Williams quoted Mack as saying, "Foxx can pitch better than half of the fellows we have on the ball club."

Jimmy Isaminger gave Mack the benefit of the doubt about his switch of Foxx to catcher, saying Connie had good reasons for such moves. However, he pointed out that few catchers play much more than 100 games in a season and that Foxx would need to be in the lineup at first base for his valuable bat on days he wasn't catching. He was worried about Foxx injuring his fingers enough to affect his batting or to sideline him altogether.

Clint Brown, veteran Cleveland Indians pitcher, had a different view of Foxx playing catcher for the A's. Mack inserted Foxx as catcher in several exhibition games in the Orient—one in which Brown pitched and two others that Clint watched from the dugout. "Foxx will be one of the standout catchers in baseball," Brown predicted. "He's a great target for pitchers to throw to, he knows what it's all about, and I have never seen his superior at throwing to the bases. There will be little stealing against the A's next summer if Jimmy gets any cooperation from the pitchers."

On January 24, before leaving for spring training in Florida, Foxx underwent a double operation in Dr. Herb Goddard's office in Philadelphia for removal of tonsils and a nasal obstruction. "The operations were easily performed and both were successful," according to Dr. Goddard. On the last day of January, while in Mr. Mack's office in Shibe Park, Jimmie convinced Connie to give Sammy Dell a tryout at the Athletics' training camp at Fort Myers. Sammy was only sixteen, the same age that Jimmie was when he joined the Macks in September 1924. Sammy was a left-handed pitcher and occasionally played in the outfield, gaining his experience with Sudlersville High School, the local sandlot games, and George Brand's semipro teams. Unlike his famous brother, Sammy was a left-handed batter. He was about an inch taller and five pounds heavier, at 195 pounds, than Jimmie. "The two brothers could pass for twins," according to AL umpire Bill McGowan, who penned a story for the *Philadelphia Public Ledger*. A photograph taken at spring training in Fort Myers illustrates how much the brothers looked alike. Jimmie and Sammy are crouched to the ground, facing each other. The resemblance of their faces is remarkable, given their difference in age, but Jimmie wore catching gear in the photo (without a mask), so it was obvious which was the established major-league star.

Mack was in dire need of left-handed pitchers and probably decided to hope for the best and invite Jimmie's brother to camp. The *Centreville Observer* didn't view Sammy's trip to the A's camp at Fort Myers a tryout; it referred to it as an opportunity to "acquire schooling" in baseball, especially pitching. Some observers from Queen Anne's County believed that Sammy had a good fastball and a fairly good "dewdrop" [curveball].

Jimmie, Helen, and Jimmie, Jr., left for Miami shortly after the January 31 conference with Mack and spent some time there before traveling across Florida to Fort Myers. Sammy joined some of the A's players in mid-February in Wilmington, Delaware, and then headed for Fort Myers by train.

On February 22, the first day of spring training for the A's, Mack was pictured with his hands on the shoulders of Jimmie and Sammy. On the same day, Sammy lined up with twelve other pitching hopefuls for photographers. Jimmie was pictured on March 4 conferring with Sammy on the pitcher's mound, but Sammy left for Sudlersville shortly thereafter. No other tryouts are known to have occurred, and it doesn't appear that he was signed to a minor-league contract. Sudlersville resident Bo Benton recalled that Sammy had a good measure of ability but not enough desire to apply himself and succeed beyond the sandlot level of competition.

After Jimmie caught six innings of an exhibition game against the Giants on March 9, Giants catcher Gus Mancuso claimed that the move from first baseman to catcher was not a good one:

Even if Foxx escapes an injury that will keep him on the bench for a few days, he's going to get weary behind the plate—And a weary player at the bat is not as dangerous as a fresh one. The labors of catching will take at least 20 points off Jimmie's batting average.

Two months after his negative remarks on the shift of Foxx from first to catcher, Joe Williams interviewed Mack about the move. Mack said, "With Foxx behind the bat, we were almost certain to finish one-two-three. With him on first base, we figure to do no better than fifth. Isn't that justification enough?" Williams saw Foxx catch for the first time during the exhibition season on March 14 and remarked on Foxx's play in the game against the World Champion St. Louis Cardinals. "His receiving was all that it should have been. He threw to bases with unerring accuracy; he fielded hits in front of the plate with great agility; he was all pepper behind the plate." Williams learned that "Mack has insured Foxx against accident and that Foxx is the only player on the team that is so protected." Joe further revealed:

The inside dope on the situation is that Foxx consented on the shift because it was the only way he could get more money from a club that has lost a lot of money for three straight years. It develops that catching right-handed curve balls is giving Foxx plenty of grief. Jimmy admits he has yet to master the detail. Foxx said, "When Mickey Cochrane broke in with us he couldn't catch a foul to save his life. Why should I get discouraged?" With experience, Foxx should get the hang of his new job, even if he never does threaten Cochrane's supremacy at the position.

Alex Hooks, a power-hitting prospect from the minor league Tulsa, Oklahoma, club who was bidding for the A's first base job now that Foxx was behind the plate, recalled Foxx's appeal to fans in spring training: "On the way north in 1935, as the Athletics played some exhibition games, Jim was so powerful, that the Athletics would let him take extra swings in batting practice to see how many home runs he could hit for the local fans." Jim finally smashed his first homer of the exhibition season on April 1 against the minor-league Griffin Red Sox at Griffin, Georgia. He played catcher for Mack in most of the games on the way north, getting an occasional rest, and was the primary catcher for Mack during the City Series with the Phillies, homering twice in one of the series games.

Now that Ruth was a National Leaguer on the Boston Braves, Connie Mack no longer viewed Jimmie Foxx as the Babe's successor. On April 12, Mack picked Cleveland's first baseman Hal Trosky, in his second year with the Indians, as "the lad likely to sit down in Babe Ruth's vacated throne as the AL 'Sultan of Swat.'" Mack said, "He promises to be Ruth's successor in baseball." Less than a year and a half earlier, Mack had proclaimed at the testimonial dinner for Foxx at Cox Memorial Hall in Sudlersville that Jimmie would break Ruth's single-season homer record. Did Mack think Foxx would be less potent in hitting homers now that he was the club's catcher? Foxx had just put together homer marks of 58, 48, and 44 the previous three seasons. In spite of Mack's lofty predictions, Trosky would hit a career-high 42 homers the following year—a good number, but hardly Ruthian.

Foxx's return to catcher was depicted on a baseball trading card made by the National Chicle Company from Cambridge, Massachusetts. Jim was pictured on the front of the card in catcher's garb. Austen Lake, from the *Boston American*, who wrote the short biographical information on the back of each card, said of Foxx: "He . . . is counted as the most likely man in the game today to break Babe's home run mark."

Jim was beginning his eleventh season with the Athletics. He was only twenty-seven, and the only remaining star player from the 1929-31 pennant winners. It was fitting that Mack made him captain of the club. While not a firebrand like Cochrane or a chatterbox like Dykes, Foxx led by example and his manner of welcoming rookies and other young players to the club.

On opening day, April 17, the Athletics visited Griffith Stadium to play the Senators. About 20,000 shivering fans watched the players warm up and cheered as President Roosevelt arrived by automobile and climbed into the presidential box by the third base dugout. Foxx joined Senator manager Bucky Harris and stood by the box seat railing near Roosevelt, Senator owner Clark Griffith, and other dignitaries for a photograph session and the throwing of the ceremonial first ball.

As Mack promised, Jimmie started the game at catcher. Foxx was now wearing uniform number two, the number often associated with catcher, in place of uniform number three, the number often worn by a club's regular first baseman. The Senators scored four runs in the first two innings and blanked the A's batters through seven innings. At one time during the game, Foxx hit the ball so hard that it knocked several numbers off the scoreboard. He also broke the A's scoring drought in the first half of the eighth inning with a long drive that sailed into the left field bleachers, scoring Wally Moses ahead of him. President Roosevelt added a loud cheer to the applause for Foxx's home run. The A's scoring ended with Jim's homer, but his initial return to catcher was a success. Foxx homered again the following day in another losing effort.

Foxx caught 13 games in a row from April 17-May 1 and played the entire game at catcher in 24 of the Athletics' first 27 games. Jimmie last played catcher for Mack during the 1935 season for part of the first game of a May 25 doubleheader. Charlie Berry replaced Jim at catcher late in the first game, and Foxx returned to full-time duty at first base in the second game.

Foxx's fielding and batting while a catcher were superb. He compiled a .992 fielding average (116 putouts, 16 assists, only 1 error and 1 passed ball). During the 24 games that Jim played catcher, he batted .352 with a .729 slugging average and homered every 10.6 at bats.

Mack had hoped that with Foxx at catcher, he could place an additional batter in the lineup who would hit for power and average, or both. But the early season trial with Alex Hooks and Lou Finney was a bust. Neither Hooks nor Finney, who played ten and eighteen games at first base, respectively, provided the kind of power hitting customarily expected from a first baseman. Hooks was released shortly after his ten-game stint. Finney remained with the club as an outfielder but hit no homers in more than 400 at bats for the season. Mack must have figured, why risk injury to his best hitter, Foxx; an injury that would be more likely to occur while playing catcher.

After two years of letting the fans have most of the control over player selection for the All-Star game, Commissioner Landis directed managers Frisch and Cochrane to name twenty players each to their teams. The July 8 All-Star game was played at Cleveland's Municipal Stadium, to the delight of more than 69,000 fans. Cochrane picked Gomez to start for the AL and Frisch picked his own hurler, Bill Walker, to start when Dodger ace Van Lingle Mungo sustained an infected finger before the game. Cochrane chose Foxx as his third baseman and cleanup hitter, and Jimmie didn't let his former teammate down.

The Sudlersville Slugger came to bat in the bottom of the first with Gehrig on first and two out. On a 3 and 2 count, Foxx lined a home run far into the left field lower grandstand. Jimmie also smashed a hard grounder through pitcher Hal Schumacher's legs in the fifth to drive in the AL's last run in a 4-1 victory. The victory was partial revenge for Cochrane's Tigers' loss to the Cardinals in the previous World Series.

As the back-slapping occurred in the AL dressing room following the game, Foxx said to Cochrane, "We got back at 'em for you."

"What was it you hit?" Cochrane asked.

"A curve," said Foxx. "They will try to hook that three-and-two ball, those National Leaguers."

While it became apparent that the Athletics would remain out of the pennant race then dominated by Cochrane's club, Foxx was still in contention for several individual batting honors, including the batting and home-run titles. On September 1, Foxx trailed Greenberg in the homer derby 34-29, and Joe Vosmik in batting average, .349-.326. From September 1-18, Jimmie batted 33 for 63 (.524) during an 18-game hitting streak that included seven doubleheaders. After the games of September 19, Foxx led the league in batting at .351, four points ahead of Vosmik and just two homers behind Greenberg, 36-34. Greenberg didn't homer in his final nine games after September 19, and Foxx waited until the last day of the season to homer twice and tie Greenberg for the AL home-run crown.

Foxx reverted to another of his specialties when he faced his nemesis, Elden Auker, on September 7. Jim solved Auker's underarm (submarine) delivery and busted up the Tiger hurler's no-hit bid with an eighth-inning double.

But Jim's chase for the batting title weakened when he could only muster 9 hits in his last 34 at bats, dropping his average from .351 to .346. Meanwhile, Senators' outfielder Buddy Myers crept by Vosmik (.348) and Foxx to end the season at .349. Foxx had come ever so close to his second batting title. However, Foxx's high average and tie for the league lead in homers gave him a league-leading slugging percentage of .636.

Although still among the league leaders, Foxx's runs scored and runs batted in totals dropped off somewhat in 1934 and 1935, compared to his MVP seasons. This reduction may have been in part due to the different supporting cast in the A's batting lineup. Although the Mackmen had hard-hitting Bob Johnson, Doc Cramer, and Pinky Higgins in 1934 and 1935, these hitters were not quite the same caliber as Simmons, Bishop, and Cochrane, who reached base more often. Jimmie played in 120 games at first base, 24 games at catcher, and split one additional game between catcher and first and another between catcher and third base. The A's finished in last place, 34 games behind the Tigers. Cramer, Johnson, and Higgins continued to star at the bat for Mack, but the only effective starter was Marcum, who went 17-12 and had 25 pinch-hitting appearances with an overall average of .311.

In October, Connie Mack's acquisition of first baseman Jim Oglesby, who hit .365 in the Pacific Coast League in 1935, ignited trade talk that Connie was ready to let Foxx go for the right price. Joe Williams asked Red Sox owner Tom Yawkey early in October about rumors that he was about to buy Foxx from the Athletics. Yawkey said that he had asked Mack for a price for Foxx and was told that nothing under $300,000 could swing the deal. Mack admitted to Williams that neither Foxx nor any player was worth anything like $300,000. "However, if Cronin was worth $250,000, Foxx should bring $300,000," said Mack.

On October 3, Tom Yawkey said he was no longer planning to spend "big money" for "big names," and Joe Cronin denied any interest in purchasing Jimmie Foxx from Mack for big money. Cronin said flatly the Red Sox did not want Foxx. The Red Sox management said it didn't believe that Foxx was worth $200,000-300,000.

"We would rather spend that kind of money on young players, if at all," said Cronin. "We have plenty of power without Foxx," he continued. Cronin couldn't be sincere about what he was saying. Foxx was still young, not quite twenty-eight, and the Red Sox had very little batting power. The highest home run production by a Red Sox hitter in 1935 was fourteen by Bill Werber, so it seems that Cronin was making statements just to reinforce Yawkey's stated position.

Over his career with the Athletics through 1935, Foxx had a .303 batting average against the Red Sox at Fenway, compared to a .369 average against the Red Sox at Shibe Park. In fact, the only enemy park where Foxx batted higher against a given team's hurlers than in Shibe Park was in Comiskey Park (.348 vs. .337). The only ballpark that thwarted Jim's normally high batting average and home-run production was Yankee Stadium, with its deep left-center and center field walls.

Several weeks later, the strongest rumors still had Jimmie going to the Red Sox, but Dan Daniel reported in his column of October 17 that Yawkey had recently insisted he was no longer interested in Foxx. Daniel referred to Yawkey's denial as "pardonable camouflage" and predicted that Foxx would be especially helpful to the Red Sox with their short distance to the left field fence in Fenway Park.

Even though the Yankees were being mentioned as another contender for Foxx's services, Daniel reasoned that Foxx's batting average at Yankee Stadium has not reached the .300 mark and his home runs there were well below his amount at most other parks. Daniel was correct. Through the 1935 season, Foxx batted .265 (85 hits in 321 at bats) in Yankee Stadium, with only 9 homers, by far his lowest total in any opponent's ballyard, and batted .354 (102 hits in 288 at bats) with 34 homers against Yankee hurlers in Shibe Park. The homer total for Foxx against Yankee pitchers in Shibe Park was his greatest amount against any opponent there.

Foxx's favorite parks to hit in for average and homers were Sportsman's Park (.355 average and 25 homers), Navin Field (.343 average and 27 homers), and Comiskey Park (.348 average and 22 homers).

During October and November, Earle Mack took an aggregation of major leaguers on a barnstorming tour. Three of the players, Foxx, Rogers Hornsby, and Earl Whitehill, brought their wives. The club played several games against semipro teams in Texas, then played 16 games in 18 days in Mexico. The major leaguers played the Negro League champion Pittsburgh Crawfords in Mexico City in a three-game series, winning two games, 11-7 and 7-2, and tying one. Foxx's teammates included Hornsby, Eric McNair, Higgins, Ralph Kress, Charlie Berry, Cramer, Heinie Manush, and pitchers Ted Lyons, Jack Knott, Vern Kennedy, and Whitehill. Jimmie and his teammates were each paid $825 plus expenses.

On December 2, Foxx announced from Philadelphia that his current contract would have to be scrapped by any club buying his release from the Athletics. Jimmie explained that, "If some American League club owner puts up a fortune for me in release money, he will have to give me a contract for more than I ever received before, even though my current contract has two more years to run." Foxx said that when he signed his last contract with the Athletics, "he did so to help the club out of financial trouble." He also said he did it because he thought he owed something to Connie Mack, who had given him his start in baseball. The following day, Foxx told the press that he had been informed by Mack several weeks earlier that he would likely be sold to another club, just as trade rumors had begun to die down. Rumors variously had Jimmie going to the Red Sox, White Sox, Yankees, and Indians. Higgins, McNair, and Cramer were also said to be on the trading block.

Two days later, Wayne Otto of the *Chicago Herald Examiner* informed his readers that he had learned that Jimmie Foxx had been purchased by the White Sox from the Athletics for $75,000. Mack would neither confirm nor deny the report that day. Meanwhile the *New York Times* reported that White Sox owner Louis Comiskey replied, "I wouldn't have Jimmie Foxx now at any price." "We don't want the grief of dealing with him," Comiskey said. "He's asking a higher salary from whatever club takes him from the Athletics and I don't want to go through all the contract negotiations with a holdout star."

White Sox Manager Dykes was much less negative in his reply to the rumored purchase of Foxx:

> There is absolutely no foundation to the report. Certainly I'd like to get Foxx. What major league club wouldn't like to have him? But I'm certain if Mr. Comiskey had made the purchase, I would have heard about it. I talked with Foxx by telephone, too, and he asked me if Chicago had bought him, and I told him the same story. So far as I know, there are no plans under way for his purchase.

Finally, on December 10, at the beginning of the winter baseball meetings, photographers recorded Connie Mack securing the signature of Yawkey, which completed a deal in which Foxx and Marcum were sold to the Red Sox for reported amounts varying from $150,000-250,000 and two "throw-in" players, pitcher Gordon Rhodes and George Savino, neither of whom were considered top major-league prospects. Rhodes had pitched briefly for the Red Sox in 1935 and was unimpressive (2-10), and Savino had caught for Syracuse and batted .265. Mack had paid $25,000 several years earlier when he purchased Marcum from Louisville. Other reports speculated that a similar deal had been struck between Mack and Yawkey on December 10 in which McNair and Cramer had been acquired by the Red Sox for outfielder Carl Reynolds and an undisclosed amount of cash. On the strength of the confirmed Foxx-Marcum trade and the unconfirmed acquisition of Cramer and McNair, the *Boston Globe*'s front page asserted that "Boston today ascended to the position of the number one baseball city in the universe on the wings of young Tom Yawkey's pocketbook." The transactions were lauded as the single most important trade in baseball history. The *Globe* went on, "In Foxx, the Red Sox have acquired the greatest right-handed slugger of all time to plug one of their most glaring weaknesses—first base."

Baseball fans and sportswriters from Boston had plenty of reason to be excited. The city had been without a serious pennant contender for NL or AL honors since the Braves won the NL pennant and World Series in 1914 and the Red Sox won the AL pennant and World Series in 1918. More often than not, both clubs finished in the second division of their league standings following those seasons through 1935. The Red Sox had been even worse than the Braves, with nine eighth-place finishes over an eighteen-year period. The Red Sox had new hope for the 1936 season, given the club's fourth-place finish in 1935 and the addition of Foxx and Marcum.

Some Boston sportswriters proposed that the team change its last name to the Red Soxx, the second "x" being in honor of Foxx's last name. Other scribes were calling Yawkey's club the "Gold Sox," referring to the exorbitant sums of money being paid out by the Red Sox' owner to purchase proven major-league talent in hopes of buying an AL pennant.

The loss of Foxx was a low point in Mack's managerial career. When interviewed by reporters, he simply said, "Well, Jimmie's gone. After this I'm right back where I started." Mack probably meant he was now at the same point he found himself shortly after the breakup of the Athletics powerhouse of 1910-1914. Mack continued, "I'm giving no reasons [for letting Foxx go to the Red Sox]. They must be obvious or remain a mystery. I am not even going to discuss the team for next year. I am not in a position to do that now."

Foxx paused briefly after he was first informed of the news at his home, then is reported to have let out a loud whoop and exclaimed, "Oh boy, what a break! Who said there isn't a Santa Claus?" Jim hugged Helen, gave six-year-old Jimmie, Jr., a big kiss, walked to the hall closet, and took out a big bat. "This is going to do alot of talking up in Boston next year," he concluded. "With good breaks, no injuries and any kind of start I believe I can break Babe Ruth's record for home runs in one season." Foxx said, "Since I was going anyway, I'm glad it's the Red Sox. There's no other city to which I'd rather go than Boston. It's the most understanding baseball town in the country."

Still, Jimmie would miss the friendly confines of Shibe Park. He had batted .358 with 168 homers in Philadelphia compared to .323 with 134 homers on the road.

Foxx began fielding questions regarding his current salary and any hopes that he may have for an increase, given the much better condition of Yawkey's pocketbook than Mack's. Foxx had just finished another year of a three-year contract of $50,000 with the A's and a contract that netted him close to $2,000 with a Philadelphia radio station. Jimmie was quoted as saying, "I have other interests in Philly [other than his playing salary] that increase my income. I'll have to give them up when I leave. But I'm sure Ed Collins and Tom Yawkey will take care of everything."

Many fans of the Athletics and scribes who had been covering the Mackmen while Foxx played for the club knew they would miss the popular player. James Isaminger reported on the trade in the December 12 issue of *The Sporting News*, recounting some of Jim's highest accomplishments, especially the 58 homers in 1932 and his back-to-back most valuable player awards in the AL in 1932 and 1933. He reminded readers that Foxx had been the last member of the 1929 champion A's that defeated the Cubs in the Series. Isaminger also asserted:

> While Jimmy was quoted a short time before the Boston deal was made that he would insist on a new contract, with more liberal salary figures, the Maryland farm boy denied this when informed of the deal. He said it was his understanding that the Boston club would assume his contract which has two years to go, and that this would be entirely satisfactory to him. It is reported that his salary runs around $18,500 a season. He signed the three-year document about a year ago. Mack regretted to dispense with the services of Foxx and Marcum, but it was explained that the Philadelphia club lost money again this year and that, in view of the failure of the fans to support his team, he felt he would have to continue rebuilding with younger and less expensive players.

On December 13, Foxx was pictured in several newspapers, wearing his perpetual grin, trying on his new Boston Red Sox uniform and cap for size. Jim and the Red Sox were both in a hurry for the 1936 season to start.

Jim visited Boston on December 30 and was greeted as the local fandom's new hero when he attended a luncheon beginning at noon and a banquet later that evening. Foxx's first stop was Fenway Park, where an elaborate luncheon was held at the Sox's headquarters by a caterer. Cameramen took a host of pictures of the new Red Sox slugger as the luncheon lasted into the early evening while he fielded questions from reporters.

The *New York Times* grossly underestimated his lifetime batting average at Fenway Park to be .235. Foxx was quoted as blaming his low average in Boston on the "strong arms of those Boston hurlers." Foxx picked Detroit to be the chief competitor of the Red Sox for the 1936 AL flag and Gehrig to be his "chief worry in the race for league honors for the home run championship."

Foxx followed the luncheon as the guest of honor at a Fathers' and Sons' night at the big synagogue for the Ohabel Shalom Brotherhood on Beacon Street. A couple of thousand men and boys roared and applauded as Jim was introduced as the new star of the Red Sox. Jim voiced his appreciation to both the lunch and dinner audiences as the seeds of mutual admiration were planted between Foxx and the Red Sox fans.

12

FOXX JOINS THE RED SOX

Shortly following Foxx's move to Boston, owner Yawkey completed another deal with Mack on January 4, 1936, when he obtained Cramer and McNair for Hank Johnson, Al Niemiec, and $75,000. Yawkey was still searching for the AL pennant with his coffers.

Then, on January 7, business manager Eddie Collins announced that Foxx had signed a one-year contract with the Red Sox the day after attending a Boston Bruins hockey game with Yawkey. Foxx's three-year contract with the A's, which had two years to run, was destroyed, and a new one was drawn up. Collins did not disclose the salary but said that Foxx had received an increase. Estimates of Foxx's new salary were given as $25,000 by the *New York World Telegram* and the *New York Times*. The Red Sox organization was not obligated to resign Jim to a different contract. "However, after Jimmy explained the matter to Mr. Yawkey," said Collins, "and pointed out that the shift to Boston was causing him to give up certain radio work [in Philadelphia]," Mr. Yawkey agreed to sign him to a new contract.

The day after Foxx signed his contract with Boston, Eddie Collins hosted a group of Philadelphia members of the Red Sox organization at the Penn Athletic Club. Foxx, Miller, Roger Cramer, Rube Walberg, Herb Pennock, and Joe Cascarella attended. They no doubt gave a few toasts of good luck for the Red Sox' 1936 edition and Collins met in private, at least momentarily, with all the attendees other than Foxx, because no one else had yet signed for the new season.

Foxx and Miller began working out hard at a Philadelphia gym in early January in preparation for their season as Red Sox teammates. Foxx promised to be at a lower weight for the 1936 season than he had been for the past several years.

While Foxx exercised on a bike in the gym that month, he said he was serious in his belief that he'd crack Ruth's home-run record for a single season in 1936. The single-season home-run record was important to Jimmie. He said several times in his career that there was only one Ruth and there would never be another one like him, but he recognized the distinction he would gain from accomplishing the feat.

Always willing to participate on the winter banquet tour and socialize with other ballplayers, Foxx served as toastmaster for a send-off for former teammate Max Bishop at the Southern Hotel in Baltimore on January 30. More than 400 players and fans wished Bishop good luck in his new job of managing the Portland (Oregon) minor-league club of the Pacific Coast League. Among Bishop's former teammates attending were Boley, Rommel, Walberg, Miller, Grove, Jack Ogden, Tommy Thomas, Bill Werber, Fritz Maisel, Dick Porter, and Foxx.

Jim had had several colorful nicknames over his career, but he would most often be referred to as "The Beast," and "Double X," while with the Red Sox. His earliest nickname had been "The Sudlersville Flash," as coined by the *Centreville Observer* during his first few years with the Athletics. That name came about as a result of his first-place finishes track-and-field sprint events. Then came nicknames recognizing his batting power and strength while with the Athletics—"The Sudlersville Slugger" and "The Maryland Broadback."

Fans and the press in Boston displayed growing optimism about the Red Sox' pennant chances. Ferrell's league-leading twenty-five wins in 1935, Grove's comeback in 1935 after a sore arm in 1934, and the acquisitions of Foxx, Marcum, and Cramer pointed to a much stronger ball club than two years previous.

In early February, Joe Williams told the story of Yawkey's disinterest in Foxx as recently as the previous October, just two months before he purchased Jimmie. Yawkey said:

> I told you I wasn't at all interested in Foxx; but that was because I had heard he lost his enthusiasm for baseball. Naturally, I didn't want that type of ballplayer. I got to thinking Foxx's case a little further. I got Mack's permission to talk with Foxx. This talk convinced me that if Foxx had lost his enthusiasm, it was due to circumstances that could be easily remedied. Thus convinced I didn't hesitate to buy him. Keep your eye on him this year. He will have one of his greatest seasons.

Red Sox manager Cronin was reached at his hometown of San Francisco, California, on February 3, singing a much different tune than he did before the Red Sox obtained Foxx:

> Foxx will come close to, if not break Babe Ruth's AL home run record this year. Foxx is the greatest player in the game [today]. The set up for Foxx to better Ruth's record of 60 is perfect. He is joining

a new club under ideal conditions. I wouldn't say Jimmy was bogged down last year, but he had reached the stage, where it was more or less routine. Our left field fence is a few feet shorter [from home plate] to aim at than in Philadelphia. [But] he'll have to hit the ball a bit higher, but when he gets a hold of one, no fence will stop him. It is a pretty big order to ask a man to hit as many homers as the Babe did in 1927, but I am confident that Jimmy has the stuff to do it.

Cronin said that Foxx had the perfect temperament. "I'll match his disposition against that of any other player in the history of the game. He is moulded from the stuff from which champions are made."

Joe praised Jim's versatility:

Having played against Foxx over a period of years, it is my opinion that he is one of the real standouts. He can play first, third, the outfield, and catch, if necessary. I haven't any doubt that if I put him in to pitch, he would make a creditable showing.

Three days after Cronin's high praise, Jimmie told the Norristown (Pennsylvania) Rotary Club that he planned to head south for the Red Sox training camp in a few more days. Jim was suffering from a severe head cold and ignored his doctor's orders not to attend the luncheon. Foxx said he couldn't leave too soon, adding, "I'm tired of this cold weather."

On February 9, fans and baseball players gave Foxx a farewell banquet in Philadelphia at the Ritz-Carlton Hotel as he said good-bye to his local friends. Collins, Miller, Walberg, Cramer, Herb Pennock, all of the Boston club, and about 250 guests attended. It was a bittersweet moment for Jimmie. He had enjoyed the baseball fans in Philadelphia, the closeness of the city to his hometown, and had had the good fortune of playing on three pennant winners and two world champions. But he had been underpaid during most of his stay with Philadelphia, and the team was now far removed from being a pennant contender. Now he was joining a team with an owner who was willing and able to spend money to purchase the necessary players to make a winning ball club, and Jim's own salary would likely increase.

Personally, the trade would be a difficult transition for Helen, Jimmie, Jr., and Jimmie. He would no longer be able to spend half the summer with Helen and Jimmie, Jr., as he had in Philadelphia during home games, because Helen had elected to stay behind and not move to Boston. About the only time he would see his wife and son during the summer would be when the Red Sox played at Shibe Park. Also, the frequent trips by Dell Foxx, family, and friends to see Jimmie play baseball were now just a memory. They would only make an occasional trip to Shibe Park when the

Red Sox visited Philadelphia, and on rarer occasions to Boston's Fenway Park. Baseball fans from Sudlersville and other Eastern Shore towns would still identify with Jimmie Foxx, but it wouldn't be with the same fervor and intensity.

By the first of March, Foxx reported to the Red Sox camp at Sarasota, "tanned, weighing [a trim] 183 pounds and asking for action." Cronin complied by making sure his pitchers gave Jim an early workout of batting practice. Foxx had tanned mostly while playing golf the last couple of weeks of February, and one Boston newspaper told its readers, "Jimmy Foxx can drive a golf ball almost as far as he can clout a horsehide, but his work falls off when he nears the greens."

On March 3, Grantland Rice wrote in his syndicated column that baseball fans throughout the country were speculating and waiting anxiously to see who would be Babe Ruth's successor to the home-run hitting crown, now that he was retired as a player. Rice said the three leading candidates were Greenberg, Gehrig, and Foxx. Cochrane talked briefly about Greenberg, McCarthy about Gehrig, and Wes Ferrell gushed about his new teammate, Foxx. Ferrell observed:

> The left field fence in Boston is about 20 feet closer than the left field fence at Shibe Park. Foxx hit many a fly ball that just missed the Philadelphia fence. A lot of those will clear the boundary in Boston. I've pitched a lot against Jimmie Foxx and I know how he can hit. He is always a hard man to handle, always dangerous. It wouldn't surprise me if Jimmy came close to 60 home runs this year. That's how good I think he is, and I think the switch to Boston will be a big help!

Jimmie compared Mack's teams of 1929-31 with the 1936 Red Sox during an interview with George Carens.

> I'd say the A's had a pretty swell outfield in Simmons, Haas, and Miller—the Red Sox outfield of Manush, Cramer, and Almada or Cooke will have to step lively to match those fellows. The infields are on about a par and the Red Sox will be pretty hot if Werber gets into top stride at third. The A's pitching just overpowered the opposition and Cochrane's batting was a big help.

Carens also inquired, "How will the Foxx of those pennant-winning Philadelphia teams compare with the Foxx of the 1936 Red Sox?"
Foxx replied:

You can always figure a ball player with ambition will do his level best—this is a great bunch of fellows to play with. Not a roughneck on the team, unless it's me. They say a ball player's best years are from 23 to 33. If that's true, I ought to be pretty near my prime, because I'm 28, and I've never felt any better. I've made quite a study of batting and the only time I hit under .300 in ten years was in 1930 [actually it was 1931].

No one ever taught me much about batting. I remember talking it over with Ty Cobb, when he joined the A's. Cobb told me, "Never take your eye off the pitcher until the ball leaves his hand, and then always follow the flight of the ball." I've done that.

Carens also reported that Jimmie and Helen were expecting a new arrival in their family before mid-summer and both parents were hoping for a girl.

The Red Sox stayed at the Sarasota Terrace Hotel during spring training. Cronin usually had no set plan for the event—just be there on time. Pitchers pitched batting practice and hitters did lots of hitting. Pitchers and regulars did their running for conditioning plus infield and outfield workouts. "The regulars were ready when the bell rang in April for the starting pitchers to go nine innings and the regulars to play in 154 games," recalled pitcher Charlie Wagner.

Early in spring training on March 9, Cronin beamed over Foxx's value to the Red Sox:

Foxx is the boy who has made this club. He added a lot of power and a lot of spirit to the team. He's one of the hardest workers in camp. He showed up in the best shape in years and looks great. He's made himself the most popular man on the club. Moreover, he's glad to be with us. Like everyone else, he feels we have a fine chance to finish on top.

On March 11, Tom Yawkey had his first view of Jimmie Foxx in a Red Sox uniform at Sarasota, and was joined by Foxx's former boss, Connie Mack, who came over from Fort Myers. Yawkey said he was thrilled when Foxx slammed three drives over the left field wall, each traveling more than 425 feet. Mack exaggerated when he exclaimed, "I've seen James hit all of his record homers, but none of them compared with the drives he hit today!"

Several days later, Foxx told Ed Rumill of the *Christian Science Monitor*, "Detroit will be tough, but we'll beat them." Rumill noted that balls hit over the left field wall at Sarasota were a rarity in the past, whether in a game or in practice, but Jim was smacking them with regularity, sometimes as many as three or four a day. Rumill added, "Such long-range hitting is a new and welcome sight in the Red Sox camp."

Joe Williams, sportswriter of the *New York World-Telegram*, interviewed Joe Cronin on March 27 while at the Red Sox training camp. Cronin's optimism for a pennant in 1936 stemmed from the 45 victories notched by Ferrell and Grove in 1935, the return of a healthy Fritz Ostermueller, and the addition of Johnny Marcum, who had won 17 games for the lowly A's in 1935. Cronin felt that the bats of Foxx, Cramer, McNair, and Manush added to the roster greatly outweighed the loss of hitters Carl Reynolds, Roy Johnson, and Babe Dahlgren.

The preseason poll to pick the AL pennant winner for 1936 was announced on April 3 and showed that 69 of 97 sports editors and baseball writers participating chose the Tigers for first place. The Red Sox finished a distant second in the poll, with 16 first-place votes.

As the season began in mid-April, Foxx was labelled "Boston's new darling" just a year after Babe Ruth had returned to the city as a Boston Brave with an overdose of fanfare, considering the Babe's retirement from the team before the end of June. Fans could expect a longer stay by Foxx, considering his much younger age of twenty-eight, compared to the Babe's age of forty.

Fenway Park had opened for baseball in 1912 with a crowd capacity of 35,000. Streets that bordered the park were Jersey Street (now Yawkey Way) alongside home plate toward first base and right field, Brookline Avenue from home plate to third base to left field, and Landsdowne Street along a line from the left field corner to center field. Landsdowne Street is where Foxx would hit many of his home runs.

In 1936, the odd-shaped outfield fence from left to right field included a 315-foot distance to the left field corner, 379 feet to the left-center corner, 388 feet to the deep left-center point in line with the flagpole, 420 feet to the deepest corner just right of dead center, and 332 feet to the right field corner. The playing field had the smallest foul territory of any major-league park.

The "Green Monster," the left field wall of today's Fenway Park, was "the Monster" then. The wall wasn't painted a solid green. Rather, the 37-foot-high tin wall that covered a frame of railroad ties behind it was splattered with advertisements, the most prominent one being for "Gem Razor Blades."

In Foxx's first year with the Red Sox, a 23-foot-high net was added on top of the tin wall to prevent most homers rapped over the wall from breaking windows in the dwellings and businesses on Landsdowne Street. It seems that this was in large part due to Foxx becoming a member of the club, considering the meager homer production of the Red Sox before his arrival.

It's believed that Foxx may have actually whaled some of his homer blasts that passed over the net as far as the tracks of the Boston and Albany Railroad. The tracks were parallel to Landsdowne Street, farther from home plate. At least one story has it that one of Foxx's homer blasts out of Fenway landed in a moving freight car on those railroad tracks, making it the "longest-traveled home run."

In 1936, a fan at Fenway Park could buy a scorecard for five cents. "Frankfurts—Our Famous Horseshoe Brand," by Handschumacher and Co., were sold at the park with Gulden's mustard on Ward's frankfurter rolls for only ten cents. Drinks such as Hi-Brow beverages, orangeade, and Coca-Cola were sold throughout the stands for only ten cents. Ballantine beer was ten cents for a draught and twenty cents for a bottle and sold only at bars below the stands. You could call out to the vendors for Lucky Strikes, Camels, Between-the-Acts Little Cigars, Muriel cigars, Schrafft's chocolate-covered bars, and Beech-Nut gums and candies. Prices for seats at Fenway were a mere $1.65 for box seats, $1.40 for reserved seats, $1.10 for grandstand, 85 cents for pavilion, and 55 cents for bleachers.

Red Sox fans could choose sports pages from a host of different newspapers in Boston in the 1930s, which also meant that Foxx and his teammates had to be very thick-skinned, since they were scrutinized by so many different sportswriters. Papers in Boston that followed the Red Sox included The Boston Herald, The Boston Post, The Boston Daily Globe, the Boston Evening Transcript, the Daily Record, the Boston Traveler, Boston American, Boston Advertiser, and The Christian Science Monitor.

Foxx made his regular season debut for the Red Sox on April 14, playing his former teammates, the A's. Connie Mack watched helplessly as Foxx, who batted cleanup, singled, doubled, and tripled in a 9-4 Red Sox win at Fenway Park. Foxx followed with a homer in his second game for the Red Sox, which also ended as a lopsided win over the A's. Jim donned the number three uniform for Boston, as he would his entire stay with the club.

After the games of May 3, Boston held a slim one-half game lead over New York with 13 wins to New York's 12. Both teams had six losses. Rookie Joe DiMaggio made his first appearance at Yankee Stadium on May 3 and had an immediate positive impact with three hits in six at bats. The Tigers suffered a severe blow to their pennant chances when Greenberg broke the same wrist as he did a year earlier, only twelve games into the season with a .348 batting average. Hank collided with Senator outfielder Jake Powell at first base and was lost to Detroit for the rest of the season. Meanwhile, on May 7, Foxx belted his seventh and eighth homers to lead the Red Sox to their eighth victory in nine games.

Then, on May 26, Jimmie celebrated the birth of his second son, William Kenneth, one day earlier, with a homer that led Boston to a 5-4 win over the Yankees to cut New York's lead to only one-half game. Kenneth was born to Helen Foxx in Germantown Hospital in Philadelphia. Meanwhile, in the loss to Boston, the Yank's Bill Dickey suffered an injury to his left kidney and was rushed to St. Elizabeth's Hospital in Boston. The injury represented a serious threat to New York's pennant hopes, considering that Dickey led the league in rbi's with fifty at the time of his injury.

On May 28, Dan Daniel predicted that Foxx would hit far more than his league-leading 36 homers of a year earlier, since he had already slugged 13 through that date. The serious injury to Greenberg meant that Gehrig and Cleveland's first baseman Hal Trosky would be Foxx's chief competitors for the AL home-run honors as the season unfolded.

Foxx showed off his tremendous power on June 16 while at Comiskey Park when he pounded two long homers off Merritt "Sugar" Cain, the first over the roof of the left field pavilion and the second into the center field stands just to the left of the center field bleachers. According to Ed Burns of the *Chicago Tribune:*

> The first one [homer by Foxx] was of the brand that no other man has knocked before at Comiskey Park. Foxx, on surveying the flight of the ball after the game, remarked that it was the longest homer he had ever hit. According to the guards outside the park, the ball cleared the grandstand roof and came down in a handball court across 34th Street. It traveled a block after coming down.

It was the second time Foxx homered over the left field roof at Comiskey, a feat accomplished only by him up to that point, and a remarkable achievement for a visiting player who played only eleven games in the park each season. Ruth was the only player up to that time to knock a homer over the right field pavilion.

From June 7-26, Jimmie hit safely in 16 of 17 games, batting 31 for 67, with 8 homers.

The fourth annual All-Star Game was played on July 7 at Braves Field in Boston. Foxx didn't start the game; Gehrig again got the nod to start at first base and Higgins at third. The AL threatened a comeback in the top of the seventh inning, trailing, 4-0. Gehrig led off the inning with a 420-foot homer followed by two consecutive outs. Then Goslin singled and Foxx batted for Higgins and sent a hard grounder to shortstop Durocher, who couldn't handle the ball smoothly enough to force Goslin at second. Foxx was credited with a hit. Appling's single to right scored Goslin and Foxx before the rally died, and Foxx replaced Higgins at third base in the bottom of the inning. Nonetheless, the NL took the game, 4-3. Foxx batted 1 for 2 and scored one run.

On September 8, the day of an exhibition game in Canton, Ohio, Cronin decided to shake up the Red Sox lineup the following day. Joe switched

Foxx from first base to left field; Babe Dahlgren, called up from the minor leagues, was assigned to first base; and Werber was moved from left field to second base. Jimmie showed off his versatility playing at both left field and at third base on September 9 and in the outfield for the last fifteen games of the season.

Foxx's hitting didn't falter while handling the outfield position. He smacked 22 hits in 59 at bats for a .373 average. Yawkey was right—Jim had one of his best overall seasons, batting .338 with 41 homers, 143 rbi's, and a slugging average of .631, only to be overshadowed by Gehrig (49 homers and 152 rbi's) and Trosky (42 homers and 162 rbi's).

Foxx's 41 homers broke the Red Sox club record of 29 set by Babe Ruth in his last season with Boston before joining the Yankees (Ruth's 29 homers were hit over a 140-game schedule during the "deadball" era). Red Sox batters were so anemic from Ruth's last season through Foxx's first with the club that no other batter even hit 20 homers in a season. Jim's rbi total was also a new Red Sox record for a single season, and he played in all 155 of Boston's games. During the first 139 games, he played exclusively at first base, and he performed in 15 games in the outfield (10 in left field and 5 in right), and split a game between left field and third base.

The Red Sox faltered badly in the second half of the season and ended with only 74 wins, 80 losses, and a tie, landing in sixth place despite Yawkey's heavy spending for new talent the winter before. C. M. Gibbs, of the *Baltimore Morning Sun,* had speculated on March 15 that if "Foxx happens to have a flat year, the machine [for the Red Sox] is going to blow itself to a cracked piston." However, Jimmie had an excellent season, but was still overshadowed by several problems. Cronin and Manush appeared in only about half of Boston's games due to broken fingers. No other Red Sox player hit as many as ten homers to help support Jimmie's run production. Grove (17-12) and Ferrell (20-15) were the only reliable starters; Marcum fell short of expectations with less than ten wins.

The pennant-winning Yankees won 102 games and finished 19 games ahead of second-place Detroit. Five players drove in 100 or more runs for New York—Gehrig, DiMaggio, Lazzeri, Dickey, and Selkirk. The Tigers stumbled partly because of Greenberg's injury and partly due to Cochrane's action being limited to only 42 games at catcher due to illness. Because of the dismal sixth-place finish for Boston, Yawkey decided he couldn't build a winning club simply by purchasing proven veteran ballplayers. It was time to build his farm system, and the club owner employed former umpire Billy Evans as farm director.

Near the end of the regular season for major leaguers, Colonel Albanus Phillips, owner of Phillips Packing Company, and Joe Fowler, owner of the local Coca-Cola plant, spurred formation of baseball teams in Cambridge, Maryland, to decide that city's "championship" in a seven-game series to be played on Sundays in September and October. After Phillips won the first two games, the Coca-Cola team used several IL players to assure its first victory in game three. The Phillips club lost to Coke again, 1-0, in game four, despite using Max Bishop and Dick Porter.

Desperate to beat Fowler, Phillips called Colonel Ruppert for help and learned that Jimmie Foxx was organizing a team for barnstorming. On the spur of the moment, Phillips convinced Foxx to come to Cambridge for game five for a sum of $300. Foxx picked up the Senators' hurler Jimmy DeShong in Philadelphia and joined other players such as Bishop, Porter, Doc Cramer, Billy Werber, and Frankie Hayes.

Just before game five began, word spread among the crowd of 3,000 fans that Foxx would be playing, and the crowd stirred with excitement. Foxx took the field in the top of the first inning for the Phillips club, playing third base, wearing his "All Americans" uniform that he used for the 1934 tour of Japan by the All-Star squad. Jimmie stepped into the batter's box to lead off the bottom of the second inning and let several pitches go by as the count mounted to three balls and two strikes. Then he smashed the pitcher's next offering and everyone knew it was gone, the longest homer of the day—by most estimates over 450 feet from home plate. The crowd exploded as Foxx trotted around the bases, loving the moment. Phillips won the game 8-2 and clinched the series the following Sunday with a 2-0 win with many of the same players (without Foxx)in the lineup and 4,000 fans on hand.

In late February 1937, Foxx was interviewed and indicated that he would not sign the contract sent to him but expected little trouble in reaching a salary agreement with Red Sox officials. Foxx had been reported to refuse signing because the Red Sox were asking him to take a $5,000 cut. Then, on March 4, General Manager Eddie Collins announced that Foxx had signed a contract offered by Joe Cronin while in Sarasota. Although Foxx's salary was not announced, it was believed that the Red Sox' proposed cut was restored. Foxx had reportedly said he would not sign unless he received at least the same salary as in 1936—variably estimated at $22,000-$25,000. What happened to Yawkey's pocketbook? If anything, Jimmie deserved a raise. He was one of the few bright spots in the Red Sox lineup in 1936, finishing among the league leaders in homers, rbi's, batting average, and slugging.

Jimmie appeared on Wheaties boxes again in 1937, in an advertisement exclaiming "Jimmie Foxx tells how to play first base—how to put 'em out." The panels on the box consisted of a series of five different illustrated instructions on fielding the first base position and a picture of Foxx leaping to catch a ball high to his glove side.

Jim had one of his worst spring trainings in 1937, in terms of power production, with only a couple of homers, and became anxious to solve his batting problems so he could regain his batting prowess of the previous season. Foxx went to Dr. Herb Goddard in Philadelphia on the morning of April 16, complaining of pain over his eyes.

"I noted he was running a temperature, so I sent him to the hospital," Goddard remarked. "I don't think it will be necessary for an operation and believe the sinus infection will respond to treatment."

Foxx was released from the Jewish Hospital in Philadelphia on April 23. He didn't play his first game for Boston until April 30, missing their first five games. In his debut for the season, Foxx slugged a three-run homer in Boston's 15-5 victory over the Athletics at Shibe Park, which must have brought another melancholy feeling to Connie Mack. Jim seemed especially tough on his former teammates.

Jimmie's average remained low for the first half of the season and was only .253 at the All-Star break. Foxx's action in the All-Star game was limited to a pinch-hitting appearance in which he grounded out in the bottom of the sixth inning when he batted for Tommy Bridges.

Tom Meany reported on July 13 in the *New York World Telegram* that "the answer to Jimmy Foxx's slump is sinus trouble." The cause of Foxx's sinus problems never seems to have been determined. If it was like the sinus problems suffered by many others in the Northeastern U.S., he had his good days and bad days, especially with regard to normal or blurred vision. Nevertheless, Foxx began to catch fire just after the All-Star game and hit two homers in each of two consecutive games on July 21 and 22, another homer in the next game, and eight homers over a nine-game period. He slugged eleven home runs in the month of July.

The Red Sox won 12 straight from July 28 through the first game of a doubleheader on August 8. Foxx batted 17 for 47 with five homers and 12 rbi's during the streak. On August 12, Jim's batting eye and mechanics were in perfect working order. Foxx became the only player other than Hank Greenberg to hit a ball out of Fenway Park to the right field side of the flag pole in deep left-center, smacking a mammoth long-distance shot off the Yankees' Kemp Wicker. The *New York Times* called the homer a "masterpiece" by the "double-X man," a shot of 450 feet or more onto the roof of a building overlooking Fenway Park.

Jimmie's late-season batting surge upped his final average to .285. He had recovered enough to smash 36 homers and drive home 127 runs for Boston, even though he had two long homerless droughts during 15 straight games in August and 26 straight games in September. Despite his sinus problems, Jim played in 150 of Boston's 155 games, missing only the first five contests. He played in 149 games at first base and split the action between first base and catcher in one other game.

Grove led the Red Sox pitching staff with 17 wins and 9 losses, despite the obvious loss of his fastball. Jack Wilson won 16 while losing 10, and

Marcum rebounded from his poor initial season with Boston to win 13 of 24.

On November 22, Foxx denied rumors that he was about to be traded to the Indians, or any other club, for that matter. He had just returned to Atlantic City from a hunting trip with Yawkey in Wyoming and said:

> When Mr. Yawkey saw reports that I was going to be traded to Cleveland, he said, "That's news to me. I guess I ought to know who is staying with the club." Maybe I'm wrong, but I don't think Mr. Yawkey would take with him a ballplayer he intends to dispose of. Of course I would like to see my batting average soar, but ballplayers should put more stress on the runs-batted-in column. Averages don't win games, runs batted in do.

On December 2, the Red Sox traded Bobo Newsom, outfielder Buster Mills, and shortstop Ralph "Red" Kress to the Browns for outfielder Joe Vosmik. Yawkey was continuing his persistent efforts to strengthen the team and find the right combination of players to claim the AL pennant in 1938.

13

FOXX MAKES A SUPERB COMEBACK

Jimmie entered the 1938 season under close scrutiny from sportswriters. Despite his good power (36 homers) and run production (127 rbi's), his season-long low batting average (below .300) in 1937 gave observers reason to wonder if his career was beginning to decline.

In early January, the IL's Baltimore Orioles sponsored a test at Oriole Park of the performance of the "jack-rabbit ball" which that league and the AL used, versus the "deadened ball" of the NL. Roughly one thousand fans attended the hitting demonstration free of charge, to watch close to two dozen players participate, most notably Foxx, Chuck Klein, and Charlie Keller, the leading hitter of the IL in 1937. Generally, the players found little or no difference in home run distance between the AL/IL and NL balls. But it was generally agreed that the livelier AL/IL ball gave off a "socking whack" and the dead ball gave a "soggy whoosh" sound when hit.

Foxx hit two balls of each type over the wall and said of the NL ball, "It's just a bit slower. You can notice it on most ground balls. I think it will help the infielders." Jimmie believed that the dead ball would shave only four or five points off the batting averages of power hitters, but as much as twenty points off the batting averages of nonsluggers. Johnny Willig, the Oriole hurler who did most of the pitching for the hitting demonstration, said, "The raised stitches on the dead ball will give the pitcher a better chance to curve the ball."

Foxx signed with the Red Sox on January 25, without any haggling, before attending the Philadelphia baseball writers' dinner. A press report speculated that Foxx might be called upon to resume catching during the coming season. The early signing by Foxx set the stage for a timely reporting date for spring training. He appeared in "ruddy, streamlined shape," hoping to avoid the setbacks he suffered a year earlier from sinusitis.

In early February, Foxx, ever honorable, paid off a bet with a five-dollar personal check to Mr. Willie Green, a black porter at the Capitol Theatre in Atlanta, to purchase a new hat. The bet was made a year earlier during the spring, when Earle Holden, manager of the theater, invited Foxx and the rest of the Red Sox to witness a show. After Jimmie and Willie engaged in baseball conversation, Foxx bet Willie that he would hit more homers than Gehrig in 1937, or buy Willie a new hat. Foxx lost the bet because he hit 36 homers against Gehrig's 37 for the same number of at bats.

It's difficult to know for certain what Foxx's attitude was toward blacks during his playing days in the majors. He didn't shy away from playing against teams of Negro League All-Stars; he played in many contests against them and no doubt developed a healthy respect for their playing abilities. Many white major leaguers felt threatened by the black players, especially those most likely to lose their spot on a major-league roster if blacks were allowed to play in the majors. But many white superstars in the majors, most notably Cap Anson, Ty Cobb, Tris Speaker, and Rogers Hornsby, were opposed to playing against blacks or alongside them as teammates.

Foxx predicted in early March that Bob Feller might win twenty-five games in the coming season, attributing Feller's effectiveness not only to his fastball and curve, but to the intimidating effect of his wildness. Foxx said, "You've got to be loose up there at the plate or he will knock your head off. I don't think he has the speed that Walter Johnson had, or Lefty Grove, but that fastball of Feller's is alive."

As the season approached in early April, an editorial by Joe Williams asked, "Is Jimmy Foxx through?" Williams retold the story that Foxx's sinuses were infected in 1937, which affected his batting eye, and that doctors said rest and sun would eliminate the condition. Williams reported, "in 1937 Foxx could follow the pitch if it was on a level with his shoulders, close enough to see clearly, but when the pitch was low, say around his waist or knees, he found himself swinging at a blurred object." Foxx's poor performance in spring training in 1938 indicated he wasn't putting good wood on the ball and was letting a lot of good pitches go by for called strikes. Was his vision permanently impaired?

Foxx had spent several weeks with Yawkey in the hills of Wyoming in December 1937 "buzzing the fuzz of native animals," and believed the time spent there might have helped his sinusitis condition. But he was probably well aware of the effects that the same condition had in prematurely ending the brilliant careers of George Sisler and Chick Hafey.

Jimmie's sinus condition must have stopped bothering him just before the season's opener, because from April 7-13, he slammed five homers during a seven-game stretch. The home-run barrage gave Foxx's critics their first hint of the kind of comeback he was preparing to mount for the 1938 season. Meanwhile, a poll of sixty sports writers and editors who participated in the annual pennant poll picked the Red Sox to finish fifth in the AL, probably due to weak pitching and little power in the lineup other than Foxx's.

Despite Foxx's heavy homer hitting during the end of the exhibition season, he started slowly in the power department as the regular 1938 season began to unfold. Still, he was steady in run production in April as the Red Sox and Yankees both played about .500 ball. While Jimmie hit only one homer, he drove across fifteen runs.

Then, in May, Foxx's bat finally exploded. He carried the Red Sox during an eight-game winning streak and asserted that the veteran makeup of the club would be an asset during a pennant race. "The loss of a few games through tough breaks might send a young club skidding, but I don't think that would happen with a club with as many cool heads as we have," Foxx said. "Vosmik's ability to get on base from his third spot in the batting order, has resulted in numerous extra runs for the team." Jimmie cooled slightly at the end of May during a 5-game losing streak, but he still was able to homer 10 times and drive across 35 runs for the month.

In June and July, Boston remained near even with New York and Cleveland in the standings, often just two games behind the pacesetters. On June 4, Foxx and Grove teamed up to defeat the Tigers, 5-3, when Jimmie slugged two homers off Tiger ace Tommy Bridges and Lefty blanked Detroit for eight innings, fanning nine batters. After the games of June 8, an article by Pat Robinson in the *New York Daily News* pointed out that Foxx's 17 homers and 66 rbi's in his first 43 games put him on a pace to hit 61 homers and drive in 236 runs, if his performance continued for the season.

On June 8, Jimmie and Helen sold their farmhouse and land in Sudlersville to J. Clauson Jones for only $7,000. The mortgage had been paid and released just two days before. Did Jimmie and Helen need the cash that badly? The sale of the land meant that they had given up on property already paid for that could have been a decent place to live and work after Jimmie's retirement from baseball. Presumably, Dell and Mattie lived there until the sale of the home, then moved to a house next to Mr. Truitt's barbershop on South Church Street, near the corner of Church and Main Streets in Sudlersville.

Jimmie Foxx's cousin Mattie Anthony recalled that Dell was not able to work enough at sixty-five to keep the farm in order. At this point in Dell and Mattie's lives, daily living was probably much less burdensome in town. It's not known whether Jimmie bought the house in town for Dell and Mattie. If they were renting the property, it's likely that Jim and Helen supported his parents by paying any rent.

Foxx was still known for his generosity. Red Sox batboy and clubhouse man Don Fitzpatrick said that Foxx, along with Ted Williams and Greenberg, were among baseball's biggest tippers, and Gehrig was among the cheapest. Jim liked paying the bill for others, especially family, friends, or players with lower salaries than his. His cousin Mattie Anthony remembered one time she visited Fenway Park to see Jim play in a Red Sox uniform. "He knocked a home run, Atlantic or some other company gave the hitter a coupon book for five dollars worth of gas. Well, that was a lot of gas! When they gave Jim the coupon book for gasoline, he walked over and gave it to me."

On June 9, Grove became the first ten-game winner in the AL with an 8-0 shutout over the first-place Indians, shaving their lead over the Red Sox and Yankees to three and one-half games. In a visit to Sportsman's Park on June 16, Foxx faced the ultimate frustration for a power hitter. Jim entered the game leading the league in homers and runs batted in, while placing fifth in batting average. He had slugged a two-run homer the day before in the ninth inning to ice the Red Sox' victory over St. Louis. Browns' manager Gabby Street decided that if Boston were to beat his club on June 16, Foxx should be as little a factor as possible. Six straight times the Browns' hurlers walked Jimmie in an effort to defuse the potency of his bat, but the Red Sox went on to win the game, 12-8, with Foxx scoring two runs. Foxx's six walks in a nine-inning game established a new modern major-league record.

The "Beast" picked up in June where he left off in May, with 11 more homers and 33 more rbi's to take a commanding league lead for runs batted in. Greenberg and Foxx ended the month tied with 22 homers each.

At the All-Star break, the Yankees and Cleveland were tied for first place in the AL with 41 wins and 25 losses, and Boston was only two and one-half games behind the league leaders, with 39 wins and 28 losses. It was the first time in many years that the Red Sox were that close to first place in the AL that late in the season.

McCarthy again served as manager for the AL and selected Foxx over Gehrig as the starting first baseman for the AL All-Stars—no surprise to most fans and sportswriters. Gehrig was slumping with a .277 batting average at the All-Star break, while Foxx was batting .348, leading the league in rbi's, and battling Greenberg for the home-run leadership. Grove had 12 wins and 3 losses for the Red Sox, second only to the Indians' Johnny Allen (11-1) in winning percentage.

The AL was stymied by excellent pitching by NL hurlers at Crosley Field in Cincinnati, losing, 4-1. Foxx managed only a scratch single in four at bats while batting cleanup, started the game at first base, and moved to third base in the bottom of the fifth to make room for Gehrig at first base. Jim's errant throw to first base of a bunt by Leo Durocher in the seventh led to two of the NL runs.

Shortly after the Red Sox lost Grove to an arm injury, the Yankees made their move in late July and early August. Beginning July 29 and ending with August 30, New York won a formidable 32 of 39 games. During that period, Foxx suffered a 12-game homerless drought at the beginning of August, which allowed Greenberg to pull away from him in the homer department. More importantly, Foxx's power slump coincided with a four-win, eight-loss slide by the Red Sox. No one else on the Red Sox picked up for Foxx during his power outage.

On August 16, Foxx once again was busting down the fences. Three times over the next eleven days, Jimmie hit two homers in single games. Meanwhile, Greenberg maintained a serious challenge to Foxx's single-season home-run record for right-handed batters as well as Babe Ruth's single-season homer record.

It became apparent in late August that the Yankees had nudged Boston out of pennant contention, so Foxx's hitting exploits now pointed to individual honors. "Double X" continued to challenge for his second batting title and remained comfortably in the league lead for rbi's.

Early in September, Foxx poled one of the longest homers ever, in Griffith Stadium against rookie Senator hurler Rene Monteagudo. The hard-hit ball landed deep in the left field bleachers. The next day, on September 7, Jimmie put on a one-man slugging show for 13,000 fans at Fenway Park. The game started during a drizzle, and after Foxx was retired in his first at bat, Jimmie reached Red Ruffing for two successive three-run homers, one landing in the screen atop the centerfield wall in the third inning, and the next in the fourth inning soaring well over the left field barrier. Foxx now had a chance to break the league record of eleven rbi's by one batter in a single game. In the fifth inning, Foxx doubled two runs across off Paul "Ivy" Andrews. He now had tallied eight rbi's after only five innings. When the drizzle turned to a heavy downpour during the top of the sixth, umpire Steve Basll halted play and waited a full half-hour before he called the game. Had the Red Sox batted in the sixth, seventh, and eighth innings, Foxx would probably have batted at least twice more with a good chance to tie, or even break, the record.

In his last game of the season on October 1, Jim slugged 2 homers and drove home 7 runs. For the season, he hit 2 homers in a game 10 times, and Greenberg smacked 2 homers in a game 11 times, a new major-league record.

Foxx sat out the last game of the season on October 2, rather than add to his individual batting totals. It was the only game he missed during the season, and it appears he was guarding against losing points from his league-leading average or being overtaken by second-place batter Jeff Heath of the Indians, who raised his average ten points over the final week to .343. By winning the batting title with a .349 average, Jim pocketed an extra $500, a cash award from either the AL office or the Commissioner's office.

Still, by sitting out the last Red Sox game of the season, Foxx disappointed some fans. When the starting lineups were announced at Fenway Park that afternoon, a large portion of the crowd of more than 12,000 fans booed when Johnny Peacock was introduced as the Red Sox' first baseman. Foxx was the most popular player on the club, the Red Sox' biggest drawing card for home and road games, and the Red Sox' fans loved to beat the Yankees, no matter what the circumstances.

Foxx never batted below .339 in 1938, beginning with games ending on June 29, and peaked at .362 on July 17. It was his second AL batting title.

Foxx was awarded the AL batting title even though he could have lost it on a technicality similar to when Dale Alexander was given the title over him in 1932. The Senators' rookie Taft Wright batted .3498 in 1938 with 92 base hits for 263 at bats in 100 games. Foxx batted .3486. Wright appeared in the minimum 100 games normally needed for consideration for the batting championship, but in 40 of those games, Wright was a pinch hitter, so he was even less of a regular in the lineup than Alexander in 1932.

Foxx had battled late-season foot, hand, and ankle injuries while staying in the lineup. Jack Malaney of the *Boston Post* said that had Foxx sat out some of the games during the peak of his nagging injuries, he may have finished the season with his highest average ever, though he would have had to eclipse his .364 mark of 1932.

Batting third and fourth in the lineup, Foxx led the league with 175 rbi's, one of the highest totals ever made by a major leaguer, and played in 149 games, all at first base. If the Red Sox had played in the customary 154 games, Foxx would have had an outside chance to break the single-season AL record for rbi's of 184 established by Gehrig.

Jim recognized the role that various Red Sox batters had in bolstering his batting figures for the season. Cramer, Vosmik, and Chapman reached base frequently before Foxx batted, and Cronin and Higgins were good run producers behind him, making it hard for pitchers to pitch around Foxx.

"Knowing that the other fellows are hitting takes much of the responsibility off you," he explained, "and you are up there swinging more freely without so much on your mind."

Jimmie also led the league in total bases, slugging percentage, and on-base percentage, and tied Greenberg for the league lead in walks. Foxx's leadership in so many batting categories paved the way for an announcement on November 2 that he had won the AL MVP award for the third time in his career, the first player in either league to accomplish the feat. It was one of the most satisfying moments of his career, considering the talk early during spring training that he might be washed up or on a serious decline. Foxx garnered 305 out of 336 points for the MVP award, to finish well ahead of Bill Dickey and Greenberg in the balloting. It was an impressive vote total for Foxx because of Greenberg's serious late-season challenge to Ruth's single-season home run record.

Gehrig slumped to 29 homers and a .295 batting average, low numbers for him, and Lou's subpar season, coupled with Greenberg's second consecutive outstanding season, made him Foxx's new chief competitor for the best hitting AL first baseman. Foxx's 50 home runs and rbi's for 1938 were new individual records for the Red Sox and remained team single-season records through 1997. During 1938, Greenberg tied Foxx's major-league mark of 58 home runs by a right-handed batter in a single season, a mark that stood through the 1997 season, when it was tied by Mark McGwire. Jim slugged 35 homers at Fenway Park during the 1938 season, more than any other Red Sox player ever hit in one season through 1997.

It was no surprise that awards and accolades kept coming Jimmie's way throughout the off-season. The New York and Boston chapters of the BBWAA voted Foxx the outstanding major-league player of 1938.

The Red Sox finished a distant second to the Yankees in the final standings but thrilled Boston fans early in the season. The club's second-place finish allowed each player on the team to pocket more than $1,000 from the 1938 World Series revenues after the Yankees swept the Cubs in four straight games.

Shortly after he was named the AL's MVP, Foxx began a tour of winter banquets. Sportsmen and officials from Atlantic City and southern New Jersey gave Jimmie a testimonial dinner at the Hotel Traymore (Atlantic City) on November 4.

Foxx was rejuvenated. His enthusiasm and confidence were never higher. He had silenced his critics, and his career was back on track. Jack Malaney said that 1938 was Foxx's most intensive spring training ever.

Foxx attributed his comeback to the fall 1937 hunting trip to Wyoming with Yawkey, Grove, and Higgins, where the high altitude cleared his sinuses, and because he quit smoking cigars in mid-season of 1938. Jim said:

> There is no questioning the fact that getting off to a good start physically this year meant everything to me. Before I went to spring training camp in Florida, I accompanied Joe Cronin to Hot Springs, Virginia. The baths there took the impurities out of my body and I felt great when I started working out at Sarasota on March 1.

Foxx also said he cut back his bat weight in 1938 from 38 or 39 ounces to 34 ounces. He recalled using bats as heavy as 42 ounces early in his career, when his eyes were younger and clearer and he had quicker reflexes.

On January 5, 1939, Foxx revealed that he intended to demand a big increase in his salary for the coming season, compared to the $20,000-$23,000 he had received in 1938. The slugger believed he deserved the highest salary in the league based on his MVP performance and was toying with a $40,000 figure. "I led the league in almost every department, so why shouldn't I get more dough?" asked Jimmy. "Lou Gehrig was the top man in money, when he was the top hitter," Foxx recalled. "On that basis I ought to get the largest paycheck for 1939 for the work I did in 1938." But with major-league clubs holding the hammer over their players because of the reserve clause, even stars like Foxx had only limited bargaining power. In the end, Jimmie decided to sign on with Yawkey's club at a fairly modest raise, given the season he had just completed. On January 26, Foxx signed his 1939 contract with the Red Sox at an estimated $30,000. Jim figured his best year was still ahead, and if he wasn't the best paid player in 1939, he'd be in the running in 1940.

Continuing on the winter banquet circuit, Foxx received a plaque as the "Outstanding Athlete of 1938" (for all sports combined) at a banquet of the Philadelphia Sporting Writers on January 31 at the Penn Athletic Club for having led the AL in batting and rbi's, following a season in which he was seriously handicapped by sinus problems. Jimmie shared the spotlight with Dizzy Dean, who received a plaque for the "Most Courageous Athlete of 1938" for helping lead the Cubs to the World Series despite an injured pitching arm. Although Connie Mack could not attend, Earle, Roy, and Connie Mack, Jr., were there. Cochrane, Dykes, Ira Thomas, Chuck Klein, Joe McCarthy, and Johnny Vander Meer joined many football stars at the banquet, especially those from nearby colleges, and about 800 other attendees in applauding Foxx and Dean for their awards. Autograph seekers made Foxx one of their most popular targets.

Just two days later, Foxx received the Baseball Writer's plaque and a $500 check from the Boston Chapter of the BBWAA at the Copley Plaza Hotel for leading the AL in hitting in 1938. Then, on February 5, Jimmie received a "Player of the Year" plaque for his "astounding comeback."

Meanwhile, the Red Sox were looking forward to a lineup that had table setters Cramer, Vosmik, and Doerr, followed by run producers Foxx, Cronin, and rookie Ted Williams. It would be difficult to deny Williams a starting position in the regular lineup before the first team practice session even began in spring training for 1939. Williams terrorized pitchers in the American Association in 1938, leading in homers, rbi's, and batting average (while with Minneapolis) and winning the Triple Crown. Foxx could have used help from a power source like Williams in 1938, considering that

Jimmie accounted for slightly more than half of the home runs produced by Boston.

It remained for Cronin to construct a pitching staff that would keep Boston in the pennant race. How much more could be expected from Grove, who was thirty-nine in March? The Red Sox needed repeat performances from Wilson and Ostermueller. Cronin hoped that the acquisition of right-hander Elden Auker from the Tigers the previous December would add greatly to his pitching staff's performance. The Red Sox had to give up Pinky Higgins and pitcher Archie McKain to get Auker, but Elden had pitched for six years for Detroit and compiled a record of 77-52 with his submarine-underhand delivery.

Foxx predicted near the end of January that Babe Ruth's record of 60 home runs would be broken—"eventually,"

Why not? Hank Greenberg of Detroit and I both have smacked 58 homers in a season—and if we can come that close, it seems likely that somebody will squeeze out three more circuit clouts for a new mark.

Foxx fell short of predicting he'd be the one to break the mark, but he asserted that, "I'll be out there trying." Foxx said:

Hitters have been handicapped [in hitting home runs] in recent years by the increasing number of rules that penalize long hits. For example, look at the high screen fences almost all the ball parks are putting up. And now there's a rule making a ball that bounces in the stands an automatic double instead of a homer.

When interviewed by a sportswriter, Foxx was willing to discuss Ruth's single-season home-run mark. However, he seldom talked about Ruth's record or any other record with his teammates or other players.

Foxx told a reporter from his home in Abingdon, Pennsylvania, that he planned to work out for a fortnight at Hot Springs before the spring training season opened around March 1. Foxx speculated, "I expect an even better season in the coming year than I had in 1938. I say that because I've been keeping in good shape all winter—better than I can remember. I wouldn't be surprised to see my batting average jump at least fifteen points."

Foxx said about the upcoming season:

I feel even more confident about our club this year than I've ever felt. This kid [Jack] Wilson is a 20-game winner, if I ever saw one, and Bagby will win nearly as many. Cronin's back in form, and so

am I. Grove will win us some games, too. I think Cronin will use
Grove once a week this year. He'll still win if he gets rest in between
starts.

Foxx saw Gehrig early during spring training and was quoted in a
Boston Globe article as saying that Lou looked like he was forty-five. Gehrig
was plagued by an obvious loss in strength and reflexes but had not yet
been diagnosed to determine the source of his problems. His manager,
teammates, and opponents noticed a change, and even many fans suspected a problem.

As the Red Sox began their homeward trip from spring training in
Florida, their first stop was at Moultrie, Georgia, on March 31 to play the
Moultrie club of the Georgia-Florida State League. The Red Sox defeated
Moultrie 13-3, despite three strikeouts of Foxx, two by pitcher Pete Dulick.
Dulick had met Foxx two years earlier at a banquet in New Jersey. "Foxx
was a fine man, very good speaker and also my idol," recalled Dulick.

After two games against the Atlanta Crackers (Southern Association)
in Atlanta, Georgia, on April 1 and 2, the Red Sox continued northward
for a series of eight exhibition games with the Cincinnati Reds beginning
in Macon, Georgia, followed by several contests in South Carolina, North
Carolina, and Virginia. Foxx had his share of base hits, including a tenth-
inning game-winning homer in one contest.

Because the Red Sox-Newark Bears game of April 13 was canceled due
to cold weather, most of the sun-tanned Red Sox players arrived in Boston
a day ahead of schedule, except for Foxx, Berg, and Cramer, who visited
their families in nearby towns. Jimmie stopped in Jenkintown (Pennsylvania) to see Helen and his sons before leaving the following day. Then Jim
homered on April 16 for the Red Sox' lone run in a 7-1 loss to the National
League's Boston Bees in the final exhibition game before the season opener
two days later.

Foxx didn't know it, but he saw Gehrig perform in Yankee pinstripes
for the last time on April 20 at Yankee Stadium. Lou retired in early May
and underwent an examination at the Mayo Clinic in Minnesota shortly
thereafter. The clinic determined that Gehrig had amyotrophic lateral
sclerosis. The robust and powerful Gehrig had succumbed rather suddenly
to a disease that ended his career prematurely at thirty-five and his life just
two years later.

Foxx was honored by the BBWAA prior to the Red Sox-Athletics game
at Fenway Park on April 23. As Connie Mack looked on from the A's
dugout, Jimmie received the MVP award for 1938. On behalf of *The Sporting
News*, Boston's Mayor Maurice Tobin presented Foxx with a handsomely
engraved Browning over-and-under shotgun made to Foxx's specifica-

tions. Foxx placed the gun to his shoulders and paraded to the Red Sox' dugout to the cheers of 12,000 fans.

Because Jimmie had led the AL in batting the previous season, he was featured on the cover of Louisville Slugger's *Famous Slugger Yearbook* for 1939, along with NL batting champion Ernie Lombardi. The inside of the booklet had batting statistics of major leaguers and batting tips from Foxx, Lombardi, and other well-known sluggers. Foxx also appeared on the front cover of the 1939 edition of *Who's Who in Baseball*.

Foxx homered for the first time in 1939 on April 24 in a losing cause in the Red Sox' fifth game of the season, but his homer the following day in the eleventh inning carried Boston past the Senators. Jimmie smashed Joe Krakauskas' first pitch over the left field wall and onto a rooftop 450 feet from home plate.

Foxx and Elden Auker were season-long roommates on road trips, and the former opponents became very close friends. Elden and his wife, Mildred, even named their son, born two years later, after Foxx: "James Emory Auker."

Jim and Helen were struggling in their marriage at this point, and Helen often called Jimmie in the middle of the night on road trips when Elden and Jim were already in bed. "He had been trying to convince Helen to move with their boys to Boston," Elden recalled. "But she never would. It made Jimmie very unhappy. And she was always asking him for money. She was also 'seeing' a banker from back home. Jimmie knew it and there was nothing he could do about it."

Foxx and Auker's routine on road trips was to get the morning paper to read during breakfast. They'd check "what Hitler was doing, how England was holding up under the military pressure from Germany and how President Franklin Roosevelt was reacting." And of course, the two ballplayers pored closely over the sports pages every day, checking how the other clubs were doing, especially the other AL pennant contenders, and how the other players were doing. They occasionally went to the movies together and sometimes went to church on Sundays.

Foxx lived at the Miles Standish Hotel that season during homestands at Boston, as did Ted Williams and some of the other Red Sox players. Auker didn't forget Jimmie and Ted during home games—Elden often would call Mildred up from the clubhouse and ask her to fix enough fried chicken for Foxx and Williams, too. Fried chicken and steak had always been two of Jimmie's favorite foods.

Foxx was hampered on and off all season with severe sinus problems, and he had some especially bad days during May. On May 11, Jim slugged his fifth homer of the season against Ted Lyons at Comiskey Park and played the entire game "despite a severe sinus attack."

On May 16, the team physician, Dr. James Conway, examined Foxx when the slugger arrived at Fenway Park before the opener of a three-game set with the White Sox. Foxx had a low fever, and Conway sent him to St. Elizabeth's Hospital with the expectation that he needed to stay there for several days. A day later, team physician Dr. Edward O' Brien said that Jim was feeling "much better." But Foxx missed four games from May 16-19 before he struck out in a pinch-hit appearance on May 20. Jim was back in the Red Sox' starting lineup on May 21, only to miss one more game on May 23 due to another sinus attack.

Jim powered four homers in a three-game sweep over St. Louis on June 8 and 9 as Joe DiMaggio returned to the Yankee lineup; but again, Jimmie soon fell into a homer slump. From June 14-July 8, he only managed one homer in 21 games, but returned to hitting consistently on June 22.

Foxx led the club by his demeanor, his coolheadedness, and his playing performance, especially his heavy hitting. "Foxx was a leader and took the pressure off of the other players," recalled Bobby Doerr. "He pretty much had his own style of hitting and would have been hard to copy, but he was easy to approach with questions," said Doerr. Ted Williams asserted, "I'm not sure if he had any favorite pitchers to hit against, but I do know that of all the hitters I saw, he was one who when somebody looked like they purposely threw at him, he was then a really fearsome hitter."

Jim was still a cutup, too. More than once, Foxx and Williams were caught bare chested in the Red Sox' locker room, comparing muscles. In one photo, Jim stood over Williams, who was sitting on a stool, and squeezed Ted's left bicep, as if searching for the source of the tall slugger's strength. In another photo, both men stood side-by-side, Williams in his boxer shorts and Foxx in his jockstrap as they flexed their biceps for comparison, Foxx grinning at Williams and Ted grinning at the photographer.

Foxx liked to chase various players in the Red Sox' locker room and wrestle them or trap them into a tight bear hug. Elden Auker recalled that both Grove and Foxx were close to owner Tom Yawkey and that Grove liked to cut off Yawkey's neckties with scissors when Tom visited the locker room. But Foxx must have felt bad when he picked Tom up, gave him a bear hug, and found later that he had cracked a few of his boss' ribs! It was painful for Tom to breathe for a couple of weeks.

Auker recalled:

> He [Foxx] was just a big kid. Just a regular guy, went about his job like he was going to the office. He never seemed to let his personal problems affect his playing performance. He seemed to forget about his problems when he stepped onto the field. He laughed alot and always seemed to be grinning.

"Foxx received a lot of mail and he had a beautiful signature," Doerr recalled. "It was always fun to watch him sign like he did, the double 'X' in 'Foxx'," he continued. Foxx and his teammates gave autographs before and after games, mostly outside the park.

Jimmie's hot hitting was interrupted briefly when he was carried off the train on a stretcher in Boston and moved to St. Elizabeth's Hospital by ambulance the night of June 28. Jimmie's temperature had climbed to 102 degrees on the train but dropped to 99 degrees overnight. Dr. Edward O'Brien accompanied Foxx to the hospital and determined he was not suffering from sinusitis.

Foxx actually missed the Red Sox-Senators' game at Griffith Stadium the day before, possibly because of the onset of a stomach disorder, and the game scheduled for June 28 was postponed due to rain. At the time of his hospitalization, he was leading the league in hitting at .353 (Joe DiMaggio had a higher average but not enough qualifying at bats due to missed time from an injury). Win Green, Red Sox club trainer, announced on June 28 that in addition to the fever, Foxx was suffering from a stomach disorder, possibly an early sign of the appendix problems he would have later in the season. When some newspapers reported that Jimmie was seriously ill, Mattie Foxx said, "This is a lot of newspaper stuff."

Jimmie missed only one more game due to his stomach disorder before returning to action on July 1. In his return to the lineup that day against the Yankees in New York, Foxx stumbled rounding first on what looked like a sure double in the seventh, then overran second and was tagged out by Joe Gordon.

One of the highlights of the season was when the Red Sox swept five straight games from the Yankees at Yankee Stadium (a single game on July 7 and doubleheaders on July 8 and 9). Foxx did his part, batting 8 for 19 in the five games, slugging 2 game-winning homers and a long triple (461 feet to dead center) that would have been a homer in most other ballparks. Red Sox pitchers were at their best, allowing three runs or less in each game, and the five-game sweep moved Boston to six and one-half games behind the Yankees. More importantly, the sweep left the Red Sox with only three more losses than New York just before the All-Star break.

Foxx was snubbed by the league's managers when they chose Greenberg to be the AL's first baseman for the July 11 All-Star game at Yankee Stadium, despite Jimmie's batting average of .358 and Hank's .286 average. Although AL manager Joe McCarthy was criticized for starting six Yankees in his lineup, he said his greatest problem was who to start at first base—Greenberg or Foxx? "When you have to leave one of those fellows sitting on your bench, that's tough," said Joe. Gehrig was honorary captain for the AL squad. The AL won over the NL, 3-1, headed by Feller's pitching and DiMaggio's long homer. Surprisingly, McCarthy never put Foxx in the game, even as a pinch hitter.

Foxx's hot hitting was especially apparent in July, when he smacked 13 homers and batted .380. He put together one of the best extended hitting streaks of his career when he batted .404 (92 hits in 228 at bats) from June 22-August 23 and scored 73 runs over a 59-game stretch due to the timely hitting of Williams and Cronin. The Red Sox stayed within striking distance of the Yankees through mid-August, but then fell out of the pennant race by the end of the month, despite the return of good starting pitching.

Although Queen Anne's County fans could no longer make the short trip to Philadelphia to see Foxx play in half of his team's games, pride still ran deep in that area's residents as Jimmie's list of accomplishments in baseball continued to mount. In its commemorative centennial issue of July 27, the *Queen Anne's Record-Observer* published a lengthy story entitled, "Jimmy Foxx—Baseball's Siege Gun," recalling Foxx's early accomplishments in high school athletics and a summary of Foxx's records. The article noted that Mattie Foxx still held many of Jimmie's medals that he won during track-and-field events in county and state meets. The medals were among her prize possessions.

Foxx complained of a severe pain in his side on September 7 and 8 while the Red Sox were finishing a road series with New York. He had been hitless in three consecutive games for the first time during the 1939 season when he surprised manager Cronin with an announcement on September 9. Foxx walked into the Red Sox dressing room at Shibe Park shortly before one o'clock in the afternoon and told Cronin that the pain was so severe the previous night he had called his physician to his home in Abingdon (Pennsylvania), where the doctor applied an ice pack to his side. Jimmie announced that after the doctor's checkup he decided to have his appendix removed. The *Inquirer* told its readers, "Six weeks ago Foxx experienced the first symptoms of the ailment, but treated the problem externally to avoid an operation while the Red Sox were still in the pennant fight."

Jim shook hands with all the boys in the Red Sox' locker room and greeted many of his old teammates who were at Shibe Park for an Old-Timer's game to be played the following day. Then Jim left for St. Joseph's Hospital in Philadelphia.

Jim's personal physician, Dr. P. S. Pasquariello, and Dr. B. G. Burden performed the operation and announced a little after 5:00 P.M. that same day that Foxx's operation was a success. He was "resting comfortably and in fine shape." The operation took little more than fifteen minutes, but the doctor recommended no visitors for a couple of days.

The doctors said that Foxx would probably be confined to the hospital for a week, but that most likely he would be unable to play any more baseball for the rest of the season. Cronin immediately decided that Foxx would be shelved until the 1940 season. There was no reason to take chances with Foxx's future in baseball now that the Red Sox were out of the pennant race. Foxx was cheered up by a floral bat from some of his friends in Philadelphia and was pictured laying in his hospital bed with the gift on September 14 in at least one Boston newspaper. Despite his season-ending illness, Foxx finished among the league leaders in various batting categories. The only time Foxx was hitless in three straight games during the 1939 season was the three-game series he played just before his appendectomy. Although he also missed the final twenty games for the Red Sox, he still led the American league in homers (35) and slugging percentage (.694), and had kept his preseason promise to raise his 1938 batting average by about fifteen points.

Jim finished third in the AL's MVP voting behind DiMaggio and Feller. Double X was outdistanced greatly in the voting by DiMaggio because Joe played on a pennant winner and came close to batting .400. Both Jimmie (124) and Joe (120) played in about the same number of games due to injury problems. Foxx had the highest on-base percentage (.464) in the league; although DiMaggio also had a fairly high number (.448), the point being, Foxx actually reached base more frequently. But such figures were not commonly calculated and publicized by sportswriters in the 1930s. Jimmie played in 122 games strictly as a first baseman, split one game between first base and pitcher, and pinch hit once.

Although Foxx had an excellent season, the Boston media turned much of its attention to the brash young rookie outfielder, Ted Williams. Not only were the sportswriters interested in Williams' playing ability, they were also fascinated by Ted's flaky personality.

Williams recalled that the first thing he heard when he came to the Red Sox was, "You should see Jimmie Foxx hit."

He had a rather big swing, but he still was extremely quick. His nickname for me, and this was before I came to the Red Sox, was "The Beast." I saw only one other player who made the bat and baseball sound like it did when he really hit one, and that guy was Mickey Mantle.

Williams was also instrumental in Foxx switching from heavier to lighter bats. "Before I came to Boston, Jimmie's bats were quite a bit heavier." Foxx's bats earlier in his career were 35 inches long and weighed 36 to 37 ounces. "When I arrived and started weighing my bats in the clubhouse, he liked the feel of my bats because they were much lighter and he realized the lighter bats could do things for him that the heavier ones wouldn't," Williams recalled.

On September 30, Jimmie agreed to terms with the Red Sox for the 1940 season. His new salary was not disclosed, but how much bargaining power had he lost, if any, because of his late-season operation? His excellent season would probably have been even more impressive. He was on a pace to hit 40 homers instead of his league-leading 35 and would probably have led the league in runs scored as well as total bases.

Following the Yankees-Reds World Series, first division shares were announced, with the second-place Red Sox and Cardinals each receiving about $33,000 per club. This amounted to over $1,000 for Foxx and each of his teammates.

Jimmie was a guest speaker for the ninth annual banquet of the Niagara Falls (Ontario, Canada) Baseball Association in the Park Restaurant on the evening of November 1. Almost 1,300 baseball supporters showed up as Foxx recounted his barnstorming tours in Mexico and Japan. He told the crowd that more than one-half million fans crowded baseball parks in Japan during the 1934 tour by the major-league All-Stars.

14

SECOND TO RUTH

Red Sox management had no reason to worry about the hitting ability of the team's lineup as the 1940 season approached. The superb rookie season of Ted Williams in 1939 and two outstanding seasons in a row for Jimmie Foxx in 1938 and 1939 meant the team could expect plenty of batting power in 1940. Additionally, Joe Cronin, Bobby Doerr, and Jim Tabor could be counted on for run production, thereby providing excellent depth in the batting order to challenge the Yankees. The Red Sox sold Joe Vosmik to the Brooklyn Dodgers in February because the club was confident that Doc Cramer and Dom DiMaggio, Joe's brother, would team up with Williams for a formidable outfield.

Starting pitching was the chief question mark for Boston, with most of the load probably resting on Jack Wilson, Joe Heving, Denny Galehouse, and Fritz Ostermueller. Grove, at the age of thirty-nine, had been the best starter for the Red Sox in 1939, posting a 15-4 record with 17 complete games in 23 starts. But Lefty was no longer able to start every fourth or fifth game because of his advancing age and all the innings he had already toiled in professional baseball. He would be a spot starter, at best, in 1940.

Foxx sat with sportswriter Joe Williams on a crude pine-tar dugout in Sarasota on March 15, a hot, steamy day. "You look light," Williams remarked.

Foxx replied:

> Down to 182. Lightest I've been in ten years. Been golfing a lot this winter. You know I'm a golf magnate now. Yep, I took over a couple of golf courses over in "St. Pete," pay-as-you-play courses, and the setup is such that I can make myself around $9,000 a year. You know I'm not getting any younger. I can get myself a string of these courses down here and it may be the answer to my old-age security.

Williams asked Foxx what important changes had taken place in the game since he first came up with Mack's Athletics. Foxx answered:

The rookies have it easier now and to their detriment, I think. It's a distinction to be a big leaguer, and it's worth fighting for, worth enduring mental anguish and heartaches. But the newcomers today are big leaguers the moment they arrive, or at least they think they are. Every one of the veterans steps aside and lets them have their own way. I think the old custom was better for the kids. The veterans if they weren't openly hostile, pretended they didn't know the rookies were around. The softening-up process had already begun by the time I came up, but even so, the veterans made you realize your place. It was days before I got a chance to take my turn in batting practice and it would have been many more days if Connie hadn't led me to the batting cage myself. And he carried the bat.

Ted Williams often expressed his admiration and fondness for Foxx and was caught in the act by Joe Williams in Sarasota. Joe reported:

Jimmy Foxx is his [Ted's] idol, or at least one of his pronounced favorites. Down here he stands behind the batting cage when old Double X is up and studies every move. Foxx will drive one over the left field wall, more than 400 feet out, and Williams will turn to whoever is close to him and exclaim, "Holy Pete, did you see that one go!"

A news article on April 8 asserted, "Ted's idol is Jimmy Foxx. He'd rather have big powerful muscles like Foxx than be president. And Foxx's desire is to be able to snap his wrists like Williams does."

Foxx enjoyed Ted's youthful enthusiasm and was impressed by his bright prospects as a major leaguer. Jimmie recalled of Ted early in 1940:

He gave me a laugh last summer. I hit ten homers in seven days. When I hit the tenth he came to me sleepy as a solemn owl, and shook my hands. "You know," Williams said, "I always suspected you could hit, but now you've convinced me."

The Red Sox and Cincinnati Reds began their annual trip north near the end of March, with games against each other in Alabama, South Carolina, North Carolina, and West Virginia. Foxx's homer stroke was in full gear. On April 7, Jimmie walloped his fifth homer in a week in a game against the Reds in Durham, North Carolina.

On April 14, baseball sportswriters from around the country made their predictions about the final standings of AL clubs and gave the Red Sox 9 first-place votes and 57 second-place votes out of 77 ballots. The Boston club placed a distant second place, overall, to the Yankees, who received

66 first-place votes and 11 second-place votes. Many writers cited a clear superiority of the Yankees' pitching and defense over the Red Sox.

Several days before the 1940 season started, Cronin announced that Foxx was being named captain of the team. "There is no question that Jimmy is a great asset as a player. He never hesitated to help young players, so we thought it would place a little more responsibility on him if we named him captain, and make him more valuable."

Herb Hash, who began with the Red Sox in 1940, remembered being a nervous rookie when Jimmie made him feel welcome

> On the first morning that we were in Boston to begin the 1940 season, I came down to breakfast in the hotel and Jimmie was sitting at a table all alone. He too, was an early riser for breakfast. I was a rookie, so I went to another table. He told me to come on over and join him. He allowed he had nothing contagious. I was a bit shy, but from then on, I was his friend.

At the same time, Tigers' manager Del Baker made a key move to bolster his lineup when he moved Greenberg from first base to left field, to replace the aging Earl Averill, and moved Rudy York from catcher to first base, leaving Birdie Tebbetts and Billy Sullivan at the catcher's position. It was a gamble, because Greenberg had never played outfield before in the majors. Speaking from his own experience of switching from first base to outfield, Foxx speculated that Greenberg's main troubles in catching a fly ball in the outfield would be in breaking for the ball. "By that I mean starting in the right direction the moment the ball is hit," Jim said.

Boston led the league by mid-May; the Yankees were struggling to stay out of last place. At one point, Foxx went on a tear with five home runs in four games, including grand-slam homers in two consecutive games.

Foxx was the starting first baseman for the AL in the 1940 All-Star game at Sportsman's Park, while Greenberg shared left field duties with Ted Williams. Jim led the AL in homers at the All-Star break with 20, compared to 17 for Trosky and Charlie Keller. Jim was second to Greenberg in rbi's, 71-68.

Several sluggers smashed long homers during batting practice into the left field stands and over the right field pavilion before the All-Star game started, but Foxx stroked an especially hard-hit ball high against the scoreboard that topped the back wall of the stadium behind the left field seats. The NL prevailed in the actual game, 4-0, behind five pitchers. Foxx played the whole game at first base, batted fifth, but went 0 for 3.

Foxx, Bill Dickey, Cronin, and Carl Hubbell were the only players on the 1940 rosters who were also members of the first All-Star teams in 1933.

Double X was the only player to be on all eight of the first All-Star rosters for either league.

Jim suffered a minor leg injury late in July in a game against the White Sox at Comiskey Park and appeared only in pinch-hitting roles (four times) in the Red Sox' next seven games. When he returned to the regular lineup on July 31, Cronin made him the team's catcher and cleanup batter, because the manager wanted to retain hot-hitting Lou Finney in the lineup and catcher Gene Desautels was bothered at the time by sciatica. Finney, stayed at first base while Foxx played catcher, and Dom DiMaggio was inserted at Finney's old position in the outfield.

Other than a pinch-hitting appearance in one game of a doubleheader, Foxx played catcher in 42 of the next 43 games, a longer stint as catcher than in 1935. In the early portion of Jimmie's stretch as catcher, he responded with an all-around increase in batting performance, even beyond his better-than-average hitting standards. Starting in his second game at that position, Jimmie smashed 12 homers in the next 21 games. According to Joe Williams, "Foxx stepped in cold and caught perfectly."

"I had to make a place for myself, and the club needed catching," Foxx beamed.

Gene Desautels said of Foxx as a catcher, "He had a real good arm and accurate, but not outstanding as a catcher. He did a good job selecting the best pitches against all hitters."

Rick Ferrell recalled, "If it wasn't for Cochrane, Foxx would have been [developed into] a great catcher. He was the greatest all-around athlete I ever saw play major league baseball."

From August 13-19, Jimmie slammed seven homers in eight games. On August 16, he hit two homers at Fenway, one in the first inning and the other in the tenth, to defeat the Senators. The two homers moved him past Gehrig to second place on the all-time homer list behind Ruth. An article in the *New York Times* soberly pointed out that "Ruth's [lifetime homer] record is unassailable. Foxx, who is 32, would have to average better than 40 homers for each of the next five years to reach Ruth's figure by the time he is 38, an age far past the prime of most major league players." Yet the two homers gave Foxx 30 or more homers 12 seasons in a row for a level of consistency unmatched by any home-run slugger in the history of the game through 1997. The two homers also gave him six more than runner-up Joe DiMaggio to that point in the season and seven more than Greenberg.

The very next day, Joe Williams tabbed Foxx as the "star of the week" for bettering Lou Gehrig's home-run mark.

Jimmy Foxx is the greatest long distance right-handed batter of all time and unquestionably the most versatile big-name player in history. No right-handed first baseman ever came in to field a bunt, turn and throw to second or third base more quickly or more accurately than the one-time Maryland boy.

Williams gave his own synopsis of Foxx's appearance, personality, and hobbies, stating that he was an accomplished after-dinner speaker, likes to be around other people, enjoys cigars, a highball, or a beer. Williams opined that Foxx was one of the better dressed men, prefers light tints, and was "addicted" to bowling, golfing, and hunting. He continued that Foxx was forced to wear glasses off the diamond as a result of his sinus problems. He stated that Foxx had tried glasses in a full exhibition game the previous spring but quickly dismissed the idea from further consideration.

Foxx wound up his stint as catcher on September 14 and returned to first base the following day in a game in Chicago, to replace the slumping Lou Finney. Four days later, Jim was moved to third base, replacing the injured Cronin. Foxx explained that shortstop, which he only played for half of one game, was the toughest position for him because of the ground that had to be covered and the many different angles from which you had to throw.

On September 24, Foxx reached another milestone when he clobbered his 500th career home run off the A's George Caster in the first game of a doubleheader at Shibe Park, becoming only the second major leaguer to reach that number of homers, but still well behind Ruth's lifetime mark. Asked to comment on the homer, Foxx said he was much more thrilled with his first major-league homer back in 1927, asserting it held much more significance to him than his 500th. Jimmie accomplished the milestone homer about a month shy of his thirty-third birthday, making him the youngest player ever to reach that number of homers in major league history through the 1997 season.

Foxx's overall slump in homers from mid-August through the rest of the season prevented him from winning another AL homer crown. Greenberg made a very strong finish to overtake Jimmie in the homer department, 41-36.

In 1940, Foxx played in 144 games: 95 games at first base, 42 games strictly as catcher, 1 game at third base, and 6 games as a pinch hitter. He batted .297 (153 base hits in 515 at bats), coaxed 101 walks, and had a slugging percentage of .581. He was still a run producer, driving home 119 runs for the Red Sox.

Boston finished in a fourth-place tie with Chicago, eight games out of first. The Red Sox failed to overcome a weak first-place record by the Tigers because Boston's pitching staff lacked the necessary dominant hurlers. Wilson and Heving won more games than they lost; Grove won seven while losing six, with only twenty-two game appearances; and Ostermueller, Denny Galehouse, Jim Bagby, Jr., rookie Mickey Harris, Emerson Dickman, and Herb Hash posted mediocre records. Meanwhile, Boston led the league in batting average and was second in runs scored, with Foxx, Williams, Tabor, and Doerr all driving home more than 100 runs.

During the winter of 1940-41, Foxx spent much of his time helping manage the golf courses at the Jungle Club Hotel on Boca Ciega Bay in St. Petersburg, Florida. On February 15, while Jim and his younger son, William Kenneth, were in St. Petersburg, Foxx had a major scare when his son fell from a moving automobile. William Kenneth had plunged head first to the ground when the automobile's door opened suddenly, but somehow he managed to escape any permanent serious injury.

Foxx hurt his right wrist when he tripped while chasing a foul on March 6 in an intrasquad game between the regulars and Yannigans. Although still nursing a sore wrist three days later, Foxx played first base and batted fourth against the New York Giants at Miami in a 4-2 Red Sox win. Jim was hitless in two at bats and was replaced late in the game by Tony Lupien. Sportswriter John Drebinger of the *New York Times* noted that Double-X played his position in fine style despite his injury and the Giants' players were "struck by the fine physical appearances of Cronin and Jimmy Foxx."

Foxx hit the ball especially hard during the last two weeks of spring training. After Jim homered on March 26 against the Phillies in Miami Beach, the Red Sox played two games in Havana, Cuba, one being a 2-1 loss to the Cuban All-Stars on March 27 and the other a 9-2 victory over the Cincinnati Reds featuring a triple by Foxx. During the Red Sox-Reds annual exhibition series while heading north, Jim hit homers on April 5, 7, and 9. His homer on April 9 was referred to as "a terrific clout over the left field wall" at Crosley Field in Cincinnati.

Once the season started, Jim suffered a prolonged batting slump. While mired at a .250 batting average on May 29, Foxx asked to be benched for the first time in his career when the Red Sox played the final game of a four-game series with the A's at Fenway Park. On June 5, New York sportswriter Dan Daniel reported:

> Jimmie Foxx may not be at first base for the Red Sox much longer. There is a report that he may quit even as early as 1942. Foxx is going through the most harrowing campaign of his life. To sinus trouble has been added a stomach ailment.

The sinus problem reportedly was affecting his vision.

In one game against Philadelphia, the A's first sacker, Dick Siebert, reached first after clouting a homer, double, and single and said to Foxx, "Guess I'm stealing your stuff." Out of his normal character, Foxx replied sarcastically, "Listen son, for you that's a good season, for me, it would only be a good day." On July 3, Foxx was rumored to have suffered a cracked rib during a friendly wrestling match with Ted Williams in the clubhouse. The official announcement said that Foxx tore some cartilage when hit by a ball.

Rudy York beat out Jimmie as the starting first baseman for the 1941 All-Star game. Jimmie, listed as a first base reserve for the game, replaced York late in the contest in Detroit and went 0 for 1, striking out on three pitches in the eighth inning with the tying runs in scoring position. Ted Williams' homer in the bottom of the ninth won the game for the AL.

On July 25, Jimmie helped Grove collect his 300th win, tripling off the center field wall to drive home DiMaggio and Cronin in the eighth inning and break a 6-6 tie. Grove pitched a complete game despite the 90-degree heat at Fenway, losing eight and one-half pounds from perspiring for two and one-half hours. "That Jimmy!" Grove grinned. "He's hit some mighty important baseballs for me over the years, but never one as important as that one today. I had a hunch Jimmie would get one for old Mose."

Lefty became a weekend pitcher during the 1941 season. Due to an injury to his pitching hand, he didn't see action in a preseason game until April 6, but won six and lost two games by July 3. His sixth victory also represented his 299th in the majors. Grove then pitched two consecutive complete games but lost both of the low-scoring contests, 2-0 and 4-3. Luckily, on the day he won his 300th game, the Red Sox wielded potent bats. Grove tried six more times during the season to win another game, but without success.

Foxx was benched again August 11, in favor of the left-handed batting Finney, as the Red Sox opened a series at Yankee Stadium. Steve O'Leary of the *Boston Globe* pointed out that Foxx never could hit in Yankee Stadium, for some peculiar reason, but was batting .301 at this point in the season. O'Leary reported:

> The thing we liked about the whole thing was the way Foxx took it. . . . Jimmie always a great team man—never showed what must, after all, have been considerable inner hurt. . . . instead he stepped out and pitched for batting practice, which is just about what you would expect the guy to do. . . .

Jim missed two more games, one against the Yankees and one versus the A's, then proved his mettle on August 14 when he returned to action against Connie Mack's club in a doubleheader at Shibe Park. Foxx smacked a three-run homer in the eleventh inning to win the first game for the Red Sox, sending relief pitcher John Babich's pitch over the left field pavilion. He also homered in the second game in a losing cause for Boston, but collected four hits in eleven at bats in the doubleheader with five runs batted in.

John Lardner criticized Foxx in his column and second guessed what Foxx's salary and public image could have been, had he been much more aggressive, outgoing, and boisterous like Ruth. Lardner complained:

> This is what Mr. Foxx should have done: 1927—punched an umpire in the nose, 1928—got into a fight with three Yankees, 1929—disappeared for two days and turned up with a perfume of corn likker clinging to his ears, 1930—publicly demanded that Connie Mack pay him $50,000 a year, 1931—publicly demand that Connie Mack pay him $75,000 a year, 1932—stole second with the bases loaded, 1933—gone to Hollywood to make a Tarzan movie, 1934—bought a second hand Jew's harp and organized Jimmie Foxx' "Mudcats," 1935— punched another umpire on the nose, 1936— publicly demanded that Tom Yawkey pay him $100,000.

Lardner speculated that had Foxx done these things he would have been part of the "national consciousness," and not forgotten when the magnates meet. Instead, Lardner reported that rumors suggested Cronin had recommended disposal of Foxx and no owners were offering him contracts to manage. Additionally, Lardner noted that Foxx had now driven in 100 or more runs in a season for thirteen years in a row, including the 1941 season, but few fans were aware of the feat because so few writers publicized it.

In making his case that Foxx should have been more like Ruth, Lardner seemed to forget that Ruth never received many offers to coach or manage after his career, but the Babe did accomplish much more through salary negotiations as a player than Foxx did. Although Foxx didn't command the salary and the attention that Ruth gained, Jim certainly had his own legion of baseball fans around the country, especially from Philadelphia, New Jersey, Boston, and the Delmarva peninsula. He had operated under a "no brag, just fact" work ethic, letting his performance do the talking. He was one of the most popular players ever to put on a uniform, as indicated in testimony received in the 1990s from former teammates and opponents. Everyone seemed to cheer up at the sight of Foxx coming their way. He was generally upbeat, almost always grinning, and a cut-up. Although Foxx didn't fit Lardner's definition for having "color," he was a showman on the field—a power hitter who often slugged the ball for long distance— and he was much more versatile than most players.

During the 1941 season, Jimmie played in 135 games: 124 at first base, 5 as a pinch hitter, 5 exclusively at third base, and 1 strictly in the outfield. Despite his slow start with the bat, Jim finished with a .300 batting average

(146 base hits in 487 at bats) and 105 runs batted in. The main difference in Jim's batting performance was in the power department. He smacked only 19 homers, the first year he belted less than 30 since 1928. The Red Sox had only two more wins and two less losses than the season before, but this season they finished in second place, a whopping seventeen games behind the Yankees. Ted Williams batted a league-leading .406, and three new pitching stars emerged for the Red Sox—Dick Newsome (19-10), Joe Dobson (12-5), and Charlie Wagner (12-8).

Because the Red Sox were unable to contend for the pennant, Cronin and Yawkey began searching for ways to improve their club for the 1942 season. Concerned about Foxx's loss in homer output and slower reflexes in the field, by the end of September 1941 they decided to start the next season with new players at first base and shortstop.

Foxx and Williams arrived in California the first week of October to play in a brief exhibition tour there organized by promoter Joe Pirrone. Jim was still a chief gate attraction for the fans, but Ted's outstanding accomplishment of batting over .400 for the 1941 season gave him first billing with the press.

Foxx called Williams the greatest natural hitter he had ever seen and said that Ted was certain to become one of the greatest hitters of all time. Both of the Red Sox players predicted the Yankees would defeat the Dodgers in the 1941 World Series because of New York's talent-laden pitching staff.

On October 8, Williams and Foxx were teammates with several players from the Pacific Coast League against the Eastern Colored Giants, an aggregate of Negro League stars. The Giants had a host of star players, including Chet Brewer, Ray Dandridge, and Biz Mackey. In a seesaw battle, "Ted Williams' All-Stars" defeated the Giants, 9-6, with Williams homering once. Foxx collected a single, played all four infield positions in different innings, and pitched in the ninth inning.

Later during the off-season, friends on the Eastern Shore honored Foxx and another Eastern Shore native, Bill "Swish" Nicholson, a hard-hitting young player with the Chicago Cubs who was born in Chestertown, Maryland, just 14 miles from Sudlersville. Swish had grown up idolizing his fellow Eastern Shoreman, followed Foxx's career closely, and even had a brief lookover by Connie Mack in 1936. But Bill went hitless in 12 at bats, mostly as a pinch hitter. After more seasoning in the minors, Bill began making his mark as a left-handed power hitter in the NL in 1939.

On November 18, Eastern Shore sportswriters, sportsmen, and fans recognized the feats of Foxx and Nicholson with a turkey and ham feed, speeches, and gifts at the Fire Engine House in Easton. Walter McCord served as toastmaster and called on Frank Baker. Frank then called Foxx, who had made the trip from Florida, to come to the podium. Baker handed

Jimmie a gold watch given to him by the Eastern Shore sportswriters. Next, Reverend Thomas Donaldson, President of the Easton Farmers when Foxx played for that club, told of the time Jimmie first came to Easton on a Sunday night in May 1924. State Senators Dudley G. Roe and Wilmer F. Davis both praised Foxx and claimed him as their own.

One group of hunting-clad players, Frankie Hayes, Max Bishop, Tommy Thomas, Rube Walberg, and George Case, arrived for the feast, as did several local baseball celebrities. Boys came into the dinner meeting for autographs in between speeches. All told, 197 people attended the banquet.

As the winter trading season drew near, newspaper reports claimed that all AL clubs had waived on Foxx by November 29. However, Red Sox general manager Collins countered, "Right now, Foxx is a member of the Red Sox and we are planning to send him a 1942 contract." Asked about the possibility that waivers had been asked to feel out other clubs, Collins responded, "It is customary to ask waivers on a lot of players at the end of the season." On December 5, a report surfaced that Giants' owner, Horace Stoneham, was not interested in obtaining Foxx, contrary to an earlier rumor. Meanwhile, the Red Sox had lost their number one candidate to replace Foxx at first base, Al Flair, to the military, leaving Tony Lupien as a possible replacement for Jimmie, if Foxx didn't make good with the 1942 club.

15

FOXX'S TWILIGHT

Cronin had confirmed in December 1941 that the Red Sox would start the season with Foxx on the roster, but he'd have to win the first base job from Tony Lupien. Harold Kaese, sportswriter for the *Boston Globe*, speculated that Cronin made the announcement to spur Foxx to try harder because he believed Foxx's subpar 1941 season resulted from lack of enthusiasm rather than diminished playing ability. But other writers felt that Foxx had slowed some in the field recently.

Foxx was preparing for his eighteenth season in the AL when he was interviewed early in February at St. Petersburg. Foxx said he expected pitchers to benefit from the increasing number of night games scheduled for the upcoming season because:

A batter only sees half a ball coming at him in a night game. . . . Since the light comes from above, the bottom half is in shadow and comes sailing up there like a half an orange. Trying to hit a whole ball is tough, but when you see only half of it, that's tougher yet. It's harder for a batter to time his swing at night, too. The tendency is to underestimate the speed of the pitch and to swing late. If a pitcher is unusually fast, like Bob Feller, the swing more than likely is too late.

Before spring training began, Foxx worked his legs into shape by playing plenty of golf. Interviewed in early February, he said:

I'll go into spring training in playing condition. I worked all winter, and in between work I'm playing 36 holes or more of golf a day, which isn't exactly easy or soft when you're shooting in the 70s and low 80s. I'll go into spring training with the thought uppermost in my mind that I am the first baseman of the Red sox, as I have been for six years. Maybe the threat of a younger man seeking my job may make a difference, but I can't realize it now. I never loafed or "jaked" in my life in spring games, exhibition games or in practice. Perhaps though, the constant knowledge my job had been safe might have made me overlook the fact that I wasn't doing as well as I thought I was. Maybe now I'll have to show Fourth of July style in exhibition games in March as a convincer.

As spring training began, Tony Lupien and Paul Campbell figured to compete with Foxx for the Red Sox' first base job. During March, Jim suffered a broken toe when he tripped over a bench in the Red Sox' clubhouse. The injury sidelined him for three weeks at a critical time during spring training.

Despite Jim's spring training mishap, he was ready to play at the start of the regular season. Foxx was more impressive with the bat in spring training than Lupien, prompting manager Cronin to put Jim in the regular lineup. Double X was still designated as team captain.

Foxx batted fourth in the lineup and played first base in an April 12 exhibition game against the Braves at Fenway Park and in the same spot in the batting order and same fielding position for the season opener against the A's on April 14. Jim batted 1 for 5 in the opener with one rbi as Boston beat Philadelphia, 8-3 while about 11,000 fans (1,200 of whom were servicemen admitted free of charge) looked on at Fenway Park.

Near the end of April, Foxx missed three games because of a sinus condition that resulted in two front teeth being extracted. But Foxx was a battler, and upon his return to the lineup on April 25, he slugged his first homer of the season. Cronin still had Jim batting fourth in the lineup.

Foxx had only two homers through the end of April, but he often started slow in the power department. He was batting .352 after the games of May 2; then, he began to slump. From May 3-17, Foxx batted only 4 for 26, to drop his average to .288. Possibly he was bothered by recurring sinus attacks.

Jim had only a few prolonged batting slumps in his major-league career, most notably in 1931 and 1937. His reaction to the booing of the Boston fans when he stepped to the plate during a batting slump typified his easy-going attitude. Ed Linn, author of a biography on Ted Williams, says, "I think it was in the *Boston Record*, I remember an article quoting Foxx during a batting slump: 'I don't consider the fans to be booing me, they're just booing their disappointment.' " Foxx was a forgiving individual.

Although Foxx had been struggling with the bat in May, he homered in his first game back in the starting lineup on May 18 after a three-game absence from the lineup, except for some pinch hitting. He homered off knuckleballer Roger Wolff of Connie Mack's A's on May 23, when the A's beat Boston at Fenway Park, 4-3. Jim played in both games of a double-header against the A's the following day, batting just 1 for 6. Foxx started both games at first base, but had been batting sixth since returning to the regular lineup on May 18. Cronin had moved Williams to cleanup and the hot-hitting Doerr to fifth in the order. Some rumors indicated that Mack was interested in reacquiring Foxx and the Red Sox were hoping to obtain catcher Frankie Hayes from the A's, but any hopes of the Red Sox trading Foxx to the A's were dashed one day later, after a freak pregame injury to Jim.

On May 25, Jimmie volunteered to pitch batting practice at Yankee Stadium and was struck in the right ribs by a line drive off the bat of Lupien. It was a hard enough blow to make the Beast buckle over and fall to the ground. Red Sox players agreed it was the hardest hit ball by Lupien so far in the season. The Red Sox trainer suspected that Jimmie might have a broken rib, and Foxx intended to have an X-ray taken of his right side. "It hurts when I breathe or move my arm," Foxx said.

Apparently, Foxx didn't suit up the following afternoon, but he did visit the press box in Yankee Stadium, telling writers he was scheduled to have X-rays done that day. The injured ribs later proved to be broken.

Foxx was discouraged by the injury and expressed his dismay to Connie Mack the last weekend in May before a Friday night game between the Red Sox and the A's in Philadelphia. "I figured I was coming along," said Jim, "and this broken rib is surely a big setback and disappointment."

Connie replied, "That's too darned bad. But keep your chin up and I know you'll be all right."

Jim said, "I hope so."

On June 1, the Red Sox announced the sale of Foxx on waivers to the Chicago Cubs for $10,000, just $2,500 above the minimum. The Cubs also had to pick up the tab for the balance of Jimmie's annual salary, estimated to be anywhere from $8,000-$16,000. No AL club put a bid in for Foxx's services. His recent decline in batting discouraged long-time opponents from adding Jim to their roster, even though he was on a pace with 450 at bats to hit 22 homers with 63 rbi's and a .270 batting average.

Many scribes complimented Foxx upon learning of his transfer to the Cubs. Ed Rumill of the *Christian Science Monitor* said:

> From clubhouse boys to rival managers, they all call him their friend—clubhouse boys because he was generous on payday; managers because he played the game clean and hard. Only those close to the Red Sox know that Jimmie was on first base many days when he should have been in his hotel room. First of all, he has been a team player.

Web Morse, sports editor of the *Monitor*, lamented:

The sale of Jimmie Foxx to the Chicago Cubs was on the surface, a cold transaction. "The Beast" as he was affectionally known to teammates, was about as close personally to his boss, Tom Yawkey, as was Lefty Grove. Foxx probably would like to retire at this stage if it were not for recent financial reverses. He deserved, but never had a "day" at Fenway Park.

One story from the press claimed that at the time of the sale, Foxx had just left his home in Jenkinstown, Pennsylvania, with his oldest son, Jimmie, Jr., by train to Boston and didn't know of his sale until he reached his room in the Miles Standish Hotel.

When Jimmie arrived at the hotel, his roommate, Dom DiMaggio, was reported to say, "Hi Jim! Well, I see you've got to keep right on going."

"What do you mean?" asked Foxx.

"What? Haven't you heard?" exclaimed DiMaggio. "They've sold you to the Chicago Cubs."

But Foxx didn't quite grasp the situation. He heard "Chicago" and thought Dom meant the White Sox. Foxx was stunned to learn he was sold to a NL club. The Cubs were able to purchase Foxx only after all seven AL clubs other than the Red Sox "waived" on purchasing him.

Foxx said, "I sort of thought I'd last the season with the Red Sox seeing that I had lasted this long. I wouldn't have been surprised a few weeks ago, but now . . ." He shrugged his shoulders.

DiMaggio, who started rooming with Foxx during home games toward the end of his first season with the Red Sox in 1940, said to Foxx, "What'll I do with the big place now, Beast?"

Foxx laughed gently but didn't reply. Jimmie turned to his son and said, "Well, Jimmy, you'll like Chicago. It's a nice city."

On the same day he found out about his sale to the Cubs, Foxx picked up his equipment at Fenway Park (an open date for all the AL teams) and said good-bye to the Red Sox players. It had to be a bitter moment for the slugger.

Yet for all the supposed surprise of the trade on the part of Foxx, an Associated Press wirephoto in the *New York Times* taken on June 1 showed a dapper, widely grinning Foxx in a coat and tie shaking Dom DiMaggio's hand. An article in the *Times* on June 2 said that Foxx learned of his transfer to the Cubs while still in Philadelphia at the bedside of his sick son, Kenneth.

Ted Williams recalled many years later, "No one felt so lost as I did when the Beast was sold to the Cubs." Charlie Wagner recalled, "When Jimmie was released it was a shock to us all, because he was greatly admired by every one of his teammates. It was apparently the thing to do, because soon after he was waived to the Cubs, his great abilities left him."

Leaving the Red Sox was disappointing to Foxx from another standpoint. Jimmie had hoped to help the Red Sox earn their first AL pennant for Boston baseball fans since 1918, but it never happened during Jim's stay with the club. The Red Sox had more first-division finishes while Jim was on the club, compared to the years leading up to his arrival, but they didn't combine enough pitching, hitting, and fielding to overpower the rest of the league. It was a letdown to Foxx to know that his best years in terms of team performance were 1929-31, when he was just 21-23 years old.

The silver lining for Foxx and the Red Sox during his stay with Boston was that the club finished in second place in 1938, 1939, and 1941, so the fans had a much more competitive club to root for during Jim's tenure. This was also the beginning of an intense rivalry between the Red Sox and the Yankees that remains to this day, regardless of the standings whenever the two clubs meet.

At the time of the trade, Foxx had 27 hits (4 doubles and 5 homers) in 100 at bats, plus a rib injury to further confound baseball observers, who wondered what kind of performance Jimmie had left in his bat. Cubs' manager, Jimmy Wilson, was gambling that Foxx's career was not over yet. After a little more time to think the trade over, Foxx said:

> Chicago is a great city, and I'll like playing for my old friend Jimmy Wilson with such others as Stan Hack, and Swish Nicholson, and Dom Dallessandro, who was with the Red Sox when I first came here in 1936. I really don't know much about the NL, for I never thought I'd be in it.

Nicholson was thrilled to have Foxx as a teammate, even though Jim was past his peak playing ability.

Foxx assured Cubs General Manager, Jim Gallagher, who called Jimmie by phone, that he'd be in Chicago by the following day, June 3, and be ready to play early the following week.

Foxx said it didn't bother him that the NL was full of curveball pitchers. He was grateful to still be in the major leagues, but said:

> I regret I have to leave Boston and the AL after all these years. I'm going to miss Boston. I think it's the greatest town in baseball. I'll always regret that I was unable to help the Red Sox win a pennant. I bet the fans will go insane with joy if they ever get one.

Harold Kaese felt that Foxx's career would not last much longer. After all, no AL club wanted him, and only one NL club claimed him. Kaese also reported that "there is a predominant belief in baseball that Foxx is just about washed up as a hitter because his eyes are bad."

The transfer of Foxx from the Red Sox was not surprising to many baseball observers. After all, Yawkey, long a "sincere admirer of Foxx," had tried in vain to convince the Indians to name Jimmie their club manager during the winter of 1941-42.

Foxx laughed at the suggestion that he was through as a player. He said: "People have been saying I was through for seven years, ever since I was traded from the Athletics to the Red Sox." Foxx said if he was used regularly, he'd do a good job for the Cubs. "I can't get going when I'm in the lineup for two or three days and then on the bench for a couple." He continued, "I regard 1938 as the greatest season of my career. That was the year after I slumped from .338 to .285, the season some of you writers said I was about washed up as a major leaguer."

During the Red Sox' first home game after Foxx was transferred to the Cubs (June 2), his absence was jeered by some fans. When Cronin stepped to the plate as a pinch hitter for Wagner in the sixth, he was loudly razzed. Shortly thereafter, one spectator jumped atop the Indians' dugout at Fenway and shouted loudly, "We want Foxx. We want Foxx." Many Red Sox fans repeated his cries and booed when police ejected him from the park.

In the umpire's room after the game at Fenway on June 3, Eddie Rommel, Cal Hubbard, and Bill McGowan lamented Foxx's sale to the Cubs. Former teammate Rommel recalled, "I've never seen Foxx do anything to embarrass a teammate, an opponent, or an umpire." Hubbard said, "Foxx never alibied a third strike, he didn't try to blame his lapse on the umpire." And former hunting buddy McGowan said:

> He'd go out of his way to give the umpire the benefit of the doubt. I've seen him agree with the umpire's decision when he undoubtedly figured the play had been missed just to prevent a needless argument. The fans would have been on his side if he had been inclined to protest openly.

On June 3, Jim arrived at Wrigley Field and conferred briefly with Gallagher before meeting players on the Cubs. The whole club gathered in the dressing room, especially so the younger players could "gaze at the mighty veteran." Foxx wasted no time in donning his new Cubs' uniform and posed with his old Philadelphia neighbor, manager Wilson, that same day. Jim flashed that familiar wide grin for photographers while holding a bat, though his rib injury kept him from playing.

On June 5, in Chicago, Foxx informed listeners that:

Everyone has been asking about my ribs ever since I got into town—women and men in the stands, people on the street, and kids on the corner. Maybe I'll be ready to play in a couple days. The "doc" says the break mended nicely but the cartilage had been torn. I don't get much pain when I swing the bat, but it's bad when I run.

Cubs first sacker Glen "Rip" Russell had clouted three homers since the arrival of Foxx, who was wearing uniform number sixteen, formerly worn by Babe Dahlgren. On June 5, Foxx took batting practice and belted the ball out of the park. When he made his debut as a pinch hitter for the Cubs, however, he flied out against the Giants. It's unknown how long the rib injury affected Foxx, but when he first began swinging the bat for the Cubs, he had to be heavily taped around the chest. Jim recalled about a year later "And with that stuff strapped around me, I couldn't get my left arm up. I couldn't swing at the ball in the natural position."

Foxx didn't hit his first homer for the Cubs until June 26 at Braves Field. The homer came with two out in the ninth with a mate on board and provided the margin of victory in a 6-4 win over Boston. Jimmie also drove home two other runs earlier in the game.

On July 4, Jimmie found his range again with a three-run homer off the Cardinals' Mort Cooper at Sportsman's Park, sending Cooper to the showers and ending his nine-game winning streak. The homer gave Chicago a 6-1 lead in a game they eventually won 6-5.

Foxx began complaining about various factors in the NL that made it harder on the batters to perform. He said:

What makes the NL hurling somewhat tougher is the strike zone. In the NL, this zone extends from your shoulder to below your knee. If you pitch a ball as low as the bottom of a batter's pants, it's a strike. In the AL, the strike zone is just from the letters on your shirt to just over your knee.

Dan Daniel reported that pitchers who had shifted from one league to another had confirmed Foxx's observations.

From June 7-July 19, Foxx played 37 games at first base, batting 29 for 138 (.210 average), with five doubles and three homers. Foxx had to be worried; it was the most prolonged and severe slump of his career.

Jim was pictured sporting his new Cubs' uniform on July 30 in the *New York World Telegram*. His uniform was tight-fitting, compared to the customary loose-fitting woolen flannels that most major leaguers wore. Ball clubs were looking for a uniform that was not as heavy as the woolen flannels yet not too light to absorb perspiration. Jimmie said he didn't like the new look and complained that the uniforms made the players look like a bunch of monkeys. The uniform had a sleeveless outer shirt and a colored long-sleeve undershirt, which meant Jimmie could no longer display his powerful biceps.

A few days later, *Baltimore Morning Sun* sportswriter Jesse Linthicum speculated that Double X was nearing the end of his playing career. Linthicum wrote:

> Foxx finds himself flirting with a .200 batting average . . . made 3 hits Sunday, but shows only brief bursts of the great punch which brought him fame and fortune, and has a $16,000 salary which made him too steep an investment for most clubs when he was put on waivers. Troubled by sinus, Foxx, who is almost 35, wears glasses off the field but insists his eyes are perfect. He reported to Boston heavier this year than ever before, then suffered a fractured rib.

A few days later, Rodger Pippen, sports editor of the *Baltimore News Post*, joined the growing legion in the press who were writing off Foxx:

> Rather than sit on the bench for the Cubs or any other club, Maryland's Jimmy Foxx will retire from baseball. Foxx has been nursing hopes of getting a shot at managing a big league club, but for obvious reasons cannot discuss reports that he is being considered as Jimmy Wilson's successor at Chicago.

Foxx's pride was beginning to suffer, and he could see the writing on the wall. Jimmie said, "The minute I'm finished as a regular, I'm going to get out and stay out. I'm not going to sit on the bench and be a pinch hitter once in awhile."

Jim appeared in just sixteen games in August, ten of which were only pinch hitting appearances. He was now assured that the 1942 season was a bust, but he tried to play out the remaining schedule.

Double X was interviewed by J. G. Taylor Spink in *The Sporting News* on August 27. Foxx recounted his release by the Red Sox, wondering if the move was made in part because Cronin may have viewed Jim as a second guesser:

> I was amazed when I was told to move to the Cubs. I felt at the time that maybe I had talked too much to Cronin. I said to Joe, "On other clubs, they establish a routine, and stick to it. They let things work themselves out. You make too many snap decisions, play too many hunches." I said that to Joe in the spirit of friendliness, with the impression that he welcomed such little conversations with me. I did not mean to criticize him, because I never made such comments

to anybody but Joe. However, I have nothing against Cronin. He felt he did not need me and that was that.

Then Jim asked Spink to clarify the record regarding his earlier comments on the Cubs' uniform:

> For heavens sake, Taylor, do me a favor! Get me straightened out on the matter of the Chicago monkey suit. While we were in Boston on our last trip, a writer came to me and asked how I liked the uniform. I replied that it did not appeal to me. I said that it was tight where it should be loose, the material does not absorb perspiration, and I do not believe it has a dignified appearance. Imagine my amazement when I read that I had said no man could be expected to hit in that kind of outfit. Now, what drivel that was. It was especially tough on me because I wasn't hitting [at the time], so it looked as if I was trying to pass the buck to the uniform.

Finally, Foxx covered many points with Spink on the differences between play in the AL and the NL. He reiterated earlier remarks about the strike zone being larger in the NL and noted the ball in both circuits was deader in 1942 than the year before. Foxx said, "The AL ball is slicker because it is put in a rolling machine. The NL cover is looser and the stitches stand out more because it is not rolled. As a consequence, the NL ball adds to the pitcher's benefit in that circuit."

Foxx continued by saying that there was more night ball in the NL; pitchers are pulled out of the game quicker there; third and first base lines are guarded more intensely in the NL; pitchers will throw a curve ball in the senior circuit even on a three ball and no strike count; and the AL has many more fastball pitchers. Jim believed that the offense and defense in the NL was built around the idea that one run might easily win or lose the game. Foxx rated Enos Slaughter as the hardest hitter in the NL and Mort Cooper was the best pitcher there, with an especially good fastball.

As late as the end of September, with only about a week remaining in the schedule, Jimmy Wilson hinted that he might try Foxx at his old position of catcher again. The armed services were grabbing up youngsters Bob Scheffing, Clyde McCullough, and Chico Hernandez, and Wilson was probably wondering who his catching prospects were for the 1943 season. Foxx said he wasn't sure how he liked the idea of returning to catcher over the long stretch, "but we might see about it in due time." As it turned out, Foxx only caught part of one game on September 22.

Jimmie barely batted above .200 for the Cubs compared to .270 for the Red Sox earlier in the season. He struck out at a much greater rate (55 strikeouts in 205 at bats) for the Cubs than he did for the Red Sox (15 strikeouts in 100 at bats) in 1942. He batted a combined .226 average for both clubs in 1942, compared to his lifetime batting average of .332 at the beginning of the season.

Was his poorer batting for the Cubs due to a worsened sinus condition, his rib injury, his eyesight, or all three? A possible additional factor contributing to his hitting problems with the Cubs could have been difficulty in adjusting to different pitchers. But it seems unlikely that a healthy Foxx in his prime would be significantly affected by new pitchers. He complained of the hitting background at Wrigley Field in 1942, but apparently not in 1929, when he batted well in the World Series at Chicago.

The Red Sox voted a meager one-quarter share ($300) for Foxx of their second-place World Series money. Tony Lupien replaced Foxx at first base for the Red Sox and played in 121 games at that position, batting .281 with 3 homers and 70 runs batted in. Lupien recalled, "I didn't succeed Foxx, I followed him, much the way Babe Dahlgren followed Gehrig."

With the end of the 1942 season, both Foxx's personal and professional lives took serious reversals. A story out of Philadelphia at the end of December 1942 said that Jimmie was employed as a salesman for a leather firm and reportedly was considering retirement from baseball as a player.

His troubled marriage with Helen became publicized early in 1943 when she sued for divorce, charging cruelty on January 29 in Norristown, Pennsylvania. It had been no secret for some time among many of Jim's friends that he and Helen were not a happily married couple.

On March 3, Foxx, now employed as a lubricating oil salesman, said he had decided to retire from baseball. He had not yet notified the Cubs of his decision but "expected to get around to doing it pretty soon." Jimmie said:

> It looks like a good time for me to quit. Baseball may not even start this season, let alone finish [because of possible wartime restrictions]. I'm about at the end anyhow, and I might as well stop while I have a good job. I want to get out of baseball before I have another season like 1942. I don't want people to remember me like that.

Cubs' General Manager Jim Gallagher said he was surprised to hear that Foxx intended to retire from baseball:

> We haven't heard from him yet. It's entirely up to him. We would like him back, of course, but if he thinks he could better himself at his present job, he's welcome to try it. He is the better judge of whether he is through or not.

A few days later, Jimmie was interviewed again, while presumably visiting his girlfriend, Dorothy Anderson Yard, in Lewiston, Maine. He and Dorothy had been seeing each other for several months. Sitting in a barbershop chair, Foxx let it be known that his "baseball days are over forever." He told a reporter that he was done. "Yes, definitely. I've had enough of it for many reasons. You know, it takes a lot of hard work to get in shape to play when you're my age [35] and I just don't feel like I can or want to do it."

A few months later, a court granted Helen a divorce from Jimmie on charges of indignities. Mrs. Foxx testified in an uncontested suit that Jimmie "is just a selfish boy who has never grown up," and said that he earned between $12,000 and $30,000 a year, but squandered most of it on himself. "He never took any interest in the children," she testified. "He never even played catch with the boys. He was more interested in the plaudits of baseball fans than in his family or our married life." She confirmed that they were married in Church Hill, Maryland, in 1928 by the justice of the peace.

The divorce decree was granted by Judge William F. Dannehower in a Montgomery County (Pennsylvania) Court. Although Mrs. Foxx had sued on additional grounds of cruelty, the court found there was no evidence that Jimmie had ever endangered Helen's life. She said he had become abusive while under the influence of alcohol. Jimmie, Jr., now twelve, was enrolled in a military academy, and his younger brother, William Kenneth, was now seven. Both were placed in their mother's custody. Helen said that Jimmie was presently employed by the E. F. Houghton Company of New York, and was living at the Sheraton Hotel in New York City.

Several factors contributed to Jimmie and Helen's divorce. According to friends and relatives still living in the 1990s, it was a troubled marriage even while the couple lived together in Philadelphia. Helen Tarring Harrison said that Helen Foxx told her once in the early 1930s that she would stay in the marriage with Jim as long as his career was on the rise, but after that, she'd be gone. Jim's move to Boston in 1936 strained their relationship further, because Helen elected not to move to Boston, even for the summer months. Both Jimmie and Helen were heavy spenders, so as a couple they didn't manage their earnings very wisely. Jimmie allowed Helen to spend freely, especially for her clothing, contrary to her testimony before the divorce court judge that Jimmie squandered his salary. In one instance, Helen refused to get out of the car when they reached their destination for an event during the 1932 season until Jimmie agreed to buy her a ring with a larger diamond to replace her wedding ring. Sometimes Jimmie was generous with family and friends to a fault, and his investments in the St. Petersburg golf courses in 1940-41 were a major financial loss (with estimates as high as $40,000), which frustrated Helen.

Just a few days after Jimmie and Helen were divorced, Jim traveled to Sudlersville. Jim's mother made a "mis-step," fell, and broke her hip on about June 11. Mattie was taken to Kent and Queen Anne's Hospital in Chestertown where her fracture was set. She was scheduled to stay in the hospital for at least several weeks. Jim stayed with his father for a few days and probably visited with his mother. No doubt he used the time to talk with his parents about his divorce and upcoming marriage.

On June 18, Jim married Dorothy at the home of friends in Short Hills, New Jersey. Jim's new marriage and positive relationship with Dorothy boosted him immensely and dampened the effects of his recent setbacks. Dorothy had been divorced from H. Nabor Yard, of Auburn, Maine, a year earlier. Although Jim never officially adopted Dorothy's son, John, and daughter, Nanci, he functioned as a fulltime father and they always called him "dad."

Dorothy was twenty-five when she wed Jim, eleven years younger than him. She was from Lewiston, Maine, the only child of Harry and Alice Anderson. Like Helen, she was attractive with dark brown eyes and brown hair. Dorothy graduated from Edward Little High School in 1936 and was active in various school organizations, including the Girls Athletic Association, the Home Economics Club, and the Glee Club. Harry Anderson was a partner in the Anderson and Briggs Drugstore in Auburn, Maine.

Jim had precious little time to fully enjoy his new marriage before his mother died either late on August 26 or early on August 27 (accounts vary) at the age of sixty-six. She suffered a heart attack and died very suddenly. Jim had always been very close to his mother. Mattie was very proud of her son, not only of his accomplishments in sports, but of the generous, friendly man he was. At the time of Mattie's death, Jim and Dorothy were visiting with Dell in Sudlersville, so the three of them were together when Dell received word of Mattie's death from the hospital in Chestertown. Staff Sergeant Sammy Dell, Jr., was overseas at the time of his mother's death. Funeral services were held on August 29 at Calvary-Asbury Methodist Church by Reverend Revelle. The next day, Dell accompanied Jim and Dorothy back to their home at Short Hills (New Jersey) for several days before he returned to Sudlersville.

On January 8, 1944, Jimmie's draft board in Newark, New Jersey, called him up for a physical examination. Jim was still employed by the oil and leather goods firm. He reported for a follow-up "final visit" for his physical exam on January 25 but was told to come back for further checks the next day. Foxx entered the induction center around 9:00 A.M. and left shortly after noon, rejected by the board. Although officials refused to disclose why Jimmie was rejected, it was believed he received a 4F classification because of his chronic sinus ailment.

About the same time that Jim was rejected from military service, his father remarried. The *Record-Observer* noted in its January 13 issue: "Mr. Dell Foxx left town very quietly Tuesday of last week [January 4] and returned home bringing with him his bride, the former Mrs. Elsie Man-love." Dell and Elsie were married by Dr. Roberts, pastor of Christ Meth-odist Church in Chestertown.

Shortly after his rejection from the military, Foxx expressed an interest in returning to the majors as a player. On February 26, Cubs' general manager Jim Gallagher said that Foxx would apply to Commissioner Landis' office for transfer from the voluntarily retired list to the active list. The Cubs reported to spring training camp at French Lick, Indiana, in March. On April 10, it was reported that Foxx had been doing well in spring training and was scheduled to experiment at his old position, catcher, in the Cubs' next game.

Infielder Roy Hughes recalled that Jimmie suffered badly from sinusitis in the spring of 1944, to the point that he often had a blind spot, "right around the letters" for a given pitch. After spring workouts at Wrigley Field, Foxx and Hughes would go back to their hotel room and put a damp towel between themselves and the radiator to keep warm. Roy had met Jimmie years earlier in the mid-1930s, when Foxx was with the Red Sox and Hughes was with the Indians. Hughes said, "Every time I would reach first base on a single and Foxx was covering the bag, Jimmie would make a fist and ram me in the butt [playfully], and say, 'Nice hitting, Slug(ger)!' "

A couple of weeks later, as the team was leaving for Pittsburgh, Man-ager Jim Wilson announced Foxx would start at third base in place of rookie Tony York. Jimmie had been used only as a pinch hitter in the Cubs' first four games. But, like some of Wilson's previous experiments with Foxx, the move to third base was short-lived. Jim appeared in only two games at third base, batting 1 for 7 with a walk and one run batted in. In early May, Foxx was demoted back to pinch hitter, appearing in that role in several games.

In mid-May, Rodger Pippen observed that Jimmie's attempted come-back appeared to be a bust. Foxx was relegated to a bullpen catcher, the same role he held as a player on the Athletics at eighteen. In one game, Foxx watched as the Cubs' new manager, Charlie Grimm, marched four other players to the plate as pinch hitters for the Cubs—never calling on Foxx. Pippen said:

> He hit the ball hard in spring training. He was used as a pinch hitter in an early game in Cincinnati, and drove one of his old-time massive clouts far over the left field fence and onto the roof of a laundry across the street from Crosley field—foul by inches. [But] Old Double X's batting eye is dim—he can't follow the low curve ball anymore.

It was time for Foxx to retire.

On the last day of May, Foxx played catcher and was hitless in two at bats. He pinch hit five times in June without reaching base. His last appearance in a game that season was as a pinch hitter on June 21, leaving him with anemic batting average of .050 (1 for 20).

On July 5, the Cubs removed Jimmie from the active players' list. He remained as a coach and bullpen catcher for the club. Little coverage occurred in newspapers about Foxx's removal from the active players' list, probably because Jim's playing had been subpar for parts of three seasons (1942-44). Sportswriter Ed Rumill interviewed Foxx shortly after July 5 for an article that appeared in *Baseball Magazine*. Jim noted without being specific that Red Sox manager Cronin "let me get away with things in Boston that Connie would have kicked me all over the clubhouse for." He added that it was a big break starting out in the majors with Connie Mack, especially at such a young age. Foxx asserted that he was definitely interested in managing a big-league club.

On August 25, Jim was named as the new player-manager for the Portsmouth, Virginia, club of the Class B Piedmont League after the team owner, Frank Lawrence, peddled catcher-manager Frank Steinecke to the New York Yankees. Foxx pitched for his club on September 5, striking out eight batters in a 3-1 win over Newport News. But Jim was now away from his expecting wife, Dorothy, for long stretches of time. Luckily, his friend Roy Hughes was there for Dorothy when the Foxxes needed him.

Late that summer during a Cubs' road trip, Hughes stayed in Chicago recovering from an injury while the Cubs traveled. Jim was in Portsmouth, Virginia. One evening in mid-September, before the Cubs and Foxx returned to town, Dorothy called Roy and asked him if he would drive her to the hospital because she believed her delivery time was imminent. Hughes got her to the hospital in twenty minutes. It's uncertain how long after her arrival Dorothy actually gave birth to her and Jim's newborn son, but it was reassuring to her to be able to call Roy rather than a taxi. Jim and Dorothy named their first and only child James Emory Foxx III, the second time Jim gave one of his sons his own name. As soon as Jim was notified of his son's birth, he began handing out cigars to practically anyone who would take one.

Ralph Daughton, President of the Piedmont League, announced on September 9 that Foxx would be ineligible to play in the league (Shaughnessy) playoffs unless the managers from the other five clubs gave their unanimous consent to Jimmie playing in the games. They didn't.

Abe Goldblatt, sportswriter for the *Virginia-Pilot*, recalled Foxx's short stay with the Portsmouth club several years later:

I found Jimmie to be a gentleman. He tolerated the second-rate hotels along the Piedmont circuit and survived the weary hours of bus travel. This manner of living must have been a novelty to a man accustomed to the swank accommodations enjoyed by major leaguers. But he endured it all with a smile.

Goldblatt also recalled that Jim gave Julius Berson, the club's handyman, a handsome tip at the end of the season in appreciation of his services. Jim and Roy Hughes went hunting together in South Dakota in the fall of 1944 during the "Baseball Phestival" held in Huron. A number of players, including Foxx, Hughes, Paul Waner, Paul Derringer, Andy Pafko, Kiki Cuyler, and Dizzy Trout, traveled on the Nickel Plate Railroad from Chicago to Huron for exhibition baseball and hunting for pheasant, ducks, and geese. Dorothy traveled with Jim and the team.

On December 7, Ival Goodman was named manager of the Portsmouth club. Foxx had to reconsider his options again. But the loss of major-league talent to the military service gave Jimmie another chance to play in the big leagues in 1945. General manager Herb Pennock and manager Fred Fitzsimmons of the Philadelphia Phillies announced the signing of Foxx to a one-year player contract on February 10. They said that Foxx was in excellent health and they expected him to be a great asset to the Phils in the coming season. They were undecided what position Foxx would play.

The Cubs listed Foxx as a coach and scout on their 1945 roster until he said he wanted to play again. "I'm not through," Foxx said. "My legs are as good as ever." But what about his batting eye? Apparently the Cubs gave Foxx his unconditional release so he could sign with Philadelphia.

Several days after Foxx signed with the Phils, there was speculation that Foxx might land the first base position with the club. Tony Lupien, who was generally figured to be the top candidate for that position, had been inducted into the Army.

Foxx played first base frequently for the Phils during their exhibition season but did not accompany the team for several games against military teams beginning March 31. Jim was troubled with foot pains and was replaced at first base by Jimmy Wasdell.

Jimmie and Dorothy, with their children John, Nanci, and newborn son, James, were still living in the Chicago area as the season began.

Foxx wore uniform number four for the Phillies (also known as the Blue Jays at this time), the number typically assigned to the club's cleanup hitter. Although his appearances in the lineup were spotty in 1945, compared to when he was a regular, his performance was better than his two stints with the Cubs in 1942 and 1944. Jim was listed in the club's scorebook as five feet, eleven and one-half inches, weighing 190 pounds (probably ten to fifteen pounds less than his actual playing weight that season).

Early in April, Foxx had two base hits and a walk in three pinch-hitting appearances. With the departure of the early season hitting sensation Elisha (Bitsy) Mott on April 28 for the Navy, Foxx was inserted at the hot corner when his ailing feet were up to the task. Foxx played in eight games at third base from April 26-May 6. On May 9, Jimmie was ordered to his bed for at least 48 hours, forcing Fitzsimmons to juggle the lineup again and replace Foxx at third base with infielder John Antonelli (not to be confused with the star pitcher of the same name from the 1950s) just when Fred had planned to switch Jimmie to first base. Jim pinch hit again on May 13, played in four straight games at third base, and then blasted his seventeenth career grand slam, a pinch-hit job, on May 18 against the Cardinals at Philadelphia before over 4,500 fans at Shibe Park.

Teammate Lou Lucier roomed with Foxx on road trips during the 1945 season and says that Jimmie had many long, enjoyable phone calls with Dorothy. Lou recalled, "He [Jim] couldn't wait to give her a call on those road trips." Jim also wrote love letters to Dorothy regularly while on the road. Nanci Foxx Canaday recalls, "Dad often arrived home before his love letters to mom did. I still have some of those love letters he sent her."

In early June, Foxx was still reported to be down to a slim 195 pounds while holding much of the first base duty for the Phils. Later that month, Arthur Daley noted that although Foxx was looking svelte, he had no illusions about it. "When the war's over, I'm through," Foxx stated flatly. "If I were to quit today, I guess I'd have played enough."

From May 30-June 12, Jimmie batted 16 for 55 with four doubles and three homers, but then slumped until mid-August. But before the season ended, the dilution of talent in the majors due to wartime activity allowed Jim to realize a longtime ambition.

One of the highlights of the 1945 season for Foxx occurred on August 19, when he started at pitcher for the Phils in the second game of a doubleheader against the Reds. Manager Ben Chapman, who had recently replaced Fitzsimmons, watched Foxx allow only a scratch single in the first six innings while striking out six Reds, driving in a run, and holding a 4-1 lead over Cincinnati with two outs in the seventh.

Foxx tired and lost control of the game when the next three batters hit safely. Chapman signaled to the bullpen for his ace reliever, Anton Karl.

As Jimmie strode off the pitching mound he received a tremendous ovation from the fans at Shibe Park. His fastball and sinking screwball baffled Cincinnati's heaviest hitters for most of the game. Karl shut down the Reds' batsmen the rest of the way, to preserve the victory for Foxx. Chapman later said in a 1990 interview, "I was short of pitching late that season and Foxx wanted to pitch. I let him and he did a pretty good job."

Although Foxx was not Babe Ruth on the mound, he did have a 1-0 lifetime pitching record with a 1.52 earned run average in his few appearances—once for the Boston Red Sox in 1939 and nine times for the Phillies in 1945.

Within about a week or two after Foxx's star pitching performance, Herb Pennock took several of the Phillies players in uniform, including Foxx, to the Valley Forge Rehabilitation Hospital for servicemen. Mark Abrams, civilian sports director of the facility, took Foxx to the center of the blind ward of the hospital and announced, "Boys, here is the fellow you've all been waiting to meet—Jimmie Foxx." Writer Spink reported the room was alive with chatter as Foxx grinned and said, "Hello, fellows. This is a great treat for me." One blinded veteran within the group now surrounding Foxx reached out, felt Foxx's big arms, and said, "Gosh, feel these muscles." Another vet said, "Oh, boy, I wish I had shoulders like that—and what a chest!"

Foxx countered after grabbing a GI by the arm, "You're a pretty big guy, too. I could use a wrist like that."

Then the boys told Foxx they had heard his pitching victory on radio and wondered when he would pitch again. Jim replied that he didn't know, but they'd have to ask manager Chapman.

Later, as Foxx left the last ward of the hospital, he called out, "Well, so long fellows. Take good care of yourselves."

The boys shouted back in chorus, "So long, Jimmie, good luck!"

Foxx smiled as he left the room, but writer Spink said there was a lump in Jim's throat after quick reflection. "Imagine," he said, "them wishing me good luck!"

Jim put together his best batting performance of the season on September 9, hitting a homer in each game of a doubleheader, driving in seven runs, and collecting five hits in eight at bats. He started two more games for the Phils at first base, then served as a mop-up pitcher for manager Chapman late in the game three times (September 14, 16, and 17), allowing only one run.

Foxx's versatility was never more evident than while playing for the Phils. He played 40 games at first base, 14 at third, and 9 as pitcher.

As the 1945 season was nearing an end on September 20, Foxx, now a resident of Needham, Massachusetts, announced his retirement from baseball to do general sales promotion work for Hathaway Bakeries, Inc. of Cambridge, Massachusetts. He said he would also be involved in a quarter-hour radio show on sports every Sunday, starting September 30.

The Phillies' general manager Herb Pennock said he was unaware of Jimmie's reported intention to resign. "He hasn't been released from the club," Pennock said. Herb said that Foxx's baseball future was up to Jim but confirmed that Jimmie's 1945 contract with the Phillies was just for that season. Meanwhile, Chapman said he knew late in the season of Foxx's intention to retire as a player but never attempted to change Jimmie's mind.

Foxx probably realized that with so many younger players planning to return to the majors for the next season he had little chance of sticking with a major league club in 1946.

In his final game at Philadelphia, he couldn't muster a base hit in a pinch-hitting appearance for starting pitcher, Tex Kraus. In his final major-league game on September 23, Jim doubled once in three at bats, driving home two runs against the Dodgers at Ebbetts Field.

Foxx's 1945 retirement as a major-league player was not front-page news. It was not a surprise—he had been playing too long below his peak performance. Baseball fans were much more interested in seeing baseball's wartime heroes, especially its star players (Ted Williams, Joe DiMaggio, Bob Feller, and Hank Greenberg) return for the 1946 season. As his playing career ended, Foxx was already somewhat of a forgotten slugger with the sportswriters and fans.

16

AFTER THE GAME WAS OVER

After the 1945 major-league baseball season, Jimmie Foxx began a long search for a second career. He was only thirty-eight, without a high school diploma, and had very little work experience to his credit other than playing baseball. He was at a financial low point, probably with little or no savings between his losses from his investment in the golf course in St. Petersburg and, presumably, costs of his divorce from Helen. He saw his sons from his first marriage—Jimmie, Jr., and William Kenneth—very little after the divorce. But, he was still in the early stages of a new life with his new wife, Dorothy, her children, and their new son, James Emory Foxx III.

Jimmie was well-known, and his name helped him. People were quick to hire Foxx, mostly in promotional or sales representative positions.

Early in 1946, Jim, Dorothy, Nanci, John, and James lived in Needham, Massachusetts, fourteen miles west of Boston. Jim worked in public relations for the bakery company in Cambridge and was beginning a part-time job as a sports commentator, especially about baseball, for radio station WEEI in Boston. It didn't take long for some listeners to criticize Foxx's Eastern Sho' accent. He said "cow" like "caow" and was reminded that voice teachers were available. Jimmie snorted good-naturedly, "I'd like to take some of these Yankees down on the shore. People there would wonder where they [New Englanders] came from." Although Foxx received criticism from some sportswriters and listeners, he continued to work on the radio throughout the summer.

Some of Jim's friends and family had hoped that he would return to Sudlersville to live after his playing days were over. Many players from his era did move back home after their playing careers ended, but Jim had grown accustomed to mingling with celebrities in the news, especially sports personalities. By remaining in the Boston area, he was able to maintain many of his more recent contacts through baseball, but it wouldn't be long before Florida lured him away from the Northeast, at least for awhile. There Foxx would enjoy the year-round warm weather and one of his favorite pastimes, golf.

Jim's father still lived in Sudlersville. Dell and his second wife, Elsie, made their home in the center of town, next to the barbershop near the corner of Church and Main Streets.

Late in 1946, Foxx was hired as manager and general manager of the St. Petersburg Saints, a new club in the Florida International League (a class C league). Foxx was cast in the same role at age forty that his onetime mentor, Frank Baker, faced at age thirty-eight—being a player-manager for a brand new club that needed to construct a players' roster from scratch. The team signed seven new players almost immediately, all from Cuba, during a trip that Jim took to that country. He probably knew some Spanish from his frequent trips to Miami over the years, but now a crash course in the language was advisable.

Foxx started the 1947 season for the Saints as a player-manager. The club owners hoped to attract some extra paying customers if they would occasionally see Jimmie appear in a game. Foxx played in several games as either a pitcher, catcher, or pinch hitter, batting only 1 for 6 before announcing during the first week of May that he was once again ending his playing career.

Foxx's club fell to last place in the league's standings early in the 1947 season—no surprise, given the newness of the club. But owners of the St. Petersburg club had unreasonable expectations and little patience. On May 17, Foxx was released as manager and replaced by former teammate Lou Finney, who had just been given his release by the Phillies.

Jim and Dorothy and their three children headed north and moved to New Jersey. Foxx worked at a tavern in Hammonton and continued to be paid by the St. Petersburg Saints during the 1947 season. Early in 1948, he became sales manager for a distributor of Rheingold Beer in Philadelphia.

Some time in 1949, Jim left the beer distributor, which had been troubled by labor strike problems, and gained employment with Mid-States Freight Lines, a trucking firm based in Philadelphia. He took a brief leave of absence from the trucking firm in August to serve as an interim manager of a minor-league professional baseball club. Foxx managed for the Bridgeport (Connecticut) Bees of the class B Colonial League in early August as a favor to Rabbit Maranville, then returned to his regular job. Jim continued to work for the trucking firm in 1950 while he and Dorothy and their children lived in the Maplewood section of Doylestown, Pennsylvania, outside Philadelphia.

Foxx continued to miss major-league baseball and hoped to eventually manage a big-league club. Often when he was interviewed by sportswriters or attended sports banquets he made it known that he still sought to wear a major-league uniform as a manager or even as a coach.

Foxx reached a well-deserved high point of his post-playing days when he was elected to the National Baseball Hall of Fame by the Baseball Writers

Association at the end of January 1951. Jim was about ready to sit down to eat dinner in his Maplewood home with Dorothy, his brother Sammy Dell, Nanci, and young James when reporters notified him of the news. Dorothy cried with joy briefly upon hearing the news, and Jim and his family posed for photographs. Jim lounged in a big easy chair, and Sammy Dell and Dorothy sat on a wide davenport across from the baseball hero. Jim posed in one photo with Jimmie III, both holding bats in the same stance. Always humble, Foxx seemed to forget the relative ranking of his baseball accomplishments. He told reporters of his election into the Hall of Fame, "All of the years I played, all the great players I saw, played against and watched, it always seemed there were so many good players. I never expected this honor. I'll never forget it." He added, "I want to thank all those who made it possible for my name to be listed with baseball's greatest."

Foxx was named on 179 out of 226 ballots; National League home run champion, Mel Ott, was named on 197. Ott and Foxx outdistanced such stars as Paul Waner (162 votes), Harry Heilmann (153), Bill Terry (148), Dizzy Dean (145), Bill Dickey (118), Al Simmons (116), Rabbit Maranville (110), and Ted Lyons (71)—all future Hall of Famers.

Jimmie's father was reached in Sudlersville by the *Queen Anne's Record-Observer*, and said of his son's honor, "I am mighty pleased." Dell continued, "Many of his friends were happy to hear that Jimmie was voted into the Hall. Many residents said, 'He should have made it a long time ago.' "

Jimmie had received 21 votes for election into the Hall as early as 1936, after which a rule was passed specifying a candidate was to be retired before being eligible for election. Since the Hall didn't officially open its doors for dedication and initial inductees until 1939, Foxx was competing in 1936 with all of the all-time greats in baseball that first election year, and the competition remained heavy for the next twenty to twenty-five years.

Amazingly, it took eight tries for Foxx to be selected into the Hall of Fame. His point totals over the years after 1936 were: 26 in 1946, 10 in 1947, 50 in 1948, 85 in the first 1949 election, 89 in the 1949 runoff election, and 103 in 1950.

No one garnered enough votes in the 1946 election. Hubbell, Frisch, Cochrane, and Grove were elected in 1947; Pennock and Pie Traynor in 1948; Gehringer in the 1949 runoff election; and no one was elected in 1950. Jimmie was third in the balloting of the 1949 runoff election behind Gehringer and Ott and third in 1950 behind Ott and Terry.

Several days after Jimmie first learned of his election into the Hall of Fame, he attended the annual meeting of the National League, seeking a job in baseball as a coach or possibly as a manager. The search didn't pay off in an offer, but he had plenty of time to visit with old friends. Cameramen caught Foxx front and center between two old Hall of Fame team-mates, Tris Speaker and Ty Cobb, who were grinning and shaking Jim's hands firmly while congratulating him on his election.

The actual induction of Foxx and Ott into the Hall of Fame took place about six months after their election, on July 23. Ott could not make the festivities because he was managing the Oakland ball club in the Pacific Coast League.

Earl Hilligan, of the American League Service Bureau, spoke on behalf of AL president, Will Harridge, who was ill. Earl spoke of Foxx's tremen-dous batting power and mentioned a homer hit by Foxx at Comiskey Park on June 16, 1936, which went over the 352-foot marker in left, cleared the roof 90 feet above the ground, and came to rest in a playground 535 feet from home plate. "Foxx was popular with the fans, and a great guy all around," Earl said.

Connie Mack and Jimmy Dykes, who had just replaced Mack as the A's manager, were at the induction to honor their old friend. Jim was extremely proud of his induction, and wore his wide dimpled grin throughout the afternoon.

Dorothy's daughter, Nanci, recalls, "I think dad went alone to the induction. I recall mom stayed home and Sammy Dell was still in the military. I don't know if his father or anyone else from Sudlersville at-tended." Dell was seventy-five at the time, but if he was physically able, it's hard to imagine him missing the event. Howard Talbot, who was still employed by the Hall of Fame in the 1990s, couldn't recall anything in particular said by Foxx at the 1951 induction, and asserted that in those days, lists of family members attending an individual's induction were not kept by Hall of Fame officials.

The A's played the Brooklyn Dodgers in the Hall of Fame Game in the afternoon at Doubleday Field, and Foxx was introduced and bowed before the crowd of 9,000 fans during pregame announcements. Dykes was managing for the A's in 1951, the first season that Mack was not manager for that team after fifty consecutive years.

As always, Foxx signed a generous number of autographs. Some former major-league stars tired early of the autograph seekers on the Hall of Fame grounds and shunned further requests or threw money in the crowd of kids to pacify them. Foxx hung tough, sat under a tree when he tired from standing, but signed autographs for more than an hour.

Jim didn't stay away from baseball too long after his induction into the Hall of Fame. On February 2, 1952, the Fort Wayne Daisies baseball club of the American Girls Baseball League (AGBL) announced that Foxx had been hired to manage the club for the coming season as a replacement for Max Carey, former NL star outfielder for the Pittsburgh Pirates.

Foxx had been working for the Mid-States Freight Lines of Philadelphia for three years when he accepted the managerial job with the Daisies. Pat Toal, an intimate friend of Foxx and a member of the Daisies' Board of Directors, had broached the subject to Jim and found he was interested. Jim came to Fort Wayne (Indiana) from Philadelphia and met with Daisy officials before agreeing to be the team's manager. News releases did not disclose the terms of his contract, but it appears that Foxx was given a leave of absence by the Mid-States Freight Lines so he could return with that company when the AGBL season ended.

Foxx's signing of the contract was pictured in the *Fort Wayne News Sentinel*. Both the *News Sentinel* and the *Fort Wayne Journal Gazette* covered the Daisies' 1952 season heavily. At the time of the signing, Jim still slicked his hair straight back and had mostly dark hair sprinkled with grey. He flashed his familiar wide grin and wore his light-colored suit with a tie. Jim was a bit heavier than his final playing days, but still a handsome man at forty-four.

Foxx's appointment as the Daisies' manager was hailed by local supporters of the club, and the team's forty-page game program featured a full-page article on Jim's previous accomplishments in baseball.

Jim's stepdaughter, Nanci, who served as the team's batgirl, recalls, "We moved to a house in Fort Wayne that we rented by a lake. My brother Jimmie and I always went fishing, using worms for bait from a nearby manure pile. I was a tomboy at heart."

The Daisies were part of a six-team league for the 1952 season and had finished in third place the previous year, just two and one-half games out of first. Foxx took over a team loaded with talent, especially the league's leading batter for two years in a row, Betty Foss, and the league's leading pitcher in 1951, Maxine Kline.

From the time of the league's formation in 1943, the official league ball slowly evolved from a softball to a hardball the same weight as a major-league baseball but not as densely packed, having a larger circumference (10 inches) compared to a major league ball (9 and 1/16 inches). The distances between bases were about 20 percent shorter, and the distance between the pitcher's mound and home plate was 5 feet shorter than in the major leagues; otherwise the girls' version of the game was very similar to the major leagues.

Foxx arrived back in Fort Wayne on April 15 and attended a fan club meeting the following evening. The club's spring training tour began in earnest on April 20, when Jimmie and most of the players waved at well-wishers and photographers as they boarded the train in Fort Wayne for a 24-hour trip to Newton, North Carolina. The Daisies and the Battle Creek Belles, one of the Daisies' regular season opponents, arrived in Newton the following day and were greeted by local dignitaries.

The Daisies and Belles, led by Guy Bush, former NL pitcher, shared Twins Park, also known as Newton-Conover baseball field, the first week of spring training. Practices were hampered by rain showers and frequently by muddy fields when it wasn't raining.

Jo Weaver, the youngest of Betty Foss's two sisters on the Daisies, proved to be a sensation in batting for the Daisies during spring training as she bid for a starting role in the outfield. Meanwhile, Foxx was bothered by bursitis beginning April 26, with one local North Carolina newspaper dryly remarking about his ailment, "thus becoming the first spring training casualty."

That same day, Herman Helms of the *Charlotte Observer* interviewed Foxx as he relaxed on the front porch swing of the boardinghouse where his team was quartered in Newton. Foxx recalled a homer that he hit off White Sox lefty Garland Braxton at Comiskey Park in 1930. He said it was the longest homer and confessed he liked playing third base the best. Jim also recalled that when he rode the bench in the first All-Star game ever played in 1933, he wasn't too disappointed that he didn't actually get to play. He remembered that the fans began to shout for him to appear on the playing field as the game wore on, that being a "thrill enough for him," given the caliber of stars already in the lineup.

Then Foxx whipped out a long cigar, lit it up, and continued. "I was all tuckered out when it [the 1945 season with the Phillies] was over. As soon as the season was over, I knew that was all for me, that I'd never be back. I was just a tired old man."

Jim also admitted in the interview that "he might be letting himself in for something by taking this job with the girls' team." It might give him the urge to return to "big-time" baseball, presumably as a manager or coach.

Foxx didn't show off his batting skills very often for the Daisies. Wilma Briggs, who played outfield that season for Foxx, recalls:

> It was very difficult for us to get Bush to throw even a few pitches and even harder to get Jimmie Foxx to take batting practice. Foxx was just not a showoff. He was very reluctant to bat, almost as if he was saying, "those days are gone." He only took batting practice a few times in spring training and a few times before home games, but never on road trips. He could still hit the ball far, but I thought that season that he was in his fifties. [She was surprised to learn he was only 44 years old.] No wonder he could still hit the ball far.

Wilma also says of Jim, "He ate a lot. He was a big man. Maybe that was his biggest weakness."

The Belles were good competition for the Daisies that spring. Bush's team dominated the early practice games, while Fort Wayne grew stronger as spring training progressed and won more games, overall, between the two rivals. Then the regular season pennant race began in mid-May with the defending champion South Bend (Indiana) Blue Sox taking an early lead in the standings over second-place Fort Wayne. The two clubs fought for first place throughout the summer.

Len Davis, sports announcer for radio station WGL in Fort Wayne, broadcast eighteen home games that season and six road games of the 110-game schedule. Some of the Daisies' games were televised directly to the Veteran's Hospital in Fort Wayne.

Foxx wore a men's white version of the Daisies' uniform with the city's emblem encircled on the chest portion of the shirt. He stationed himself at the third base coach's position whenever the Daisies batted, and various players on the team took turns working as the first base coach. Foxx was not much of a chatterbox, but gave the signals typically flashed by a third base coach. Briggs says:

> Jimmie was not the teacher/instructor that Max Carey was, but he knew his baseball. He was knowledgeable of the game's strategies. He was not at all like the manager portrayed by actor Tom Hanks in the movie, "A League of Their Own." Jim did enjoy his drinks. He occasionally took a swig from a bottle in the bus on road trips, but it never changed his behavior or demeanor. He never lost his temper; he was never violent. He was a kind man, a gentleman to me and all my teammates. He never used bad language. He was very soft spoken.

Briggs' teammate Dottie Schroeder recalls:

> Jimmie Foxx was very generous. I liked him immensely. He was a nice person. I held him in high respect. He did enjoy to drink [an alcoholic beverage], but it never affected his performance on the ball field. He was a good manager. He never lost his temper. I don't remember him ever talking about his past accomplishments in baseball. I remember him as a good family man.

The regular season for the AGBL started in mid-May and within a couple weeks, the defending champion South Bend Blue Sox took over first place, remaining there much of the season, while the Daisies applied steady pressure to take over the league lead. Foxx displayed a rare show of frustration when he played a game under protest about the second week of the season because a balk was called against Daisies' pitcher Eleanor Moore which nullified a successful hidden ball trick against the Blue Sox. During the rhubarb that resulted from the play, Jean Weaver was tossed out of the game. The play occurred with Blue Sox runners on first and second and one out in the sixth. Daisies' second baseman Jean Geissinger pulled the trick on base runner Betty Mueller of the Blue Sox, tagging her when she strayed off second base. But instead of Mueller being called out, she was waved to third base by the umpire, and Blue Sox runner Shirley Stovroff was waved from first to second. A hit and two runs followed for a 3-0 Blue Sox lead and eventual win.

Foxx strengthened the Daisies by trading Geissinger, Mary Rountree, and Eleanor Moore to Grand Rapids for catcher Lavonne "Pepper" Paire and pitcher Jayne Bittner. Dolly Brumfield returned to the club in June following the end of the school year, and Foxx made Brumfield the regular second baseman and Katie Horstman the regular third baseman. Jo Weaver maintained a stronghold on the league batting lead with an average over .400 well into June, with her sister Betty Foss usually second in the league in batting.

Seven years after his retirement as a player, Jim was still recognized for his past accomplishments. He took several days off from managing the club while the team chaperon, Doris Tetzlaff, served as a substitute manager so he could travel and attend the Reds-Braves game at Cincinnati's Crosley Field on July 10. About eighteen Hall of Famers gathered for the game, including Foxx, Hornsby, Hubbell, Cochrane, and Paul Waner.

He was still asked occasionally to endorse a product. The Hillerich and Bradsby Company wrote Foxx that summer and asked for his permission to use his name on some of their bats. Foxx wrote back, saying in effect, "The original set of [golf] clubs is pretty worn out, so send me another and I hope I shall be able to use the new set for another 25 years, or so." It was only a few days before a new set of clubs arrived.

There's no doubt that Jim's players were flattered when Fox Movietone Company sent a six-man crew to film part of the first game of a double-header between the Daisies and Belles on July 16. The company used "sidelight shots" from games around the league for a two-reel film that included Foxx on camera, to be used for the theater and television.

Jo Weaver was lost to the Daisies' lineup for almost two weeks from late July to mid-August. Still, the Daisies stayed within striking distance of the Blue Sox.

Foxx missed several games in the third week in August with a viral infection and high fever, while Doris Tetzlaff subbed for him as manager. Jim returned to the club as manager on August 23, as the Daisies overtook the Blue Sox for first-place honors for the rest of the regular season that ended September 1. Foxx and the Daisies lined up for a team photograph in the *News Sentinel* that day, but the team's glory was short-lived, as the Rockford Peaches defeated Fort Wayne in the first round of the league's playoffs.

Wilma Briggs doesn't know why Foxx failed to return to manage another year. She says, "We were all very disappointed that he didn't come back to manage again for the 1953 season."

Briggs says, "I never thought to get an autographed ball with Jimmie's signature on it for myself, but I did get one for my brother, Jimmie." Ironically, Wilma's dad had named one of his sons James Emory Foxx Briggs in honor of Foxx many years before Wilma played for Jimmie in 1952. Foxx had been one of Wilma's dad's favorite players.

Wilma says:

> Dad admired Jimmie Foxx for his power hitting, and his fielding ability, too. Dad was very excited when Jimmie became a member of the Red Sox. He took us to Fenway Park, usually once a year, to see the Red Sox play the Yankees. We went to an afternoon game so we could be back home on our farm near Narragansett, Rhode Island, to milk the cows before we went to bed.

Shortly after the 1952 season, Jim and Dorothy and the children moved from Fort Wayne back to Philadelphia, where he became a paint salesman. During 1953, Jim and Dorothy decided on a major change in scenery when they moved to St. Petersburg, Florida. Jim enjoyed playing in golf tourneys featuring celebrities, especially in the Miami area. He often took all three children to the golf driving range, and Johnny often caddied when Jim golfed. He didn't bowl as often as he had when he lived in Philadelphia, but he enjoyed saltwater fishing, especially deep-sea fishing. Nanci Foxx Canaday recalls, "He went every chance he could."

In 1954, Foxx went to a number of sports banquets along the East Coast and moved to Miami. Jim channeled a lot of time and effort for several months to help spearhead a program using baseball to curb juvenile delinquency. By October, a report out of Scranton, Pennsylvania, stated that thirty-two major-league baseball players agreed to join "Jimmie Foxx's Baseball Stars on Parade." Gene Woodling, Yankees' outfielder, represented the players on the board of directors. Mickey Vernon, Gil Hodges, Sal Maglie and eleven Yankees, including Whitey Ford, Hank Bauer, and Gil McDougald, were among the player members.

Foxx said he expected to have 120 players become members by 1955 and gained early support from Baseball Commissioner Ford Frick. The initial plan was to pay the players as much as they would make if they had gone barnstorming. Local groups that sponsored the tour of All-Stars were intended to be nonprofit organizations such as the American Legion or other civic groups. The baseball players would not be playing in front of crowds. Rather they would speak on the merits of baseball, how to be a good citizen and team player, and the boys would get a chance to meet and talk with baseball greats. But finances for the program were never firmly secured, so the project died before it ever got started, despite the efforts of Foxx and others.

The City of Miami gave Jimmie a testimonial dinner at Ramon's Restaurant in early April, just as the 1955 baseball season was beginning. He was given the key to the city by commissioner, Randy Christmas, explaining that meant Miami and Coral Gables, where Jimmie was making his home. Foxx shared the spotlight with his former teammate Ted Williams, who attended the dinner in honor of Foxx. Ted was hammered hard by the press at the dinner about his future plans for baseball. Ted was retired for the moment, despite an excellent season in 1954. His divorce proceedings prompted him to stay out of baseball; his salary was much lower for purposes of determining alimony payments. Ted said, "After Jimmie retired [left Boston], I sure missed him batting in back of me. When I got back from Korea, I told Jimmie to get back in shape. Those banjo hitters made me keep sliding into second." Fred "Lefty" Heimach, a former teammate and roommate of Foxx, also attended, and Connie Mack, Jr., came over from Fort Myers. Friends presented Foxx with a television set.

On June 26, the Baltimore Orioles honored Frank Baker at Memorial Stadium for his recent election into the Baseball Hall of Fame by the Veterans Committee. Jimmie was there, along with Lefty Grove, Dan Danforth, Frank Brower, Merwin Jacobsen, George Maisel, Fritz Maisel, Max Bishop, Bill Nicholson, Rube Marquard, and former Washington College baseball coach and Eastern Shore League president Tom Kibler. Foxx always enjoyed the camaraderie of any kind of reunion with his former teammates and athletes from the Eastern Shore, and this event had all the ingredients.

Foxx was interviewed by Neil Eskridge, of the *Baltimore News Post*, and laughed off "those 450-foot fences" in Memorial Stadium. Asked whether he would have liked to have spent his career at the Stadium instead of Shibe Park and Fenway Park, Foxx replied, "It would have been all right with me. Seems if you get hold of the ball like you should, you ought not have any trouble. It'll go."

Foxx would have had an easier time hitting homers near the foul poles at Memorial Stadium, but a harder time making round trippers in the power alleys at Baltimore. In 1955, Memorial Stadium had distances of 309 feet down the foul lines, 447 feet in the power alleys, and 450 feet to the center field wall. At Shibe Park when Jimmie played there, the distances were 334 feet to the wall at the foul lines, 405 feet to left-center, 390 feet to right-center, and 468 feet to the center field wall.

Always the teaser, Foxx leaned over in the dugout during the ceremony for Baker and said to Mr. Mack, "This fella [Grove] here would have been a pretty good pitcher, wouldn't he, if he'd just had a fastball?"

In July, Foxx headed back out to Kansas City for a reunion with many of the former A's from Connie Mack's last championship years. Bing Miller, Connie Mack III, Connie Mack in a straw hat, Foxx in a white suit and dark striped tie, and Mickey Cochrane met at Municipal Airport in Kansas City. Connie and many of the former Mackmen attended Hall of Fame activities in honor of former A's players before that night's games between the Red Sox and Athletics. Foxx looked healthy, only slightly overweight, some gray hair, and was still not wearing glasses in public.

In September, University of Miami Athletic Director Jack Harding hired Foxx as the university's baseball coach for the 1956 season. Foxx had been living in Miami for a couple of years, had served as Commissioner of the Junior Baseball Program in Coral Gables during the summer of 1955, and was an automobile salesman for Leo Adeeb Chevrolet at the time of Harding's announcement. Jimmie planned to handle both jobs at the same time.

Foxx was out on the University of Miami diamond six days a week in February 1956, from mid-afternoon until "the sun began to dip between the pines," preparing the club for its regular season. He piloted the University of Miami baseball team to a 9-8 record that season, a moderate success, given it was his first season leading the club.

Right after the University of Miami baseball season ended, Foxx took over as batting coach for the Miami Marlins, who had moved from Syracuse (New York) before the 1956 season after being bought by baseball magnate Bill Veeck. Jim was credited in part by some writers and players for the club's better-than-average hitting as the season unfolded.

Jim was greatly saddened when he learned that his father died suddenly in his home in Sudlersville on January 15, 1957. Dell had been such a staunch supporter of Jimmie and the most important early mentor for the development of his baseball skills. Dell had been in "poor health for some time, but his death came suddenly," according to the *Queen Anne's Record-Observer*. The same article noted that Dell had spent fifty years farming in Sudlersville before his retirement. Other than attending Jimmie's games at Shibe Park, Dell's chief source of enjoyment was harness racing in Harrington, Delaware, and at nearby Maryland racetracks. Jimmie and Sammy Dell flew up from Florida for funeral services on January 18 at Calvary Asbury Methodist Church. Reverend William Hemphill gave the funeral services, and interment was at Sudlersville Cemetery.

Jim brought back various family artifacts, mostly photographs, to Miami after Dell's death. In addition to his two sons, Dell was survived by his second wife, Elsie Manlove Foxx.

The 1957 baseball season was bit of a disappointment for Foxx when the University of Miami managed only a 11-12 record in his second year as manager. He was released from his duties as head coach after that season. According to one report, his lack of a college degree was the reason. Jimmie continued to struggle in his search for permanent work. Early in January 1958, the Boston Chapter of the Baseball Writer's Association located him at a South Miami address. They wanted to invite him to their annual dinner on January 22.

At the time, all three children, John (18), Nanci (16), and James (13), were still living with Jim and Dorothy. Jim was out of work, and John was working for Eastern Airlines, providing the only family income for several months. Foxx was reportedly several months behind in his rent and received money from several sources to make his trip to Boston.

Jimmy Silin, who had been one of Foxx's financial managers during some of his years in Boston, heard of Foxx's plight and sent him a check for $400. Foxx said, "Until that check, I didn't have a dime. Now I can hold my head up a little." Jimmie also said, "I don't feel badly for myself. The money I lost and blew was my own fault. But I'd like to give my children something."

Red Sox General Manager Joe Cronin was gravely concerned upon hearing of Foxx's financial woes. "I'll be looking forward to seeing Jimmie next week, so that we can discuss this situation. I was shocked to hear of his predicament," said Cronin.

Columnist Joe Williams offered a mixed review and opinion of Foxx's struggle with money. On the one hand he pointed to the fact that Foxx lost heavily in the golf course investment with the Jungle Club in 1941 or 1942, and limited blame, if any, could be placed on Foxx's judgment for that financial loss. He also recognized that Foxx was not a benefactor of major-league baseball's initial pension plan, which included players who played in 1946, but not players who retired before that year, so Foxx missed eligibility by a single season. Williams said, "The initial pension plan disregarded many old-timers who paved the way for the current players' salaries and luxuries."

But Williams claimed that Foxx made "no serious attempt to prove he can teach, coach, or manage in the big leagues." Maybe Foxx wasn't cut out to be a manager. He may have been too easy on the players. Still, his true calling after his playing days may have been as a hitting instructor or public relations officer, as suggested by author Ed Linn. Foxx's personality and general knowledge of baseball and the operations of major-league teams might have suited him well in either job.

The Red Sox signed Jimmie as a coach for their minor league club in the American Association, the Minneapolis Millers, and as a special batting instructor for the entire Red Sox farm chain for the 1958 season. Foxx turned down many job offers at about the same time, including one by the National Bohemian brewery, which sponsored radio and television for the Baltimore Orioles. Jimmy Silin said Foxx had more than 200 job offers with salaries ranging from about $5,000-$45,000, annually, and that Foxx's final decision was based less on money than on a job he would enjoy.

Joe McKenney, public relations director for the Red Sox, announced at a news conference, "It's a great personal pleasure for Tom Yawkey and Joe Cronin to have Jimmie Foxx back in baseball, where he belongs." Foxx started work with the Millers and their manager, Gene Mauch, the first week in March.

Foxx recalled that the first money he ever received was when a semipro team (probably from Caroline County) hired him to play second base, the only position he never played in the majors. He was probably thirteen or fourteen and received one dollar for his performance in the game.

Even after Foxx received his job with the Red Sox, job offers, letters, and small cash contributions continued to trickle in to him for several weeks. The king of generosity didn't stash the loot in a savings account; he handed the letters and contents over to Ted Williams at the Sportsman's show in Boston on February 8 and said, "Ted, a lot of kids are worse off than I'll ever be. Take this money over to your Jimmy Fund and put it to work."

In late April, Foxx was thoroughly at home in his new coaching job, bantering with ballplayers and the press, and occasionally even taking a few swings near the end of batting practice. In the early part of the season, Foxx's health began to plague him again. Near the end of June, Jimmie was admitted to a Minneapolis hospital for several days with high blood pressure. After his release from the hospital, his health was somewhat better for most of the second half of the season.

In October, Tommy Thomas, general manager of the Millers, notified Foxx of his release from the Red Sox' minor-league club. The Millers wanted to hire a player-coach for the upcoming season, rather than just rehire a coach. Thomas said it was one of the hardest things he ever had to do, but doubted that Foxx would have returned to Minneapolis, anyway. Tommy said Foxx's sinus condition made him completely miserable at times, and noted Jimmie's heart condition, too. It seems that the real reason the Red Sox released Foxx was because of his health problems, not the need of a player-coach.

Thomas said he was under the impression that both Jimmie and his wife had obtained good jobs in Arizona. Foxx was probably trying out the Scottsdale area to escape or minimize serious sinus trouble and seek relief for their son, James' asthma problems. But the move backfired; if anything James' asthma problems became worse, according to Nanci Foxx Canaday.

In mid-May, 1959, Foxx was hired by three businessmen in Galesburg, Illinois, to be the front man for a steak house. Foxx would be the manager of the Jimmy Foxx Restaurant, and his wife and two boys were looking for a home in the area. He was reported to have been out of a job and in financial straits at the time he was hired.

That summer, Foxx joined Grove, Cobb, Paul Waner, Hornsby, and others as the Kansas City Athletics honored fellow Missourian Zach Wheat in their home park for his recent induction into the Baseball Hall of Fame. Wheat, Foxx, and Grove had been teammates on the Athletics during the 1927 season.

Several months later, on September 1, Jim was confined briefly to St. Mary's Hospital in Galesburg after fainting in a doctor's office. Jimmie had brought Dorothy to a physician for treatment of her sprained wrist and fainted while she was being treated. The doctors initially blamed high blood pressure and fatigue as the causes of Foxx's latest health woes.

A day later, Dr. Graham amended his remarks and said, "There is a strong possibility that Jimmie suffered a heart attack yesterday in the doctor's office. His electrocardiogram certainly was suggestive of a recent heart attack." After Jim recuperated, he began working for the restaurant that bore his name and continued there until the following June.

Foxx's health continued to plague him. On August 24, 1960, he suffered a back injury, skull fracture, and concussion when he was trying to move a trunk and fell down the basement stairs in his home in Galesburg. The fall resulted in a fractured spinal disc and permanent partial paralysis of his left side. Jim had been scheduled to start a new job the following day with a horticultural nursery owned by former catcher Mickey O'Neil in Rocky River, Ohio, but his injuries kept him from working for O'Neil.

Jim's finances hit rock-bottom a year later in November 1961, when he filed a voluntary petition for bankruptcy. His attorney, John V. Donnelly, said that Jim had been down on his luck for some time and that bankruptcy action was meant to give him some breathing room. Foxx was living in Lakewood, Ohio, a suburb of Cleveland, at the time. Jimmie's salary for 1959 and 1960 averaged $3,400 per year, and his debts were listed as $4,260. He was employed as a contact man for the Bureau of Unemployment Compensation at $4,000 per year, but was released shortly after he filed for bankruptcy because the Civil Service stepped in and said he lacked qualifications.

As Roger Maris and Mickey Mantle pursued Babe Ruth's single-season home-run record in early September 1961, the *Cleveland Press* published an interview with Foxx. Although the media coverage on Mantle and Maris was more intense than on Foxx in 1932 and Greenberg in 1938, Jimmie seemed to forget that there was heavy interest and expectations by the fans and considerable coverage by the media during his chase of Ruth's record. Foxx recalled:

There wasn't stress on beating the Babe, probably because his mark was set just 5 years earlier and he was still playing. I was more concerned with winning the batting title than breaking the record [Ruth's]. I think I had about 41 homers by the first week in August. Then I hurt my left wrist sliding into second to break up a double play. I stayed in the lineup, but later found out I had a chipped bone. I was able to get base hits, but for three weeks I just didn't have the power to hit for distance.

Foxx's former teammate Bing Miller was interviewed by writer Hugh Brown at about the same time: "Jimmy should have had at least 65 homers in 1932 . . . rainouts robbed him of two and the right field screen at Sportsman's Park in St. Louis robbed him of at least five more." Miller recalled Foxx's injury in August as being a broken finger, not a broken wrist. Miller continued, "I've never seen anybody hit a ball harder than Foxx. He hit them on a line. They tried to curve Jimmy to death [in 1932]." Bing said Foxx used the standard 38- to 39-ounce bat of that era.

In January 1962, Jim was employed in the sporting goods section of a Cleveland department store. James was a sophomore athlete at Lakewood High School, and Jim appeared on the road to financial recovery. Whereas Jim's bats and gloves were once the hot items in sporting goods departments, now Roger Maris gloves and bats reflected the biggest demand.

Jimmie and Dorothy's stay in the Lakewood area served a very useful purpose for their son, James. It allowed him to attend the same high school for three years, where he lettered three times in football as the team's quarterback, captained the football team as a senior, led it to the league championship as a junior, and batted .320 for the baseball team as a senior. Jimmie advised his son to continue with his education, causing James to forego an offer by the Red Sox to join that club's entry in the Florida Winter Instructional League.

"Dad and I decided education comes first," James said.

James proceeded to attend Kent State University in Ohio in the spring of 1965 and never seriously pursued a professional athletic career.

Foxx attended a $20-a-plate testimonial dinner for retiring Cardinal star Stan Musial in St. Louis in late October 1963, and was introduced to the 1,500 attendees. The next morning before leaving his hotel, the swank Chase Park Plaza, Jim woke up to dizzy spells and sent for the house physician, Dr. J. W. Probstein. Dr. Probstein said Foxx suffered from a "decompensation of the heart." Foxx's heart sounded like "a trip hammer, but I wouldn't call it a coronary." Foxx was taken to Faith Hospital in St. Louis and remained there for several days.

Jim and Dorothy left Cleveland in the summer of 1964 and returned to Miami, Florida. For the most part, Jim was retired and only worked an occasional part-time job.

Dorothy died suddenly of asphyxiation on May 7, 1966, when a piece of pork lodged in her throat (according to her daughter, Nanci Foxx Canaday). She was pronounced dead at Baptist Hospital in Miami. She was only forty-eight. It was big blow to Jimmie, given the closeness of their relationship over the entire marriage. Funeral services were held for Dorothy on May 10, and she was laid to rest in Flagler Memorial Park in Miami. Jim's son, Kenneth Foxx, came from Alabama for Dorothy's funeral to support his dad. It was one of the rare times that Jim and his second-oldest son were together following Jim's divorce from Helen. Jim remained in Miami after Dorothy's death along with his brother, Sammy Dell, while none of his children lived with him any longer. They were all young adults now.

On August 17, 1966, Giants outfielder Willie Mays passed Foxx as second highest on the all-time home-run list with his 535th career homer. Foxx sent a telegram congratulating Willie and said, "I hope he hits 600. For 25 years they thought only left-handers could hit the long ones. They even teach right-handed youngsters to hit left-handed."

Foxx said that Mays didn't have a chance to break Ruth's lifetime total of 714 homers. Jim added that the only player who may have had a chance was Ted Williams, but Williams lost five playing seasons to military service and had a farther distance to hit homers as a left-handed batter in Fenway Park than in many other AL parks. "Can you imagine what Williams would have done in Yankee Stadium?" Foxx added.

Jim lamented a bit about not having broken Ruth's single-season homer record in 1932 when he had his best chance and fell only two homers short of tying the mark. He said, " Oh, it might have put a few more bucks in my pocket. But there was only one Ruth!"

Foxx's loneliness made him restless and spurred a rare trip from Miami to Sudlersville by car with his brother, Sammy Dell, in August 1966. One of his first stops was to the Kent Island Pharmacy in Queen Anne's County. Jim's visit to the pharmacy proved to be fortuitous in opening the door for older fans to recall—and future baseball fans to learn about—his exploits as a baseball player. Gil Dunn, owner of the pharmacy, had contacted Jimmie by letter several times to tell him that he had dedicated a portion of his store to memorabilia and information about Foxx's baseball career.

Foxx had been Dunn's idol when Gil was a boy growing up in Baltimore. Gil had moved to Kent Island in 1953 and was amazed at the quiet approach most Eastern Shore natives had toward Jimmie in the 1960s in and around Sudlersville. Gil decided to restore some of the luster to Foxx's name and his baseball exploits by creating a display in his store to honor Jimmie.

Gil's impression was that "the people in Sudlersville wanted Foxx to do something after his playing days were over that would bring dignity to his career and his hometown." Some people may have been upset that he was reported to be having some drinking problems and wasn't able to hold a steady job. Still, others stuck by Jimmie, especially many of his relatives.

Slowly, word trickled out to local residents and tourists about Dunn's tribute to Foxx. Most importantly, it stimulated discussions and reminiscences about Jimmie's career and the generous nature of his personality, especially through periodic articles written by various sportswriters for local newspapers on the Eastern Shore.

When Jimmie, white-haired with a Boston Red Sox cap fixed squarely on his head, showed up with Sammy Dell outside the front door of the pharmacy, Dunn couldn't believe his eyes. Gil recognized Jimmie Foxx immediately, even though his health problems had taken their toll. Jimmie gave Gil a host of personal articles and trophies, including some of his MVP trophies, a Red Sox uniform, and the All-Star uniform that he wore with the touring All-Stars on their 1934 trip through Japan. Foxx was flattered deeply that someone cared enough about his accomplishments to memorialize them in such a manner. He asked "Doc" Dunn to cash a check and went on his way to Sudlersville, where he stopped at Tarbutton's Tavern for a few beers just outside town. It was to be Jimmie's last time in his hometown.

Jimmie died suddenly while eating dinner at his brother's house in Miami the evening of Friday, July 21, 1967. He was taken to Baptist Hospital after some meat lodged in his throat, but was pronounced dead on arrival. Sheriff's detective Walter Seward said that Sammy Dell told him Jim had a history of heart ailments. An autopsy performed by the Dade County medical examiner's office revealed on July 22 that Foxx died on the previous day from asphyxiation due to the meat lodging in his throat, not due to any heart ailment. So, if the information about the cause of death of Dorothy is correct, they both died in the same manner.

The National Baseball Hall of Fame provided Max Carey and Jim's former A's teammate Rube Walberg as pallbearers for Foxx's funeral on Tuesday, July 25. The funeral services were held at the flower-bedecked Van Orsdel Bird Road Chapel in Miami. Reverend Jiles Kirkland, pastor of the First Methodist Church of South Miami, delivered the eulogy, saying, "His feats and exploits on the baseball diamond are too well known to mention, too many to enumerate. His name held something of a magic for me."

Connie Mack, Jr., lamented, "We'll all miss Jimmy. He was such a likable guy. He always had a smile and a pat on the back for everybody. He was a great competitor, but it was impossible to make him lose his temper. He was never thrown out of a ball game in his life."

Jim was buried next to Dorothy in Flagler Memorial Park, not far from the chapel, while the annual Hall of Fame game was being played in Cooperstown. Foxx's plaque was draped in a black shroud. Jim had planned to attend the annual induction ceremony.

Just two months later, Sammy Dell died in Miami of a heart ailment. He was only forty-nine, although listed as fifty-one in some newspaper articles. Jimmie was no ordinary brother to Sammy Dell; they were lifelong best friends.

Foxx seemed to be a poor judge of his own abilities and interests when it came to making the right choices of job offers or options available to him. Hindsight indicates he would have been better off remaining independent of contacts he had made during his playing days. But how does one stay clear of such people when he is a celebrity like Foxx?

Jim kept very few jobs he had after baseball for more than a year. Did employers release him because he wasn't working up to expectations, or did he typically not keep a job long because he "burned out" early? He never accrued valuable experience over a long enough period to reach any kind of job seniority. It's a bit of a mystery why Jim never received a job as a coach, manager, or in the front office of a major-league club after his 1944 coaching job with the Chicago Cubs. But some of Jim's inability to hold jobs, especially in the '50s and '60s, was blamed on serious health problems by newspaper accounts—for example, the coaching job with the Minneapolis Millers in 1958 and some of his attempts in the '60s. His financial troubles occurred from a combination of bad investment decisions, poor judgment about his own abilities and interests, and serious health problems.

Jimmie Foxx's failure in the job market after his baseball-playing days did not go unnoticed by other professional athletes, nor did similar problems encountered by many of his one-time teammates and opponents. His financial woes served as an important lesson for major-league baseball players who followed him.

Major-league players have made remarkable progress in their knowledge of personal finance and their earning power while playing. They've strengthened their union, obtained the right to free agency after a certain number of years at the major-league level, hired highly qualified agents to negotiate on their behalf, and on average have learned a lot more about viable options for investment of extra monies.

Foxx would have derived immense satisfaction from the benefits gained by players. The "other guy" always seemed to be his top priority.

17

FOXX IN BASEBALL HISTORY

After Jimmie Foxx's death, there was a certain quiet and tight-lip approach that townspeople of Sudlersville and nearby areas showed toward outsiders who inquired about his life, his childhood, and the recollections that friends and family had of him. Some people were probably ashamed of Jimmie's life during his declining years or frustrated with his infrequent visits back home. Author James Michener observed such behavior toward Foxx in the early 1970s in researching his book *Sports in America*, but he only spoke with a handful of people in and around Sudlersville.

About ten years after Jimmie's death people began to focus on his good qualities again. There was pride in his accomplishments in major-league baseball, and everyone remembered his warm, generous, unselfish personality.

Several small community meetings commemorated Foxx and his baseball abilities. Various speakers shared memories of their associations with Jim, whether they were schoolmates, relatives, or just close friends. The speakers re-created the excitement everyone felt as they followed Foxx's exploits in professional baseball. In 1981, Sudlersville hung a wooden sign alongside the road near the main intersection in town, declaring Sudlersville "the birthplace of Jimmy Foxx."

In October 1987, to celebrate the 80th anniversary of Jimmie's birth, the Sudlersville Community Betterment Club organized and sponsored an unveiling of a marble base for the flag in the center of the town, with an inscription on the front pronouncing Sudlersville "the birthplace of James E. (Jimmy) Foxx, Baseball Hall of Fame," immediately followed by a commemorative dinner with speakers.

Jimmie's oldest son (Jimmie Emory, Jr.) could not be located for a possible invitation to the event. The last time anyone connected with the Foxx family knew of his whereabouts was in the early 1970s, when his brother, William Kenneth, established contact with him in California. William Kenneth and Jimmie's youngest son, Jimmie III, attended with their families. Speeches were given by several local sportswriters, including John Steadman from the *Baltimore Sun;* former clubhouse errand boy for the Philadelphia Athletics, Al Ruggieri; and the former National League slugger Bill Nicholson from Chestertown, Maryland. Several hundred other people attended the event. "The Pride of Sudlersville" had returned in the hearts of his towns people.

Despite Foxx's major achievements during his career, he still does not command the respect and attention from baseball followers that he deserves. Foxx's career closely paralleled Lou Gehrig in terms of the same years played, in the same league, facing mostly the same pitchers. Gehrig and Foxx were very similar in terms of batting accomplishments, but Lou retains a much bigger name, especially with baseball fans born since the playing careers of Foxx and Gehrig ended. Gehrig is much better known today, in part because he played in New York, was a teammate of Babe Ruth, appeared in more World Series over a longer stretch of his career from beginning to end, and held the consecutive-games-played streak for over sixty years before it was broken by Cal Ripken in 1995. Because Gehrig died prematurely at the age of thirty-eight from amyotrophic lateral sclerosis (ALS), often called "Lou Gehrig's disease," he is still known by the general public even into the 1990s.

Most former major-league players who played against Jimmie and Lou, who I polled between 1989 and 1992 by telephone and letter, rated Foxx and Gehrig very close—if not even—in batting, hitting with power, fielding, and base running. Some players rated them even, and about an equal number gave a slight edge to either Foxx or Gehrig.

Ted Williams rates Foxx as the third best hitter of all-time behind Ruth (first), and Gehrig (second). In his book, *Ted Williams' Hit List,* co-authored with Jim Prime, Ted excludes himself from the list and points out that the difference between Gehrig and Foxx is a very close call, "an awfully tough matchup." Williams says, "Gehrig's statistics suggests he was better than Foxx." But he acknowledges that ballparks in general favor left-handed hitters. Williams further points out, "Foxx was definitely the most productive right-handed hitter I ever saw."

Foxx and Gehrig both played as full-time regulars in the lineup simultaneously for eleven years from 1928-38. During that period, Gehrig had an edge in runs scored, rbi's, and batting average, and Foxx had an edge in home runs. Gehrig's team, the Yankees, outscored Foxx's teams, the Athletics and Red Sox, every season except 1929, by much more than the difference in run production between the two players, so that the players surrounding Gehrig and Foxx in their lineups had some effect on Jimmie and Lou's batting statistics. For instance, during that eleven-year period, Foxx had Simmons batting in the lineup before him from 1928-32, but no one of quite the caliber of Simmons from 1933-38. Gehrig had Ruth batting before him from 1928-34 and Joe DiMaggio next to him in the lineup from

1936-38. Examining home runs, runs batted in, batting average, and slugging percentage, Foxx had better years than Gehrig in 1929, 1932, 1933, 1935, and 1938; Gehrig had better statistics in the other six seasons. Foxx gets the nod over Gehrig in terms of long-distance hitting ability. William Jenkinson has researched the long-distance hitting ability of all the great home-run hitters exhaustively and rates Ruth as the top hitter for distance. In Ruth's best year for long-distance homers (1921), Ruth hit at least one homer over 500 feet in each of the eight AL parks. Jenkinson rates Foxx second to Ruth in long-distance hitting ability, asserting that Ruth and Foxx's longest homers were 50 feet further than those of Gehrig and Greenberg.

Foxx still holds the AL major-league record along with Greenberg and McGwire for home runs in one season by a right-handed batter with 58. The record has stood for 72 years. Jimmie also still holds the Boston Red Sox club record for homers (50) and runs batted in (175)—records that have stood for 66 years. John Lardner once said that Jimmie didn't promote himself enough, especially compared to Babe Ruth, but few players promoted themselves like Ruth. The Babe overshadowed all other major leaguers. The Yankees' trips north near the end of spring training, with stops at various cities, illustrated his overwhelming national appeal. The fans, press, and photographers couldn't get enough of him.

Did Foxx hurt his image during his declining years after baseball? Probably to some degree, but Jim didn't command the respect he deserved even while he was playing baseball. An example is the All-Star balloting from year to year for the first base position and the Hall of Fame balloting the years he was eligible before he was elected to the Hall in 1951. Foxx should have been the starting first baseman for the AL in 1933, the first year the All-Star game was played. Jim had slugged 58 homers in 1932, won the AL MVP award for that season, and was heading for his second straight AL MVP award in 1933, but Gehrig completely overshadowed Foxx in balloting by the fans. Although Foxx was a slightly better player than Mel Ott, he finished behind the NL slugger in the 1951 Hall of Fame balloting. Foxx arguably should have been elected into the Hall earlier, even though he had heavy competition.

In terms of his popularity among his peers, players that played with or against Foxx were unanimous in their praise of him.

Ted Williams said, " He was one of the nicest guys in baseball and extremely well-liked."

"He was a super gentleman, and I always wished we had him on our team," said the former Tiger Charlie Gehringer.

"He was always affable," recalled Tony Giuliani.

"He was very pleasant, especially to youngsters," said Harry Eisenstat.

Former teammate Tony Lupien said, "Jimmie was one of the most generous men who ever lived."

Former pitching opponents Art Herring asserted, "Jimmie was a fun-loving man," and Bud Thomas said, "Jimmie was a jolly-go-lucky fellow. He liked to talk."

Former St. Louis Browns' star third baseman Harlond Clift gushed, "Jimmie Foxx was one of my personal friends. I loved him as a great ballplayer. Every ballplayer admired Jimmie Foxx."

Teammate Herb Hash said, "Jimmie had lots of close friends on the Red Sox team in 1940. I was privileged to be one of them."

Former Indians' hurler Mel Harder said, "Jimmie Foxx had a fine disposition. He took things in stride."

Former pitching opponent Vern Kennedy stated, "I considered Jimmie one of my best friends, and I don't think he had an enemy any place at that time."

"Jimmie was the perfect gentleman," recalled Dom DiMaggio.

Teammate Gene Desautels said, "Jimmie was close to everyone on the Red Sox, and we all liked him tremendously."

Bill Werber added, "A real nice guy, Jimmie Foxx. Everyone liked the guy."

"Jimmie Foxx was a very popular ballplayer and a first class fellow," said Jimmy DeShong.

Some sportswriters would have preferred Foxx to have had a little more of the aggressiveness of Ty Cobb, the showmanship of Babe Ruth, or the shrewdness of John McGraw. But Hurtt Deringer, the longtime newspaperman of the *Kent County News*, may have paid Jimmie Foxx the best compliment of all at the October 24, 1987, dedication and dinner for Jimmie in Sudlersville, Maryland: "I've heard it said that if Jimmie Foxx had a true killer instinct, he might have been even better. But I think he was best as he was, a man genuinely liked by everyone in baseball. His niceness just shone through."

The causes for Foxx's rapid decline in baseball after 1940 are very much open to debate. He still holds the distinction of hitting his 500th homer at the youngest age (32 years) in major-league history. He had already played parts of 16 major-league seasons when he hit his 500th homer in 1940. But 1940 was the last season that he combined 30 or more homers with 100 or more rbi's. In contrast, Ruth still hit 34 homers and drove in over 100 runs at the age of 38. Foxx's yearly output quickly declined after 1940. The best evidence for Foxx's decline seems to be his frequent problem with sinus conditions, even though some newspaper articles published after Foxx retired reported that Jimmie had a drinking problem. Such claims are hard to support or refute. Foxx loved to socialize and enjoyed parties. On the other hand, he was not a heavy reader and only occasionally played cards, even on train trips, according to Red Sox players Bobby Doerr and Charlie Wagner. Some individuals recalled Jimmie did enjoy drinking, but Foxx was not a rowdy drinker; in fact he often served the role of peacemaker to calm down a heated argument.

If Foxx had put himself on a conditioning and strengthening program at this point in the late 1930s or slightly earlier, he might have delayed his decline, at least to some extent. However, major leaguers didn't take such an approach in the 1930s and 1940s, whereas many did in the 1980s and 1990s. Any contribution that drinking habits may have had in slowing Jim is difficult to measure. His sinus problems are much better documented in quotes from him, his teammates, and opponents.

Jimmie Foxx deserves mention on equal ground with Lou Gehrig, in terms of the greatest major-league baseball first baseman, ever. Additionally, Foxx might be the most versatile player ever to play in the majors.

The town of Sudlersville continues to publicize its hometown hero and elevate awareness of his baseball accomplishments to individuals of all ages and walks of life.

After several years of fundraising and preparation, a life-size statue of Jimmie Foxx was unveiled in the center of Sudlersville on October 25, 1997, three days after the 90th anniversary of his birth there. The Sudlersville Community Betterment Club spearheaded the event, especially its chairman, Ms. Loretta Walls, who was also the chairperson for the "Foxx Statue Committee." Despite heavy rain the evening before and threatening skies that morning, about 500 onlookers attended the statue dedication as the sun peeked through the clouds at about 11 A.M., the starting time of the dedication. The sunshine remained only for minutes before retreating behind the clouds for the remainder of the day, which featured chilly breezes. Trucks occasionally rolled along Church Street during the event, much the way they will on a routine basis in the future, this being a major trucking route.

Hurtt Deringer, former editor and publisher for the *Kent County News,* was master of ceremonies and narrated the proceedings with his typical enthusiasm and humor. John Steadman, sportswriter of the *Baltimore Sun* and formerly with the *Baltimore News American,* told the audience that, with apologies to Hank Aaron, Willie Mays, Ralph Kiner, and others, Jimmie Foxx was (and still is) the greatest righthanded slugger of all time. Katie Horstman, who played for Jimmie Foxx on the 1952 Fort Wayne Daisies, emphasized that Jim was a very kind and gentle man, the best manager in the world to play for, and nothing like the character played by Tom Hanks in the movie "A League of Their Own." Former Maryland Governor Harry Hughes read the dedication of the statue, and some of Jimmie Foxx's grandchildren pulled off the black cloth draped over the statue as Jim's sons, Kenneth and James Emory Foxx III, and stepdaughter

Nanci Foxx Canaday looked on. Nanci, and possibly the sons, too, had to fight back tears because it was such an emotional, yet happy moment.

Sculptor Ken Herlihy's rendition of Jimmie Foxx has him in a pose of a completed swing, and its likeness to Jimmie, especially in the face, is remarkable. Ken was aided by Jim's nephew, Dell Foxx, III, who visited the sculptor's studio on several occasions because his facial features resemble his uncle so strongly.

At a luncheon program following the dedication, additional speeches recalled Foxx's baseball exploits and his warm personality. Speakers included Ted Taylor, president of the Philadelphia A's Historical Society, SABR president Larry Gerlach, and sportscaster Phil Woods. The whole event captured the appreciation, warm memories, and pride that many people still hold for Jimmie Foxx on the Eastern Shore. The lasting quality of the bronze life-size statue of Jimmie Foxx and plaque in the center of town ensure that the memory of Jimmie Foxx, "The Pride of Sudlersville," will be handed down to future generations.

Jimmie Foxx fared well in two polls that ranked the Top 100 Players of the Twentieth Century. In *The Sporting News Selects Baseball's 100 Greatest Players* published in 1998, Foxx was ranked as the 15th best of the century. Similarly, in 1999 the Society of American Baseball Research ranked Foxx as the 14th best major league player of the century.

BIBLIOGRAPHY

Books and Periodicals

Baumgartner, Stan. "Legs and Eyes Sound, Declares Foxx, at 37." *The Sporting News*, February 22, 1945.

Broeg, Bob. "Awesome Sight—Mighty Foxx Swinging the Bat." *The Sporting News*, June 27, 1970.

Burns, Jimmy. "Players Just as Good Now, But Fewer, Says Double X." *The Sporting News*, March 14, 1956.

_____. "Foxx Takes Post as Miller Coach: Many Offer Help." *The Sporting News*, January 29, 1958.

Carter, Craig. *The Sporting News Complete Baseball Record Book.* St. Louis: The Sporting News, 1997.

_____. *Babe: The Legend Comes to Life.* New York: Penguin, 1974.

Creamer, Robert W. *Baseball in '41.* New York: Penguin, 1992.

Daniel, Dan. *The Real Babe Ruth.* St. Louis: The Sporting News, 1948.

Daniel, W. Harrison. *Jimmie Foxx: The Life and Times of a Baseball Hall of Famer.* Jefferson, NC: McFarland, 1996.

Dickson, Paul. *The Dickson Baseball Dictionary.* New York: Avon, 1989.

DiMaggio, Dom, with Bill Gilbert. *Real Grass, Real Heroes.* New York: Zebra Books, Kensington, 1990.

Doerer, Tom. "Jimmie Foxx and His Brilliant Future." *Baseball Magazine*, October 1928.

Feldman, Chic. "Foxx Starts Kid Program to Promote Game's Ideal." *The Sporting News*, October 27, 1954.

Feller, Bob, with Bill Gilbert. *Now Pitching: Bob Feller.* New York: Birch Lane, 1990.

Foxx, Jimmie (ed. Bill Cunningham, George C. Carens, Austen Lake, and A. Linde Fowler). *How I Bat.* Boston: Courier-Citizens Publishing, 1933.

Foxx, Jimmy. "The Secret of Jimmy Foxx's Slugging Power." *Baseball Magazine*, August 1934.

Gorman, Bob. *Double X: The Story of Jimmie Foxx—Baseball's Forgotten Slugger.* New York: Bill Goff, 1990.

Greenberg, Hank, with Ira Berkow. *The Story of My Life.* New York: Times Books, 1989.

Gregory, Robert. *Diz: Dizzy Dean and Baseball During the Great Depression.* New York: Viking, 1992.

Holway, John B. *The Last .400 Hitter.* Dubuque, IA: William C. Brown, 1992

Honig, Donald. *The Greatest First Basemen of All Time.* New York: Crown, 1988.

_____. *The Power Hitters.* New York: Crescent, 1989.

James, Bill. *The Bill James Historical Baseball Abstract.* New York: Villard, 1988.

_____. *The Politics of Glory: How Baseball's Hall of Fame Really Works.* New York: Macmillan, 1994.

_____. *The Bill James Guide to Baseball Managers From 1870 to Today.* New York: Scribner, 1997.

Keene, Kerry, Raymond Sinibaldi, and David Hickey. *The Babe in Red Stockings: An In-Depth Chronicle of Babe Ruth with the Boston Red Sox, 1914-1919,* Champaign, IL: Sagamore, 1997.

Kuklick, Bruce. *To Every Thing A Season: Shibe Park and Urban Philadelphia, 1909-1976.* Princeton, NJ: Princeton University Press, 1991.

Lane, Frank C. "The Strong Arm Slugger of the Fighting Athletics." *Baseball Magazine,* September 1929.

_____. "A New Home Run King." *Baseball Magazine,* October 1932.

_____. "The Greatest Player in the American League." *Baseball Magazine,* March 1933.

_____. "The Greatest Individual Punch in the American League." *Baseball Magazine,* March 1934.

Lieb, Fred. "Foxx, No. 3 on All-Time Homer List, Dead." *The Sporting News,* August 5, 1967.

_____. *Baseball As I Have Known It.* New York: Coward, McCann & Geoghegan, 1977.

Linn, Ed. *Hitter: The Life and Turmoils of Ted Williams.* New York: Harcourt Brace, 1993.

Lowery, Philip J. *Green Cathedrals.* Reading, MA: Addison-Wesley, 1992.

Macht, Norman. *Jimmie Foxx.* New York: Chelsea House, 1991.

Mack, Connie (Cornelius McGillicuddy). *My 66 Years in the Big Leagues.* Philadelphia: Winston, 1950.

Meany, Tom. *Baseball's Greatest Hitters.* New York: A. S. Barnes, 1950.

Nack, William. "Lost in History." *Sports Illustrated,* August 19, 1996.

Okkonen, Marc. *Baseball Uniforms of the 20th Century: The Official Major League Baseball Guide.* New York: Sterling, 1993.

_____. *Baseball Memories 1930-1939: A Complete Pictorial History of the "Hall-of-Fame" Decade.* New York: Sterling, 1994.

Ritter, Lawrence. *Lost Ballparks.* New York: Viking, 1992.

Robinson, Ray. *Iron Horse: Lou Gehrig in His Time.* New York: Harper, 1990.

Rogers, Charles M. "Jimmy Foxx: Friends on the Shore Remember the Strong Arm of Baseball." *The Star-Democrat Weekend Magazine*, August 28, 1981.

Rumill, Ed. "Looking Backward with Jimmie Foxx." *Baseball Magazine*, November 1944.

SABR (ed. Bob McConnell and David Vincent). *The Home Run Encyclopedia*. New York: Macmillan, 1996.

Seymour, Harold. *Baseball: The Golden Age*. New York: Oxford University Press, 1971.

Spink, J. G. T. "Looping the Loops. Two X-A No. 1 Guy." *The Sporting News*, August 30, 1945.

Stump, Al. *Cobb: A Biography*. Chapel Hill, NC: Algonquin, 1994.

Thorn, John, Pete Palmer, Michael Gershman, and David Pietrusza. *Total Baseball: The Official Encyclopedia of Major League Baseball*. New York: Viking, 1997.

Westcott, Richard. *Philadelphia's Old Ballparks*. Philadelphia: Temple University Press, 1996.

Williams, Ted, and Jim Prime. *Ted Williams' Hit List*. Indianapolis: Masters Press, 1996.

Williams, Ted, with John Underwood. *My Turn at Bat: The Story of My Life*. New York: Fireside, 1988.

Yuetter, Frank. "Art of Home-Run Hitting Dying, Declares Foxx." *The Sporting News*, February 14, 1951.

Newspapers

Accomack News — 1924.

Baltimore Morning Sun and *Evening Sun* — 1923-1945 (except 1944), 1951, 1967.

Boston Daily Record — 1932.

Boston Globe — 1933, 1935-1942, 1951, 1958.

Cambridge *Daily Banner* — 1923-1924, 1928-1933, 1936.

Centreville Observer — 1919-1933.

Centreville Record — 1907-1924.

Chicago Tribune — 1927-1928, 1936, 1942.

Dover Delaware Republican — 1924.

Dover State Sentinel — 1924

Easton Star-Democrat — 1915, 1923-1925, 1928-1933, 1940-1941

Fort Myers News Press — 1925, 1933, 1935.

Kent News — 1904

Los Angeles Times — 1929, 1932, 1941.

New Orleans Times-Picayune — 1930.

New York *Times* — 1925-1945, 1951, 1958, 1967.

New York World-Telegam — 1929-1945

Peninsula Enterprise — 1924
Philadephia Evening Bulletin — 1926-1935.
Philadelphia Inquirer — 1924, 1925-1933.
Providence Journal — 1925
Queen Anne's Record Observer — 1939, 1942, 1943, 1951, 1957, 1958, 1967.
Salisbury Times — 1924, 1929-1933.
Smyrna Times — 1902
The Sporting News — 1923-1945, 1951, 1956, 1967.

INDEX

ABOUT THE AUTHOR

Mark Millikin was born in Baltimore and currently resides with his wife Debbie in Chesapeake Beach, Maryland. He received a Bachelor of Science degree from the University of Maryland and a Masters of Science degree from the College of Charleston (South Carolina). He is a fishery manager for the National Marine Fisheries Service (U.S. Department of Commerce) and has worked for that organization for 31 years. Mark has published various articles in fishery research journals and articles on Jimmie Foxx and other major league players for the Baltimore Orioles, Boston Red Sox, and various local newspapers.